MEDICINE PRICE SURVEYS, ANALYSES, AND COMPARISONS

MEDICINE PRICE SURVEYS, ANALYSES, AND COMPARISONS

Evidence, Methodology and Guidance

Edited by

SABINE VOGLER

WHO Collaborating Centre for Pharmaceutical Pricing and Reimbursement Policies, Pharmacoeconomics Department, Gesundheit Österreich GmbH (GÖG/Austrian Public Health Institute), Vienna, Austria

ELSEVIER

ACADEMIC PRESS

An imprint of Elsevier

Academic Press is an imprint of Elsevier
125 London Wall, London EC2Y 5AS, United Kingdom
525 B Street, Suite 1800, San Diego, CA 92101-4495, United States
50 Hampshire Street, 5th Floor, Cambridge, MA 02139, United States
The Boulevard, Langford Lane, Kidlington, Oxford OX5 1GB, United Kingdom

Library of Congress Cataloging-in-Publication Data
A catalog record for this book is available from the Library of Congress

British Library Cataloguing-in-Publication Data
A catalogue record for this book is available from the British Library

ISBN: 978-0-12-813166-4

Publisher: Candice Janco
Acquisition Editor: Scott J. Bentley
Editorial Project Manager: Gabriella D. Capille
Production Project Manager: Swapna Srinivasan
Cover Designer: Christian J. Bilbow

Typeset by TNQ Technologies

To my parents

I dedicate this book to two great individuals who have always been a model for me:
To my father who taught me the values of solidarity, equity and social rights; and
To my mother for her kindness, attentiveness and support.

CONTENTS

Part 3: Using Medicine Price Comparisons for Policy-Making

CONTRIBUTORS

Zaheer Ud-din Babar
University of Huddersfield, Huddersfield, West Yorkshire, United Kingdom &
University of Auckland, Auckland, New Zealand

Jaime Espín Balbino
Escuela Andaluza de Salud Pública, Granada, Spain

Joan Rovira Forns
Universidad de Barcelona, Spain

Claudia Vaca González
Universidad Nacional de Colombia, Bogota, Colombia

Paul Grootendorst
University of Toronto, Toronto, Ontario, Canada

Syed Shahzad Hasan
University of Huddersfield, Huddersfield, West Yorkshire, United Kingdom &
University of Newcastle, Newcastle, New South Wales, Australia

Aidan Hollis
University of Calgary, Calgary, Alberta, Canada

Rabia Hussain
University Sains Malaysia, Penang, Malaysia

Swathi Iyengar
Division of Pharmacoepidemiology & Clinical Pharmacology, Utrecht Institute for Pharmaceutical Sciences, Utrecht University, Utrecht, Netherlands
World Health Organization, Geneva, Switzerland

Mitja Kos
University of Ljubljana, Faculty of Pharmacy, Ljubljana, Slovenia

Priyanka Konduru Subramani Raju
Boston University, Boston, United States

Peter Schneider
WHO Collaborating Centre for Pharmaceutical Pricing and Reimbursement Policies, Pharmacoeconomics Department, Gesundheit Österreich GmbH (GÖG/Austrian Public Health Institute), Vienna, Austria

Fatima Suleman
Faculty of Sciences, Utrecht University, Utrecht, The Netherlands
School of Health Sciences, College of Health Sciences, Westville Campus, University of KwaZulu-Natal, South Africa

Rianne van den Ham
Division of Pharmacoepidemiology & Clinical Pharmacology, Utrecht Institute for Pharmaceutical Sciences, Utrecht University, Utrecht, Netherlands

Sabine Vogler
WHO Collaborating Centre for Pharmaceutical Pricing and Reimbursement Policies, Pharmacoeconomics Department, Gesundheit Österreich GmbH (GÖG/Austrian Public Health Institute), Vienna, Austria

Nina Zimmermann
WHO Collaborating Centre for Pharmaceutical Pricing and Reimbursement Policies, Pharmacoeconomics Department, Gesundheit Österreich GmbH (GÖG/Austrian Public Health Institute), Vienna, Austria

ACKNOWLEDGEMENTS

This book would have never been possible without several individuals, whom I wish to thank.

I am very grateful to the authors of this book who were committed to contribute by sharing their knowledge and expertise. Special thanks go to my colleagues Nina Zimmermann and Peter Schneider who accepted to embark with me on this journey of preparing a book manuscript and who supported me by writing chapters and being available for discussions.

I thank colleagues from all over the world who readily agreed to review one or more chapters and provided valuable and comprehensive comments. I gratefully acknowledge the support of the following reviewers: Gustavo Luís Meffe Andreoli, Ministry of Health, Brazil; Jaime Espin-Balbino, Andalusian School of Public Health, Spain; Marg Ewen, Health Action International; Alessandra Ferrario, Harvard Medical School and Harvard Pilgrim Health Care Institute, USA; Mitja Kos, University of Ljubljana, Slovenia; Daniela Denisse Moye Holz, University Medical Center Groningen, University of Groningen, the Netherlands; Claudia Garcia Serpa Osorio de Castro, Sergio Arouca National School of Public Health, Fundação Oswaldo Cruz, Brazil; Jane Robertson, consultant to World Health Organization Regional Office for Europe; Joan Rovira, University of Barcelona, Spain; Yared Santa Ana Tellez, Utrecht University, the Netherlands; Nicolas Silva, School of Public Health, University of Chile, Chile and School of Health and Related Research, University of Sheffield, UK; Fatima Suleman, University of KwaZulu-Natal, South Africa and Agnes Vitry, University of South Australia, Australia.

The book is based on my understanding that knowledge transfer about medicine prices is a key element in the endeavour to achieve more affordable and equitable access to essential medicines globally. Health Action International (HAI) envisions "a world with safe, effective, affordable and quality-assured medicines for everyone, everywhere". To acknowledge HAI's excellent work in research and advocacy to advance policies that enable access to medicines and rational medicine use for all people around the world, it is a pleasure to donate my royalties of this book to Health Action International.

My deepest appreciation goes to my family for their patience and encouragement during the process and for enduring the numerous evenings and weekends that I invested in this book. I am very grateful that my husband and my son were not only willing to sacrifice time they might have spent with me but that they were extremely supportive of the book project.

CHAPTER 1

Introduction

Sabine Vogler
WHO Collaborating Centre for Pharmaceutical Pricing and Reimbursement Policies, Pharmacoeconomics Department, Gesundheit Österreich GmbH (GÖG/Austrian Public Health Institute), Vienna, Austria

LIST OF ABBREVIATIONS

EU	European Union
HIC	High-income country/ies
LMIC	Low- and middle-income country/ies
PPRI	Pharmaceutical Pricing and Reimbursement Information
SDG	Sustainable Development Goals
US	United States
WHO	World Health Organization

1.1 BACKGROUND AND RATIONALE

Experience 1:	*"I am working on a briefing paper for the Minister who aims to change the price regulation. We assume that medicine prices in our country are higher than in other countries of a similar income level. Do you know about price studies in other regions of the world?" (technical staff of a Ministry of Health)*
Experience 2:	*"I like your article that you recently published about the comparison of medicine prices in European countries. [...] Our group has been considering doing a similar research. However, we aim to focus on a specific therapeutic group, namely [...] We were also thinking of a different country basket. [...] We have been offered price data from [...] Do you know this data source? Is it reliable? Have you also used it? Are there any caveats? [...] We aim to apply a similar method as you did. Do you have a more detailed description of the methodology for price comparisons? Do you know about guidance documents for performing price surveys?" (a researcher interested in doing a price analysis)*

(*Continued*)

Medicine Price Surveys, Analyses, and Comparisons
ISBN 978-0-12-813166-4
https://doi.org/10.1016/B978-0-12-813166-4.00001-2

Experience 3: *"We have to extend the scope of price regulation to the private sector if we want to control rising prices. We were considering introducing international price benchmarking for originator medicines, which our neighboring countries have already implemented. Can you provide us with guidance of how to best do this? Are there any pitfalls we should be aware of? Do you have a written summary that we could translate and provide to the Members of Parliament?" (senior management of a pharmaceutical pricing agency)*

Affordable access to essential medicines has been acknowledged as a major policy objective under the Sustainable Development Goals (SDG). SDG 3.8 calls for achieving "universal health coverage, including financial risk protection, access to quality essential health-care services, and access to safe, effective, quality, and affordable essential medicines and vaccines for all" [1]. The World Health Organization estimated that one-third of the world's population has no access to essential medicines (and less than half in some areas) [2]. Major barriers are nonavailability of safe and high-quality medicines (pharmaceuticals are not brought on the market or they are only available in substandard quality), high medicine prices and, as a result, nonaffordability of medicines for governments and patients. In low- and middle-countries (LMIC), patients pay 50%—90% of the medicine prices because public pharmaceutical expenditure does not cover basic medicine needs of the majority of the population [3]. This makes medicines the largest family expenditure item after food [4] and can result in high catastrophic payments of patients and their carers [5,6].

Thirty years after the 1985 Nairobi Conference on the Rational Use of Drugs, The Lancet's Commission on Essential Medicines Policies explored the state of progress made and called for the implementation of a comprehensive set of policies to achieve affordable prices for essential medicines. The Lancet's Commission recommended that governments create and maintain information systems for routine monitoring of data on the affordability of essential medicines, as well as price and availability, in the public and private sectors [7].

Medicine prices are a key component to ensure affordable access to medicines. Similar to the two other Ps (patents and promotion) related to pharmaceuticals, pricing is a sensitive issue. Nonaffordability of medicines is no longer a sole issue for LMIC; the challenge of high medicine prices is also on the political agenda in high-income countries (HIC). In the United States, price increases were documented for anticancer medicines, and concerns were raised about the limited affordability of cancer therapy [8–10]. In European countries, the solidarity-based health-care systems aim to make needed medicines available. Public payers of lower-income European countries, however, cannot afford all medicines, and even payers in HIC have been struggling to ensure access to new high-priced medicines without jeopardizing the financial sustainability of their health-care system. In recent years, nearly all Presidencies of the Council of the European Union (EU)—the chairing and coordinating Member State in a 6-month rotation system—addressed affordability limitations of medicines given their high prices [11–13].

Interest in medicine prices has been growing, and studies that compare the own country's prices or analyze price developments have attracted the attention of policy-makers and stakeholders. Members of the scientific community are not the only ones interested in conducting price comparisons correctly. Public authorities require foreign price data and a robust methodology when they set their medicine prices using prices of the same medicine in other countries. This policy is called external price referencing (similar names such as international price benchmark are also applied), and it has been implemented in an increasing number of countries. Further countries consider its introduction.

These developments suggest a need for a compilation that reviews, analyses, and discusses findings, methodologies, and policies related to medicine prices. The three scenarios presented at the beginning of this chapter describe the rationale why the editor of this book felt motivated to embark on this book project journey. Several times I was approached by researchers and experts in public authorities who asked for advice on planning and performing medicine price surveys, analyses, and comparisons and for guidance on how to design or optimize the external price referencing policy. Together with team members, I used to react by providing ad hoc advice, developing and offering trainings and doing consultancy. Still, I kept being asked to provide, in writing, a summary, a review, or a guidance document. This book aims to respond to this request.

1.2 AIM AND OUTLINE

In line with the abovementioned rationale, the overall aim of the book is to contribute to more in-depth insight and improved understanding of medicine price surveys, analyses, and comparisons—may they be used for scientific publications or for pricing purposes.

Specific objectives of the book are

- to present and discuss evidence about medicine prices in different regions of the world;
- to provide advice about how to conduct medicine price studies; and
- to inform about options of how to design the external price referencing policy.

The book is organized in three parts that address these objectives:

- Part 1: Evidence—Findings of medicine price studies (Chapters 2–5)

Chapter 2 provides a review of medicine price studies in different regions of the world (Europe, the United States and Canada, Asia–Pacific, Latin America, and Africa). Chapter 3 presents results of price analyses for specific groups of medicines, and Chapter 4 explores evidence on price developments.

- Part 2: Training—How to conduct medicine price surveys, analyses, and comparisons? (Chapters 6–10)

After an introductory review of existing methodologies for price studies (Chapter 6), the subsequent chapters introduce key terminology, provide support in identifying data sources and assessing their reliability, and provide advice for planning and performing price studies. Theoretical background information will be supplemented by teaching materials (training exercises).

- Part 3: Guidance—Using medicine price comparisons for policy-making (Chapters 11–15).

This part is focused on the use of price data for pricing purposes. The external price referencing policy is presented and critically assessed, supplemented by options for improvement and alternative pricing polices. Chapter 15 summarizes main pieces of evidence and recommendations in a policy brief.

Chapter 16 concludes the book by discussing key findings of all three parts.

1.3 METHODOLOGY

The book is based on a mix of methodological approaches:

- literature review (peer-reviewed and gray literature),
- surveys with competent authorities for pharmaceutical pricing and reimbursement (particularly members of the Pharmaceutical Pricing and Reimbursement Information/PPRI network of competent authorities responsible for pricing and reimbursement policies [14] were addressed),

- practice in performing medicine price comparisons and expertise in offering advice to policy-makers and technical experts about the external price referencing policy, and
- teaching and capacity-building experience.

Further details of the methods applied are provided in respective chapters if applicable.

1.4 TARGET AUDIENCE

In line with the objectives defined, this book addresses any reader who is interested in learning more about medicine prices, in conducting, supervising, and teaching price surveys and comparisons, in analyzing and interpreting their results, and/or in using price data for pricing purposes.

Key target audiences include

- researchers,
- trainers and students,
- technical staff of public pricing authorities and policy-makers.

REFERENCES

[1] United Nations. Sustainable development knowledge plattform. 2017. Available from: http://www.un.org/millenniumgoals/.
[2] WHO. The world medicines situation. Access to essential medicines as path of the right to health. Geneva: World Health Organization; 2011. Available from: http://apps.who.int/medicinedocs/documents/s18772en/s18772en.pdf.
[3] World Health Organization. Equitable access to essential medicines: a framework for collective action. Geneva. 2004. Available from: http://apps.who.int/medicinedocs/pdf/s4962e/s4962e.pdf.
[4] Cameron A, Ewen M, Ross-Degnan D, Ball D, Laing R. Medicine prices, availability, and affordability in 36 developing and middle-income countries: a secondary analysis. The Lancet 2009;373(9659):240–9.
[5] Wagner AK, Graves AJ, Reiss SK, LeCates R, Zhang F, Ross-Degnan D. Access to care and medicines, burden of health care expenditures, and risk protection: results from the World Health Survey. Health Policy 2011;100(2):151–8.
[6] Xu K, Evans DB, Kawabata K, Zeramdini R, Klavus J, Murray CJ. Household catastrophic health expenditure: a multicountry analysis. The Lancet 2003;362 (9378):111–7.
[7] Wirtz VJ, Hogerzeil HV, Gray AL, Bigdeli M, de Joncheere CP, Ewen MA, et al. Essential medicines for universal health coverage. The Lancet 2017;389 (10067):403–76.
[8] Kelly RJ, Smith TJ. Delivering maximum clinical benefit at an affordable price: engaging stakeholders in cancer care. The Lancet Oncology 2014;15(3):e112–8.
[9] Kantarjian HM, Fojo T, Mathisen M, Zwelling LA. Cancer drugs in the United States: *Justum Pretium*—the just price. Journal of Clinical Oncology 2013;31 (28):3600–4.

[10] Abboud C, Berman E, Cohen A, Cortes J, DeAngelo D, Deininger M, et al. The price of drugs for chronic myeloid leukemia (CML) is a reflection of the unsustainable prices of cancer drugs: from the perspective of a large group of CML experts. Blood 2013;121(22):4439–42.
[11] Council of the European Union. Council conclusions on innovation for the benefit of patients (2014/C 438/06). December 6, 2014. Available from: http://eur-lex.europa.eu/legal-content/EN/TXT/?uri=uriserv:OJ.C_.2014.438.01.0012.01.ENG&toc=OJ:C:2014:438:FULL.
[12] Council of the European Union. Council conclusions on strengthening the balance in the pharmaceutical systems in the EU and its Member States. June 17, 2016. Available from: http://www.consilium.europa.eu/press-releases-pdf/2016/6/47244642812_en.pdf.
[13] Council of the European Union. Council conclusions on encouraging member states-driven voluntary cooperation between health system. June 16, 2017. Available from: http://data.consilium.europa.eu/doc/document/ST-10381-2017-INIT/en/pdf.
[14] Vogler S, Leopold C, Zimmermann N, Habl C, de Joncheere K. The Pharmaceutical Pricing and Reimbursement Information (PPRI) initiative—experiences from engaging with pharmaceutical policy makers. Health Policy and Technology 2014;3(2):139–48.

PART 1

Evidence — Findings of Medicine Price Studies

CHAPTER 2

International Comparison of Medicine Prices

Sabine Vogler
WHO Collaborating Centre for Pharmaceutical Pricing and Reimbursement Policies, Pharmacoeconomics Department, Gesundheit Österreich GmbH (GÖG/Austrian Public Health Institute), Vienna, Austria

LIST OF ABBREVIATIONS

HAI	Health Action International
WHO	World Health Organization

Chapter 2 is one of the flagship chapters of the book: its aim is to provide an overview of medicine prices in different parts of the world.

Renowned experts in the field of pharmaceutical pricing and medicine prices in the defined regions wrote the following subchapters:

- Mitja Kos of the University of Ljubljana analyzes medicine price levels in different European countries based on a careful selection of price studies for this region.
- Canadian researchers, Aidan Hollis and Paul Grootendorst, investigate the medicine price arena in the United States and Canada.
- Zaheer Ud-din Babar et al. present findings of price studies for different types of medicines in the Asian—Pacific region.
- Jaime Espin Balbino et al. explore the pharmaceutical pricing policy framework and price data sources in Latin American countries and compare their price data.
- Fatima Suleiman et al. survey the existing evidence about medicine prices in Africa.

Although all authors of the regional subchapters worked on the same task, i.e., to present the pharmaceutical pricing framework and to identify evidence of price studies, their findings vary considerably, thus reflecting differences between the regions of the world. There is large variation between the income of the countries and their health-care systems in terms of organization, funding schemes, and progresses toward universal health coverage. This results in differences in access to medicine price data and in availability and prices of medicines. There is a dearth of evidence on price

Medicine Price Surveys, Analyses, and Comparisons
ISBN 978-0-12-813166-4
https://doi.org/10.1016/B978-0-12-813166-4.00002-4

studies in several regions of the world though for a few regions the challenge is rather to select, out of a larger range of surveys and comparisons, the most meaningful price studies that meet best methodological requirements.

This chapter offers more than a sole presentation of evidence on medicine prices all over the world. By identifying key price studies, it also sets the path for the chapters to follow. For instance, the findings indicate which medicine groups are in the focus of price studies (a more in-depth analysis will be provided in Chapter 3). Identified studies also point to the importance of the WHO/HAI methodology that was developed to survey medicine prices in settings with a lack of price regulation (cf. Chapter 6.2).

By bringing together evidence on medicine prices, the authors of the subchapters contribute to shedding a light into the "black box" of medicine prices in different regions of the world.

CHAPTER 2.1

Medicine Prices in European Countries

Mitja Kos
University of Ljubljana, Faculty of Pharmacy, Ljubljana, Slovenia

LIST OF ABBREVIATIONS

ACE	Angiotensin-converting enzyme
CML	Myeloid Leukemia
DAA	Developed direct-acting antiviral
EPR	External price referencing
EU	European Union
EUR	Euro
FD	Fabry Disease
GDP	Gross domestic product
HAE	Hereditary Angioedema Chronic
HCV	Hepatitis C virus
MS	Member State(s)
OECD	Organisation for Economic Co-operation and Development
PAH	Pulmonary Arterial Hypertension
PPI	Pharma Price Information (information service of the Austrian Public Health Institute)
TPE	Total pharmaceutical expenditure
US	United States
USD FOREX	United States Dollar foreign exchange rate

2.1.1 INTRODUCTION

The chapter presents a review of price comparison studies in European countries. The review is of pragmatic type and is based on an established expertise by the WHO Collaborating Centre for Pharmaceutical Pricing and Reimbursement Policies in Vienna and continuous monitoring of the research area. The main objective of the review was to detect main challenges and rationale for the price comparison studies of medicines in the last decade and present their key findings.

Medicine Price Surveys, Analyses, and Comparisons
ISBN 978-0-12-813166-4
https://doi.org/10.1016/B978-0-12-813166-4.00003-6

Studies that include European countries as recognized by WHO classification were relevant for inclusion in the analysis: Albania, Andorra, Armenia, Austria, Azerbaijan, Belarus, Belgium, Bosnia and Herzegovina, Bulgaria, Croatia, Cyprus, Czech Republic, Denmark, Estonia, Finland, France, Georgia, Germany, Greece, Hungary, Iceland, Ireland, Israel, Italy, Kazakhstan, Kyrgyzstan, Latvia, Lithuania, Luxembourg, Malta, Monaco, Montenegro, Netherlands, Norway, Poland, Portugal, Republic of Moldova, Romania, Russian Federation, San Marino, Serbia, Slovakia, Slovenia, Spain, Sweden, Switzerland, Tajikistan, The former Yugoslav Republic of Macedonia, Turkey, Turkmenistan, Ukraine, the United Kingdom, and Uzbekistan [1].

2.1.2 HIGH-COST MEDICINES

Several studies have focused on high-cost medicines, which increasingly challenge public health-care systems. Moreover, they can also represent a considerable burden to patients who have to pay for them out of pocket. A recent report by the WHO defined a medicine as high-priced if the therapy for one patient exceeds €10,000/year to be reimbursed by a public payer [2]. However, price alone is not the only factor that impacts the pharmaceutical expenditure in health budgets.

Vogler et al. [3] investigated prices of medicines that likely contribute to high expenditure for the public payers in high-income countries. The ex-factory price data of 30 medicines in 16 European countries were collected in national databases accessible through the Pharmaceutical Price Information (PPI) service of Gesundheit Österreich GmbH (Austrian Public Health Institute) in April 2013. The study reports considerable difference in medicine prices. A total of 53% of the medicines surveyed had a unit ex-factory price (median) above 200 Euro. For two-thirds of the medicines, price differences between the highest-priced country and lowest-priced country ranged between 25% and 100%; the remaining medicines, mainly low-priced medicines, had higher price differential up to 251%. Medicine prices of Greece, Hungary, Slovakia, and the United Kingdom were frequently at the lower end; German and Swedish, as well as Danish and Irish prices were at the upper end.

Vogler et al. [4] also studied high-cost medicines specifically used in hospitals. Ex-factory prices for 15 medicines from the hospital sector that accounted for high expenditure for public payers in Austria were surveyed for 16 European countries in April 2013 (same data set as for the previous study). The comparison showed that Sweden had most frequently unit ex-factory prices in the fourth (i.e., highest) quartile (in 83% of the 15 medicines), followed by Germany (73%) and Finland (53%). Countries that most frequently had prices in the first (i.e., lowest) quartile were Hungary (90% of medicines), Greece (85%), and the United Kingdom (67%). In 74% of the medicines in the sample, Greek prices were the lowest of the analyzed countries. The price in the highest-priced country and the lowest-priced country ranged between 25% (ipilimumab) and 132% (pemetrexed).

2.1.2.1 Oncology

Research on high-priced medicines has also focused on some specific disease areas. Cancer, which is a major cause of morbidity and mortality worldwide, especially in high-income countries, represents one of such groups [5—7]. Cancer medicines were evaluated in the study of Vogler et al. [8] in a selection of high-income countries in Europe, Australia, and New Zealand. Although prices of cancer medicines were included in the panels of some price studies or were analyzed for individual countries or a few countries, no cross-country price comparison of this group of medicines for a larger number of countries has been published before this study. Official list prices per unit were surveyed at ex-factory price level for 31 originator cancer medicines in 16 European countries, Australia, and New Zealand as of June, 2013. Medicine price data for the European countries were provided by the Pharma Price Information (PPI) service; Australian and New Zealand medicine price data were retrieved from the respective pharmaceutical schedules.

Similarly to the previous findings, results of the study showed variations in ex-factory prices also for the originator cancer medicines. The difference of a medicine price between the highest-priced country and the lowest-priced country varied between 28% and 388%. A few medicines had lower outliers, especially Greek and UK prices, and upper outliers (particularly prices in Switzerland, Germany, and Sweden). Overall, Greek prices ranked at a low level, whereas Sweden, Switzerland, and Germany showed price data in similarly high ranges.

2.1.2.2 Hepatitis C

Recently, the introduction of new hepatitis C virus (HCV) medicines prompted a wide debate about fair and affordable prices. Hepatitis C is a blood-borne viral infection that can lead to liver cirrhosis, cancer, and death [9]. Newly developed direct-acting antivirals (DAAs) have markedly improved treatment efficacy, as well as shortened and simplified the treatment regimen. However, the high cost of HCV medicines has caused significant financial strain for patients and the health-care system and limited their access.

For that purpose Iyengar et al. [10] systematically compared the price and affordability of sofosbuvir and ledipasvir/sofosbuvir, the two most widely used DAAs, across 30 countries. Apart from the Organisation for Economic Co-operation and Development (OECD) member countries, a selection of low- and middle-income countries was included in the study. Published 2015 ex-factory prices for a 12-week course of treatment were provided by the Pharma Price Information (PPI) service of the Austrian public health institute Gesundheit Österreich GmbH or were obtained from national government or medicine reimbursement authorities and recent press releases. Prices were converted to US dollars using period average exchange rates and were adjusted for purchasing power parity (PPP). An additional 23% price reduction was assumed to exist in practice. All data were compiled between July 17, 2015 and January 25, 2016.

The median nominal price of a 12-week course of sofosbuvir across 26 OECD countries was US$54,568, ranging from US$48,999 in Japan to US$84,000 in the United States. Assuming a 23% price reduction on the list ex-factory price, the differences between countries were somewhat smaller. The median nominal price of a 12-week course of sofosbuvir across 26 OECD countries was US$42,017, ranging from US$37,729 in Japan to US$64,680 in the United States. Comparison of nominal prices of sofosbuvir for a 12-week course is presented in Fig. 2.1.1.

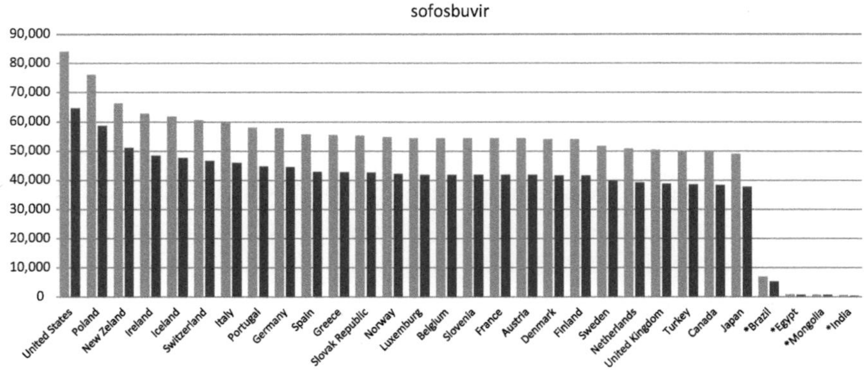

Figure 2.1.1 Comparison of the nominal (United States dollar foreign exchange rate [USD FOREX]) prices of sofosbuvir for a 12-week course, with and without a 23% rebate (or price reduction). *Not Organisation for Economic Co-operation and Development (OECD) member. *(Adopted from Iyengar S, et al. Prices, costs, and affordability of new medicines for hepatitis C in 30 countries: an economic analysis. PLoS Med 2016;13(5):e1002032.)*

2.1.2.3 Rare Diseases

Medicines for rare disease seem to receive a growing attention in the past decade. Rare diseases are usually chronic, life-threatening, or chronically debilitating and affect up to 5 in 10,000 people. They are often poorly diagnosed and treated. Although each rare disease affects only a few individuals, together they affect around 6%–8% of the total European population. Hence, they are recognized as a health-care priority in Europe [11–14].

Blankart et al. [15] published an international comparison of pharmaceutical treatments for rare diseases: pulmonary arterial hypertension (PAH), Fabry disease (FD), hereditary angioedema (HAE), and chronic myeloid leukemia (CML). The article aimed to identify differences in the availability of orphan medicines and in patient access to them in 11 pharmaceutical markets: Australia, Canada, England, France, Germany, Hungary, The Netherlands, Poland, Slovakia, Switzerland, and the United States.

Price comparison formed one of the three indicators of patients' access to the medicines for rare diseases besides the outcomes of technology appraisals and the extent of coverage provided by health-care payers. For each of the rare disease, a selection of the most relevant medicines was analyzed: for PAH bosentan, iloprost, sildenafil, treprostinil (intravenous and inhaled), as well as sitaxsentan and ambrisentan; for FD agalsidase alfa and agalsidase beta; for HAE icatibant, ecallantide, and two complement C1s inhibitors; and for CML imatinib, dasatinib, and nilotinib.

The highest prices for the included medicines were found in Germany and the United States, and the lowest in Canada, Australia, and England. Authors explained that this is related with a more centralized price control or centralized commissioning mechanisms. They also concluded that the development of medicines for rare diseases has been neglected in the past and would remain neglected if special incentives such as market exclusivity, including higher prices and more generous reimbursement conditions, were not in place.

Furthermore, Aballéa et al. [16] reported the annual average cost of 19 common orphan medicines in five European countries using public prices. Fig. 2.1.2 shows the disparities between those countries.

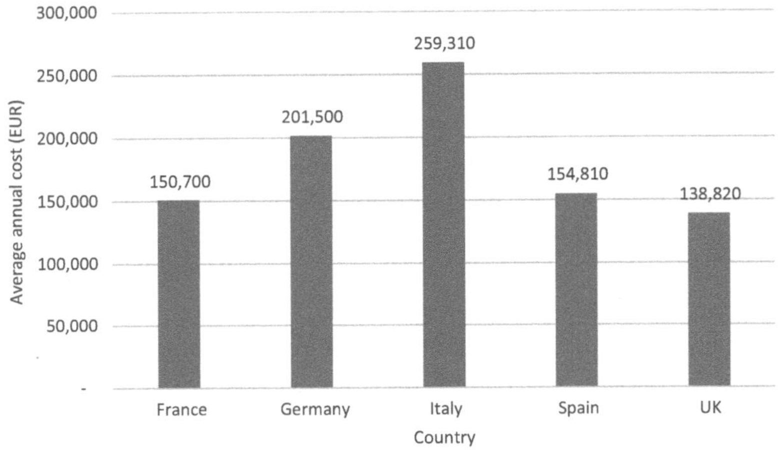

Figure 2.1.2 Comparison of average annual cost of 19 orphan medicines in Europe using public prices (in Euro (EUR)). *(Adopted from: Aballéa S, et al. Quantitative analysis of the influence of disease and product characteristics on orphan medicine prices in Europe. Poster Presented at: 15th ISPOR international meeting. Atlanta, GA, USA, 15–19 May 2010; 2010.)*

2.1.2.4 Concordance of Prices With Purchasing Power

On the contrary to what one could expect, prices of original medicines were not concordant with purchasing power as it was also showed in the two studies of medicines for rare diseases and hepatitis. Blankart et al. [15] found out that companies usually do not differentiate prices of orphan medicines according to the purchasing power of different countries. Therefore, purchasing power–adjusted prices gave different rankings compared with the nominal results as prices in Eastern Europe that are lower-income countries within Europe were similar to those in Western Europe, while purchasing power was lower. When prices were converted using PPP, prices were highest in Slovakia and Poland followed by the United States, Germany, Hungary, The Netherlands, France, Switzerland, Canada, England, and Australia.

Similarly, the study by Iyengar et al. [10] on hepatitis C medicines showed that lower-income countries such as those in Central and Eastern Europe had higher PPP-adjusted prices than other countries: prices of sofosbuvir in Poland and Turkey (PPP$101,063 and PPP$70,331) and of ledipasvir/sofosbuvir in Poland (PPP$118,754) were at least 1.09 and 1.63 times higher, respectively than in the United States (PPP$64,680 and PPP$72,765). Comparison of nominal and PPP-adjusted prices of sofosbuvir is presented in Fig. 2.1.3.

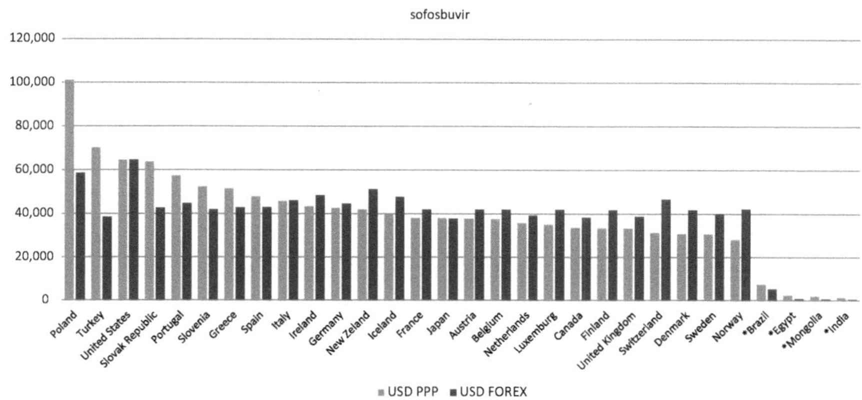

Figure 2.1.3 Comparison of the nominal (United States Dollar foreign exchange rate [USD FOREX]) and purchasing power parity–adjusted (USD PPP) prices of sofosbuvir for a 12-week course, with a 23% rebate (or price reduction). *Not Organisation for Economic Co-operation and Development (OECD) member *(Adopted from Iyengar S, et al. Prices, costs, and affordability of new medicines for hepatitis C in 30 countries: an economic analysis. PLoS Med 2016;13(5):e1002032.)*

2.1.3 GENERIC MEDICINES

Generic medicine may enter the market, once pharmaceutical patents of the originator medicines expire. A generic medicine is equivalent to a brand name product in dosage, strength, route of administration, quality, performance, and intended use. Therefore, they are certified to be perfect substitutes to the original branded medicines. In competitive markets, entry of firms producing perfect substitutes would trigger fierce price competition, bringing monopoly rents enjoyed by the original patent holder to an end.

The question of how large are the differences between originator and generic prices and what is the potential for cost-saving generic medicines policy was evaluated by Vogler [17]. Ex-factory prices as of November 2011 of five molecules provided from the Pharma Price Information (PPI) service of the Austrian Public Health Institute were analyzed for 16 European countries. The selected molecules were gemcitabine, mycophenolate mofetil, olanzapine, risperidone, and sumatriptan. For a specific presentation (same pack size, dosage, and pharmaceutical form) of each molecule, the prices of the original product and the "most common generic" as defined by PPI were compared.

Considerable variations among the extent of price differences between originator and generic were identified (gemcitabine: lowest price difference of 1.4% between originator and generic in Belgium and highest difference of 73.4% in Portugal; mycophenolate mofetil: 3.4% Norway—71.7% Netherlands; olanzapine: 0.1% Spain—97.1% Sweden; risperidone: 0.9% Netherlands—97.3% United Kingdom; sumatriptan: 5.8% Greece—95.0% Denmark).

Furthermore, no difference at all between originator and generic prices was found for some molecules in a few countries (Norway: for 4 of the 5 molecules analyzed; Spain: 3; Belgium: 2; in Austria, France, and Greece for 1 molecule, respectively). For the five molecules of the sample, Greece, Spain, Ireland, and Norway consistently displayed lower price differences, whereas Denmark, Finland, and Sweden tended to show higher differences between originator and generic prices.

2.1.4 IMPACT OF POLICY MEASURES

The special nature of pharmaceutical markets (due to patent protection, third-party payers, and low-price elasticity) has led to the introduction of regulation in European markets. A variety of policy measures have been implemented to control pharmaceutical prices. From the study by Vogler [17], it appears that countries (e.g., Denmark, Sweden) with strong generic policies, particularly based on competition and involving elements of enforcement, tend to have higher differences between originator and generic prices. More policy measures exist in practice and differ significantly across countries. They can target both the demand and supply side (see Table 2.1.1). However, although the aim of regulation is usually to decrease costs, it is not always the case that regulatory measures have the desired effect on prices and sales volume because of market distortions.

The study by von der Schulenburg et al. [18] provides an overview of policy measures targeting pharmaceutical expenditure in Europe and analyzes their impact on originator pharmaceutical prices, specifically focusing on the market of angiotensin-converting enzyme (ACE) inhibitors. Panel data methods were used to examine the market of ACE inhibitors in six European countries (Denmark, France, Germany, the Netherlands, Sweden, and the United Kingdom) over period 1991—2006. The sample includes all available ACE inhibitors (captopril, enalapril, lisinopril, quinapril, ramipril, trandolapril, perindopril, moexipril, fosinopril, benazepril, cilazapril, zofenopril, imidapril).

Table 2.1.1 Overview of policy options in regulated markets on the supply- and demand-side

Supply-side	Demand-side
Price controls based on:	**Physicians:**
Clinical performance	Clinical practice
Economic performance	Prescription guidelines
Cost of existing treatments	Education
Cost-plus calculations	Information
International prices	Monitoring/audit
Controlled price update	Prescription quotas
	Pharmaceutical budgeting
	Overall budgets
Expenditure Control:	**Patients:**
Discounts	Cost sharing
Rebates	Information
Payback	Education
Price–volume agreements	OTC spending
Price freeze/price cuts	
Industrial regulation:	**Pharmacies:**
Profit controls/Rate of return	Generic substitution
Tax benefits	Monetary incentives
	Clawbacks
	Margins
	Discounts

Adapted from von der Schulenburg F, et al. The effects of medicine market regulation on pharmaceutical prices in Europe: overview and evidence from the market of ACE inhibitors. Health Economics Review 2011;1(1):1–8.

Results suggest that supply-side measures such as mandatory generic substitution, regressive pharmacy markups, and clawbacks are effective in reducing pharmaceuticals prices. Results are not as strong for demand-side measures. Profit controls and the use of cost-effectiveness analysis appear to have a negative effect on prices, whereas results on internal price referencing are inconclusive. Findings also indicate that, although originator prices are not immediately affected by generic entry, they may be influenced by changes in generic prices postpatent expiry.

2.1.4.1 External Price Referencing

External price referencing (EPR) has become one of the most common cost-containment tools to reduce prices for in-patent pharmaceuticals in the European Union (EU) Member States (MS) [19,20]. The WHO

Collaborating Centre for Pricing and Reimbursement Policies defines EPR as: "The practice of using the price(s) of a medicine in one or several countries in order to derive a benchmark or reference price for the purposes of setting or negotiating the price of the product in a given country" [21]. As such, medicine price changes in one country will influence the prices in the other countries. However, the actual performance of such schemes in practice was questioned through time.

Leopold et al. [22] examined the impact of EPR on on-patent medicine prices, adjusting for other factors that may affect price levels such as sales volume, exchange rates, gross domestic product per capita, total pharmaceutical expenditure, and size of the pharmaceutical industry. Ex-factory price data of 14 on-patent products in 14 European countries in 2007 and 2008 were obtained from the Pharma Price Information Service (PPI) of the Austrian Public Health Institute.

Out of the 14 analyzed countries, three did not apply EPR (Germany, Denmark, and Sweden) at the time of investigation. This study showed that on average EPR as a pricing policy leads to lower prices. Namely, two of the countries that do not apply EPR (Germany and Denmark) had the highest prices. However, the large variation in price levels among countries using EPR confirmed that the price level is not only driven by EPR. Price differences are presented in Fig. 2.1.4.

Similar findings were obtained also in other studies, which also give an insight into the performance of individual countries. Brekke et al. [23,24] compared prices of pharmaceuticals in Norway with nine European countries and also presented a report for the Nordic countries separately. They used a sample of the 300 most selling substances as the basis for comparison, and computed a wide set of price indices to measure the price levels for all substances and for various submarkets such as the on-patent and off-patent market segments. IMS Health with monthly information about prices and sales volumes for all prescription bound products for the first half of 2010 was used for this purpose.

Fig. 2.1.5 reports the price indices for the Nordic countries with Norway as the base country with a price index normalized to zero. The results show that the Norwegian price level tends to be the lowest among the Nordic countries. The price differences are higher in the on-patent market segment, whereas for substances in the off-patent market segment with generic competition Sweden does, in fact, have a lower price level than Norway. This result is perhaps not surprising because of the strict price cap regulation that is in place in Norway. In the off-patent market segment,

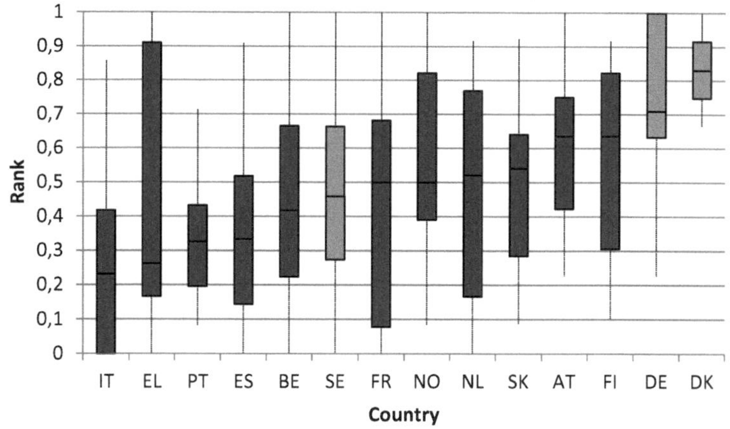

Figure 2.1.4 Impact of external reference pricing on scaled ranks. Prices were converted to scaled ranks so that different price levels were ineffectual and it guaranteed a robust data set. A higher scaled rank represents a higher price of medicines in the country. *AT*, Austria; *BE*, Belgium; *C*, country; *DE*, Germany; *DK*, Denmark; *EL*, Greece; *ES*, Spain; *FI*, Finland; *FR*, France; *IT*, Italy; *NL*, Netherlands; *NO*, Norway; *PT*, Portugal; *SE*, Sweden; *SK*, Slovak Republic. *Reading support:* blue boxes (dark gray in print version) are countries that apply external price referencing (EPR), orange boxes (light gray in print version) are countries that do not apply EPR. The line in each box equals the median of the scaled ranks per country. *(Adopted from Leopold C, et al. Impact of EPR on medicine prices—a price comparison among 14 European countries. Southern Med Review 2012;5(1).)*

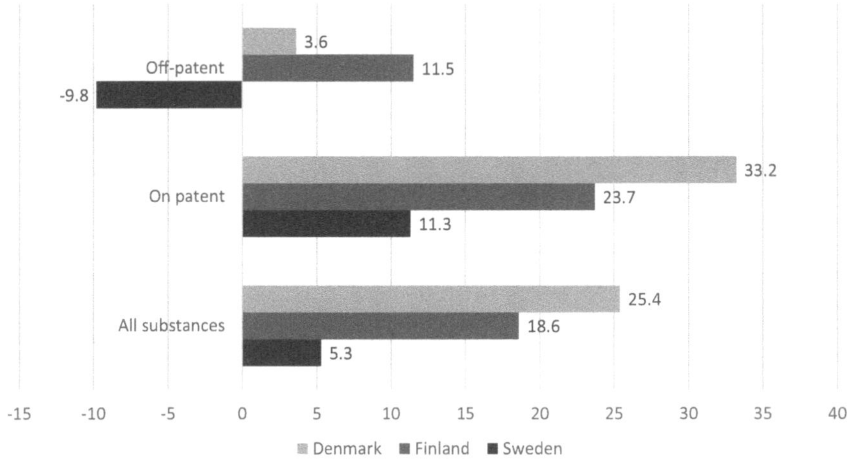

Figure 2.1.5 Bilateral price indices in comparison to Norway based on average substance prices at pharmacy levels, 2010. *(Adopted from Brekke KR, et al. Should pharmaceutical costs be curbed? Nordic Economic Policy Review 2012; Number 2/2012.)*

Table 2.1.2 Impact of a EUR 1.00 price reduction in Germany on cross-referencing countries

Country	Direct impact	Indirect impact	Total impact
Austria	0.07	0.08	0.15
Italy	0.30–0.33	0.03	0.33–0.36
Ireland	0.21–0.23	0.05–0.06	0.27–0.29
Portugal	0.00	0.33–0.36	0.33–0.36
The Netherlands	0.27–0.29	0.00	0.27–0.29

Adapted from Stargardt T, Schreyogg J. Impact of cross-reference pricing on pharmaceutical prices: manufacturers' pricing strategies and price regulation. Applied Health Economics and Health Policy 2006;5(4):235–47.

where brand names face competition from generic products, Sweden tends to have lower prices than Norway, whereas Denmark has about the same price level.

Stargardt and Schreyogg [25] aimed to quantify the cross-border effects of reference pricing schemes from the perspective of Germany. For that purpose they developed an analytical model to estimate the impact of pharmaceutical price changes in Germany on pharmaceutical prices in other countries in the EU-15[1] using cross-reference pricing. They differentiated between the direct impact (from referencing to Germany directly) and the indirect impact (from referencing to other countries that conduct their own cross-reference pricing schemes).

If the respective medicine is marketed in all referenced countries and prices are regularly updated, a price reduction of 1.00 Euro in Germany would reduce maximum reimbursement prices in the EU-15 countries from 0.15 Euro in Austria to 0.36 Euro in Italy. Impact of price changes in Germany on cross-referencing countries is presented in Table 2.1.2.

2.1.4.1.1 Challenges Related to External Reference Pricing

Authors of the last two studies exposed two different challenges related to external reference pricing. Firstly, based on the results by Brekke et al. [24], one would expect that if price indices show that the Norwegian consumption of pharmaceuticals would be 10% more expensive if using e.g., Swedish prices, the reverse is not necessarily true. The reason is that we

[1] EU-15 represents countries that were members of the European Union before enlargement in 2004: Austria, Belgium, Denmark, Finland, France, Germany, Greece, Ireland, Italy, Luxembourg, The Netherlands, Portugal, Spain, Sweden, and the United Kingdom.

then need to replace the Norwegian consumption weights with the Swedish consumption weights, implying that although the prices are the same, the price indices would be different. Nonetheless, the challenge is how to extract the potential for cost savings. This would crucially depend on the chosen policy scheme and the market dynamics.

Secondly, cross-border spillover effects of price reductions are undoubtedly welcomed by decision-makers and may be favorable to the health-care system in general. However, Stargardt and Schreyogg [25] also warned that these cross-border spillover effects provide strong incentives for strategic product launches, launch delays, and lobbying activities and can affect the effectiveness of the policy (see also Part 3, in particular Chapter 13 for further information on this topic). They also proposed to use a weighted index of prices from as many countries as possible to determine reimbursement prices to avoid the negative effects of cross-reference pricing by reducing the direct and indirect impact of individual countries.

2.1.4.2 Convergence of Medicine Prices Over Time

Previous studies have suggested that on-patent medicine prices in Europe converge over time as a result of policy measures at the level of single MS, parallel trade, and EPR [26]. The European Competiveness Report 2006 illustrated that EU price convergence for medicines was more rapid in the second half of the 1990s as a result of the process of EU monetary convergence [27]. Starting from 2000, two clusters of countries were identified: the core EU countries (France, Italy, Belgium, The Netherlands and Luxembourg, Denmark, Finland, Sweden, United Kingdom, and Ireland) with a 15% average price gap; and the cluster of newer EU MS, as well as Spain, Portugal, and Greece, who had average prices almost 40% lower than the EU-15 level [28].

Since the economic recession in 2008, many European countries have been forced to implement cost-containment policies to maintain their high-level health-care services. As a consequence these policy changes may have had an influence on medicine prices and on European price convergence. Therefore, Leopold et al. [29] questioned whether Europe price convergence of on-patented medicines in Western European countries remains in times of economic recession (2007–12).

Prices of 10 on-patent medicines in 5 years (2007, 2008, and 2010–12) of 15 Western European countries were analyzed. The unit of analysis was the ex-factory price in Euro per defined daily dose (exchange rate indexed to 2007). A score (deviation from the average price) per country and the ranges were calculated for all medicines.

Instead of the price convergence, between 2008 and 2012, a price divergence was seen, which was fully driven by two countries, Germany (up to 27% more expensive than the average) and Greece (up to 32% cheaper than the average). All other countries had stable prices and centered around the country average. Prices of less expensive and expensive medicines remained relatively stable or decreased over time, while only the price of sirolimus relatively increased. The authors commented that several pricing policy measures may had affected the prices of medicines as a reaction to the recession.

2.1.5 ACTUAL PRICES

Most of the European price studies published in the international literature do not report the actual prices that would become a real cost to the payer. Actual paid prices are likely to be lower because of confidential discounts and similar funding arrangements between industry and public payers. According to Vogler et al. [3] this could be particularly evident for high-priced medicines. Therefore, pricing authorities refer to the higher undiscounted prices when they use price data from other countries for their pricing decisions with a risk of overpaying.

An insight into actual prices gives us a study by Vogler [30] that surveyed price reductions such as discounts and rebates granted for medicines used in hospitals. They collected official list prices and actual hospital prices

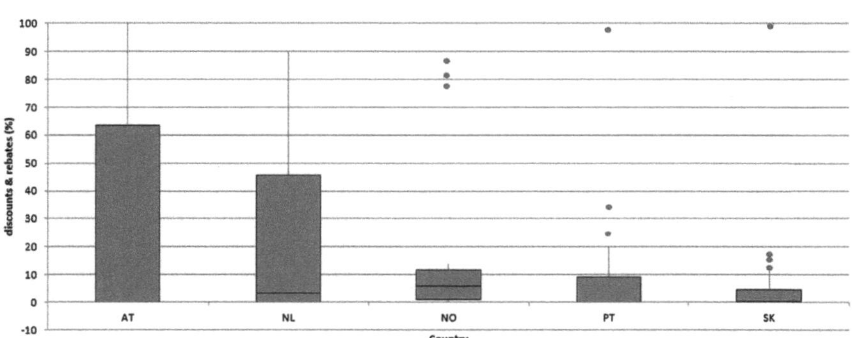

Figure 2.1.6 Range of discounts and rebates granted for medicines per country (boxplot). *AT,* Austria; *NL,* The Netherlands; *NO,* Norway; *PT,* Portugal; *SK,* Slovakia. *(Adopted from: Vogler S, et al. Discounts and rebates granted for medicines for hospital use in five European countries. The Open Pharmacoeconomics & Health Economics Journal 2013;5:1–10.)*

of 12 medicines in 25 hospitals in five European countries (Austria, The Netherlands, Norway, Portugal, and Slovakia).

In all five countries, price reductions were granted for some of the medicines surveyed. Range of price reductions granted for medicines per country is presented in Fig. 2.1.6. They usually had the form of discounts; additionally, ex-post rebates were reported from Austria and Portugal. For oncology, antiinflammatory diseases, neurology, multiple sclerosis, and blood, no price reductions or only minor discounts/rebates on medicines prices were surveyed, whereas discounts/rebates were routinely granted for cardiovascular medicines and medicines for immunomodulation. Price reductions of 100% were found in Austria, Portugal, and Slovakia. With the exception of Slovakia, the extent of the discounts/rebates did not differ substantially among the hospitals of a country. The highest median price reductions were identified in Norway, followed by The Netherlands. Price reductions for medicines procured by central tendering tended to be higher than those obtained in decentralized procurement.

The box displays the interquartile range (IQR): the bottom and top of the box are the 25th and 75th percentiles (the first and third quartiles, respectively), and the band near the middle of the box is the median. The dashed lines describe the bottom and top whiskers. Please note that whiskers can be no longer than a certain length; in R the default is that whiskers can be no longer than 1.5 times the IQR. The small circles indicate extreme data points (commonly referred to as "outliers").

The study shows the existence of discounts and rebates granted for specific medicines for hospital use. The results suggest product-specific patterns. Hospitals appear to have little leeway to negotiate price reductions for medicines to which no therapeutic alternatives are available. High-price reductions, including cost-free provision of medicines, tend to be granted for medicines whose treatment is likely to continue in primary care after discharge of the patient.

Furthermore, a study by Kanavos and Vandoros [31] analyzed price levels for a basket of prescription medicines and their differences in 15 OECD countries, including the United States and key European countries, by using volume-weighted price indices. The study showed that large differences in prices are mainly observed at an ex-factory level. Cross-country differences in retail prices are actually not as high as expected, and, when controlling for exchange rates, these differences can be even smaller as can been seen from Fig. 2.1.7.

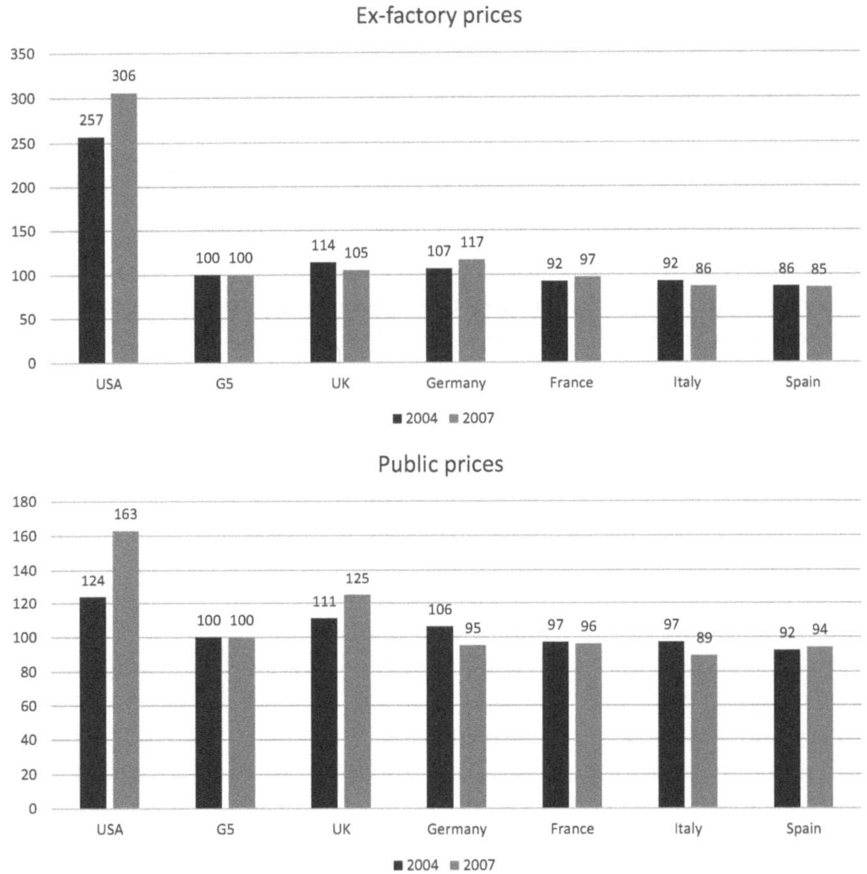

Figure 2.1.7 Price levels of United States versus European Union (EU) countries, United Kingdom, Germany, France, Italy, and Spain (EU G5): ex-factory and public prices at current exchange rates, 2004 and 2007, price indices FSS = federal supply schedule (FSS). *Note:* For the United States, the wholesaler acquisition cost is taken into account. *(Adopted from: Kanavos PG, Vandoros S. Determinants of branded prescription medicine prices in OECD countries. Health Economics Policy and Law 2011;6(3):337.)*

Furthermore, the study by Schneider and Vogler [32] analyzed ex-factory prices of 30 medicines (15 medicines from the outpatient sector and 15 medicines from the inpatient sector) that accounted for high expenditure for public payers in Austria and was surveyed for 16 European countries. In addition to these official list prices, the statutorily discounted ex-factory medicines in Germany were collected and compared.

Overall, for the 30 selected medicines, Germany was the country that had most frequently the highest prices (in 40% of the 30 medicines), followed by Sweden (23%), and Denmark (13%). If discounted medicines instead of list prices were considered for Germany, Sweden was most frequently the highest-priced country (37% of the medicines), followed by Denmark (17%). Together with Austria and the United Kingdom, Germany ranked third (10%). Among the analyzed medicines, the impact on the price level was strongest for medicines with the comparably highest prices.

Similarly, the study by van Harten et al. [33] surveyed prices for nine cancer medicines in 15 European countries in July 2015. The study reported that both official/list prices and actual prices differ substantially between countries (up to 92% for official/list prices and 58% for actual prices lower than the highest). Additionally, reductions on list prices were very different between countries. From the study, it is also evident that the research of actual prices presents a considerable challenge. The survey was sent to 51 members of the European Organization of Cancer Institutes (OECI) and Cancer Core Europe. However, only 21 centers reported the prices for the nine oncology medicines in question. Furthermore, colleagues from Belgium questioned whether the reported prices were in fact actual prices based on the discrepancies they observed for their country [34].

2.1.6 FINAL REMARKS

The number of studies that would systematically compare medicine prices in European countries is scarce. Moreover, published studies normally include only a selection of countries. For example, none of the reported studies included all EU countries. The methodology often uses a small selection of medicines, which could bias or limit the findings. Because of the great variation across countries in both the range of medicine compounds available and the dosage forms, strengths and pack sizes for each compound, obtaining a broadly comprehensive or representative sample are problematical. If products are required to match on all dimensions, then only a very small and unrepresentative sample of the medicines available in each country can be included in the analysis [35]. Finally, most of the studies report publically stated prices and do not reveal discounts or rebates and other agreements that would reveal the actual prices. Therefore, the conclusions based on the existing studies are limited and a conscious interpretation is necessary.

REFERENCES

[1] European countries as recognised by WHO classification. http://www.euro.who.int/en/countries.

[2] WHO, Regional office for Europe. Access to new medicines in Europe: technical review of policy initiatives and opportunities for collaboration and research. 2015.

[3] Vogler S, et al. Price comparison of high-cost originator medicines in European countries. Expert Review of Pharmacoeconomics & Outcomes Research 2016.

[4] Vogler S, et al. European price comparison of high cost hospital medicines. European Journal of Hospital Pharmacy 2016b;23(Suppl. 1):A163–4.

[5] Sullivan R, et al. Delivering affordable cancer care in high-income countries. Lancet Oncol 2011;12:933–80.

[6] OECD. Cancer care. Assuring quality to improve survival. OECD Health Policy Studies: OECD Publishing; 2013.

[7] Lozano R, et al. 2012 Global and regional mortality from 235 causes of death for 20 age groups in 1990 and 2010: a systematic analysis for the Global Burden of Disease Study. Lancet 2010;380:2095–128.

[8] Vogler S, et al. Cancer medicines in 16 European countries, Australia, and New Zealand: a cross-country price comparison study. The Lancet Oncology 2015; 17(1):39–47.

[9] Hepatitis C. WHO fact sheet. Updated. July 2017. http://www.who.int/mediacentre/factsheets/fs164/en/.

[10] Iyengar S, et al. Prices, costs, and affordability of new medicines for hepatitis C in 30 countries: an economic analysis. PLoS Med 2016;13(5):e1002032.

[11] European Medicines Agency. Medicines for rare diseases [Internet]. Available from: http://www.ema.europa.eu/ema/index.jsp?curl=pages/special_topics/general/general_content_000034.jsp&mid=WC0b01ac058002d4eb.

[12] Orphanet. Rare disease registries in Europe [Internet]. 2016. Available from: http://www.orpha.net/orphacom/cahiers/docs/GB/Registries.pdf.

[13] The European Organisation for Rare Diseases (EURORDIS). About rare diseases [Internet]. Available from: http://www.eurordis.org/about-rare-diseases.

[14] Richter T, et al. Rare disease terminology and definitions—a systematic global review: report of the ISPOR rare disease special interest group. Value Health 2015;18(6): 906–14.

[15] Blankart CR, et al. Availability of and access to orphan medicines: an international comparison of pharmaceutical treatments for pulmonary arterial hypertension, Fabry disease, hereditary angioedema and chronic myeloid leukaemia. Pharmacoeconomics 2011;29(1):63–82.

[16] Aballéa S, et al. Quantitative analysis of the influence of disease and product characteristics on orphan medicine prices in Europe. Poster presented at: 15th ISPOR international meeting. Atlanta, GA, USA, 15–19 May 2010; 2010.

[17] Vogler S. How large are the differences between originator and generic prices? Analysis of five molecules in 16 European countries. Farmeconomia Health Economics and Therapeutic Pathways 2012;13(Suppl. 3):29–41.

[18] von der Schulenburg F, et al. The effects of medicine market regulation on pharmaceutical prices in Europe: overview and evidence from the market of ACE inhibitors. Health Economics Review 2011;1(1):1–8.

[19] Toumi, et al. External reference pricing of medicinal products: simulation based considerations for cross country coordination. 2014. https://ec.europa.eu/health//sites/health/files/systems_performance_assessment/docs/erp_reimbursement_medicinal_products_en.pdf.

[20] Vogler S, et al. Study on enhanced cross-country coordination in the area of pharmaceutical product pricing. Brussels: Publications Office of the European Union; 2016.
[21] Glossary of pharmaceutical terms. GOEG. http://whocc.goeg.at/Glossary/About.
[22] Leopold C, et al. Impact of external price referencing on medicine prices—a price comparison among 14 European countries. Southern Med Review 2012;5(1).
[23] Brekke KR, et al. Comparing pharmaceutical prices in Europe. A comparison of prescription medicine prices in Norway with nine western European countries. Report 11/11. Bergen: Institute of Research in Economics and Business Administration; 2011.
[24] Brekke KR, et al. Should pharmaceutical costs be curbed? Nordic Economic Policy Review 2012. Number 2/2012.
[25] Stargardt T, Schreyogg J. Impact of cross-reference pricing on pharmaceutical prices: manufacturers' pricing strategies and price regulation. Applied Health Economics and Health Policy 2006;5(4):235—47.
[26] Kanavos P, Vandoros S. Differences in costs of and access to pharmaceutical products in the EU. Brussels: European Parliament; 2011. IP/A/ENVI/ST/2010-12.
[27] European Commission European Competitiveness Report. Economic reforms and competitiveness. Key messages from the European Competitiveness Report. 2006. http://ec.europa.eu/enterprise/sectors/ict/files/euro comp report 2006 en.pdf.
[28] Cambridge Pharma Consulting. Pricing and market access review 2005. IMS Intelligence 2006.
[29] Leopold C, et al. Is Europe still heading to a common price level for on-patent medicines? An exploratory study among 15 Western European countries. Health Policy 2013;112:209—16.
[30] Vogler S, et al. Discounts and rebates granted for medicines for hospital use in five European countries. The Open Pharmacoeconomics & Health Economics Journal 2013;5:1—10.
[31] Kanavos PG, Vandoros S. Determinants of branded prescription medicine prices in OECD countries. Health Economics Policy and Law 2011;6(3):337.
[32] Schneider P, Vogler S. Impact of discounts on medicine prices. Journal of Pharmaceutical Policy and Practice 2015;8(Suppl. 1):O4.
[33] van Harten WH, et al. Actual costs of cancer drugs in 15 European countries. The Lancet Oncology 2015;17(1):18—20.
[34] De Block M. The difficulty of comparing drug prices between countries. The Lancet Oncology 2016;17(4):e125.
[35] Danzon PM, Kim JD. International price comparisons for pharmaceuticals. Pharmacoeconomics 1998;14(1):115—28.

CHAPTER 2.2

Medicine Prices in the United States and Canada

Aidan Hollis[1], **Paul Grootendorst**[2]
[1]University of Calgary, Calgary, Alberta, Canada; [2]University of Toronto, Toronto, Ontario, Canada

LIST OF ABBREVIATIONS

PMPRB	Patented Medicine Prices Review Board
UK	United Kingdom
US	United States
ICER	Incremental Cost Effectiveness
CADTH	Canadian Agency for Drugs and Technologies in Health
pCPA	pan-Canadian Pharmaceutical Alliance
OECD	Organisation for Economic Co-operation and Development
PMPI	Patented Medicines Price Index
CPI	Consumer Price Index
DMARD	*Disease-modifying anti-rheumatic drugs*
PBM	Pharmacy Benefit Managers
GBP	Great Britain Pound

2.2.1 CANADA

2.2.1.1 Policies

Canada is a federation and constitutionally health falls under provincial jurisdiction. As a result, each provincial government operates its own prescription drug insurance plan and is free to set plan parameters, including which residents are covered, copayments and other cost-sharing rules, and the price at which drugs are reimbursed. These plans mainly cover seniors, those with low income, residents of long-term care facilities, and others with high drug costs relative to income. There are also federal government plans for active and retired military personnel, aboriginals, and various smaller groups. Collectively, these public plans account for about 43% of national prescription drug spending [1]. Employer-sponsored drug plans also operate across provinces; these plans account for 35% of total spending.

Medicine Price Surveys, Analyses, and Comparisons
ISBN 978-0-12-813166-4
https://doi.org/10.1016/B978-0-12-813166-4.00004-8

Out-of-pocket spending (mainly on drug copayments and deductibles) accounts for the remaining 22%. This complex arrangement is relatively ineffective in controlling prices as we discuss below.

2.2.1.1.1 Federal Patented Drug Price Regulation

The federal government operates the Patented Medicine Prices Review Board (PMPRB). This agency regulates both the introductory prices and subsequent price increases of patented drugs. Introductory prices are regulated on the basis of a test that considers the therapeutic benefit provided by the new patented drug relative to similar drugs on the Canadian market. Innovative drugs—ones that are considered at least a "moderate improvement" over existing drugs—generally are allowed higher prices than new products that fall into the "slight or no improvement" category.

Innovative drugs can be priced no higher than the median of the factory-gate prices of the same patented drug in the so-called PMPRB7 countries: France, Germany, Italy, Sweden, Switzerland, the United Kingdom (UK) and the United States (US) [2]. Other new drugs can be priced no higher than similar drugs on the Canadian market. In addition, the prices of all patented drugs are constrained to be no greater than the highest price of the same drug charged across the PMPRB7 countries. Patented drug price inflation cannot exceed overall price inflation.

The PMPRB rules are somewhat ineffective. First, the actual transaction prices paid in the PMPRB7 countries are almost certainly lower due to the widespread use of confidential rebates and discounts. A recent survey of rebates in drug plans operating in 11 countries, including 4 PMPRB7 comparator countries (Germany, England, Sweden, and the United States), found discounts in excess of 20% off list prices [3]. Thus the median PMPRB7 price threshold is likely inflated. (To the PMPRB's credit, however, prices in Canada have been well below the median PMPRB7 price [4]). Second, the PMPRB7 countries include those with the most expensive prices worldwide [5]. The PMPRB is currently reviewing its policies in light of these concerns. Among other changes it is considering, is a change in the comparator countries, removing the United States and other countries with very high list prices and including Spain and other countries with lower list prices [2].

2.2.1.1.2 Drug Plan Reimbursement of Brand Drugs

Since the mid-1990s, the public plans have relied on health technology assessments to determine which drugs they will pay for and how much. Manufacturers submit evidence on the incremental cost effectiveness (ICER) of new drugs; a drug's ICER is the ratio of the additional health benefits to the additional cost of the new drug relative to the standard of care. This evidence is reviewed by the Canadian Agency for Drugs and Technologies in Health (CADTH). (Québec uses its own agency, the Institute National d'Excellence en Santé et Services Sociaux.) After assessing the quality of the clinical evidence, the estimated health benefits, and the price, CADTH will then recommend that the drug be approved or not [6]. If the agency approves a new drug, then another agency, the pan-Canadian Pharmaceutical Alliance (pCPA), will negotiate on behalf of the public drug plans over the size of a secret discount off of the list price. Then each of the public drug plans will consider covering the drug at this discounted price.

Private drug plans do not participate in these negotiations, although some larger insurers are reported to be engaging in price negotiations with manufacturers [7]. It appears, however, that private plans pay higher prices than the public plans, something that the brand drug trade association, Innovative Medicines Canada, admits [4].

2.2.1.1.3 Drug Plan Reimbursement of Generic Drugs

Public plan coverage of generic drugs is more streamlined. Health Canada approves generic drugs on the basis of its bioequivalence to a reference brand drug. Each of the public plans then reviews these same bioequivalence data for generics that Health Canada approved. Generics deemed to be interchangeable with the brand drug are listed on a formulary. Pharmacists are then allowed and in some provinces are required to substitute between interchangeable formulary drugs. All public drug plans and about two-thirds of private plans [8] limit reimbursement of the brand drug to the generic reimbursement price.

Over the first 30 years of their history, the public plans paid relatively generous amounts for generic drugs, well in excess of the average cost to generic firms to supply these drugs, leading to substantial profits. A generic manufacturer would typically share some of these profits with pharmacies that stocked its products. The pharmacy portion is called an "off invoice" rebate. In 2006, the Ontario public drug plan, aware of these rebates, reduced its reimbursement price, and over the next 10 years, all other public plans unilaterally reduced their prices as well. Since 2013, the pCPA, operating on behalf of the public plans outside Quebec, has limited reimbursement of various high-volume generic drugs to 18% (and in some cases 15%) of the reference brand name drug price. Quebec has recently announced its intention of tendering generic drugs [9].

Other generic drugs are paid on a declining price schedule whereby the reimbursement price declines, the larger the number of generics on the market. This approach has the advantage that generic firms will keep entering the market—and knocking down the price—as long as it is profitable to do so [10]. The lowest price under this scheme, however, is 25% of the reference brand price, which is much higher than generic prices in many other countries.

Some of the provincial governments have also introduced legislation that lowers generic drug prices paid by private plans. Before this, some private plans attempted to negotiate lower generic prices with pharmacies but were ultimately unsuccessful [11].

2.2.1.1.4 Biosimilars

Public drug plan policy regarding the coverage and pricing of biosimilar drugs is still being developed. The pCPA, however, has revealed some aspects of its forthcoming policy [12,13]. In particular, it intends to force the biosimilar price to be lower than the price of the pioneer biologic.

2.2.1.2 Canada Drug Price Studies

2.2.1.2.1 Brand Drugs

The PMPRB regularly reports on patented drug prices in Canada relative to those paid in the seven comparator countries. (Foreign prices are converted to Canadian dollars at market exchange rates.) The most recent published comparison reveals that Canada pays substantially more than France and Italy, modestly more than Sweden and the United Kingdom, about the same as Switzerland, and substantially less than the United States and Germany [14]. As is true for most price studies, these price comparisons are of limited value because there are unreported rebates in all countries. It seems likely, however, that even net of confidential rebates, UK prices are considerably lower than Canadian prices, which are in turn considerably lower than US prices on average.

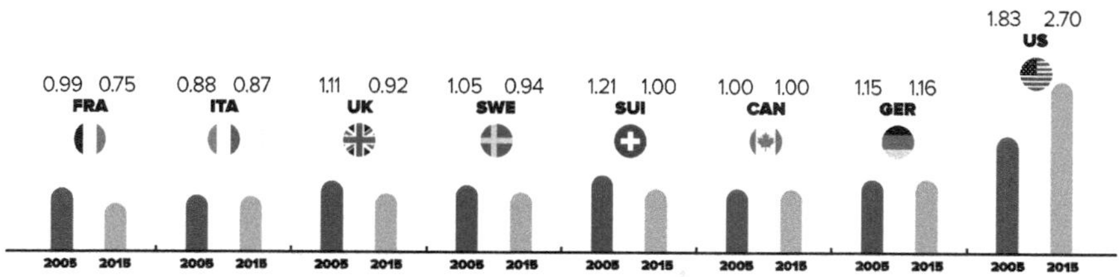

Average foreign-to-Canadian price ratios: 2005, 2015. *(Reproduced from 2015 PMPRB Annual Report.)*

The PMPRB has also compared domestic patented drug prices to those charged in the Organisation for Economic Co-operation and Development (OECD) member countries. The median OECD prices are on average ~22% below prices in Canada.

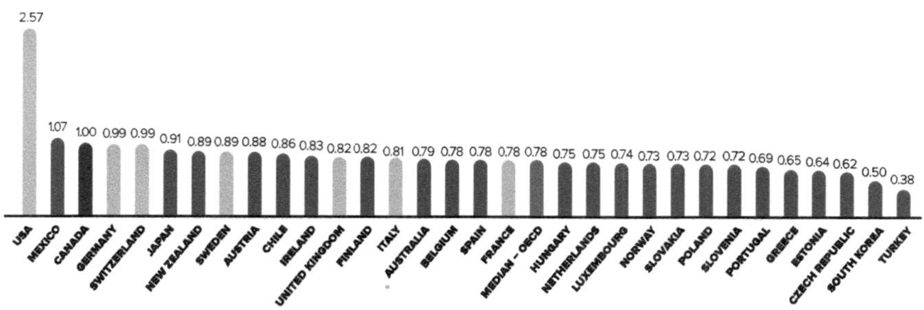

Average foreign-to-Canadian price ratios, patented drugs, OECD, 2015. *(Reproduced from 2015 PMPRB Annual Report.)*

The PMPRB also reports the annual rate of change in domestic patented drug prices, using the "Patented Medicines Price Index" (PMPI). The PMPI uses a sales-weighted average of price changes observed at the level of individual drug products.

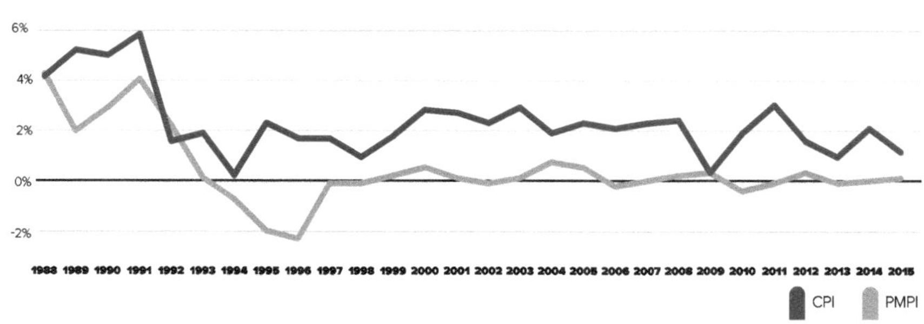

Annual rate of change, patented medicines price index (PMPI), and consumer price index (CPI), 1988–2015. *(Reproduced from 2015 PMPRB Annual Report.)*

As several of the provincial drug plans do not generally permit price increases, it is not surprising that the PMPI has been essentially flat since 1993. This index, however, does not account for the incorporation of new drugs that often replace existing lower-priced drugs or indeed the increase over time in the entry prices of new drugs. Morgan and colleagues [15] carefully explore the reasons for the changes in drug expenditures in Canada from 2007/8–2012/3. They find that price decreases led to a 0.5% expenditure decrease over that period, whereas the choices of drugs across or within therapeutic classes led to a 2.2% increase in total expenditures.

2.2.1.2.2 Biologics

Biologic drugs constitute a growing share of total drug spending in Canada. The PMPRB recently examined prices of a subset of biologics which they refer to as "biologic disease-modifying antirheumatic drugs" or biologic DMARDs for short [16]. These consist of the drugs Enbrel, Remicade, Kineret, Humira, Rituxan, Orencia, Simponi, Cimzia, and Actemra. These six drugs accounted for 10.3% of the Canadian pharmaceutical market in 2015.

The list prices of these drugs were compared with international list prices. The agency found that the median PMPRB7 (France, Germany, Italy, Sweden, Switzerland, the United Kingdom and the United States)-to-Canadian price ratio was 0.89, suggesting that the median prices for biologic DMARDs in the PMPRB7 markets were, on average, 11% lower than in Canada. In addition, the median OECD-to-Canadian price ratio was 0.78, indicating that the median prices in the OECD markets were, on average, 22% lower than in Canada.

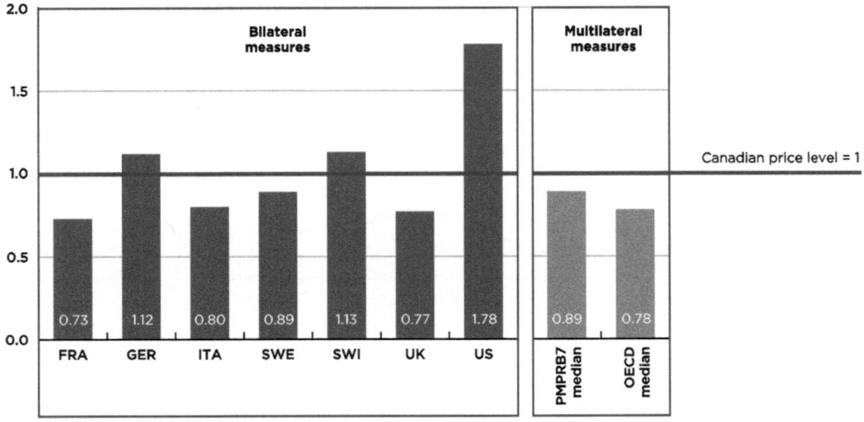

Average foreign-to-Canadian price ratios for biologic DMARDs. Canada versus PMPRB7 (comparator countries: France, Germany, Italy, Sweden, Switzerland, UK and US) and OECD countries, 2015. *(Reproduced from Patented Medicine Prices Review Board. Market intelligence report: biologic Response modifier agents 2015. Ottawa: Patented Medicine Prices Review Board; October 2016.)*

2.2.1.2.3 Generics

Over the period 2010–14, the changes to generic drug reimbursement described earlier lead to significant price decreases, relative to international averages. Nevertheless, domestic generic prices remained higher than those paid elsewhere. In 2014, the mean price of a subsample of generic drugs available in both Canada and in the comparator countries referenced by the PMPRB was 0.81 of the corresponding Canadian prices, whereas the median foreign price was 0.69 of the Canadian price [18].

Numerous studies (e.g., Beall et al. [19]) have documented that generic drug prices are much lower in many comparable countries, in part no doubt because the limit for reimbursement is set based on a relatively high price ceiling, even for high-volume drugs.

2.2.1.2.4 All Prescribed Drugs

Morgan et al. [20] find expenditures on primary care prescription drugs in Canada were much higher than in comparator countries, with higher Canadian prices driving most of the difference. They report that list prices in Canada were 61% higher than in nine other countries. They also observe that countries with single-payer financing systems seem to obtain lower prices and lower-cost selection of treatment options within therapeutic categories, compared with countries with mixed systems or social insurance models.

2.2.2 UNITED STATES

The United States is the world's largest market for pharmaceuticals, with high prices and high utilization of new pharmaceuticals [21]. It is also a particularly complex market, with national, state, and private insurance systems and many intermediaries in both distribution and insurance. We first summarize some of the key policies and then briefly review some recent studies on pricing.

2.2.2.1 Policies

The US system of drug insurance is similar in many respects to the system in Canada. There is a mixed public–private system, with public subsidies for individuals and households who do not have comprehensive employer-sponsored coverage and who have limited means to pay out of pocket. These include seniors (Medicare part D), households with very low income (Medicaid), children of households with incomes that are modest but too high to qualify for Medicaid (The State Children's Health Insurance Program), active and retired military personnel (Department of Defense and Department of Veterans Affairs, respectively), and others without access to private employer-sponsored health-care coverage (Affordable Care Act).

There are, however, several differences between the systems in the United States and Canada. First, unlike in Canada, the largest US public drug plans—Medicare Part D and Affordable Care Act coverage—are not publically administered. Instead, they are offered by private insurers whose coverage meets federal standards. These standards specify maximum out-of-pocket spending over a 12-month period and the drugs that must be reimbursed. The reliance on private insurers provides beneficiaries a wider range of insurance packages than would be available under a publicly administered plan, and this was thought to improve welfare. Although there are indeed a large variety of plans, with different premiums and copayments and formularies, it is challenging for beneficiaries to choose the optimal plan from the large choice set [22].

Second, there is no federal price regulation in the United States. Some federal drug plans, however, require price discounts from manufacturers who wish to have their drugs covered. Medicaid requires that brand drug manufacturers offer rebates that reduce prices to the lower of 23.1% less than the average price paid for the drug by other buyers, or the lowest price at which the drug is sold to other (nonfederal) buyers [23]. (In addition to these mandatory rebates, state Medicaid programs can negotiate further discounts.) The Veterans Health Administration and the Department of Defense impose similar rules. Moreover, these two programs also directly negotiate lower prices with drug manufacturers [23]. The 340 B program requires drug manufacturers to offer discounts on outpatient drugs to certain hospitals, community health centers, and other facilities that treat large numbers of low-income patients [23]. Unusually, Medicare Part D is barred from engaging in drug price negotiations, although private insurers that serve Medicare beneficiaries are free to negotiate.

Third, the public plans in Canada use health technology assessments to determine which drugs offer acceptable value for money. The US public plans have no formalized health technology assessment procedures. Instead, these plans tend to cover most of the drugs produced by the manufacturers that agree to provide statutorily defined price discounts [24].

A final key difference between the two countries is the prominent role of pharmacy benefit managers (PBMs) in the United States to negotiate on drug prices and pharmacy fees for employer-sponsored and other drug plans. In general, PBMs offer suppliers (i.e., pharmacies and branded drugs manufacturers) higher unit sales volumes in exchange for lower prices. PBMs can increase a supplier's unit sales volumes by providing drug plan beneficiaries with financial incentives to use the supplier. This is accomplished by structuring beneficiary copayments such that copayments are lowest for a "preferred" supplier. The size of the discount extracted from a brand drug manufacturer presumably depends on the number of therapeutically similar drugs it competes with.

PBM penetration is much lower in Canada. Although private drug plans tend to use beneficiary cost sharing [8], this cost sharing is not used to steer patients to particular branded drugs or pharmacies.

Cost sharing in the United States likely exerts some downward pressure on US drug prices. About one quarter of people taking a prescription drug in the United States reports that it is either somewhat or very difficult to afford it [25].

Kesselheim et al. [26] argue that the high drug prices observed in the United States are the consequence of coverage requirements imposed on government-sponsored drug plans, which cannot bargain effectively (if at all) when they are constrained to provide insurance for a patented drug. Private insurance has also been relatively ineffective for achieving price reductions on branded drugs. Smaller employers will typically rely on one of the large PBMs which, however, are at least partly motivated to capture price reductions for themselves and may not pass all savings on to the employers or insured. Kesselheim et al. [26] argue further that self-insured large employers have historically not been successful in taking a tough bargaining stance since they have used open formularies.

2.2.2.2 US Price Studies

Kanavos et al. [27] compare US with foreign prices using two indices: Laspeyres and Paasche, with the difference being that the former is weighted based on US consumption volumes and the latter based on the comparator country volumes. As they show, when using the Laspeyres index, the US prices are higher, but not as much higher as when the Paasche index is used. The implication they draw from this is the United States uses relatively more expensive drugs. They also find that taxes and wholesale and retail markups add less to drug cost than in comparator OECD countries, which somewhat mitigates the difference in ex-factory drug pricing. The scale of price differences between countries, however, is impressive, with the United States paying markedly higher prices than other countries. For example, the PMPRB estimates that patented drug prices in the United States are about 2.7 times higher than those in Canada [14], although the presence of confidential rebates makes it difficult to be precise about the price difference.

Dusetzina [28] examined the prices of new oncology medicines. She finds that the average monthly price of new drugs increased from $1869 in 2000 to $11,325 in 2014 (both in 2014 dollars). These numbers exclude any confidential rebates or discounts. Prasad and Mailankody [35], looking back even further, propose that prices for new cancer drugs have soared from roughly $100 per month of therapy in the 1960s to roughly $10,000 today.

Howard et al. [29], also focusing on oncology drugs, model the relationship between drug price per life year gained and the year a drug was introduced. They show that there has been a steady increase in the price per year of life gained: it rose from around $54,000 in 1995 to $139,000 in 2005, to $207,000 in 2015. (All figures are reported in 2013 US dollars.) This approach shows that even accounting for the therapeutic value of drugs, new drug prices have risen at an extraordinary pace—approximately 7% per year over a period of 20 years. They suggest, following a group of over 100 oncologists [30] that this increase in prices is due to a pricing system in which each successive cancer drug is priced a little higher than whatever came before.

Jorgensen and Kefalas [31] examine the relationship between nominal prices of newly launched patented drugs in the United Kingdom and United States. Although they adjust for wholesale markups, they lack information on confidential discounts, which of course occur at different levels in both countries. They find that the mean US/UK price ratio was 3.64 for drugs that cost less than GBP 2500 per patient per year, whereas the ratio fell consistently as the number of patients for whom the drug indicated was decreased. That is, prices are more similar for very high-priced drugs with smaller patient populations.

2.2.2.2.1 Generics

The United States has historically had a robustly competitive generic drug market; it is not surprising, then, that generic prices in the United States were on average lower than prices in Canada in 2010 and 2014 [6]. These differences in average generic price levels, however, mask substantial variation in relative prices of individual generic drugs with some generics being markedly less expensive in Canada [32]. Indeed, there has been some concern about very large price increases on a few generic drugs in the United States observed recently. This led to a study by the Government Accountability Office, which found that US generic prices declined on average from 2010 to 2015, but that prices had at least doubled for 315 out of 1441 "established" drugs [33]. Forty-eight generics drugs had a price increase of over 500%. Most products with large price increases had relatively small volume, and the study noted that lack of competition was likely one of the causes of price increases.

Dave et al. performed a comprehensive analysis of prices for established generic drugs during the period 2008–13, using detailed insurance claims records [34]. They explicitly modeled the effect of competition. Their analysis showed that, on average, when there were four interchangeable generic products in the market, prices fell over their study period by 32%; and when there was a monopoly, prices increased by 47%. Intermediate levels of competition led to intermediate price changes. The authors do not try to explain either of these outcomes, both of which are somewhat perplexing: why had prices not already adjusted to the existing level of competition by the beginning of the period? They do, however, show that changes in the number of competitors were associated with predictably inverse change in price.

2.2.3 CONCLUSION

Although it is difficult to make international drug price comparisons, it is safe to say that branded drug prices are higher on average in the United States than in Canada. This could reflect in part the role of Canadian drug price regulation or higher incomes in the United States. In both countries, private payers pay markedly more than public drug plans. The US public drug plans require manufacturers provide discounts off of the prices charged to private payers. In exchange, the public plans will cover most of the manufacturer's drugs. Canadian public plans rely on price negotiations, which are informed by the use of economic appraisals. Canadian public plans are more selective in their uptake of new drugs. US private drug plans use PBMs to secure discounts off of list prices; some of these discounts are retained by the PBM. Canadian private drug plans typically pay list prices. Generic drug prices tend to be lower in the United States than in Canada, likely because the US market is more competitive than the Canadian market. Recently in the United States, however, the prices charged for certain generics have increased markedly.

REFERENCES

[1] Canadian Institute for Health Information. Prescribed drug spending in Canada, 2016; a focus on public drug programs. Report No.: 978-1-77109-551-8. Ottawa: Canadian Institute for Health Information; December 15, 2016.

[2] Patented Medicine Prices Review Board. PMPRB guidelines modernization – discussion paper. Ottawa: Patented Medicine Prices Review Board; June 2016.

[3] Morgan SG, Vogler S, Wagner AK. Payers' experiences with confidential pharmaceutical price discounts: a survey of public and statutory health systems in North America, Europe, and Australasia. Health Policy 2017;121(4):354–62.

[4] Innovative Medicines Canada. Submission to the patendted medicine prices review board. October 24, 2016. Ottawa.

[5] Gagnon M-A, Hébert G. The economic case for universal pharmacare: costs and benefits of publicly funded drug coverage for all Canadians. Report No.: 978-1-926888-13-2. Ottawa: The Canadian Centre for Policy Alternatives; Institut de recherche et d'informations socio-économiques; 2010.

[6] Rocchi A, Miller E, Hopkins RB, Goeree R. Common drug review recommendations. Pharmacoeconomics 2012;30(3):229–46.

[7] Nelson J. Manulife begins program to scrutinize coverage of pricey drugs. The Globe and Mail 2015. https://www.theglobeandmail.com/report-on-business/manulife-launched-drugwatch-program-to-scrutinize-coverage-of-pricey-drugs/article27265898/.

[8] Kratzer J, McGrail K, Strumpf E, Law MR. Cost-control mechanisms in Canadian private drug plans. Healthcare Policy 2013;9(1):35.

[9] Perreaux L. Quebec expects to save millions with overhaul of generic-drug purchasing process. The Globe and Mail 2017. https://www.theglobeandmail.com/news/national/quebec-expects-to-save-millions-with-overhaul-of-generic-drug-purchasing-process/article35484903/.

[10] Hollis A, Grootendorst P. A comparison of mechanisms for setting generic drug prices in Canada. Journal of Generic Medicines 2017;13(1):19–27.

[11] Ismail E. Generic drug pricing and substitution in private drug plans in Canada. Toronto: University of Toronto; 2014.

[12] Pan-Canadian Pharmaceutical Alliance. Subsequent entry biologics (SEBs) - first principles. 2016. p. 1.

[13] Vogler S, Österle A, Mayer S. Inequalities in medicine use in Central Eastern Europe: an empirical investigation of socioeconomic determinants in eight countries. International Journal for Equity in Health 2015;14(1):124.

[14] Patented Medicine Prices Review Board. Annual report 2015. Report No.: 1495–0561. Ottawa: Patented Medicine Prices Review Board; 2015.

[15] Morgan S, Smolina K, Mooney D, Raymond C, Bowen ML, Gorczynski C, et al. The Canadian Rx atlas. 3rd ed. British Columbia, CA: The Centre for Health Services and Policy Research; 2013.

[16] Patented Medicine Prices Review Board. Market intelligence report: biologic Response modifier agents 2015. Ottawa: Patented Medicine Prices Review Board; October 2016.

[17] Patented Medicine Prices Review Board. Market intelligence report: biologic response modifier agents 2015. Ottawa: Patented Medicine Prices Review Board; October 2016.

[18] Patented Medicine Prices Review Board. Generics360. Ottawa: Patented Medicine Prices Review Board; 2014.

[19] Beall RF, Nickerson JW, Attaran A. Pan-Canadian overpricing of medicines: a 6-country study of cost control for generic medicines. Open Medicine 2014;8(4):e130–5.

[20] Morgan SG, Leopold C, Wagner AK. Drivers of expenditure on primary care prescription drugs in 10 high-income countries with universal health coverage. CMAJ: Canadian Medical Association Journal 2017;189(23):E794–9.
[21] Danzon PM, Furukawa MF. International prices and availability of pharmaceuticals in 2005. Health Affairs (Project Hope) 2008;27(1):221–33.
[22] Abaluck J, Gruber J. Choice inconsistencies among the elderly: evidence from plan choice in the Medicare Part D program. The American Economic Review 2011;101(4):1180–210.
[23] Blumenthal D, Squires D. Drug price control: how some government programs do it. To The Point 2016. http://www.commonwealthfund.org/publications/blog/2016/may/drug-price-control-how-some-government-programs-do-it.
[24] Medicaid.gov. Medicaid drug rebate program. Baltimore (MD): Centers for Medicare and Medicaid Services; 2013.
[25] Cox C, Kamal R, Jankiewicz A, Rousseau D, for the Kaiser Family F. Recent trends in prescription drug costs. JAMA 2016;315(13):1326.
[26] Kesselheim AS, Avorn J, Sarpatwari A. The high cost of prescription drugs in the United States: origins and prospects for reform. JAMA 2016;316(8):858–71.
[27] Kanavos P, Ferrario A, Vandoros S, Anderson GF. Higher US branded drug prices and spending compared to other countries may stem partly from quick uptake of new drugs. Health Affairs (Project Hope) 2013;32(4):753–61.
[28] Dusetzina SB. Drug pricing trends for orally administered anticancer medications reimbursed by commercial health plans, 2000–2014. JAMA Oncology 2016;2(7):960–1.
[29] Howard DH, Bach PB, Berndt ER, Conti RM. Pricing in the market for anticancer drugs. Journal of Economic Perspectives 2015;29(1):139–62.
[30] Abboud C, Berman E, Cohen A, Cortes J, DeAngelo D, Deininger M, et al. The price of drugs for chronic myeloid leukemia (CML) is a reflection of the unsustainable prices of cancer drugs: from the perspective of a large group of CML experts. Blood 2013;121(22):4439–42.
[31] Jørgensen J, Kefalas P. A price comparison of recently launched proprietary pharmaceuticals in the UK and the US. Journal of Market Access & Health Policy 2016;4:32754.
[32] Gooi M, Bell CM. Differences in generic drug prices between the US and Canada. Applied Health Economics and Health Policy 2008;6(1):19–26.
[33] United States Government Accountability Office. Generic drugs under Medicare: Part D generic drug prices declined overall, but some had extraordinary price increases. Report No.: GAO-16-706. August 2016.
[34] Dave CV, Kesselheim AS, Fox ER, Qiu P, Hartzema A. High generic drug prices and market competition: a retrospective cohort study. Annals of Internal Medicine 2017;167(3):145–51.
[35] Prasad V, Mailankody S. Research and Development Spending to Bring a Single Cancer Drug to Market and Revenues After Approval. JAMA Internal Medicine 2017;177(11):1569–75.

CHAPTER 2.3

Medicine Prices in Asia—Pacific Countries

Zaheer Ud-din Babar[1], Rabia Hussain[2], Syed Shahzad Hasan[3]
[1]University of Huddersfield, Huddersfield, West Yorkshire, United Kingdom & University of Auckland, Auckland, New Zealand; [2]University Sains Malaysia, Penang, Malaysia; [3]University of Huddersfield, Huddersfield, West Yorkshire, United Kingdom & University of Newcastle, Newcastle, New South Wales, Australia

LIST OF ABBREVIATIONS

AEDs	Antiepileptic drugs
ARV	Antiretroviral
CNS	Central nervous system
HAI	Health Action International
IRP	International reference price
LMIC	Low- and middle-income country/ies
NDRC	National Development and Reform Commission
NLEM	National List of Essential Medicines
OECD	Organisation for Economic Co-operation and Development
PPPs	Purchasing power parities
US	United States
WHO	World Health Organization

2.3.1 INTRODUCTION

The chapter includes the studies that evaluated medicine prices and affordability in countries located in Asia—Pacific region. The region includes culturally and economically diverse nations and typically includes East Asia, South Asia, Southeast Asia, and Oceania. Despite the heterogeneity, most individual countries within the region are emerging markets showing rapid growth and development. The primary aim of this review was to report medicine prices in Asia—Pacific region in the last decade and document their significant findings. All studies that include countries located in Asia—Pacific region and depicted medicine prices data using World Health Organization/Health Action International (WHO/HAI) methodology were relevant for inclusion in the analysis. Many countries in

Medicine Price Surveys, Analyses, and Comparisons
ISBN 978-0-12-813166-4
https://doi.org/10.1016/B978-0-12-813166-4.00005-X

this region often supply medicines free of charge in the public sector, but public sector availability of medicines is reported as consistently low [1]. Some of the possible reasons of low availability are discrepancies in the medicines listed in the national essential medicines and poor compliance with their recommendations [1].

2.3.2 PRICE STUDIES FOR SPECIFIC MEDICINES GROUPS

2.3.2.1 High-Cost Medicines

Increasing costs of prescription medicines are evident, which have become a major public health challenge to health-care systems worldwide [1]. Accessibility and affordability of high-cost medicines are two major challenges confronting the global pharmaceutical pricing policy. In 2011, WHO reported that one-third of the world's population and half of the population in the poorest countries of Asia and Africa lack a regular access to essential medicines [2]. It is argued that medicines are often too expensive for people to afford [2]. According to the WHO, "expenditure on medicines accounts for a major proportion of health costs in developing countries and therefore access to treatment is heavily dependent on the availability of affordable medicines" [3].

In a WHO report, it was suggested as definition for a high-priced medicine if the therapy for one patient exceeds €10,000/year to be reimbursed by a public payer [4]. In low- to middle-income countries of Asia—Pacific region, most of the patients who need medicines must pay for them out of their own pockets [1]. Therefore, high-cost medicines are challenging the public health-care systems and represent a considerable burden to patients in this region. Some middle-income countries in this region such as Thailand have taken important initiatives to cover for high-cost specialty medicines by launching a new subcategory in the National List of Essential Medicines (NLEM): the E2 category of high-cost medicines for specific conditions [5]. At 1 year after the E2 program was implemented, the quarterly health-care cost savings were US$1253.66 per patient for all patients and were US$2896.69 per patient for universal coverage category, respectively [5]. High-income countries of this region have also introduced different schemes to provide coverage for high-cost medicines. Most of the schemes involved pricing arrangements and are related to treatments for cancer and inflammatory diseases [6]. The number of studies evaluating price of high-cost medicines in Asia—Pacific countries is limited.

2.3.2.2 Medicines for Cancer

Access to medicines used for the treatment of cancer is a major health concern, particularly for those who cannot afford these medicines. Generally, cancer medicines are unaffordable in many low-income to middle-income countries located in Asia—Pacific region. Vogler et al. surveyed the prices of 31 cancer medicines in 18 high-income countries: European countries, Australia, and New Zealand [7]. The results showed that the prices of cancer medicines varied across the surveyed countries, with the difference of a cancer medicine price between the highest-priced country and the lowest-priced country ranged from 28% to 388% [7]. The prices of 24 of the 31 cancer medicines in Greece ranked in the first quartile, and their prices were the lowest for 14 of the medicines. The prices in Switzerland were the highest for 9 of the 26 cancer medicines with available data, whereas in Germany and Sweden, prices of 8 of the 31 cancer medicines in both countries were the highest, respectively [7]. No substantial differences in the prices of cancer medicines in European countries and Australia and New Zealand were noticed [7].

Recently, Goldstein et al. measured the differences in both prices of eight patented cancer drugs (e.g., bevacizumab, dasatinib, erlotinib, trastuzumab) and wealth levels between high-income countries, including Australia, Israel, the United Kingdom, and the United States, upper middle-income countries, including China and South Africa, and lower middle-income country, including India to make indications about affordability of cancer drugs [8]. Regardless of the method used to convert local currencies into US dollars, the median cancer medicine price was highest in the United States (foreign exchange rates method: US$8694; purchasing power parities (PPPs) method: US$8694). When using foreign exchange rates method, the median cancer medicine price was lowest in India (US$1515), while using PPPs method, the median cancer medicine price of Israel was the lowest globally (US$2531). In terms of affordability, cancer medicines appeared to be most affordable in Australia, with monthly medicine price of 71% of the domestic product per capita at PPP. Cancer drugs were least affordable in India, with monthly medicine price of 313% of the domestic product per capita at PPP [8].

2.3.2.3 Medicines for Central Nervous System—Related Diseases

Central nervous system (CNS)—related diseases are chronically debilitating and life-threatening, whereas some of them are degenerative in nature.

CNS medicines are generally affordable in developing countries, whereas medicines for some CNS conditions such as dementia and Alzheimer are only affordable in developed countries. In 2007, an international survey was conducted in 21 countries across six continents to examine the price and affordability of drugs to treat Alzheimer's disease (donepezil, galantamine, rivastigmine, memantine) [9]. Both currency-converted prices (US$) and the PPPs-converted prices of Alzheimer's drugs were reported. It was reported that both currency-converted prices and PPPs-converted prices in Mexico were lowest for all the available Alzheimer's drugs and their strengths in the country. On the other hand, prices of Alzheimer's drugs in Philippines were among the highest, with the PPP-converted prices for both donepezil and memantine and their available strengths, as well as for 8 mg tablet of galantamine, being the most expensive among the surveyed countries [9]. Mexico had the highest affordability index (the total number of units purchasable with one's daily income) for all the available Alzheimer's drugs and their strengths, whereas Philippines had the lowest affordability index for three of the four available Alzheimer's drugs in the country. It is worth pointing out that the affordability index was less than 1 for 5 mg tablet of donepezil in Uganda (0.6), Nigeria (0.2), and Philippines (0.9), indicating that the daily income of people in these countries was not enough for purchasing even one 5 mg tablet of donepezil [9].

Epilepsy, another common CNS-related disease is highly prevalent in Asian countries (about 23 million Asians have epilepsy) [10]. Because of larger population of Asia, with greater treatment cost, Asia has more untreated patients than Africa [10]. In 2012, Cameron et al. evaluated the price and affordability of antiepileptic drugs in 46 countries [11]. The procurement prices for generic carbamazepine and phenytoin in public sector were on average 1.6 and 2.5 times higher than that of the international reference prices (IRPs) of Management Sciences for Health (for further information about the IPR see Chapter 6.2), whereas originator brands were on average 6.2 and 5.2 times higher [11]. In countries where individuals pay for their medications in the public sector, PPP-adjusted patient prices of generic carbamazepine and phenytoin were 5.0 and 17.5 times higher than IRPs, whereas the originator brands typically cost 2.4 and 2.8 times higher than their lowest-priced generic equivalents [11]. Prices from the private sector were even more striking for carbamazepine and phenytoin with PPP-adjusted patient prices 11.3 and 24.8 times the IRPs, whereas originator brands for both drugs were more than 30 times higher [11].

2.3.2.4 Medicines for Hepatitis C

Novel direct-acting antivirals, sofosbuvir, daclatasvir, and ledipasvir have improved treatment options and prognosis for patients with chronic hepatitis C infection [12]. The treatment of hepatitis C with new novel drugs such as sofosbuvir and ledipasvir is causing huge burden on health institutions and on patients. According to the manufacturer of an originator brand, the usual course of 12 weeks' therapy with branded sofosbuvir costs up to US$900/12 weeks in 101 low-income countries [13]. Treatment of hepatitis C with a 12-week course of daclatasvir is priced at US$63,000 in the United States [14].

Iyengar et al. systematically reviewed and compared the price and affordability of sofosbuvir and ledipasvir/sofosbuvir across 26 Organisation for Economic Co-operation and Development (OECD) member countries and four developing (low- and middle-income) countries [15]. The nominal adjusted price of sofosbuvir for a 12-week course across the OECD countries ranged from US$37,729 in Japan to US$64,680 in the United States. The nominal prices of sofosbuvir in low- and middle-income countries such as India (US$539) and Mongolia (US$900) were up to 120 times lower than the nominal price in the United States (US$64,680) because of negotiated pricing arrangements and licensing agreements [15]. The median PPP-adjusted price among OECD countries was PPP US$38,884. Overall, the PPP-adjusted prices of sofosbuvir ranged from PPP US$1861 in India to PPP US$131,250 in Poland [15]. The nominal adjusted price of ledipasvir/sofosbuvir for a 12-week course was highest in the United States (US$72,765) and lowest in the United Kingdom (US$43,215) among the OECD countries. The nominal adjusted price of ledipasvir/sofosbuvir of ledipasvir/sofosbuvir in India (US$655), which was the lowest across the 30 studied countries, was 1.2% of the price in the United Kingdom [15].

The PPPs-adjusted prices of ledipasvir/sofosbuvir ranged from PPP US$2260 in India to PPP U$118,754 in Poland, with a median price of PPP U$46,035 across the OECD countries [15]. The PPPs-adjusted price of a full course of sofosbuvir would be equivalent to at least 1 year of the PPPs-adjusted average earnings for individuals in 12 of the 27 countries analyzed and at least 2 years of earnings for individuals in 4 of the 27 countries analyzed. Sofosbuvir was most affordable in Egypt (0.2 year of average annual wages) and least affordable in Turkey (5.3 years of average annual wages) [15]. For ledipasvir/sofosbuvir, individuals in 10 of the 21 countries and 3 of the 21 countries analyzed would require at least 1 year and 2 years, respectively, of the PPP-adjusted average earnings to afford a course of ledipasvir/sofosbuvir [15].

Patent holders of sofosbuvir (Gilead Sciences) and daclatasvir (Bristol-Myers Squibb) have taken important initiatives to make high cost novel direct-acting antivirals affordable in low-income and middle-income countries. For example, Gilead Sciences has allowed 11 Indian generic manufacturers to produce generic sofosbuvir with a 7% royalty payment to Gilead [12]. The export of active pharmaceutical ingredients at reduced price has also accelerated the generic production of sofosbuvir and daclatasvir and cost of therapy are rapidly decreasing [12].

2.3.2.5 Antiretroviral Medicines

Sagaon-Teyssier et al. analyzed the data on effective procurement prices of antiretroviral (ARV) medicines in developing countries obtained from the Global Price Reporting Mechanism between 2003 and 2015 [16]. It was reported that costs for yearly treatment of adults with ARV decreased from US$464.3 to less than US$136.8 between 2003 and 2015. This was driven mainly by the decrease in average generic prices (decrease of 69% by 2015 as compared to the average yearly treatment price of US$300 in 2003) [16]. The average price of yearly treatment with originator ARV decreased by only 52% during the same period (as compared to the average yearly treatment price of US$862 in 2003). Estimations for the general market show that originator ARV medicines were on average 42.5% more expensive than generic medicines. Sub-Saharan African countries paid on average the lowest price for originator ARV medicines, in which the prices for countries of other geographical regions were on average 36.1%—136.0% higher than those paid in sub-Saharan African countries. In contrast, sub-Saharan African countries seemed to purchase generic ARV medicines at the highest prices. The prices for countries of other geographical regions were on average 8.6%—24.4% lower than that for sub-Saharan African countries [16].

The originator ARV medicines purchased 18 years before the expiry of the patent were on average 155% more costly compared with medicines bought in the year of patent expiration [16]. Generic ARV medicines bought 18 years before the expiry of the initial patent were on average 64% more costly compared with those whose patent just expired [16]. Five years after the expiry of the initial patent, prices of originator ARV medicines were 68% more costly compared with they were in the year of the initial patent expiry, whereas the generic ARV medicines were still 8% less costly, although the prices had increased as compared to the year of the initial patent expiry [16].

2.3.2.6 Generic Medicines

Generally, patients living in low-income countries (including many Asia—Pacific countries) require long-term medicines to treat chronic conditions as several countries in this region are undergoing a rise in the prevalence of patients suffering from noncommunicable diseases (e.g., diabetes, cardiovascular disease) [17]. The use of generic medicines is one of the key strategies employed by governments and third-party payers to control the costs of medicines and to improve patients' access to essential medicines [18].

Generic medicines give low-income and middle-income countries in Asia—Pacific region an affordable treatment option. Cameron et al. were the first who measured the access to medicines in developing and middle-income countries using the WHO/HAI methodology [19]. They included 45 national and subnational surveys of medicine prices and affordability from 36 developing and middle-income countries [19]. Public sector procurement prices of lowest-priced generics varied according to the geographical regions, in which the southeast Asia (0.63) achieved median price ratios (for explanation cf. Chapter 6.2) that was lower than IRPs, whereas in Africa (1.34), Europe (1.40), and western Pacific (1.44), the prices averaged 34%—44% more than IRPs. The price ratios (median) of lowest-priced generics in lower middle-income countries ranged from 0.33 (Jordan) to 2.94 (Philippines) [19]. In countries where public sector patients pay for their medicines, the regional median price ratios for the basket of 15 medicines varied from 3.18 in the Americas to 11.95 in western Pacific countries [19]. However, prices paid by the patients in the public sector were still generally lower than prices paid by the private sector patients in most regions. The percentage difference in price between originator brands and lowest-priced generics in the private sector was only 6% in India but was 300% higher in lower middle- and in low-income countries, whereas it was 152% in upper middle-income countries [19].

Wang et al. undertook secondary analysis of the composite data on medicine prices from the HAI database to examine the prices and affordability of 15 medicines for common chronic diseases in the Asia—Pacific region [20]. Among the 11 countries analyzed, the procurement price was 1.4 times the IRPs for lowest-priced generic equivalents and 9.1 times for innovator brands. Fiji and India achieved a lower-than-IRP procurement price for lowest-priced generics, whereas Laos, Mongolia, Philippines, and

Vietnam had to pay more than two times the IRP to purchase lowest-priced generics. Indonesia (1.13) and Malaysia (1.17) had a procurement price close to the IRP [20]. In general, prices were lower in the public sector than in the private sector, except for China and Vietnam, where the prices being higher in the public sector than in the private sector for both innovator brands and lowest-priced generics. In general, prices for innovator brands were often several times higher when compared with those of lowest-priced generics [20].

A study of the price and affordability of 32 essential medicines was carried out by Mendis et al. in defined areas in Bangladesh, Brazil, Malawi, Nepal, Pakistan, and Sri Lanka [21]. They expressed prices and affordability as the median price ratios and the number of days' wages it would cost the lowest-paid government worker to purchase 1 month of treatment, respectively [21]. Like many other middle- and low-income countries, generic medicines were the predominant type of product available in the public sector of the surveyed low- and middle-income countries, with most priced between 0.5 and 1.5 times their IRPs. Where the innovator brands were available, their prices were about 2−3 times their IRPs. In the private sector, innovator brands were priced 1.31 times their IRPs in Bangladesh [21]. Regarding the generics medicines, Sri Lanka had the lowest median value of median price ratios in which the prices for both the most sold generics (0.97) and lowest price generics (1.05) were close to the IRPs. Comparison between innovator brands and generic equivalents revealed that the prices of brands were 34% higher than the lowest-priced generics in Bangladesh, 40% higher in Nepal, 90% higher in Pakistan, and 175% higher in Sri Lanka [21].

Vogler et al. surveyed the prices of 14 medicines, both originators and generics, in New Zealand and 16 European countries [22]. There was a high variation in medicine prices in European countries and New Zealand. In 8 out of 14 selected medicines, the price of the medicine in the highest-priced country was more than twice the price of the medicine in the lowest-priced country. For three generic medicines (venlafaxine, pioglitazone, mycophenolate mofetil), the differences between highest-priced and lowest-priced country amounted more than 1000% [22].

2.3.3 CONCORDANCE OF PRICES WITH AFFORDABILITY

2.3.3.1 China (Upper Middle-Income Country)

Historically, in China, the Bureau of Pricing of the National Development and Reform Commission (NDRC), at both the national and provincial levels, was responsible for the retail pricing of all medicines and medical devices included in the drug formulary for reimbursement under publicly funded medical insurance programs. Although products not covered in the drug formularies can be priced freely by market forces, their prices are still required to be registered with the government pricing authority.

A study of prices and affordability of 50 essential medicines in the public and private sectors was conducted in Jiangsu, China using the WHO/HAI methodology [23]. They expressed prices as median price ratios while affordability was estimated by comparing the total cost of a medicine for a standard course of treatment to the daily wage of the lowest-paid unskilled government worker [23]. The median price ratios for the lowest-priced generics ranged from 1.26 in primary health-care facilities to 2.05 in secondary and tertiary health-care facilities [23]. In contrast, the prices of innovator brand medicines were above the threshold level to be considered acceptable, with median price ratios ranging from 3.76 to 27.22. The median price ratios of most innovator brand medicines were about 2—7 times higher in public sector outlets than in private pharmacies. In terms of affordability, it would require between 0.1 and 0.8 days' wages to purchase the lowest-priced generic of the surveyed medicines. However, innovator brand medicines were less affordable, ranging from 0.2 days' wages to 10.8 days' wages [23].

Another study in Shaanxi province of China [24] by Jiang et al. compared the prices with IRPs (median price ratios) and measured affordability as the number of days' wages required for the lowest-paid unskilled government worker to purchase standard treatments for common conditions [24]. Overall, the public sector procures 15 originator medicines at 8.49 times their IRPs and 28 generic medicines at 0.75 times their IRPs. However, the public retail prices were higher, with 10.16 times and 0.97 times their IRPs for originator and generic equivalents, respectively, indicating markup of prices [24]. The variations in markup rates among the 28 generic medicines were more significant compared with the 15 originator brand medicines, ranging from 3.3% to 80.0% for generic medicines while ranging only from 14.7% to 48.1% for originator brand medicines. The markup rates were higher for generic medicines procured at below IRP (27.2%) compared with those procured above IRP (15.1%) [24]. In the private retail pharmacies, the originator brand medicines were priced at 8.36 times the IRP, whereas for the generics, they were priced at 1.53 times the IRP. Analysis of the 11 medicines for which both originator brands and generically equivalent products were available reported that, on average, originator brands cost 390.7% more than their generic equivalents in the private retail pharmacies. On the other hand, analysis of medicines that were found in both public and private sector showed that patient paid 16.5% lower prices for originator brands and paid 17.3% higher prices for generic equivalents in the private sector [24]. In general, originator brand medicines were less affordable than their generic equivalents in both the public and private sectors. The treatment costs with some originator brand medicines were strikingly high, including omeprazole which required 15.6 days' wages for the treatment of peptic ulcer and fluoxetine which would cost 11.5 days' wages for the treatment of depression [24].

Yang et al. investigated the prices of 39 essential medicines at different medicines outlets in Hubei province, China [25]. There was wide variation in the median price ratios of 25 lowest-priced generics, ranging from 0.07 to 18.38. Sixteen lowest-priced generics were procured at lower prices than the IRPs, whereas five lowest-priced generics were more than twice the IRPs. The procurement prices of lowest-priced generics were lower than innovator brands, in which the median value of median price ratio for 25 lowest-priced generics was 0.74, whereas for seven innovators brands the median value of median price ratio was 9.78 [25]. The same was observed for retail prices in the public sector where the 25 lowest-priced generics (1.04; range: 0.09−22.05) reported a lower median value of median price ratio than the seven innovator brands (11.25; range: 2.35−35.88) [25]. Majority of the lowest-priced generics were under the so-called acceptable price line (median price ratio of 1.5 or less), whereas eight medicines were above the warning level (if a median price ratio is twice the IRP for a generic equivalent is considered a warning level), with some medicines such as albendazole, fluconazole, and amlodipine, had prices with six times the IRPs [25]. In the private sector, the median value of median price ratio for the five innovator brands was found to be 19.94 (range: 1.29−28.48), whereas the median value of median price ratio of 20 lowest-priced generics was 0.68 (range: 0.08−2.82). Only 3 out of 20 generics had median price ratios that were above the warning level [25]. Interestingly, the median value of median price ratios of all generic medicines in the public sector was higher than that in the private sector. Regarding affordability, the authors found that half of the surveyed medicines would cost more than 1 day's income of the low-income population, with the situation generally being worse in the public than in the private sector [25].

2.3.3.2 Sri Lanka (Lower Middle-Income Country)

Health care is delivered by both government and private sectors in Sri Lanka, but the private sector accounts for majority of outpatient care. Dabare et al. conducted a national survey to reveal the prices of 50 essential medicines prescribed for noncommunicable diseases in Sri Lanka [26]. Among the 50 medicines surveyed, the prices of 41 medicines were less than US$1 and only two medicines were priced more than US$10. In addition, the prices of 21 medicines were less than IRP of the generic medicine. The median price ratio was more than 5 for one medicine. When the median price ratios of originator brands were compared with the lowest-priced generics, it was found that the prices of 10 originator brands were 10—100 times higher than their lowest-priced generics [26]. In most instances (96.6%) the price of originator brand was higher than lowest-priced generics. In terms of affordability, more than 67% of medicines required less than a single day's wages of the lowest-paid unskilled government worker to purchase for 1-month supply. There was one medicine which required more than 10 days' wages of the lowest-paid unskilled government worker to buy a month's supply (levodopa/carbidopa tablets) [26].

Senarathna et al. determined the prices of 28 essential medicines in the private sector of Sri Lanka [27]. They expressed prices of medicines as median price ratios and affordability as the daily wage of the lowest-paid government worker. In privately owned pharmacies, the median value of median price ratios of 19 innovator brands was 4.72 times the IRP in 2009. In addition, the 22 most sold generics and cheapest generic products had median value of median price ratios of 0.75 and 0.44, respectively, in 2009 [27]. Generally, the innovator brands had higher prices than their generic equivalents, and the price differences showed an increasing trend. In 2003, the prices for innovator brands were 6.58 times higher than most sold generics and 8.12 times higher than lowest-priced generics, however, the innovator brands were 6.71 times and 8.45 times more expensive than the most sold generics and lowest-priced generics, respectively, in 2009 [27]. Diazepam had the highest price difference between the innovator brand and its lowest-priced generic equivalent, in which the innovator brand was more than 100 times the median price ratio of the lowest-priced generic product (164.55 times in 2009). Monthly hypertensive treatment with the innovator brand atenolol (50 mg once daily) required 1.22 days' wages in privately owned pharmacies, but only 0.03 days' wages were required for both the most sold generic product and the lowest-priced generic products [27].

Furthermore, a month's treatment of epilepsy with innovator brand carbamazepine (200 mg twice daily) required 6.78 days' wages, but only half a day salary was required for the most sold generic product and the lowest-priced generic product [27].

A national survey was conducted to evaluate the price of 25 key essential medicines for children in Sri Lanka using WHO/HAI medicine price methodology [28]. The prices for innovator brands were higher than the generic brands for all the 14 medicines, which were available in both innovator brands and generic version, except for ibuprofen syrup. Among the innovator brands, highest median price ratio was reported for mebendazole chewable tablet (19.89), whereas salbutamol respiratory solution (0.23) had the lowest median price ratio. There were five innovator brand medicines with a median price ratio of more than 5: ceftriaxone injection (14.46), mebendazole syrup (7.70), mebendazole chewable tablet (19.89), diazepam injection (7.69), and metronidazole tablet (5.87). Among the lowest-priced generics, clotrimazole topical cream (3.74) and salbutamol respiratory solution (0.05) had the highest and lowest median price ratio, respectively [28]. Prices of the lowest-priced generics of the majority of medicines were above the IRPs except for amoxicillin–clavulanic acid suspension, diethylcarbamazine citrate tablet, mebendazole chewable tablet, salbutamol metered-dose inhaler, and salbutamol respiratory solution. Regarding affordability, it would require 0.3 days' wages to purchase 1-month supply of beclomethasone (100 mcg twice a day) [28]. In addition, for a Sri Lankan child on 150 mg carbamazepine per day, purchasing of 1-month supply of carbamazepine would cost 5 days' wages, which was considered unaffordable. The treatments of lower respiratory tract infection with amoxicillin suspension and acute gastroenteritis with oral rehydration salt were considered affordable in Sri Lanka. Purchasing of amoxicillin suspension (125 mg three times a day for 7 days) would cost between 0.22 (lowest-priced generics) and 0.53 (innovator brands) days' wages, whereas 1-week supply of oral rehydration salt (one packet per day) would cost 0.31 days' wages [28].

2.3.3.3 Malaysia (Upper Middle-Income Country)

Over the years, owing to free pricing policy, high drugs prices have been reported in Malaysia in literature, and Malaysia has been known as a "high price island" for pharmaceutical prices. Babar et al. measured prices of 48 medicines and their affordability in the public and the private retail pharmacy sectors, as well as in dispensing doctors' clinics of Malaysia [29].

Procurement prices of innovator brand medicines in the public sector were higher compared to their generic equivalents, where the median value of the median price ratios of 14 innovator brands was 2.41, whereas for 26 most sold generic and lowest-priced generic products, median values of the median price ratios were 1.56 and 1.09 times the IRPs, respectively. It was reported that the innovator brand of four medicines (fluoxetine, loratadine, amlodipine, and simvastatin) had median price ratios of more than 10 [29]. The same was observed in private sector retail pharmacies, where the median value of median price ratios for 32 innovator brands (16.35) was higher than both the most sold generics (6.89) and lowest-priced generics (6.57). There were four innovator brands in the private sector with median price ratio of more than 50 (fluconazole, ciprofloxacin, furosemide, fluoxetine), whereas their generic equivalents only had median price ratios ranging from 10.9 to 39.3. In the dispensing doctor's clinics, the median value of the median price ratios for the 17 innovator brands (15.40) was almost twice their generic equivalents (7.76 for both most sold generics and lowest-priced generics). Some of the generics in dispensing doctors' clinics, such as metformin, hydrochlorothiazide, and isosorbide dinitrate, had prices which were twice the prices that they were in private sector retail pharmacies [29].

One-month treatment using innovator brand ranitidine (150 mg twice daily) for peptic ulcer required 7.5 days' wages when bought from private pharmacies and 8 days' wages from dispensing doctors' clinics [29]. On the other hand, the cost of generic versions of ranitidine was about two times lower, required only 3 days' wages in the pharmacies and 3.7 days' wages from the dispensing doctors' clinics [29]. Innovator brand omeprazole (20 mg daily) costs 14—15 days' wages for 1-month treatment, whereas its lowest-priced generic costs about five times lower (3—4 days' wages) in both private sector retail pharmacies and dispensing doctor's clinics [29]. Purchasing of innovator brand simvastatin (20 mg daily) required 7.5 days' wages in private pharmacies and 6 days' in dispensing doctors' clinics, whereas its generic equivalent costs about 2.3 days' wages in both facilities [29].

2.3.4 IMPACT OF POLICY MEASURES

The medicines pricing policy has seen dramatic changes over the past decades in countries located in Asia—Pacific region. The development of drug pricing policy is extremely difficult throughout the health-care system in this region due to complex bureaucratic procedures. In some countries, pricing agreements are kept confidential so the prices paid by the government in one country cannot be compared with prices paid in other countries.

In China, higher markups are given to new drugs and drug under patents (manufacturers) to encourage innovations [30]. Pharmaceutical manufacturers could apply to government for a higher price than the existed official price if they could prove that a certain drug demonstrates superiority in terms of therapeutic effectiveness and safety over the other drugs of the same kind or if the treatment cycle and expenses are much lower than those of other manufacturers producing the same drug. To be eligible for setting prices higher than recommended prices, pharmaceutical companies are required to meet conditions, such as having at least one peer-reviewed article published to show safety and effectiveness and establishing a drug surveillance system for adverse drug reaction [30].

In Australia, public pricing policies have been aiming at the generic formulations, but there are pharmaceutical industries requesting high prices for their new medicines. To counter the high prices of some new medicines, Australia has introduced managed entry agreements for several medicines, with the objective of permitting access to patients for medicines found to be cost-effective, but to restrict use outside of these indications [31]. The postmarket reviews to assess medicines utilization and to strengthen medicine pricing management may also result in changes to the medicine prices [31]. For instance, a review undertaken for antidementia drugs to treat Alzheimer's disease in 2013 resulted in a 40% decrement in the medicine prices because these medicines were being used in a much wider population and for longer duration than originally agreed as cost-effective [31,32]. In addition, the review of biological disease modifying antirheumatic drugs in 2009 also resulted in price reductions [33].

The uncontrolled drugs prices or unregulated drug pricing poses serious problems for the health-care system and threatens its financial stability and drug spending plan. This problem could trigger a series of events, affecting patient access to drug therapies, patient affordability to bear the cost of drugs and health-care providers' competencies to provide the highest quality of care. The countries in Asia—Pacific region have introduced a series of legislative and policy reforms to control drug pricing, giving patients and communities some relief, but more viable policy reforms are required to make drugs accessible at an affordable price [30,33].

2.3.5 FINAL REMARKS

There are several methodology-related limitations associated with the included studies that may affect the generalizability or limit the findings. Firstly, the data on medicine prices from majority of the countries located in Asia—Pacific region are not always available. Some of the published studies involve only a selection of countries. Secondly, most of the published studies use a small selection of medicines, causing a greater risk of selection bias. Thirdly, due to great heterogeneity across the countries in this region in both the medicine prices and the affordability, drawing definite conclusions based on limited or small representative sample from selected countries will be questionable. Lastly, most of the published studies utilize publicly stated prices for comparison and do not present data on actual prices and offer no information on discount or markups.

REFERENCES

[1] Suh GH. High medicine prices and poor affordability. Current Opinion in Psychiatry 2011;24(4):341—5.
[2] Hogerzeil HV, Mirza Z. World medicines situation: access to essential medicines as part of the right to health. World Health Organisation; 2011.
[3] Everard M. Drugs and money - prices, affordability and cost containment. World Health Organisation; 2003.
[4] World Health Organization. Access to new medicines in Europe: technical review of policy initiatives and opportunities for collaboration and research. 2015.
[5] Sruamsiri R, et al. Expanding access to high-cost medicines through the E2 access program in Thailand: effects on utilisation, health outcomes and cost using an interrupted time-series analysis. BMJ Open 2016;6(3):e008671.
[6] Lu CY, et al. Patient access schemes in Asia-pacific markets: current experience and future potential. Journal of Pharmaceutical Policy and Practice 2015;8(1):6.
[7] Vogler S, Vitry A, Babar ZU. Cancer drugs in 16 European countries, Australia, and New Zealand: a cross-country price comparison study. The Lancet Oncology 2016;17(1):39—47.
[8] Goldstein DA, Clark J, Tu Y, Zhang J, Fang F, Goldstein R, Stemmer SM, Rosenbaum E. A global comparison of the cost of patented cancer drugs in relation to global differences in wealth. 2017.
[9] Suh GH, et al. International price comparisons of Alzheimer's drugs: a way to close the affordability gap. International Psychogeriatrics 2009;21(6):1116—26.
[10] Bhalla D, et al. Epilepsy: Asia versus Africa. Epilepsia 2014;55(9):1317—21.
[11] Cameron A, et al. Mapping the availability, price, and affordability of antiepileptic drugs in 46 countries. Epilepsia 2012;53(6):962—9.
[12] Hill A, et al. Rapid reductions in prices for generic sofosbuvir and daclatasvir to treat hepatitis C. Journal of Virus Eradication 2016;2(1):28—31.

[13] Gilead. Chronic hepatitis C treatment expansion: generic manufacturing for developing countries. 2015.
[14] Hepatitis C onlie - AWS. Hepatitis C treatments. 2017. Available from: https://www.hepatitisc.uw.edu/page/treatment/drugs.
[15] Iyengar S, et al. Prices, costs, and affordability of new medicines for hepatitis C in 30 countries: an economic analysis. PLoS Medicine 2016;13(5):e1002032.
[16] Sagaon-Teyssier L, et al. Affordability of adult HIV/AIDS treatment in developing countries: modelling price determinants for a better insight of the market functioning. Journal of the International AIDS Society 2016;19(1):20619.
[17] Srivastava D, McGuire A. Patient access to health care and medicines across low-income countries. Social Science & Medicine 2015;133:21–7.
[18] Nguyen TA, Hassali MAA, McLachlan A. Generic medicines policies in the Asia Pacific region: ways forward. WHO South-East Asia Journal of Public Health 2013;2(1):72–4.
[19] Cameron A, et al. Medicine prices, availability, and affordability in 36 developing and middle-income countries: a secondary analysis. Lancet 2009;373(9659):240–9.
[20] Wang H, et al. Availability, price, and affordability of selected essential medicines for chronic diseases in 11 countries of the Asia Pacific Region: a secondary analysis. Asia-Pacific Journal of Public Health 2017;29(4):268–77.
[21] Mendis S, et al. The availability and affordability of selected essential medicines for chronic diseases in six low- and middle-income countries. Bulletin of the World Health Organization 2007;85(4):279–88.
[22] Vogler S, Kilpatrick K, Babar ZU. Analysis of medicine prices in New Zealand and 16 European countries. Value in Health 2015;18(4):484–92.
[23] Xi X, et al. A survey of the availability, prices and affordability of essential medicines in Jiangsu Province, China. BMC Health Services Research 2015;15:345.
[24] Jiang M, et al. Measuring access to medicines: a survey of prices, availability and affordability in Shaanxi province of China. PLoS One 2013;8(8):e70836.
[25] Yang H, et al. Prices, availability and affordability of essential medicines in rural areas of Hubei Province, China. Health Policy and Planning 2010;25(3):219–29.
[26] Dabare PR, Wanigatunge CA, Beneragama BH. A national survey on availability, price and affordability of selected essential medicines for non communicable diseases in Sri Lanka. BMC Public Health 2014;14:817.
[27] Senarathna SM, Mannapperuma U, Fernandopulle BM. Medicine prices, availability and affordability in Sri Lanka. Indian Journal of Pharmacology 2011;43(1):60–3.
[28] Balasubramaniam R, Benaragama BV, Sri Ranganathan S. A national survey of price and affordability of key essential medicines for children in Sri Lanka. Indian Journal of Pediatrics 2014;81(4):362–7.
[29] Babar ZU, et al. Evaluating drug prices, availability, affordability, and price components: implications for access to drugs in Malaysia. PLoS Medicine 2007;4(3):e82.
[30] Chen Y, Li L. Drug procurement bidding. 2010. Available from: https://www.chinabusinessreview.com/drug-procurement-bidding/.
[31] Vitry A, Roughead E. Managed entry agreements for pharmaceuticals in Australia. Health Policy 2014;117(3):345–52.
[32] The Pharmaceutical Benefits Scheme. PBAC recommendations from the review of pharmaceutical benefits scheme anti-dementia drugs to treat Alzheimer disease. 2013. Available from: http://www.pbs.gov.au/info/reviews/pbac-minutes-alzheimers.
[33] The Pharmaceutical Benefits Scheme. PBAC review of bDMARDs for the treatment of severe active rheumatoid arthritis. 2010. Available from: http://www.pbs.gov.au/info/industry/listing/elements/pbac-meetings/psd/2009-12/pbac-psd-bdmards-dec09.

CHAPTER 2.4

Medicine Prices in Latin American Countries

Jaime Espín Balbino[1], Joan Rovira Forns[2], Claudia Vaca González[3]
[1]Escuela Andaluza de Salud Pública, Granada, Spain; [2]Universidad de Barcelona, Spain; [3]Universidad Nacional de Colombia, Bogota, Colombia

LIST OF ABBREVIATIONS

ANMAT	Administración Nacional de Medicamentos, Alimentos y Tecnología Medica/National Administration of Medicines, Food and Medical Technology
ANVISA	Agência Nacional de Vigilância Sanitária/National Health Surveillance Agency (Brazil)
CIF	Cost, Insurance, and Freight
CMED	Câmara de Regulação do Mercado de Medicamentos/Pharmaceutical Market Regulation Council (Brazil)
CONCADECO	Centroamericano de Protección al Consumidor/Central American Council of Consumer Protection
DIME	Decisiones Informadas sobre Medicamentos de alto impacto financiero/Informed Decision about high-budget impact
EPR	External Price Referencing
GATT	General Agreement on Tariffs and Trade
GAUMU	Grupo Técnico de Acceso Universal a Medicamentos/Technical Group of Universal Access to Medicines
HAI	Health Action International
HBP	Health benefits package
HHI	Herfindahl–Hirschman index
HIC	High-income country/countries
IADB	Interamerican Development Bank
IMSS	Instituto mexicano del Seguro Social
INN	International Nonproprietary Name
IPR	Intellectual Property Rights
IRP	International reference pricing (a pricing policy that is also known under different names such as external price referencing, external reference pricing, international price referencing)
ISAGS	Instituto Suramericano de Gobierno en Salud/South American Health Government
IU	International Unit

Medicine Price Surveys, Analyses, and Comparisons
ISBN 978-0-12-813166-4
https://doi.org/10.1016/B978-0-12-813166-4.00006-1

LA	Latin America(n)
LIC	Low-income country/countries
LMIC	Lower middle-income country/countries
MoH	Ministry of Health
MPR	median price ratio(s)
OECD	Organisation for Economic Co-operation and Development
PAHO	Pan American Health Organization
PP	Pharmaceutical policy
PROAM	Programa de Accesibilidad a los Medicamentos/Program of Access to Medicines
R&D	Research and Development
SISMED	Sistema de Información de Precios de Medicamentos/ Information system of medicine prices (Colombia)
UMIC	Upper middle-income country/countries
UNASUR	Unión de Naciones Suramericanas/Union of South American Nations
WB	World Bank
WHO	World Health Organization
WTO	World Trade Organization

2.4.1 THE PRICE OF MEDICINES IN LATIN AMERICAN COUNTRIES

2.4.1.1 Introduction

To adequately understand the dynamics of medicines markets when analyzing the evolution of prices and quantities, it is essential to identify and assess the factors that determine them, such as the structure of the demand and supply and the role and policies of the public authorities. Unfortunately, there are few detailed and up-to-date studies of the medicines markets and policies in Latin American (LA) countries, including price regulation. From the perspective of the global pharmaceutical market, LA countries can be considered, mainly consumers, rather than producers of medicines, although in a number of countries—especially in Brazil, Mexico, Colombia, etc.—a relevant domestic industry has emerged, usually a generics manufacturing industry, with limited innovative and exporting capacity and aimed at supplying local and regional markets. In that context, one would expect national authorities to be more sensitive and inclined to support the needs and interests of the consumers and the health system rather than those of the industry. Although this is often the case, national authorities and regulators are often under big pressure by both the domestic and the foreign regional and multinational industry, with the ideological and political support of the governments of industrialized countries and some international organizations, such as the World Bank (WB) and the International Monetary Fund, which in line with the prescriptions of the "Washington Consensus," favored deregulation, international trade, and stronger intellectual property protection, as well as the noninvolvement of governments in pharmaceutical production. Around the 1990s, governments in LA were first pressured to abandon price regulation in the name of the virtues of the "free market" and later, as part of the globalization trends lead by the General Agreement on Tariffs and Trade and the World Trade Organization, to consolidate and reinforce monopolistic market structures by introducing and strengthening intellectual property rights (IPR), which were told to be required to secure the level of investment in R&D that would lead to the continuous flow of technological innovations needed to bring solutions to all pending health problems [1].

As governments started to take responsibility for the access of their citizens to health services, the price of health technologies became a policy concern, especially, when the involvement of the public sector implied some form of collective financing or mandatory insurance. The options available to authorities to contain or reduce medicine prices are manifold. Traditionally, analysts have distinguished two types of public market intervention approaches, namely, demand-side and supply-side policies, according to the market actors at which measures are aimed at [2].

Tobar et al. [3] take a different perspective by distinguishing between two basic approaches to contain prices: procompetitive approaches, aimed at promoting competition in the medicines markets, and direct intervention of medicine prices, which aims at substituting or correcting an inefficient market mechanism. The authors classify the medicine price control systems of LA countries in 2008 in three models:

1. Free pricing: Argentina, Bolivia, Chile, Costa Rica, El Salvador, Guatemala, Panama (with direct price control between 2001 and 2004), Peru, Dominican Republic, and Uruguay.
2. Price regulation: Brazil, Ecuador, Honduras, Nicaragua, and Paraguay.
3. Mixed systems: Colombia, México, and Venezuela.

Tobar et al. state that while in Europe most countries have increased the degree of price intervention, in LA the trend is less clear, and several countries have turned to more unregulated regimes. A second difference is that medicine price regulation systems are more heterogeneous and frequently changing than in Europe. Finally, the enforcement of price regulation is weaker in LA than in Europe, probably due to the limited institutional capacity in this area.

The description of medicine regulation systems of individual LA countries provided by Tobar et al. [3] is very brief and does not allow readers to obtain a precise understanding of how regulation works either in theory or in practice. Some of the information of this study has nevertheless been used below, complemented with other sources, to provide a brief country overview of price regulation in LA.

There are other reports that include a description of the pricing regulation system in LA countries. For example, Chapter 4 of the PAHO report "Access to High-Cost Medicines in the Americas: Situation, Challenges, and Perspectives" includes a summary of negotiation and regulatory practices in LA countries (Table 2.4.1).

The information provided in the PAHO report is based on a survey made by ANVISA and PAHO in 2009. According to the survey, six countries—Brazil, Colombia, Cuba, Ecuador, Mexico, and Nicaragua—were using at that time some form of price regulation, whereas Panama had used it from 2001 to 2004. The two most frequent criteria for determining the price were international prices (six countries) and production costs (four countries). The report also mentions public procurement as a powerful tool to improve access to medicines and quotes some experiences in this domain in countries of the region.

A recent study [5] focused on international reference pricing (IRP, also called external price referencing/EPR, this term being used in other chapters) retrieved information from 100 countries worldwide (for further in-depth findings of this study, not only on LA, see Chapter 12). 55 out of the 100 respondents declared to be using an IRP system. In LA, Colombia, and Brazil, they declared that they were using IRP, whereas Argentina, Ecuador, Grenada, and Haiti used other price regulation systems. Chile was using no price regulation. Moreover, informants from 14 countries with and without price regulation—three of them in LA (Chile, Ecuador, and Haiti)—stated that they were planning to use IRP in the future.

Impact studies that try to assess the effects of regulatory and other pharmaceutical policies in LA are even scarcer than descriptive studies [6–8]. A recent study [9] published by Prada et al., stated that "The Colombian experience clearly shows that price controls do not necessarily decrease overall real pharmaceutical expenditures," mainly due to the increase of the demand. In this sense, the authors commented that "Increased demand of pharmaceutical products may be a positive thing, as long as the increase is the result of greater access to effective medicines rather than the result of induced demand by pharmaceutical producers."

Table 2.4.1 Economic regulation of pharmaceuticals in the Americas

			Price criteria based on:					
Country	**Pharmaceutical price regulation**	**Responsible institutions**	**Therapeutic efficacy**	**Economic evaluation**	**Cost of similar treatment**	**International price**	**Production cost**	**Others**
Brazil	×	Interministerial board, presided by the Ministry of Heath, with ANVISA acting as the executive secretariat	×	×	×	×		×
Colombia	×	Ministry of Social Protection, Ministry of Trade, Industry, and Tourism, and a delegate representing the Office of the President of the Republic				×	×	
Cuba	×	Ministry of Finance and Ministry of Public Health	×		×	×	×	

Continued

Table 2.4.1 Economic regulation of pharmaceuticals in the Americas—cont'd

Country	Pharmaceutical price regulation	Responsible institutions	Price criteria based on:					
			Therapeutic efficacy	Economic evaluation	Cost of similar treatment	International price	Production cost	Others
Ecuador	×	Ministry of Health, Ministry of Industry, and the National Federation of Chemical and Biochemical Pharmaceutical Industries					×	
Mexico	×	Secretariat of the Economy and Office of the Federal Prosecutor for Consumer Affairs				×		
Nicaragua	×	Ministry of Public Works, Industry, and Trade		×		×		×
Panama	2001–2004	Executive Branch and Consumer Protection Authority				×	×	

Reproduced from Pan America Health Organization. Access to high-cost medicines in the Americas: situation, challenges and perspectives. Technical series No. 1 essential medicines, access, and innovation. Washington; 2010.

In conclusion, the available knowledge on medicine price regulation regimes and other medicine market regulations in LA countries is very limited. This applies both to descriptive and to analytical studies. Most documents are informal reports and gray literature, which raises some concerns about the validity of the information provided.

2.4.1.2 Examples of Price Regulation in the Latin America Region

2.4.1.2.1 Colombian Medicines Pricing Regulation

Colombia is moving faster than other LA countries toward universal health coverage. Nearly 97% of its citizens have access to health insurance. Furthermore, income does not determine the health benefits package (HBP) whatsoever, and out-of-pocket expenses are the lowest in the region [10]. Over the past 4 years, the HBP has grown more than those in other countries, and coverage goes beyond the recommendations of the latest update of the World Health Organization (WHO) Essential Medicines List, including biological medicines for cancer, diabetes, and rheumatoid arthritis [11].

Expanding the Essential Medicines List poses a huge financial challenge for the Colombian government. To manage this burden, the Ministry of Health (MoH) issued a pharmaceutical policy (PP) based on three components: strengthening of health technology assessment processes, price control of medicines, and the promotion of competition in the pharmaceutical market. Since then, Colombia has been implementing price control mechanisms for medicines, using national and international price references.[1]

In 2011, the MoH introduced a price cap on medicines reimbursements by active ingredient. The price cap was calculated as the median Colombian wholesaler price less a fixed percentage (20%). Two years later, another price control reform was introduced using IRP systems. The IRP system includes three main phases: (1) identification of relevant markets; (2) analysis of market power using the Herfindahl–Hirschman index; and (3) setting up of IRP for each relevant market, using available information of wholesaler prices of 17 countries from the Americas, Europe, and Australia. The IRP reflects the percentile 25 of the observed prices [12].

Until 2013, the IRP system had been applied to 837 medicines. 576 medicines (69% of those analyzed) had a national average price higher than

[1] Departamento Nacional de Planeación Gobierno de Colombia. Conpes 155 de 2012 "Política Farmacéutica Nacional". Available from: https://www.minsalud.gov.co/Documentos%20y%20Publicaciones/Politica%20Farmac%C3%A9utica%20Nacional.pdf.

the IRP and enjoyed some degree of market power, and therefore their prices were regulated. They represented 80% of public expenditure on medicines not covered by the HBP. The average price reduction for those medicines was 40% [13].

Recently (2017) the MoH started preparing a regulatory proposal of value-based pricing linked to the marketing authorization, like Brazil does since the early 2000s.

Colombia was able to apply the IRP system thanks to the existence of its information system of medicine prices (SISMED), an official source of Colombian prices and quantities of medicines sold in the market. Since 2010, it is mandatory to quarterly report all medicines trade transactions in the market.

2.4.1.2.2 Brazilian Medicines Pricing Regulation

The Brazilian pharmaceutical market is the second largest in the emerging world. The medicines pricing regulation in Brazil was set up in 2004. It establishes that once the market authorization for a pharmaceutical product has been granted, the supplier must file for a list pricing registry at the Pharmaceutical Market Regulation Council (CMED), which sets prices for the public and private sector. The list price is the official fixed price for a product. In the case of generics, this price might be adjusted annually according to which market it is sold into.

CMED sets the prices according to specific criteria that apply for the six categories a substance can fall under:

Category I. New patent-protected medicines that present better efficacy or safety profile compared with established treatments. The price is set by the IPR system and must not exceed the medicine's lowest price in any of the following countries—Australia, Canada, France, Greece, Italy, New Zealand, Portugal, Spain, the United States, and the country of origin.

Category II. "Me-too" medicines, where a cost minimization assessment applies.

Category III. New presentation in the same dosage of a medicine already marketed. The price is worked out based on the arithmetic mean of the prices of previously launched products.

Category IV. New presentations in a different dosage of a medicine already marketed. The price must not exceed the average price, weighted by sales, of available presentations of the medicine that have the same active ingredients, strength, and dosage form.

Category V. New presentations of a medicine that is a new dosage form in Brazil or a new combination of active ingredients already available in Brazil. The price is set by IRP and must not exceed the medicine's lowest price in any of the countries listed in category I.

Category VI. Generic medicine cannot have a price that exceeds 65% of the respective reference medicine.

2.4.1.2.3 Price Regulation in Other Latin American Countries

Ecuador had a direct price control mechanism based on the costs declared by the manufacturer or importer plus a profit markup (20% of the total cost). A system established in 2011 set up three regimes: monitored freedom, regulated freedom, and direct control. At present (2018), Ecuador is trying to implement a new system approved in 2014, which is based on IRP for new medicines that show a therapeutic advantage or are supplied under monopolistic conditions and on internal prices for multisource medicines.

El Salvador applies an IRP system, where the maximum price is set as the average of the Central American countries.

Honduras regulates the maximum profit.

Mexico calculates international reference prices, but suppliers define the maximum selling price based on the estimated cost structure plus a defined profit margin.

Nicaragua fixes cost, insurance, and freight prices for imported products. Comparative prices are calculated for locally manufactured products. Wholesale and retail markups are also regulated.

Paraguay applies different coefficients to locally manufactured products, imported finished products, and in bulk imported products. Negotiations are carried out with the pharmaceutical sector to reduce prices.

Venezuela only regulates the price of essential medicines, by setting a maximum profit margin [3].

2.4.2 ONLINE SOURCES OF MEDICINES PRICES IN LATIN AMERICA

Online sources of medicines prices are few, maybe because, as it has been shown in the previous section, medicines pricing policies and regulation are also incipient.

Nevertheless, nine LA countries have developed some form of online information systems and platforms: Argentina, Brazil, Colombia, Chile,

Ecuador, Mexico, Panama, Peru, and Uruguay (see Table 2.4.2). Eighteen different online sources, apps, or databases to consult medicines prices are available for these seven countries. Some countries have more than one online source of medicine prices (Brazil, 2; Chile, 2; Colombia, 3; and Peru, 4). None of these online sources are documented at the publications revised for this chapter, except that of Brazil (ANVISA, the Drug Regulatory Authority from Brazil), which was mentioned at a working paper on International Reference Price Systems [14].

Only one platform has been developed so far at regional level to provide comparative medicines prices, even though there are some ongoing initiatives.

The type of price usually included at platforms is the official or institutional price (in 12 out of the 18 online sources), which represents the price to governmental institutions and is often associated to a centralized negotiation or to a tendering process. The ANVISA database provides three kinds of prices (ex-factory, institutional/regulated, and retail). Two of the online sources, Argentina and Peru, provide information of retail prices both of them belonging to the Drug Regulatory Authority. Only Colombia's medicine price databases include wholesaler price information.

Some of the online sources of medicines prices (Brazil, Colombia, and Peru) are based on robust information systems, and two of them (Colombia and Brazil) offer the possibility to download excel files, which allows external analysts to build time series of prices. The Colombian database also includes quantities sold. These databases constitute an adequate source for conducting econometric and impact studies.

Almost all databases reflect either observed or reported prices,[2] whereas two countries provide regulated prices (Brazil and Colombia).

It is also worthwhile to highlight the Colombian effort to ensure the transparency of the medicines prices throughout apps focused on the consumer. One of them provides national mean prices of medicines on competition and without any regulation, and is implemented as a mobile app called Clic salud.[3] This mobile app allows to consult the price by active ingredient, brand name, or specific market presentation and it shows the

[2] Reported prices: pharmaceutical market sellers are obliged by the government to report its prices. Observed prices: price observed (by independent body or researcher) on the market.

[3] TERMÓMETRO DE PRECIOS DE MEDICAMENTOS. Available from: https://www.minsalud.gov.co/salud/MT/Paginas/termometro-de-precios.aspx.

Table 2.4.2 List of medicines prices databases in the Americas

	Country	Source	Medicines price setting	Website	Price type	Unit of price
1	Argentina	Administración Nacional de Medicamentos, Alimentos y Tecnología Medica (ANMAT)	ANMAT is a Drug Regulatory Authority. Its website includes information of retail prices.	https://servicios.pami.org.ar/vademecum/views/consultaPublica/listado.zul	Retail	Price per trade package
2	Brazil	Banco de Preços Em Saude[a]	The data bank of health prices is a government's system of purchase prices of medicines and other medical products	http://bps.saude.gov.br/login.jsf	Institutional (price to government institutions)	Price per unit
3		Agênda Nacional de Vigilância Sanitária (ANVISA)	Agênda Nacional de Vigiláncia Sanitaria (ANVISA) is a Drug Regulatory Authority. Its website includes information of retail, ex-factory, and institutional prices.	http://portal.anvisa.gov.br/listas-de-precos	Ex-factory institutional retail	Price per trade package
4	Colombia	SISMED	The medicines prices system is a compulsory report system of prices for every medicine seller (companies, wholesale, hospitals, insurers, etc.). It does neither include pharmacy information neither retail prices. It includes the updated price (minimun, median and max price) every three months.	http://www.sispro.gov.co/recursosapp/app/Pages/SISMED.aspx	Ex-factory Wholesale	Price per trade package

Continued

Table 2.4.2 List of medicines prices databases in the Americas—cont'd

	Country	Source	Medicines price setting	Website	Price type	Unit of price
5		Clic salud	It is a mobile app (it is an app web, too) to consult a median wholesale price from SISMED by international nonproprietary name (INN), trade package, and trade name for every medicine in the market.	https://www.minsalud.gov.co/salud/MT/Paginas/termometro-de-precios.aspx	Wholesale	
6		Termómetro de precios internacionales[a]	It is a web app to consult the international reference prices (IRP) by INN, trade package, and trade name. It includes the latest wholesale regulated price based on IRP for more than 350 medicines.	https://www.minsalud.gov.co/salud/MT/Paginas/herramienta-interactiva-de-consulta-de-precios-regulados-de-medicamentos.aspx	Wholesale	
7	Chile	Portal de compras públicas (Chilecompra)	Chilecompra is the electronic platform where the 850 public agencies in Chile carry out their purchasing processes and suppliers offer their products and services. Any transaction with medicines from public health institutions and the lowest prices achieved can be consulted.	http://www.mercadopublico.cl/Portal/Modules/Site/Busquedas/BuscadorAvanzado.aspx?qs=2	Institutional (price to government institutions)	Price per unit
8		Central de abastecimiento del Sistema Nacional de servicios de Salud (CENABAST)	It is the Chilean National Health Supply Service System for the customers belonging to the National Health Services. It reflects the minimun prices achieved for public tendering. It allows the access to the discounts to the Ministry of Health.	http://www.cenabast.cl/precio-y-cantidad-de-productos-adjudicados/	Institutional (price to government institutions)	Price per unit

9	Ecuador	Sistema Oficial de Contratación Pública	Government Procurement System is the organization that leads and regulates the public procurement services which include medicines.	https://www.compraspublicas.gob.ec/ProcesoContratacion/compras/PC/buscarProceso.cpe?sg=1	Institutional (price to government institutions)	Price per unit
10	Mexico	Instituto mexicano del Seguro Social (IMSS)	The Mexican Institute of Social Security it is a national public health-care supplier for formal workers and their families. It includes minimum prices achieved throughout tendering and negotiation process.	http://compras.imss.gob.mx/?P=search_alt	Institutional (price to government institutions)	Price per unit
11		Instituto mexicano del Seguro Social—Rubro Medicinas	The Mexican Institute of Social Security it is a national public health-care supplier for formal workers and their families. It includes minimum prices achieved throughout tendering and negotiation process.	http://compras.imss.gob.mx/?P=imsscomprotipoproddet&tip=l&sub=010&pr=2016&corder=mn&corderdir=do#detailresultane	Institutional (price to government institutions)	Price per unit
12	Panama	Plataforma de compras públicas (Panamacompra)	Panamacompra is the public procurement platform, managed by the General Directorate of Public Procurement, which carries out the selection of government suppliers	http://www.panamacompra.gob.pa/ambientepublico/AP_BusquedaAvanzada.aspx	Institutional (price to government institutions)	Price per unit

Continued

Table 2.4.2 List of medicines prices databases in the Americas—cont'd

	Country	Source	Medicines price setting	Website	Price type	Unit of price
13	Peru	Observatorio de Precios de DIGEMID	DIGEMID is a Drug Regulatory Authority. Its website hosts a platform that provides information of retail prices	http://observatorio.digemid.minsa.gob.pe/	Retail	Price per trade package
14		Sistema Electrónico de Contratación del estado (SEACE 2)	The SEACE is the electronic system that allows the exchange of information on the government contracting and the accomplishment of electronic transactions. It is administered by the State Procurement Supervisory Agency.	http://www2.seace.gob.pe/?scriptdo=PKU_CONSULTA_TOP.doview&_CALIFICADOR_=P0RTLET.1.117.0.21.81&_REGIONID_=1&_PORTLETID_=117&_ORDERID_=0&_PAGEID_=21&_CONTENTID_=81&_USERID_=%3c%21–USERID–%3e&_PRIVILEGED_=1	Institutional (price to government institutions)	Price per unit
15		Sistema Electrónico de Contratación del estado (SEACE 3)	The SEACE is the electronic system that allows the exchange of information on the government contracting and the accomplishment of electronic transactions. It is administered by the State Procurement Supervisory Agency.	http://prodapp2.seace.gob.pe/seacebus-uiwd-pub/buscadorPublico/buscadorPublico.xhtml	Institutional (price to government institutions)	Price per unit

16		Dirección de Abastecimiento de Recursos Estratégicos en Salud (DARES)	The Directorate for Supply of Strategic Health Resources (DARES) acquires and distributes vaccines, antiretrovi rais, antituberculosis, contraceptive methods, antimalarials, among other products for the supply of health services at the national level.	http://intranet.cenares.minsa.gob.pe/DARES/ABASTECIMIENTO/COMPRAS/wf_BusquedaProducto.aspx	Institutional (price to government institutions)	Price per unit
17	Uruguay	Unidad Centralizada de Adquisiciones	The Centralized Procurement Unit is in charge of acquiring food, food services, medicines, medical supplies, and related products according to the quantity and quality required, in conditions of transparency and accessibility for suppliers, with opportunity and at a minimum price.	https://www.mef.gub.uy/480/13/areas/insumos-medicos.html	Institutional (price to government institutions)	Price per trade package
18	Latin America online source	Decisiones Informadas sobre Medicamentos de alto impacto financiero (DIME)	DIME is a platform that includes comparative information of minimum prices from eight Latin American countries. It includes other comparative information about coverage, health technology assessment and patent status for a priority medicine list.[b] It is a regional public good impulse by Inter-American Development Bank.	www.proyectodime.info	Institutional (price to government institutions)	Price per Defined Daily Dose

[a]Regulated prices.
[b]DIME tutorial to consult international prices. Modified from Ministry of Health Colombia tool for calculation International Reference Prices, www.proyectodime.info.

mean prices ordered from the lowest price (on green) to the highest price (on red).

The other tool available to consult prices is a web app called *thermometer of international reference prices.*[4] This web app allows to consult the international reference price established in 2013 for more than 800 medicines in the market, most of them are single source products. The web app allows consulting the price by active ingredient, brand name, or specific market presentation and it shows the price by minimum unit of active ingredient, ordered from the highest to the lowest country's prices. Fig. 2.4.1 is the output of a query at the web app thermometer of international reference prices. It shows 12 different referenced prices. The Colombian regulated price corresponds to the percentile 25. United States has the highest price per International Unit (IU) and Norway, the lowest one.

There have been many efforts in the region to develop a regional medicine prices observatory to support joint negotiation strategies or to leverage the negotiating capacities of countries vis à vis pharmaceutical

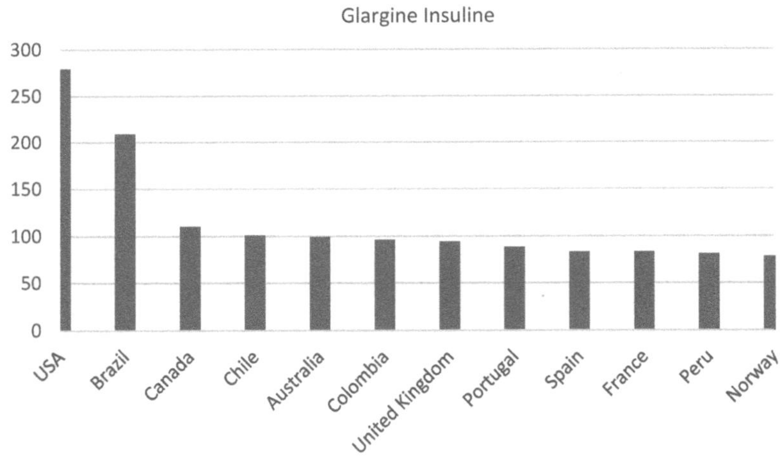

Figure 2.4.1 Comparison of Prices (in Colombian Pesos) for Glargine Insuline in IU. *(Reproduced from: https://www.minsalud.gov.co/salud/MT/Paginas/herramienta-interactiva-de-consulta-de-precios-regulados-de-medicamentos.aspx)*

[4] TERMÓMETRO DE PRECIOS DE REFERENCIA INTERNACIONAL DE MEDICAMENTOS. Available from: https://www.minsalud.gov.co/salud/MT/Paginas/herramienta-interactiva-de-consulta-de-precios-regulados-de-medicamentos.aspx.

suppliers. There is an ongoing initiative led by ISAGS and UNASUR,[5] still at the design stage. Perhaps the most advanced initiative in this regard is the platform called Decisiones Informadas sobre Medicamentos de alto costo (DIME), a regional public good sponsored by the Inter-American Development Bank (IADB). DIME is a platform that includes comparative information of the minimum public purchase prices for a list of 38 medicines selected for its high financial impact on the public budgets of eight LA countries (Mexico, Costa Rica, El Salvador, Dominican Republic, Colombia, Ecuador, Peru, and Chile).[6] The platform includes other important information for those managing the pressure of technologies over public health expenditure (coverage, health technology assessment, competition, and patent status). The most important weakness of this platform, as other similar projects, is the lack of updating along time.

Fig. 2.4.2 displays the output of a query of the DIME project. It shows the minimum price of public purchase for 12 different countries, included 8 LA countries.

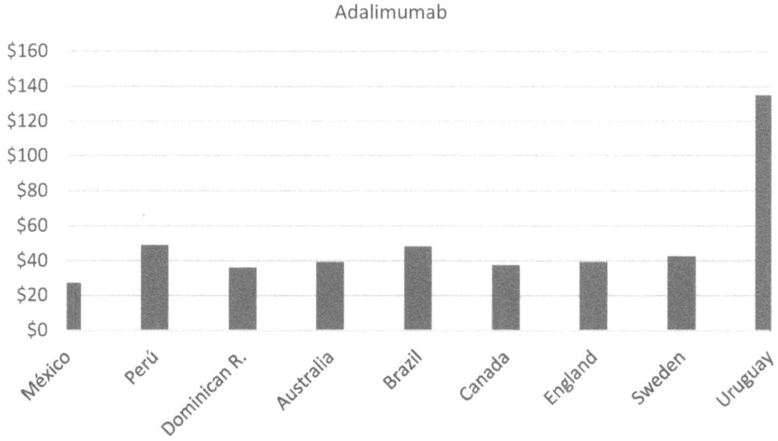

Figure 2.4.2 Comparison of prices for Adalimumab (in Defined Daily Dosis). *(Reproduced from: http://www.proyectodime.info/.)*

[5] Grupo Técnico de Acceso Universal a Medicamentos (GAUMU) y el Instituto Suramericano de Gobierno en Salud (ISAGS) impulsan banco de precios de medicamentos de UNASUR (Unión de Naciones Suramericanas). http://www.isags-unasur.org/uploads/eventos/ev[3117]ling[2]anx[569].pdf.

[6] http://www.proyectodime.info/.

2.4.3 MEDICINE PRICE STUDIES IN LATIN AMERICAN COUNTRIES

2.4.3.1 Introduction

There are few studies in LA comparing medicines prices. The main likely reason that accounts for this situation is the lack of price regulation in most countries. When prices are regulated it is relatively simple to provide a list of regulated prices; in its absence, time-consuming data collection procedures are necessary to build price databases; the absence of public prices databases makes it difficult to carry out analyses of the market dynamics and inte-country comparisons. During the last few years more countries have been starting to regulate medicines prices, trying to control or lower them. At the same time, there are new initiatives to build medicine price databases, as explained in Section 2.4.2 of this chapter. Unfortunately, these initiatives do not use a common methodology, which limits the comparability and hence the usefulness of the available information. In the past, several countries made studies using the WHO/(Health Action International) HAI methodology to survey the price, availability, and affordability of medicines (see Chapter 6.2 in Part 2 for further information on this methodology). These studies focused on low- and middle-income countries, where some LA countries were selected. The results of the studies were used in some countries (El Salvador, Colombia, and Perú, for example) as an argument for a more rational approach to medicines pricing.

2.4.3.2 Methodology

To identify articles and studies on medicine prices in the region, we carried out two literature searches in February 2017. The first search was on Pubmed and Econlit, two academic databases focusing on medicine and economy, respectively. The second literature search was based on Google Scholar, which provides both academic articles and gray literature.

Six articles were identified: four studies on medicine prices in LA [15-18] and two international medicine prices studies [19-20] that included at least one country from LA in the analysis. Most studies reported results not only on prices but also on availability. Additionally, we found a press release of the Ministerio de Economia, Industria y Comercio of Costa Rica, reporting a comparative study of medicines prices in the Centro American region done by CONCADECO, the Centro American Council of Consumer Protection Agencies that has been also mentioned in the results.

2.4.3.3 Results and Findings

In a study made in Guatemala by Anson et al., [15] using WHO/HAI methodology, the authors found that public programs (for example, the Programa de Accesibilidad a los Medicamentos/PROAM) had a lower average availability than the private sector (25% vs. 35%), and that the prices in the private sector were on average 16.7 times more expensive than the international prices used for comparison (highest 22.7; lowest 10.7 times). They concluded that medicines were generally unaffordable for the majority of the population.

In a study made in Haiti by Chahal et al., [16] the availability of medicines was found higher in the private retail sector (37%) than in public (20%) and nonprofit (23%) sectors. As an example, they reported that a government worker needed 2.5 days' wages to treat an adult respiratory infection with generic medicines from public sector, but the treatment for hyperlipidemia would require 13.7 days' wages. As a result of the study, the authors concluded that medicine prices were lower in Bolivia, Colombia, Mexico, and Nicaragua (see Table 2.4.3). As in the previous study [15] in Guatemala, most medicines were priced higher than the international reference prices used in the WHO/HAI methodology.

Madden et al. [17] published in 2010 a study in Peru using WHO/HAI survey methodology, and, contrary to the previous studies in other LA countries, they did not find significant differences in overall availability or prices by retail location (urban, semiurban, and rural). It was not possible to compare the medicine prices between public and private sector because in the public sector of Peru there is normally only one generic version of each medicine and, consequently, comparisons between alternative products in the public sector are only occasionally possible.

An earlier study [18] in Peru by WHO/HAI found similar results: the private sector originator brands were approximately 28 times the international reference price and the lowest priced generics in the private sector were almost four times the price of those in the public sector, but in the public sector generics were approximately 1.3 times the reference price.

The study by De Lima et al. [19] focuses on opioids; price comparisons are made at global level. The countries are categorized according to the WB classification: high-income country (HIC), upper middle-income country (UMIC), lower middle-income country (LMIC), and low-income country (LIC). The LA countries included are Chile, Argentina, Brazil, Uruguay, and Guatemala; all these countries are classified as UMIC, except for

Table 2.4.3 Availability and median price ratios (MPR) of 12 essential lowest priced generic medications in Haiti compared with four neighboring countries

	Haiti		Nicaragua		Mexico		Colombia		Bolivia	
Medication (strength)	**Availability (%)[a]**	**MPR**	**Availability (%)**	**MPR**	**Availability (%)**	**MPR**	**Availability (%)**	**MPR**	**Availability (%)**	**MPR**
Amitriptyline 25 mg	11.4	13.3	51.6	11.2	0	N/A	93.2	6.4	50	3.3
Amoxicillin 500 mg	97.1	4.3	100	2.2	53.3	4.3	96.6	2.5	100	2.3
Atenolol 50 mg	74.3	15.9	61.3	4	6.7	N/A	11.9	10.1	73.3	6.15
Captopril 25 mg	57.1	10.5	93.5	4	86.7	5.5	96.6	1.5	0	N/A
Ceftriaxone 1 g/vial	71.4	5.5	90.3	3.6	73.3	6.6	49.2	3	93.3	1.1
Ciprofloxacin 500 mg	91.4	5.1	100	8	80	12.7	100	4.8	96.7	4.4
Co-trimoxazole 8 + 40 mg/mL	62.9	4.5	83.9	4.2	80	4.5	86.4	4	86.7	4
Diclofenac 50 mg	85.7	25.2	96.8	11.3	6.7	N/A	96.6	7.9	100	7.9
Glibenclamide 5 mg	80	20.4	83.9	10.4	46.7	5.2	91.5	7.3	90	13
Omeprazole 20 mg	97.1	4.2	96.8	6.3	80	9.3	94.9	2.2	96.7	3.3
Salbutamol 100 μg/dose	85.7	2.3	71	3	53.3	2.1	96.6	1.4	60	2.4
Simvastatin 20 mg	57.1	N/A	83.9	N/A	6.7	N/A	35.6	N/A	6.7	N/A

N/A, not available or not applicable.
[a]Percent (%) of retail outlets with medication.
(Reproduced from: Chahal HS, St Fort N, Bero L. Availability, prices and affordability of essential medicines in Haiti. Journal of Global Health 2013;3:020405).

Guatemala, which is an LMIC. Curiously, in spite of its classification, Guatemala had an availability of opioids of 61.5%, compared with 7.7% in Uruguay and Brazil. In relation to affordability, the results show that for a 30-day treatment of morphine oral medication 6.5 days wages are needed in Argentina and 8.1 in Guatemala.

The study by Cameron et al. [20] reports the differences between country groups, aggregated by income level according to the WB classification, but not individually, and it is therefore not possible to derive specific information for LA countries.

A press release of the Ministerio de Economia, Industria y Comercio of Costa Rica, 2009, reports a comparative study of medicines prices in the Centro American region done by CONCADECO, the Centro American Council of Consumer Protection Agencies. The comparison was based on a basket of 30 medicines, both in their originator as in generic versions. The information was collected between October and November 2008 in pharmacies of the respective capitals following the WHO/HAI methodology. The values in US$ of the originators and the generics baskets were Nicaragua 54/10, Honduras 63/15, Panama 69/21, Costa Rica 62/22, El Salvador 76/32, and Guatemala 78/35, respectively. The price differentials between originators and generics that can be derived from the previous figures are larger for the lower-priced countries, for instance, 424% in Nicaragua versus 122% in Guatemala. The report states that out of the six countries analyzed, only Nicaragua has regulated prices.[7]

2.4.4 CONCLUSIONS

Available studies on medicine prices in LA are scarce and carried out in different years. Moreover, the methodologies are often heterogeneous and, hence, the results are not comparable. It is therefore difficult to draw reliable conclusions on medicine price differences across LA countries.

Most of the studies found in the literature used the standardized methodology developed by the WHO and HAI to survey the price, availability, and affordability of medicines; in fact, the results focus more often on availability than on affordability, i.e., on the price—income relationship.

[7] Unfortunately, we have not been able to identify the original study summarized in the press release, because the link it referred to for the original information was not available on July 2017.

Medicine price databases are needed to increase and improve transparency on medicine prices and to assess the effectiveness and impact of pricing policies applied in the countries. The scarcity of medicine price information in LA countries might be related to the limited use of price regulation. The situation seems to be changing (the availability of information on medicine prices seems to be associated to the development of an explicit regulatory system of medicines prices in the country), but there is still a long way ahead. National authorities and international organizations should promote the establishment of publicly available, national, and multicountry medicine prices databases to (1) enhance competition in the drug markets, (2) reduce prices and hence affordability, (3) facilitate and improve the accountability of regulatory and procurement agencies, and (4) make possible studies on the evolution of medicine prices and on the impact of policy measures.

REFERENCES

[1] Homedes N, Ugalde A, Rovira J. The World Bank, pharmaceutical policies, and health reforms in Latin America. International Journal of Health Services 2005;35(4):691–717.

[2] Espín J, Rovira J. Analysis of differences and commonalities in pricing and reimbursement systems in Europe. A study funded by DG Enterprise and Industry of the European Commission. EASP Final Report. June 2007.

[3] Tobar F, Drake I, Martich E. Alternativas para la adopción de políticas centradas en el acceso a medicamentos. Revista Panamericana de Salud Pública 2012;32(6):457–63.

[4] Pan American Health Organization. Access to high-cost medicines in the Americas: situation, challenges and perspectives. In: Technical series No. 1 essential medicines, access, and innovation. Washington; 2010.

[5] Espin J, Rovira J, Ewen M, Laing R. Mapping external reference pricing practices for medicines. HAI/EASP; September 2014.

[6] Balmaceda C, et al. Impacto de una Política de Equivalencia Terapéutica en el Precio de Medicamentos en Chile. Value in Health Regional Issues 2015;8C(2015):43–8.

[7] Vaca C, Acosta A, Rodriguez I. Precios de Referencia Internacional y Análisis de Costo Minimización para la Regulación de Precios de Medicamentos en Colombia. Value in Health 2011;14(2011):S16–9.

[8] Prada SI, et al. Evaluación del impacto de la regulación de precios de medicamentos, de Colombia. Universidad Nacional de Colombia, ICESI; 2015.

[9] Prada SI, et al. Higher pharmaceutical public expenditure after direct price control: improved access or induced demand? The Colombian case. Cost Effectiveness and Resource Allocation 2018;16:8.

[10] OECD. Reviews of Health Systems: Colombia 2016.

[11] Ministerio de Salud y Protección Social – MINSALUD (2011). 'Acuerdo 029 de 2011'. Comisión de Regulación en Salud. http://www.minsalud.gov.co/Ministerio de Salud y Protección Social. Resolución 5521 Bogotá, 2013. Available from: http://www.minsalud.gov.co/sites/rid/Lists/BibliotecaDigital/RIDE/DE/DIJ/Resoluci per centC3 per centB3n 5521 de 2013.pdf.

[12] Comisión Nacional de Precios de Medicamentos y Dispositivos Médicos Circular 03 de. Por la cual se establece la metodología para la aplicación del régimen de control directo de precios para los medicamentos que se comercialicen en el territorio nacional. 2013. Available from: https://www.minsalud.gov.co/Normatividad_Nuevo/Circular%20 Externa%20Conjunta%200003%20de%202013.pdf.
[13] Andia T, Gaviria A, Gomez C, Jaramillo LF, Marquez S, Rodríguez I, Vaca C. First evaluation of Colombian's external reference pricing system. Value in Health. May 2014;17(3):A15.
[14] Espin J, Rovira J, Olry de Labry A. Review series on pharmaceutical pricing policies and interventions: working paper 1: external reference pricing. WHO/HAI Policy Review 2011.
[15] Anson A, Ramay B, Ruiz de Esparza A, Bero L. Availability, prices and affordability of the World Health Organization's essential medicines for children in Guatemala. Global Health 2012;8:22.
[16] Chahal HS, St Fort N, Bero L. Availability, prices and affordability of essential medicines in Haiti. Journal of Global Health 2013;3:020405.
[17] Madden JM, Meza E, Ewen M, Laing RO, Stephens P, Ross-Degnan D. Measuring medicine prices in Peru: validation of key aspects of WHO/HAI survey methodology. Revista Panamericana de Salud Pública 2010;27(4):291–9.
[18] Health Action International. Medicine prices, availability, affordability and price components in Peru. 2007.
[19] De Lima L, Pastrana T, Radbruch L, Wenk R. Cross-sectional pilot study to monitor the availability, dispensed prices, and affordability of opioids around the globe. Journal of Pain and Symptom Management 2014;48(4):649–59.
[20] Cameron A, Bansal A, Dua T, Hill SR, Moshe SL, Mantel-Teeuwisse AK, Saxena S. Mapping the availability, price, and affordability of antiepileptic drugs in 46 countries. Epilepsia 2012;53(6):962–9.

FURTHER READING

Tobar F. Referenciación internacional sobre políticas de regulación de precios de medicamentos. Noviembre 2011.
Homedes N, Ugalde A. Availability and affordability of new medicines in Latin American countries where pivotal clinical trials were conducted. Bulletin of the World Health Organization 2015;93(10):674–83.
Organización Panamericana de la Salud. La Situación Farmacéutica en la Región de las Américas: Indicadores de Estructura y Proceso. Washington; 2007.
República de Colombia. Ley 1753 de 2015. Plan Nacional del plan de desarrollo. Art. 72. Available from: https://colaboracion.dnp.gov.co/CDT/Prensa/LEY%201753%20 DEL%2009%20DE%20JUNIO%20DE%202015.pdf - consulted: 27/07/2017.
Tobar F. Política de Medicamentos en América Latina. Buenos Aires: Fundación Salud y Fármacos; 2007.
Universidad Nacional de Colombia. Determinación de precios de Nuevas tecnologías considerando su aporte terapéutico. Recomendaciones para la reglamentación del Artículo 72 de la Ley 1753 de 2015; 2015. Available from: http://investigacion.unal.edu.co/fileadmin/recursos/siun/docs/escuela-pensamiento/medicamentos/propuesta-determinacion-precio-nuevas-tecnologias-aporte-terapeutico-20160830-un-uniandes.pdf.

CHAPTER 2.5

Medicine Prices in Africa

Swathi Iyengar[1,2] Rianne van den Ham[1], Fatima Suleman[3,4]

[1]Division of Pharmacoepidemiology & Clinical Pharmacology, Utrecht Institute for Pharmaceutical Sciences, Utrecht University, Utrecht, Netherlands; [2]World Health Organization, Geneva, Switzerland; [3]Faculty of Sciences, Utrecht University, Utrecht, The Netherlands; [4]School of Health Sciences, College of Health Sciences, Westville Campus, University of KwaZulu-Natal, South Africa

LIST OF ABBREVIATIONS

ABC Analysis	Inventory categorization method that consists in dividing items into three categories (A, B, C): A being the most valuable items and C being the least valuable ones.
ACT	Artemisinin-based combination therapy
AL	Artemether/lumefantrine
ASAQ	A fixed-dose artesunate—amodiaquine combination therapy
EML	Essential medicines list
GDP	Gross domestic product
GNI	Gross national income
HAI	Health Action International
HIV	Human immunodeficiency virus
IB	Innovator brand
IDPIG	Drug Price Indicator Guide
MSH	Management Sciences for Health
MPR	Median price ratio
MESH	Medical Subject Headings
NCDs	Noncommunicable diseases
NGO	Nongovernment organization
QAART	Quality-assured artemisinin-based combination therapies
SARA	Service Availability and Readiness Assessment
SGDs	Sustainable Development Goals
STI	Sexually transmitted infection
UN	United Nations
WHO	World Health Organization
WHO AFRO	World Health Organization Regional Office for Africa
WHO/HAI	World Health Organization/Health Action International

Medicine Price Surveys, Analyses, and Comparisons
ISBN 978-0-12-813166-4
https://doi.org/10.1016/B978-0-12-813166-4.00007-3

2.5.1 INTRODUCTION

Africa, as a whole, has six Portuguese-speaking, or Lusophone, African countries consisting of Angola, Cape Verde, Guinea-Bissau, Mozambique, São Tomé and Príncipe, and, since 2011, Equatorial Guinea. There are 31 Francophone, or French-speaking, countries in Africa. Anglophone, or English-speaking, Africa includes five countries in West Africa (The Gambia, Sierra Leone, Liberia, Ghana, and Nigeria, as well as a part of Cameroon), South Sudan, a large continuous area in Southern Africa, and the African Great Lakes. The Arabophone, or Arabic-speaking, Africa includes Egypt, Sudan, Morocco, Algeria, and Tunisia, Mauritania, and Chad. Of these, 47 countries are in the World Health Organization Regional Office for Africa (WHO AFRO) oversight, which share some common culture and history.

Africa's health challenges are numerous and wide-ranging. Most countries face a double burden of traditional, persisting health challenges, such as infectious diseases, malnutrition, and child and maternal mortality, and emerging health challenges from an increasing prevalence of chronic conditions, mental health disorders, injuries, and health problems related to climate change and environmental degradation. Africa's health indicators remain behind those of other continents, and major health inequities exist. Health outcomes are worst in fragile countries, rural areas, urban slums, and conflict zones, and among poor, disabled, and marginalized people.

Access to medicines is an important part of health services delivery. The Sustainable Development Goals adopted in September 2015, by the member states of the United Nations (UN), recognize that equitable access to affordable, quality-assured essential medicines is a crucial step in achieving universal health coverage. Many factors affect access to medicines. Availability has been one of these factors. This chapter looks at what information has been published concerning medicines availability, and pricing in Africa, after first presenting a background on health and health systems in Africa.

2.5.2 BACKGROUND TO HEALTH AND HEALTH SYSTEMS IN AFRICA

2.5.2.1 Growth in Sub-Saharan Africa

Gross domestic product (GDP) in sub-Saharan Africa grew by 4.5% in 2014% and 3.0% in 2015 [1]. Sub-Saharan Africa's collective annual GDP is anticipated to increase to $3.5 trillion by 2025, from US$1.573 trillion in

2015, according to an estimate [2]. Gross national income (GNI) per capita has gone up from $505 in 2000 to $803 in 2005 to $1628 in 2015 [1]. Economic growth and per capita GNI, however, differs remarkably among and within African countries, and there is still a high burden of poverty in the sub-Saharan African population.

Sub-Saharan Africa's population is expected to rise from 1.02 billion people in 2017 to 1.42 billion by 2030. More than half of the world's population growth from 2017 to 2050 will be concentrated in 10 countries, and 5 of these are in sub-Saharan Africa: Nigeria, DR Congo, Ethiopia, Tanzania, and Uganda [3]. Moreover, sub-Saharan Africa is facing the challenges and opportunities of the largest-projected population growth of young people in history, with the population aged under 25 years predicted to almost double from 230 million to 450 million by 2050. Life expectancy in sub-Saharan Africa is still far behind the rest of the world, but it has been steadily increasing since 2000.

Urbanization and population density has also increased, with the number of megacities in sub-Saharan Africa rising from 10 in 1990 to 28 in 2014 [4]. Just over one-third (37%) of the population in sub-Saharan Africa was living in urban areas in 2014, and this is projected to rise to 45% by 2030, with a continued rise thereafter.

2.5.2.2 Health Care in Africa

Prior to European colonization, health-care services were based on indigenous knowledge systems and were widely available in urban and rural communities. People trusted traditional practitioners, who used plants, herbs, and other remedies to treat various ailments. The popularity of traditional medicine is present today. The type of European colonization affected how different public health systems emerged in Africa. For instance, francophone countries often have very centralized services, rather than decentralized health-care services.

In general, African public health systems are fragmented and under-resourced. The systems are often disease-specific in focus, with multiple systems running in parallel (donor services, nongovernment organization (NGO) services, government public health services, etc.) [5]. Of the 47 countries in the WHO African region, only 17 have designated as national institutes of public health [6], and fewer than 400 laboratories are accredited to international standards, of which 90% are in South Africa [7]. Almost half of all African countries do not have basic capacity for public health workforce training and development, with only 23 countries offering postgraduate public health education [8]. Lengthy periods of armed conflict and political instability have created additional challenges in terms of health system financing and human resources. Additionally, health systems in several sub-Saharan countries are yet to recover from the impact of structural adjustments and other economic reforms imposed by international agencies in the wake of the economic downturn in the 1970s. Financial fragmentation has led many countries to have a health system under their respective Ministry of Health and other parallel health systems managed by funders and NGOs.

2.5.2.3 Provision of Health Care in Africa

In African countries, e.g., DR Congo, Malawi, and Nigeria, the majority of health care is provided by the private sector, including faith-based NGOs and traditional healers, and numerous community and prevention programs are run by NGOs [9]. Two issues are important and critical to all African countries from a sustainability perspective: the reliance on out-of-pocket payments and the substantive contribution of external funding. Out-of-pocket payments remain a large contributor to financing health services. Regardless of the overall progress during the past decade, some sub-Saharan countries have not decreased out-of-pocket payments as a share of total health expenditure. In more than a third of such countries, these payments make up more than 40% of total health expenditure [10]. In only five countries (Botswana, Mozambique, Namibia, Seychelles, and South Africa) out-of-pocket contributions represent less than 10% of total health expenditure. External assistance for health as a percentage of total health expenditure has grown to four times baseline in the entire African region over the past two decades and remains comfortably higher than in any other region [11]. Some countries have had constant external assistance relative to total health expenditure since 2000 (e.g., Cameroon and Malawi), others have seen substantial increases (e.g., DR Congo, Kenya, and Mali), and others have relied less and less on external funding (e.g., Chad). Human immunodeficiency virus (HIV), malaria, and maternal and child health have received the most attention, with some countries highly dependent on foreign funding for their HIV-treatment programmes, but donor funding for noncommunicable diseases (NCDs) has been minimal.

The share of external funding for health is variable across the countries, with some impressive progress (e.g., 8% average annual decrease as a share of total health expenditure in Namibia and 7% in South Africa). By contrast, Senegal and Swaziland have increasingly used external resources, thus increasing donor dependency, by an annual average of 11% and 21%, respectively. Most countries have had stable progress in the proportion of out-of-pocket payments, with Chad and DR Congo maintaining continuous reductions in out-of-pocket payments, and Botswana, Mozambique, and Tanzania having substantial increases.

2.5.3 THE AFRICAN MEDICINES ENVIRONMENT

African governments are all grappling with the issue of high medicine prices. Together with the increasing move to develop local pharmaceutical industries, the issue of medicine prices and how to contain them has been a key focus area for policy makers. These policy makers are also aware of measures implemented by other countries around the world to contain rising health-care costs, and especially pharmaceutical expenditure. Although price controls are important policy instruments, they are not without controversy.

From the perspective of medicine-production capabilities, ~70% of the African pharmaceutical market is imported, and although more than 30 sub-Saharan countries have some form of pharmaceutical production capabilities, only South African companies produce active pharmaceutical ingredients [12]. Substantial foreign aid received by African countries during the past decades to support tuberculosis, HIV, and malaria medicines has led to large-scale generic drug imports, primarily from Indian companies [13,14]. Although the availability of generic antiretroviral medicines from India has made it possible to treat over 10 million people with HIV in sub-Saharan Africa, a pilot study found that antibiotics and tuberculosis drugs of Indian origin are more likely to be of substandard quality in Africa compared with other markets [15]. More broadly, the issue of counterfeit medicines is of global concern, but it is considered to be even more of a problem in sub-Saharan Africa than in other regions [16,17], with a median of 20% of the population reporting to have been a victim of counterfeit drugs [18].

More than 30 sub-Saharan countries are classified by the UN as least developed countries and, as such, are eligible to refuse to grant patents for pharmaceuticals until July 2021, under the transitional provisions in the Trade-Related Aspects of Intellectual Property Rights agreement [19]. Most national regulatory agencies in sub-Saharan countries do not have the capacity to perform their basic functions, such as conducting timely, good-quality technical assessments of product dossiers and verifying the marketing authorization of products on importation [20]. To give one example, only five countries (Kenya, South Africa, Tanzania, Uganda, and Zimbabwe) have WHO prequalified laboratories for drug-quality testing [21]. For medicines to become available for African patients, it can take 5 years or longer than in other parts of the world [22].

The regional pharmaceutical sector consists of manufacturers, distributors, wholesalers, retail pharmacies, hospitals, and clinics. Pharmaceutical manufacturers are either local or multinationals. Few multinationals have local manufacturing plants, rather there are local agents who distribute their products. Multinational firms generally have brand-name products in the market, whereas local manufacturers provide lower-priced generics [23]. There has been a move to look at medicine pricing across the world in terms of affordability and access to patients. There is also a growing interest in the pricing strategies of pharmaceutical manufacturers in a global market and determining whether low- and middle-income countries can secure competitive prices for their medicines. The section that follows will look at surveys that look at or include medicine pricing in Africa, especially the WHO AFRO region.

2.5.4 METHODS FOR SELECTING STUDIES ON PRICING AND AVAILABILITY

The literature search was conducted using the following terms "medicine" (and the Medical Subject Headings equivalents) and "price" or "pricing" and "Africa" in Google Scholar and PubMed. As studies looked at pricing that in turn looked at availability as well, studies that looked at either aspects were included. The inclusion criteria were thus scope prices only, availability only, or price and availability and the WHO AFRO region. The exclusion criteria included vaccines, health system financing without specific discussion of medicines financing, and articles published before 2007. Studies available on the WHO or Health Action International (HAI) sites were also included.

Using this strategy, the search initially identified 98 articles based on abstracts (and after duplicates were excluded). The papers were extracted and stratified by criteria such as scope (e.g., availability survey, expenditure survey, price and availability survey only, etc.), focus country, standardized methods used, and therapeutic area. Forty-nine articles focused primarily on national surveys in a specific country in the African region. These are presented in the results section by region, followed by overall assessment of pricing surveys in the WHO AFRO region.

2.5.5 OVERVIEW OF FINDINGS

The findings are presented by the different regions in Africa, viz. Eastern Region, Central Region, Western Region, and the Southern Region and in terms of the tools used to capture the information. In each case, the table presents the overview of the findings by region, year, country, authors, use of standardized tools (and the indicators measured), therapeutic focus of the study, outcome focus (price vs. availability) of the study as well as the sectors included, and the facilities and products surveyed. The second part of the table for each region presents the results from the pricing surveys (where available) as well as results from the studies looking at availability only. Of the 47 WHO AFRO countries, only 23 of these are represented in these results.

As can be seen from Table 2.5.1 for Eastern Africa, the main tool utilized in the pricing surveys has been the WHO/HAI pricing and availability survey. The WHO/HAI surveys the price and availability of innovator brand, most sold generic and lowest priced generic. Price results of the three types for each medicine are presented in terms of automatically computer-generated median price ratio (MPR), which is the ratio of the median price for each medicine across facilities divided by an international reference price converted into local currency. The international reference price, using the Management Sciences for Health (MSH) International Drug Price Indicator Guide, is the median prices from not-for-profit wholesalers to developing countries. Affordability calculations are based on simple model treatments and the minimum daily wages of the lowest-paid unskilled worker in government service (refer to Chapter 6.2 in Part 2, which explains the WHO/HAI methodology further).

Essential medicines have been the focus of the surveys, though there have been surveys looking at the pricing and availability of malaria medicines specifically. Table 2.5.1 also demonstrates that aside from Tanzania and Uganda, pricing surveys are not conducted consistently in these countries and that there are large gaps between surveys. This could be due to the large number of facilities that have been sampled in these countries (e.g., 565 facilities in Zambia). Private-sector prices are generally higher than public-sector prices for medicines, with Mozambique showing the largest difference. There is a large variation in availability of medicines in both the public and the private-sector facilities. Detailed results are provided in Table 2.5.1.

Table 2.5.1 Overview of country pricing surveys in Eastern Africa

Year	Country	Authors	Standardized tool	Therapeutic focus	Focus (price vs. availability)	Sectors	Facilities surveyed	Products surveyed	Median public availability (%)	Median public price	Median private availability (%)	Median private price	Median NGO availability (%)	Median NGO price
2007	Burundi	WHO PSCP [24]	Availability on day, MPR, days wages	Essential medicines	Availability, price	Public, private, NGO			46.7	MPR 1.7	58.3	MPR 2.56		
2011	Burundi	Amuasi et al. [25]	Availability on day, MPR, days wages	Malaria	Availability, price	Public (24), private (36), NGO (10)	70	7	95.8	ASAQ 0.16 (0.16–0.16), Quinine 0.59 (0.03 −1.77), Nonpolicy antimalarials 8.90 (0.32 −11.29)	77.8	ASAQ 0.56 (0.16–2.82), Quinine 1.09 (0.24 −3.39), Nonpolicy antimalarials 8.55 (8.35 −9.44)	90	ASAQ 0.16 (0.08 −2.42), Quinine 1.19 (0.16 −2.58)
2013	Burundi	WHO/ HAI/MoH [26]	Availability on day, MPR, days wages	Essential medicines	Availability, price	Public, private, NGO	60	50	42.8	MPR 1.27	42	MPR 1.91	42.9	MPR 2.1
2007	Ethiopia	Carasso [27]	Availability on day, ratio of medicines dispensed over those prescribed, percent share by pharmacy of medicines dispensed, price of standard treatment for course, price with and without waiver	Essential medicines	Availability, price	Public, private	16	12			85	5.2 ± 2.6		
2013	Ethiopia	Ewen, Kaplan, Tedrif [28]	Availability on day, MPR, days wages	Essential medicines	Availability, price	Public, private, NGO	82	25	63.9	MPR 1.28	71.7	MPR 1.70	73%	MPR 1.47
2016	Ethiopia	Sado and Sufa [29]	Availability on day, MPR, days wages	Essential medicines for children	Availability, price	Public, private	55	22	43	MPR 1.18	43.8	MPR 1.54		

2011	Kenya	Smith et al. [30]	Stocking practices, median price	Malaria	Availability, price, access	Public, private	110				AL 43.5	2.73	AL 44.3	
2013	Kenya	O'Meara et al. [31]	Stocking practices, median price	Malaria	Availability, price	Private	97				22	AL $2.73 (0.38–7.50)		
2013	Kenya	WHO SARA [32]	Availability on day	Essential medicines	Availability	Public, private	1991 –7995	16+	85					
2016	Kenya	Kioko et al. [33]	Availability on day, median price	Malaria	Availability, price	Private	179	10			95.8	AL $0.94 (range $0.35 –4.71)		
2007	Malawi	Mendis et al. [34]	Availability on day, MPR, days wages	NCDs	Availability, price	Public, private	36	32	5.0 (0.0 –40.0)	Free	37.5 (0.0 –87.5	MPR 4.51 (n = 17)		
2017	Malawi	Khuluza and Heide [35]	Availability on day, MPR, days wages	Malaria and antibiotics	Availability, price	Public, private	31	12	38	Free	42	MPR 2.3	52	MPR 2.8
2008	Mauritius	WHO/ HAI/MoH [36]	Availability on day, MPR, days wages	Essential medicines	Availability, price	Public, private, NGO	61	50	68.6	Free	55.8	MPR 5.93		
2009	Mozambique	Russo and McPake [37]	Availability on day, MPR, days wages	Essential medicines	Availability, price	Public, private	56	25	60	MPR 0.41	73.5	MPR 5.19		
2008	Tanzania	WHO SARA [38]	Availability on day	Essential medicines	Availability	Public, private	691	13+	21		48			
2008	Tanzania	Mackintosh et al. [39]	Availability on day, median price, patient exit interviews, prescribing/ dispensing practices	Essential medicines	Availability, price	Public, private, NGO	69	31						
2008	Tanzania	Saulo et al. [40]	Price and willingness to pay (contingent valuation method)	Malaria	Price, affordability	Households	269 adults	1						
2009	Tanzania	WHO/ HAI/MOH [41]	Availability on day, MPR, days wages	Essential medicines	Availability, price	Public, private, NGO	92	40						

Continued

Table 2.5.1 Overview of country pricing surveys in Eastern Africa—cont'd

Year	Country	Authors	Standardized tool	Therapeutic focus	Focus (price vs. availability)	Sectors	Facilities surveyed	Products surveyed	Median public availability (%)	Median public price	Median private availability (%)	Median private price	Median NGO availability (%)	Median NGO price
2010/2012	Tanzania	Thomson et al. [42]	Stocking practices, median price	Malaria	Availability, price	Public, private	709/799		80.1 QAART()	Free	4.3 (QAART—general retailer)	Free		
2012	Tanzania	WHO/HAI/MoH [43]	Availability on day, MPR, days wages	Essential medicines	Availability, price	Public, private, NGO	97	50	81.4 QAART()	Free	20.6 (QAART—general retailer)	Free		
2012	Tanzania	WHO SARA [44]	Availability on day	Essential medicines	Availability	Public, private	32–1297	14+	43.3	MPR 2.18	54.3	MPR 3.14	57.9	MPR 3.9
2012	Tanzania	Roberston et al. [45]	Availability on day	Hypertension and diabetes	Availability	Public, private, NGO	24, 107, 1297	11	37		55			
2013	Tanzania	Ewen et al. [46]	Availability on day, MPR, days wages	Essential medicines	Availability, price	Public, private, NGO	93	24						
2013	Uganda	WHO/HAI/MoH [47]	Availability on day, MPR, days wages	Essential medicines	Availability, price	Public, private, NGO	114	40	52	MPR local 1.67, MPR import 2.2	82	MPR local 2.01, MPR import 3.01	70	MPR local 1.89, MPR Import 2.81
2014	Uganda	WHO/HAI/MoH [48]	Availability on day, MPR, days wages	Essential medicines	Availability, price	Public, private, NGO	123	40	60.3	Free	61.8	MPR 2.68	72	MPR 2.82
2015	Uganda	WHO/HAI/MoH [49]	Availability on day, MPR, days wages	Essential medicines	Availability, price	Public, private, NGO	109	39	57.3	Free	73.5	MPR 2.73	74	MPR 2.57
2010	Zambia	WHO SARA [50]	Availability on day	Essential medicines	Availability	Public, private, NGO	565	14+	58.1	Free	68.1	MPR 2.07	65.9	MPR 2.32

Shaded areas indicate no data available or not reported/collected.

Notes: AL, artemether/lumefantrine; *ASAQ*, a fixed-dose artesunate–amodiaquine combination therapy; *MPR*, median price ratio; *QAART*, quality-assured artemisinin-based combination therapies.QAACT also refers to quality-assured artemisin based therapies.

Table 2.5.2 presents the results for Central Africa, in terms of included studies. There are fewer studies from this region with most countries only being surveyed once and mostly for prices of essential medicines. From Table 2.5.2, it is evident from the two studies on pricing that private sector prices are very high compared with those of other countries in Africa. From where information on availability of medicines has been recorded, the results indicate low levels of medicine availability.

Table 2.5.3 presents the results for Western Africa. The reports are mainly from Service Availability and Readiness Assessment (SARA), which are submitted to WHO. In most cases these studies have looked at availability of medicines and not prices of medicines, and for the therapeutic focus area of malaria. Again, in most cases, medicines availability is low.

Table 2.5.4 looks at Southern Africa, where results are found for just two countries. This latter region has the least number of studies on pricing of medicines. None have used the standard WHO/HAI basket of medicines, with one adapting the survey for NCDs. With South Africa being one of the few countries in this region to implement pricing policies, the lack of studies into the impact of these is worrying.

2.5.6 DISCUSSION ON MEDICINES AVAILABILITY AND PRICING IN AFRICA

2.5.6.1 Measurement of Availability of Medicines

In terms of the issue of availability of medicines, 17 of 49 studies [32,38,44,45,50,51,54,56,57,59,60,62–64,66,67,69] reported availability only. The standard approach to measure availability of medicines was the WHO SARA. This approach provides a snapshot of availability, i.e., availability of a product on the day of the survey only. SARA surveys include sections for measuring a mix of core essential medicines, as well as medicines for family planning, prenatal care, obstetrics and neonatal care, child and adolescent health, maternal and child health, communicable diseases such as malaria, HIV/AIDS, sexually transmitted infections, and malaria, NCDs, medicines for surgery, and hospital-only products. All products surveyed are on the model essential medicines list (EML). However, products and strengths may differ slightly by country based on national standard treatment guidelines and national EMLs.

Publicly available SARA-survey reports provide aggregate measures of availability at the national level and, often, but not always, disaggregation by sector and facility type. The total number of medicines surveyed in the

Table 2.5.2 Overview of country pricing surveys in Central Africa

Year of survey	Country	Authors	Standardized tool	Therapeutic focus	Focus (price vs. availability)	Sectors	Facilities surveyed	Products surveyed	Median public availability	Median public price	Median private availability	Median private price	Median NGO availability	Median NGO price
2009	Cameroon	Sayang et al. [51]	Drug registers (consumption)	Malaria	Availability	Public, private	23	27	Quinine is most available, ACT was only available in private drug stores					
2014	Cameroon	Jingi et al. [52]	Availability on day, MPR, days wages	CVD, diabetes	Availability, price	Public, private	11	20						
2007	Congo	WHO/ HAI/ MoH [53]	Availability on day, MPR, days wages	Essential medicines	Availability, price	Public, private, NGO	59	32		MPR 6.51		MPR 11.54		MPR 6.66
2014	DRC	WHO SARA [54]	Availability on day	Essential medicines	Availability	Public, private	447 −1555	20+	19		22			
2008	Sao Tome en Principe	WHO/ HAI/ MoH [55]	Availability on day, MPR, days wages	Essential medicines	Availability, price	Public, private, NGO	43	50	55.1	MPR 2.41	24.3	MPR 13.76	82	MPR 2.5

Shaded areas indicate no data available or not reported/collected.

Table 2.5.3 Overview of country pricing surveys in Western Africa

Year of survey	Country	Authors	Standardized tool	Therapeutic focus	Focus (price vs. availability)	Sectors	Facilities surveyed	Products surveyed	Median public availability	Median public price	Median private availability	Median private price	Median NGO availability	Median NGO price
2013	Benin	WHO SARA [56]	Availability on day	Essential medicines	Availability	Public, private	44–189	14+	38		38			
2015	Benin	WHO SARA [57]	Availability on day	Essential medicines	Availability	Public, private	153–788	24+	40		42			
2009	Burkina Faso	WHO/HAI/MoH [58]	Availability on day, MPR, days wages	Essential medicines	Availability, price	Public, private, NGO	108	50	72.5	MPR 2.17	63.5	MPR 2.92	*52*	MPR 2.72
2012	Burkina Faso	WHO SARA [59]	Availability on day	Essential medicines	Availability	Public, private		14+						
2014	Burkina Faso	WHO SARA [60]	Availability on day	Essential medicines	Availability	Public, private	13–766	24+	41		41			
2010	Mali	Maiga and William-Jones [61]	Availability on day, Price pre-post intervention	Essential medicines	Availability, price	Public, private	47	49			66.60%			
2013	Mauritania	WHO SARA [62]	Availability on day	Essential medicines	Availability	Public, private	19–232	14+						
2016	Mauritania	WHO SARA [63]	Availability on day	Essential medicines	Availability	Public, private	29–288	24+						
2015	Niger	WHO SARA [64]	Availability on day	Essential medicines	Availability	Public, private	27–372	24+	41		33			
2011	Nigeria	Oladepo et al. [65]	Stocking Practices, Median Price	Malaria	Availability, price	Public, private	110	3+						

Continued

Table 2.5.3 Overview of country pricing surveys in Western Africa—cont'd

Year of survey	Country	Authors	Standardized tool	Therapeutic focus	Focus (price vs. availability)	Sectors	Facilities surveyed	Products surveyed	Median public availability	Median public price	Median private availability	Median private price	Median NGO availability	Median NGO price
2011	Sierra Leone	WHO SARA [66]	Availability on day	Essential medicines	Availability	Public, private	35–207	14+	31		61			
2012	Sierra Leone	WHO SARA [67]	Availability on day	Essential medicines	Availability	Public, private	18–106	14+						
2012	Sierra Leone	Amuasi et al. [68]	Availability on day, MPR, days wages	Malaria	Availability, price	Public, private, NGO	127	15	First line ACT 96.5, Policy antimalarials 64.9, Nonpolicy 5.3	First line ACT 1.5 (1.56–2.50), Policy antimalarials 0.31 (0.16 –3.75), Nonpolicy 0.39 (0.28 –0.94)	First line ACT 56.8, Policy antimalarials 38.6, Nonpolicy 79.5	First line ACT 1.56 (0.16–9.38, Policy Antimalarials 0.63 (0.76 –7.81), Nonpolicy 0.78 (0.09 –12.50)	First line ACT 76.9, Policy Antimalarials 65.4, Nonpolicy 30.8	First line ACT 0.47 (0.16–5.31), Policy Antimalarials 0.31 (0.09 –1.56), Nonpolicy 0.47 (0.31 –5.31)
2012	Togo	WHO SARA [69]	Availability on day	Essential medicines	Availability	Public, private, NGO	20–100	14+						

Shaded areas indicate no data available or not reported/collected.

Table 2.5.4 Overview of country pricing surveys in Southern Africa

Year of survey	Country	Authors	Standardized tool	Therapeutic focus	Focus (price vs. availability)	Sectors	Facilities surveyed	Products surveyed	Median public availability	Median public price	Median private availability	Median private price	Median NGO availability	Median NGO price
2007	South Africa	Jonsson et al. [70]	Price and affordability index	Rheumatoid arthritis	Price, affordability	Manufacturer prices, national expenditure								
2009	South Africa	Gray [71]	Mediscor medicines review	Generic use	Expenditure	Public, private								
2014	Swaziland	Mhlanga and Suleman [72]	Availability on day, MPR, days wages	NCDs	Availability, price	Public, private	20	16	68	0.79–7.56	77.5	1.68–53.66		

Shaded areas indicate no data available or not reported/collected.

assessment is not explicit as medicines are split up among various health-service categories. Because SARA surveys provide comprehensive reports on health-services readiness, they are resource intensive. To date, most countries that have participated in SARA assessments have only completed two rounds—suggesting that this is an ad-hoc form of data collection.

One article [51] measured availability of malaria medicines, specifically, through examination of drug registers and consumption data. Antimalarial information at facilities was analyzed retrospectively from drug registers, and authors used structured questionnaires to assess prescribing knowledge and behaviors of pharmacists. This approach measures availability as the products that are most sold at pharmacy level. However, information on stock-outs was not reported. Also, analysis of drug registers may be time intensive, especially without electronic data systems, which may underscore why this method has not gained more popularity in the AFRO region. One article [45] examined the consistency of different snapshot availability surveys using a case example of hypertension and diabetes in Tanzania.

Robertson et al. [45] compared WHO SARA surveys, WHO/HAI surveys, and another independent survey, which all provided availability data on specific medicines for hypertension and diabetes between 2012 and 2013. Although the overall conclusions of the studies were consistent, availability of key NCD medicines is suboptimal, the range of availability among the surveys varied significantly (e.g., Metformin 500 mg tablets were reported to be available in 46% of facilities in the WHO/HAI survey, 33% in the independent survey and 57% in the SARA surveys) depending on the time of survey. This indicates that using snapshot-availability indicators via ad hoc surveys will make it challenging for countries to judge the extent of access problems in countries. Robertson et al. [45] suggested that there is a need to identify a different, more reliable approach to measure availability to support decision-making.

2.5.6.2 Measurement of Availability and Price

There were 29 of 49 studies [24–31,33–37,39–43,46–49,52,53,55, 58,61,65,68,72] that reported on availability and price. The most common methodology represented was the WHO/HAI approach (n = 25), which measures snapshot availability and measures price and affordability through collection of unit price data in the public, private, and often mission or other sectors in a range of facility types. MPR is the ratio (or quantitative relation) of the unit price of a product in the country and an international reference price (e.g., prices reported by the MSH international price indicator guide). MPRs greater than 1 indicate that the price in country is more expensive than the global benchmark. However, this approach has limitations due to the occasionally small sample sizes in the MSH guide. The WHO/HAI methodology also measures affordability as the number of days' wages of the lowest-paid government employee required to pay for a course of treatment. This measure of affordability may be an overestimate as patients with jobs in the informal sector may have even lower wages.

There were 18 studies [24,26–28,36,37,39–41,43,46–49,53,55,58,61] that used the traditional WHO/HAI methodology, using the 2008 WHO/HAI recommended global, regional, and supplementary list of medicines. Twelve studies [25,29–31,33–35,42,52,65,68,72] modified the traditional WHO/HAI methodology medicines list to focus on specific therapeutic groups, such as malaria, antibiotics, NCDs, or medicines for children. Two articles surveying Ethiopia [29] and Mali [61] modified the WHO/HAI methodology, both in terms of medicines surveyed and methodology for price analysis. In Ethiopia, highest-selling essential medicines were measured in terms of snapshot availability, ratio of medicines dispensed versus prescribed, price for a standard course of treatment, and price with and without health insurance waiver. The Mali study focused on essential medicines that would treat the leading causes of morbidity and analyzed the price of these medicines before and after a regulation intervention.

In terms of specific therapeutic groups, there were four studies [25,33,35,68] diverted from the WHO/HAI methodology to examine availability and price of antimalarial medicines. ACTwatch Outlet questionnaires (that were multicountry research projects designed to fill evidence gaps in malaria) were used to measure availability of the number of brands in stock during the time of a structured interview. Prices were reported as the mean or median price for a product, and market shares were also reported through the outlet questionnaires. By examining stocking practices, ACTwatch could identify persistent stock-outs of antimalarials, such as those occurring in public facilities in Tanzania [42]. One ACTwatch study [30] further studied access to antimalarials, in addition to the traditional examination of price and availability. Access, in this case, was defined as physical access to an outlet where antimalarials could be obtained (i.e., were stores open).

2.5.6.3 Measurement of Pricing of Medicines

There were 3 of 49 studies [40,70,71] that examined price only. One study in Tanzania [40] sought to determine affordability of antimalarials using household surveys and the contingent valuation method to determine willingness to pay for artemisinin-based combination therapies (ACTs). Willingness to pay was then compared to actual prices of subsidized and nonsubsidized ACTs. Opportunity cost of using these products on the total expenditure on food was also reported. Reporting of opportunity costs may be another interesting way of putting medicines prices into context, if there are questions about the reliability of international benchmarks.

One study, focusing on South Africa and high- and upper—middle income countries in other regions, examined the price and uptake of TNF-inhibitors for rheumatoid arthritis [70]. This study reported affordability as an index, calculated by comparing relative health expenditures per capita with the relative price index for TNF-inhibitors. Uptake was measured by national expenditures and consumption for the TNF-inhibitors.

One study examined the success of various price regulation policies in South Africa [71]. Mediscor (a South African pharmaceutical benefits management organization) publishes an overview of key trends in medicine expenditure, focusing on the member's experience at point of dispensing and highlighting other specific areas of interest. The medicines review data and insurance claims data were used as the main sources of quantitative information for analysis in the South African study. Mediscor noted that use of generics in South Africa had steadily risen from 2005 to 2007, likely because of mandatory offer of generic substitution. Medicines expenditures for insurers in South Africa during this period had increased; however, the increases may have been driven by the increase in the average cost per claimed item.

2.5.6.4 Multicountry Comparisons

There were 14 articles on multicountry studies, which included countries in the African Region. There were a number of international multicountry comparative studies that included African countries. Fernandez [73] studied the global availability of misoprostol and found that sales in sub-Saharan Africa were reported to be low (with no amounts provided), but that could be due to limited availability of information for the African countries. Some African countries were included in the Bazargani et al. study [74] in terms of assessing the availability of essential medicines versus other medicines. Voman [75] studied Zambia, Mozambique, and Mali in addition to a non-African country, in terms of costs and availability of diabetic medicines. Overall, the availability of insulin and supplies was low, and the procurement price of insulin was high. Van Mourik et al. [76] studied the availability, pricing, and affordability of cardiovascular medicines across a number of countries worldwide, including a few African countries, and found that problems remain with availability and pricing of these medicines. Babar et al. [77] found similar results when looking at essential asthma medicines, as did Cameron et al. [78] for antiepileptic medicines. Simmons et al. [79] on the other hand found that pharmaceutical companies were selling antiretrovirals to non-African middle-income countries at prices 74%–541% higher than African countries with similar GNIs. Palafox et al. [80] found that retailers applied the highest percentage mark-ups on non-artemisinin therapies.

Some multicountry studies focused on African countries only. Robertson et al. [81] focused on medicines for children and found that the availability of key essential medicines for children was poor in the 14 countries surveyed in central Africa. In addition, there was considerable variability in prices, with retail pharmacies having higher prices. Twagirumukiza et al. [82] examined the availability of antihypertensive medicines across 13 sub-Saharan countries and found that medicines on national essential medicines list were cheaper, but prices were still more expensive that those found on the International Drug Price Indicator Guide (IDPIG). O'Connell et al. [83] surveyed six sub-Saharan African countries and investigated the price of antimalarials in public and private sectors. In general, in the private sector, the first-line quality-assured ACT was 5–24 times more expensive than nonartemisinin therapies. Tougher et al. [21] looked at the availability and pricing of antimalarials and found that there were large falls in median price of antimalarials, after the delivery of subsidized ACTs in Ghana, Kenya, Madagascar, Niger, Nigeria, Uganda, and Tanzania (including Zanzibar). The ACTwatch group [84] found that mixed results after the Affordable Medicines Facility-malaria pilot. Private sector quality-assured artemisinin-based combination therapies (QAACT) prices were maintained or further reduced in Tanzania, Nigeria, and Uganda, but prices increased significantly in Kenya and Madagascar. Ewen et al. [85] looked at the impact of local production on medicines prices in Tanzania and Ethiopia and found mixed results.

In general, the availability of essential medicines has been problematic in sub-Saharan Africa, more than in any other region [86]. The average availability of essential medicines in sub-Saharan Africa is around 40% in the public sector and 60% in the private sector, substantially below the WHO target of 80% medicines availability in all sectors [87]. The target is nearly met in countries such as Sudan [88] and Burkina Faso [89], but not in others, such as Malawi [72], and data gaps remain pronounced for many countries [90]. Moreover, the availability of essential medicines is often superior in the private sector compared with the public sector, for essential medicines compared with nonessential medicines, and in urban compared with rural settings [74,91]. Medicines for the treatment of chronic conditions have on average nearly 40% less availability (absolute terms) in the public sector compared to medicines for the treatment of acute conditions [1,91], a reflection of health priorities to date.

In terms of affordability, buying medicines in sub-Saharan Africa can have devastating impoverishing effects for households [92]. There is evidence that large-scale multistakeholder initiatives such as the Affordable Medicines Facility-malaria can lower prices and improve access through manufacturer negotiations, subsidies, and communication campaigns but cannot be reproduced to cover the entire spectrum of health needs [21]. The rise of chronic conditions will add to the growing need for affordable quality medicines, although most of the drugs needed to treat common chronic conditions are available as generics.

2.5.7 CONCLUSIONS: SUMMARY AND WAY FORWARD

Not all African countries have information on medicine prices in their country. The search results have indicated that there are countries where surveys have not been conducted. In countries where surveys have been done, they have not been conducted consistently, with large gaps between surveys. Thus, using cross-sectional surveys of availability indicators on an ad-hoc basis will make it challenging for countries to judge the extent of access, availability, and pricing problems in countries. Also, the results of the search have indicated that very few pricing studies have been conducted and that availability, affordability, and medicine prices have been linked in surveys. Perhaps the focus should shift to comparing prices across countries in a region/continent, or across common income levels. There is still much to be researched and standardized in terms of pricing surveys in Africa, and globally.

2.5.8 GAPS IN THE LITERATURE

Gaps of current methods were identified in the studies extracted. In terms of availability of medicines, the current survey methods do not lead to easy trend analysis without heavy resource investment. In addition, stock-out information is difficult to discern unless drug registers are examined.

In terms of pricing studies, the MPRs can be suitable, but MSH might not be the most appropriate benchmark as global information may blur specific regional differences. MPRs against neighboring countries may be more relevant. Additionally, volumes are often not noted in these studies.

In terms of affordability studies, comparison to a day's wage is still a valid method of comparison, but opportunity cost estimates might be more contextual for policy makers, especially to help relate medicines expenditures to other necessary commodities.

There were also gaps in the medicines surveyed. WHO provides a suggested core basket; however, countries may take this as a prescription rather than performing an ABC analysis to compare expenditures with leading causes of morbidity and mortality. Regularly conducted surveys are also critical to monitor changes and problems and can be a useful tool if pricing policies are implemented or changed.

REFERENCES

[1] World Bank Group. Global economic prospects: divergence and risks. Washington: World Bank; 2016. Available from: http://pubdocs.worldbank.org/en/842861463605615468/Global-Economic-Prospects-June-2016-Divergences-and-risks.pdf.

[2] McKinsey Global Institute. Lions on the move II: realizing the potential of Africa's economies. New York City: McKinsey & Company; 2016. Available from: https://www.mckinsey.com/~/media/McKinsey/Global%20Themes/Middle%20East%20and%20Africa/Realizing%20the%20potential%20of%20Africas%20economies/MGI-Lions-on-the-Move-2-Full-report-September-2016v2.ashx.

[3] United Nations, Department of Economic and Social Affairs, Population Division. World population prospects: the 2017 revision, key findings and advance tables. Working Paper No. ESA/P/WP/248. New York: United Nations; 2017. Available from: https://esa.un.org/unpd/wpp/Publications/Files/WPP2017_KeyFindings.pdf.

[4] United Nations, Department of Economic and Social Affairs, Population Division. World urbanization prospects: the 2014 revision (ST/ESA/SER.A/366). New York: United Nations; 2015. Available from: https://esa.un.org/unpd/wup/publications/files/wup2014-report.pdf.

[5] Phalkey RK, Yamamoto S, Awate P, Marx M. Challenges with the implementation of an Integrated Disease Surveillance and Response (IDSR) system: systematic review of the lessons learned. Health Policy and Planning 2015;30(1):131−43.

[6] The International Association of National Public Health Institutes. Our members. Available from: http://ianphi.org/membercountries/index.html.

[7] African Society for Laboratory Medicine. ASLM2020: strategies and vision to strengthen public health laboratory medicine in Africa. Available from: https://aslm.org/what-we-do/aslm2020-vision/.

[8] African Field Epidemiology Network. AFENET Training Programs. Available from: http://www.afenet.net/new/index.php?option=com_content&view=article&id=113&Itemid=115&lang=en.

[9] Olivier J, Tsimpo C, Gemignani R, Shojo M, Coulombe H, Dimmock F, et al. Understanding the roles of faith-based health-care providers in Africa: review of the evidence with a focus on magnitude, reach, cost, and satisfaction. Lancet 2015;386(10005):1765–75.
[10] WHO Regional Office for Africa. WHO African region expenditure atlas, November 2014. Brazzaville: World Health Organization, Regional Office for Africa; 2014. Available from: http://www.afro.who.int/sites/default/files/2017-06/who-african-region-expenditure-atlas_-november-2014.pdf.
[11] WHO Regional Office for Africa. Atlas of African health statistics 2014: health situation analysis of African region. Brazzaville: World Health Organization Regional Office for Africa; 2014. Available from: https://www.aho.afro.who.int/en/publication/921/atlas-african-health-statistics-2014-health-situation-analysis-african-region.
[12] Lopes C. Manufacturing pharmaceuticals: an untapped opportunity. Addis Ababa: United Nations Economic Commission for Africa; 2014. Available from: http://www.uneca.org/es-blog/manufacturingpharmaceuticals-untapped-opportunity.
[13] Empower School of Health. Dynamics of pharmaceutical quality systems for export of pharmaceuticals from India to Africa. London. 2014. Available from: http://www.ipekpp.com/admin/upload_files/Report_2_20_Dynamics_4145711718.pdf.
[14] Chaudhuri S, Mackintosh M, Mujinja PGM. Indian generics producers, access to essential medicines and local production in Africa: an argument with reference to Tanzania. European Journal of Development Research 2010;22(4):451–68.
[15] Bate R, Jin GZ, Mathur A, Attaran A. Poor quality drugs and global trade: a pilot study. The American Journal of Health Economics 2016;2(3):373–98.
[16] Almuzaini T, Choonara I, Sammons H. Substandard and counterfeit medicines: a systematic review of the literature. BMJ Open 2013;3(8):e002923.
[17] Nayyar GML, Breman JG, Newton PN, Herrington J. Poor-quality antimalarial drugs in southeast Asia and sub-Saharan Africa. The Lancet Infectious Diseases 2012;12(6):488–96.
[18] Ogisi M. Fake medicine common in many Sub-Saharan African countries. Gallup News. 2011. Available from: http://www.gallup.com/poll/149942/fakemedicine-common-sub-saharan-african-countries.aspx.
[19] Owoeye OA. Compulsory patent licensing and local drug manufacturing capacity in Africa. Bulletin of the World Health Organization 2014;92:214–9.
[20] World Health Organization. Assessment of medicines regulatory systems in sub-Saharan African countries: an overview of findings from 26 assessment reports. Geneva: World Health Organization; 2010. Available from: http://apps.who.int/medicinedocs/en/d/Js17577en/.
[21] Tougher S, ACTwatch Group, Ye Y, Amuasi JH, Kourgueni IA, Thomson R, et al. Effect of the Affordable Medicines Facility—malaria (AMFm) on the availability, price, and market share of quality-assured artemisinin-based combination therapies in seven countries: a before-and-after analysis of outlet survey data. Lancet 2012;380:1916–26.
[22] IFPMA. Africa needs more efficient regulatory systems to improve access to medicines. Dakar. 2015. Available from: https://www.ifpma.org/wp-content/uploads/2016/02/PR_-_ARC-FINALENG.pdf.
[23] East African Community. EAC regional manufacturing plan of action, 2012–2016. Arusha: EAC; 2012. Available from: https://www.unido.org/sites/default/files/2016-01/EAC_Regional_Pharmaceutical_Manufacturing_Plan_of_Action_0.pdf.
[24] Ministère de la Santé au Burundi and l'Organisation mondiale de la Santé. Burundi: Profil Pharmaceutique du pays. Geneva: World Health Organization; 2011. Available from: http://apps.who.int/medicinedocs/documents/s19099fr/s19099fr.pdf.

[25] Amuasi JH, Diap G, Blay-Nguah S, Boakye I, Karikari PE, Dismas B, et al. Access to artesunate-amodiaquine, quinine and other anti-malarials: policy and markets in Burundi. Malaria Journal 2011;10:34.
[26] World Health Organization. Enquete sur la disponibilite et les prix des medicaments au Burundi. Bujumbura: World Health Organization; 2014.
[27] Carasso BS, Lagarde M, Tesfaye A, Palmer N. Availability of essential medicines in Ethiopia: an efficiency-equity trade-off? Tropical Medicine and International Health 2009;14(11):1394–400.
[28] Ewen M, Kaplan W, Gedif T. Prices and availability of locally produced and imported medicines in Ethiopia: report of a survey conducted in August 2013. Geneva: World Health Organization; 2016. Available from: http://apps.who.int/medicinedocs/documents/s23207en/s23207en.pdf.
[29] Sado E, Sufa A. Availability and affordability of essential medicines for children in the Western part of Ethiopia: implication for access. BMC Pediatrics 2016;16:40.
[30] Smith N, Obala A, Simiyu C, Menya D, Khwa-Otsyula B, O'Meara WP. Accessibility, availability and affordability of anti-malarials in a rural district in Kenya after implementation of a national subsidy scheme. Malaria Journal 2011;10:316.
[31] O'Meara WP, Obala A, Thirumurthy H, Khwa-Otsyula B. The association between price, competition, and demand factors on private sector anti-malarial stocking and sales in western Kenya: considerations for the AMFm subsidy. Malaria Journal 2013;12:186.
[32] Ministry of Health, Government of Kenya. Kenya service availability and readiness assessment mapping (SARAM) 2013.. Geneva: World Health Organization; 2014. Available from: http://apps.who.int/healthinfo/systems/datacatalog/index.php/ddibrowser/42/download/145.
[33] Kioko U, Riley C, Dellicour S, Were V, Ouma P, Gutman J, et al. A cross-sectional study of the availability and price of anti-malarial medicines and malaria rapid diagnostic tests in private sector retail drug outlets in rural Western Kenya, 2013. Malaria Journal 2016;15(1):359.
[34] Mendis S, Fukino K, Cameron A, Laing R, Filipe AJ, Khatib O, et al. The availability and affordability of selected essential medicines for chronic diseases in six low- and middle-income countries. Bulletin of the World Health Organization 2007;85:279–88.
[35] Khuluza F, Heide L. Availability and affordability of antimalarial and antibiotic medicines in Malawi. PLoS One 2017;12(4):e0175399.
[36] Mauritius Institute of Health and Ministry of Health & Quality of Life. Medicine prices, availability, affordability and price components in the republic of Mauritius - report of a survey conducted in August 2008. Geneva: World Health Organization; 2009. Available from: http://mih.govmu.org/English/Research/Documents/Research/Report.pdf.
[37] Russo G, McPake B. Medicine prices in urban Mozambique: a public health and economic study of pharmaceutical markets and price determinants in low-income settings. Health Policy and Planning 2010;25(1):70–84.
[38] National Institute for Medical Research (NIMR) Tanzania. Tanzania district health assessment 2008–2009 summary report. Tanzania. Geneva: World Health Organization; 2011. Available from: http://apps.who.int/healthinfo/systems/datacatalog/index.php/ddibrowser/26/download/97.
[39] Mackintosh M, Mujinja PGM. Pricing and competition in essential medicines markets: the supply chain to Tanzania and the role of NGOs. Working Paper No. 32. Open University Research Centre on Innovation Knowledge and Development; 2008. Available from:, http://www.open.ac.uk/ikd/sites/www.open.ac.uk.ikd/files/files/working-papers/ikd-working-paper-32.pdf.

[40] Saulo EC, Forsberg BC, Premji Z, Montgomery SM, Björkman A. Willingness and ability to pay for artemisinin-based combination therapy in rural Tanzania. Malaria Journal 2008;7:227.
[41] Mujinja PG, Mackintosh M, Justin-Temu M, Wuyts M. Local production of pharmaceuticals in Africa and access to essential medicines: 'urban bias' in access to imported medicines in Tanzania and its policy implications. Globalization and Health 2014;10:12.
[42] Thomson R, Festo C, Johanes B, Kalolella A, Bruxvoort K, Nchimbi H. Has Tanzania embraced the green leaf? Results from outlet and household surveys before and after implementation of the Affordable Medicines Facility-malaria. PLoS One 2014;9(5):e95607.
[43] World Health Organization/Health Action International, Tanzania. Medicine prices, availability, affordability & price components database. September 2012. Available from: http://haiweb.org/what-we-do/price-availability-affordability/price-availability-data/.
[44] Ministry of Health and Social Welfare, United Republic of Tanzania. Tanzania service availability and readiness assessment (SARA) 2012.. Geneva: World Health Organization; 2013. Available from: http://apps.who.int/healthinfo/systems/datacatalog/index.php/ddibrowser/58/download/179.
[45] Robertson J, Macé C, Forte G, de Joncheere K, Beran D. Medicines availability for non-communicable diseases: the case for standardized monitoring. Globalization and Health 2015;11:18.
[46] Ewen M, Kaplan W, Justin-Temu M. Prices and availability of locally produced and imported medicines in Tanzania: report of a survey conducted in August 2013. Geneva: World Health Organisation; 2016. Available from: http://apps.who.int/medicinedocs/documents/s23206en/s23206en.pdf.
[47] World Health Organization/Health Action International Uganda. Medicine prices, availability, affordability & price components database. September 2013. Available from: http://haiweb.org/what-we-do/price-availability-affordability/price-availability-data/.
[48] World Health Organization/Health Action International Uganda. Medicine prices, availability, affordability & price components database. July 2014. Available from: http://haiweb.org/what-we-do/price-availability-affordability/price-availability-data/.
[49] World Health Organization/Health Action International Uganda. Medicine prices, availability, affordability & price components database. June 2015. Available from: http://haiweb.org/what-we-do/price-availability-affordability/price-availability-data/.
[50] Ministry of Health, Republic of Zambia. Zambia service availability and readiness assessment 2010 summary report.. Geneva: World Health Organization; 2010. Available from: http://apps.who.int/healthinfo/systems/datacatalog/index.php/ddibrowser/36/download/131.
[51] Sayang C, Gausseres M, Vernazza-Licht N, Malvy D, Bley D, Millet P. Treatment of malaria from monotherapy to artemisinin-based combination therapy by health professionals in urban health facilities in Yaoundé, Central Province, Cameroon. Malaria Journal 2009;8:176.
[52] Jingi AM, Noubiap JJ, Ewane Onana A, Nansseu JR, Wang B, Kingue S, et al. Access to diagnostic tests and essential medicines for cardiovascular diseases and diabetes care: cost, availability and affordability in the West Region of Cameroon. PLoS One 2014;9(11):e111812.
[53] World Health Organization/Health Action International Congo. Medicine prices, availability, affordability & price components database. June 2007. Available from: http://haiweb.org/what-we-do/price-availability-affordability/price-availability-data/.

[54] Ministère de la Santé Publique, République Démocratique du Congo. Indice de disponibilité et de capacité opérationnelle des services de santé (SARA RDC 2014).. Geneva: World Health Organization; 2014. Available from: http://apps.who.int/healthinfo/systems/datacatalog/index.php/ddibrowser/54/download/165.
[55] World Health Organization/Health Action International Sao Tome en Principe. Medicine prices, availability, affordability & price components database. 2008. Available from: http://haiweb.org/what-we-do/price-availability-affordability/price-availability-data/.
[56] Ministère de la Santé, Republique du Benin. Rapport d'enquête sur les services de sante: disponibilité et capacité opérationnelle des services de santé au Bénin 2013. Geneva: World Health Organziation; 2013. Available from: http://apps.who.int/healthinfo/systems/datacatalog/index.php/ddibrowser/38/download/137.
[57] Ministère de la Santé, Republique du Benin. Disponibilite et capacite operationnelle des services de sante - Enquête SARA 2015. Geneva: World Health Organization; 2015. Available from: http://www.who.int/healthinfo/systems/SARA_BEN_2015_Report.pdf?ua=1.
[58] World Health Organization/Health Action International. Burkina Faso. Medicine prices, availability, affordability & price components database. 2009. Available from: http://haiweb.org/what-we-do/price-availability-affordability/price-availability-data/.
[59] Le Ministre de la santé Burkina Faso. Enquete nationale sur les presentations des services de sante et la qualite des donnees sanitaires 2012. Geneva: World Health Organization; 2012. Available from: http://apps.who.int/healthinfo/systems/datacatalog/index.php/ddibrowser/39/download/138.
[60] Le Ministre de la santé Burkina Faso. Enquete nationale sur les prestations des services de sante et la qualite des donnees sanitaires 2014. Geneva: World Health Organization; 2014. Available from: http://apps.who.int/healthinfo/systems/datacatalog/index.php/ddibrowser/50/download/152.
[61] Maïga D, Williams-Jones B. Assessment of the impact of market regulation in Mali on the price of essential medicines provided through the private sector. Health Policy 2010;97(2–3):130–5.
[62] République Islamique de la Mauritanie, Ministère de la Santé. Indice de disponibilité et de capacité opérationnelle des services de santé (SARA) Mauritanie, 2013. Geneva: World Health Organization; 2013. Available from: http://apps.who.int/healthinfo/systems/datacatalog/index.php/ddibrowser/45/download/151.
[63] République Islamique de la Mauritanie, Ministère de la Santé. Indice de disponibilité et de capacité opérationnelle des services de santé (SARA) Mauritanie, 2016.. Geneva: World Health Organization; 2016. Available from: http://apps.who.int/healthinfo/systems/datacatalog/index.php/ddibrowser/55/download/168.
[64] Ministere de la Sante Publique, Republique du Niger. Rapport de l'evaluation de la disponibilite de la capacite operationnelle des services de sante avec les outils SARA et DQR 2015. Geneva: World Health Organization; 2016. Available from: http://www.who.int/healthinfo/systems/SARA_NER_2015_Report.pdf?ua=1.
[65] Oladepo O, Brieger W, Adeoye B, Lawal B, Peters DH. Awareness of anti-malarial policy and malaria treatment practices of patent medicine vendors in three Nigerian states. African Journal of Medical Sciences 2011;40(4):345–52.
[66] Government of Sierra Leone, Ministry of Health and Sanitation. Sierra Leone service availability and readiness assessment (SARA) 2011 report. Geneva: World Health Organization; 2011. Available from: http://apps.who.int/healthinfo/systems/datacatalog/index.php/ddibrowser/25/download/94.

[67] Government of Sierra Leone, Ministry of Health and Sanitation. Sierra Leone service availability and readiness assessment (SARA) 2012 report.. Geneva: World Health Organization; 2012. Available from: http://apps.who.int/healthinfo/systems/datacatalog/index.php/ddibrowser/27/download/103.
[68] Amuasi JH, Diap G, Nguah SB, Karikari P, Boakye I, Jambai A, et al. Access to artemisinin-combination therapy (ACT) and other anti-malarials: national policy and markets in Sierra Leone. PLoS One 2012;7(10):e47733.
[69] Word Health Organization. Indice de disponibilité et de capacité opérationnelle des services (SARA): Togo. Geneva: World Health Organization; 2012. Available from: http://apps.who.int/healthinfo/systems/datacatalog/index.php/catalog/56/reports.
[70] Jonsson B, Kobelt G, Smolen J. The burden of rheumatoid arthritis and access to treatment: uptake of new therapies. The European Journal of Health Economics 2008;8(Suppl. 2):S61–86.
[71] Gray AL. Medicine pricing interventions – the South African experience. Southern Med Review 2009;2:15–9.
[72] Mhlanga BS, Suleman F. Price, availability and affordability of medicines. The African Journal of Primary Health Care & Family Medicine 2014;6:E1–6.
[73] Fernandez MM, Coeytaux F, de León RG, Harrison DL. Assessing the global availability of misoprostol. International Journal of Gynecology and Obstetrics 2009;105:180–6.
[74] Bazargani YT, Ewen M, de Boer A, Leufkens HGM, Mantel-Teeuwisse AK. Essential medicines are more available than other medicines around the globe. PLoS One 2014;9(2):e87576.
[75] Voman B. Direct costs and availability of diabetes medicines in low-income and middle-income countries. Geneva: World Health Organization and Amsterdam: Health Action International; 2008. Available from: http://apps.who.int/medicinedocs/documents/s18387en/s18387en.pdf.
[76] van Mourik MS, Cameron A, Ewen M, Laing RO. Availability, price and affordability of cardiovascular medicines: a comparison across 36 countries using WHO/HAI data. BMC Cardiovascular Disorders 2010;10:25.
[77] Babar ZU, Lessing C, Mace C, Bissell K. The availability, pricing and affordability of three essential asthma medicines in 52 low- and middle-income countries. PharmacoEconomics 2013;31(11):1063–82.
[78] Cameron A, Bansal A, Dua T, Hill SR, Moshe SL, Mantel-Teeuwisse AK, Saxena S. Mapping the availability, price, and affordability of antiepileptic drugs in 46 countries. Epilepsia 2012;53(6):962–9.
[79] Simmons B, Hill A, Ford N, Ruxrungtham K, Ananworanich J. Prices of second-line antiretroviral treatment for middle-income countries inside versus outside sub-Saharan Africa. Journal of the International AIDS Society 2014;17(4 Suppl. 3):19604.
[80] Palafox B, Patouillard E, Tougher S, Goodman C, Hanson K, Kleinschmidt I, et al. Prices and mark-ups on antimalarials: evidence from nationally representative studies in six malaria-endemic countries. Health Policy and Planning 2016;31(2):148–60.
[81] Robertson J, Forte G, Trapsida JM, Hill S. What essential medicines for children are on the shelf? Bulletin of the World Health Organization 2009;87:231–7.
[82] Twagirumukiza M, Annemans L, Kips JG, Bienvenu E, Van Bortel LM. Price of antihypertensive medicines in sub-Saharan Africa. Tropical Medicine and International Health 2010;15(3):350–61.
[83] O'Connell KA, Gatakaa H, Poyer S, Njogu J, Evance I, Munroe E, et al. Got ACTs? Availability, price, market share and provider knowledge of anti-malarial medicines in public and private sector outlets in six malaria-endemic countries. Malaria Journal 2011;10:326.

[84] ACTwatch Group, Tougher S, Hanson K, Goodman C. What happened to anti-malarial markets after the Affordable Medicines Facility-malaria pilot? Trends in ACT availability, price and market share from five African countries under continuation of the private sector co-payment mechanism. Malaria Journal 2017;16:173.
[85] Ewen M, Kaplan W, Gedif T, Justin-Temu M, Vialle-Valentin C, Mizra Z, Regeer B, Zweekhorst M, Laing R. Prices and availability of locally produced and imported medicines in Ethiopia and Tanzania. Journal of Pharmaceutical Policy and Practice. 2017;10:7.
[86] Cameron A, Ewen M, Ross-Degnan D, Ball D, Laing R. Medicine prices, availability, and affordability in 36 developing and middle-income countries: a secondary analysis. Lancet 2009;373:240–9.
[87] World Health Organization. Medium-term strategic plan 2008–2013. Geneva: World Health Organization; 2009. Available from: http://apps.who.int/gb/ebwha/pdf_files/MTSP2009/MTSP1-en.pdf.
[88] Cheraghali AM, Idries AM. Availability, affordability, and prescribing pattern of medicines in Sudan. Pharmacy World and Science 2009;31:209–15.
[89] Saouadogo H. Measuring availability, affordability and management of essential medicines in public hospitals of Burkina Faso. World Hospitals and Health Services 2011;47:8–11.
[90] World Health Organization. World Health Statistics 2015. Geneva: World Health Organization; 2015. Available from: http://apps.who.int/iris/bitstream/10665/170250/1/9789240694439_eng.pdf.
[91] Cameron A, Roubos I, Ewen M, Mantel-Teeuwisse AK, Leufkens HGM, Laing RO. Differences in the availability of medicines for chronic and acute conditions in the public and private sectors of developing countries. Bulletin of the World Health Organization 2011;89:412–21.
[92] Niëns LM, Cameron A, Van de Poel E, Ewen M, Brouwer WBF, Laing R. Quantifying the impoverishing effects of purchasing medicines: a cross-country comparison of the affordability of medicines in the developing world. PLoS Medicine 2010;7:e1000333.

CHAPTER 3

Price Studies for Specific Medicines

Peter Schneider, Sabine Vogler
WHO Collaborating Centre for Pharmaceutical Pricing and Reimbursement Policies, Pharmacoeconomics Department, Gesundheit Österreich GmbH (GÖG/Austrian Public Health Institute), Vienna, Austria

LIST OF ABBREVIATIONS

AHUS	Atypical haemolytic uremic syndrome
AIDS	Acquired immune deficiency syndrome
ARV	Antiretroviral(s)
DAA	Direct acting antiviral(s)
DDD	Defined daily dose(s)
EMA	European Medicines Agency
EU	European Union
EURIPID	EURopean Integrated Price Information Database
GDP	Gross domestic product
HAI	Health Action International
HCV	Hepatitis C virus
HIC	High-income country/ies
HIV	Human immunodeficiency virus
IQR	Interquartile range
IRP	International reference price(s)
LAC	Latin American countries
LIC	Low-income country/ies
LMIC	Low- and middle-income country/ies
MAH	Marketing Authorisation Holder
MPR	Median price ratio(s)
NPM	Non-prescription medicine(s)
OECD	Organisation for Economic Co-operation and Development
OMP	Orphan medicinal product(s)
PNH	Paroxysmal nocturnal haemoglobinuria
PPI	Pharmaceutical price information
PPP	Purchasing power parities
R&D	Research & development

Medicine Price Surveys, Analyses, and Comparisons
ISBN 978-0-12-813166-4
https://doi.org/10.1016/B978-0-12-813166-4.00008-5

SVR	Sustained virological response
TLV	Tandvårds- och läkemedelsförmånsverket (Medicines Agency in Sweden)
UK	United Kingdom
US	United States
WHO	World Health Organization

This chapter presents available price studies for the following group of medicines: (1) generic and biosimilar medicines, (2) high-priced medicines including orphan medicinal products (OMP), (3) medicines for specific indications (e.g., HIV/AIDS, cancer), (4) hospital medicines and (5) non-prescription medicines. This classification is not intended to be an exhaustive and mutually exclusive set of categories, but was rather chosen due to the identified articles. The chapter adds to the previous chapter that identified medicine price studies in different regions of the world (cf. Chapter 2) and presented their findings in the context of country-specific pricing policies. In this chapter, medicine price studies and their findings will be again described, but a different perspective is applied. Independently from the studies' geographic coverage, medicine price studies are presented with regard to the group of medicines they focus on. Group of medicines can refer to the patent expiry or prescription status, to specific diseases and indications, or legal specifications. The groups of medicines were selected according to their relevance in terms of price studies (i.e., a high number of studies about generic medicines) or their policy relevance (e.g., studies that addressed the issue of high medicine prices). Given the difference in focus, Chapter 3 also relates to studies that were described in Chapter 2, and, additionally, it considers further studies that comply with the aim of this chapter. The literature search based on existing knowledge of articles was accompanied with backward and forward reference searching. The main inclusion criterion for articles was 'comparison of prices'. The chapter includes studies that were identified of key relevance from the perspective of an analysis per medicine groups: thus the literature review was designed to be thematically focused, and it is not intended to be comprehensive to cover all studies about medicine prices.

Table 3.1 provides an overview of relevant studies. Relevant subgroups were built. Since the authors are fully aware that some studies may cover more than one medicine group, and that the groups (e.g., high-priced medicines, orphan medicines, cancer medicines) might overlap. In addition,

Table 3.1 Key price studies for different medicine groups

Author/year	Title	Publication type	Med. group(s)	Country/ region	Methods/data source	Price type[a]	Year(s)	Key results	References
Generic medicines									
Cameron et al., 2009	Medicine prices, availability, and affordability in 36 developing and middle-income countries: a secondary analysis	Article published in *The Lancet*	Med. included in at least 80% of WHO/HAI surveys; originator and generic med.	Global. 36 countries (35 LIC or lower-middle income countries, Kuwait = HIC)	Secondary data analysis of medicine price data in 45 national and subnational WHO/HAI surveys Price data adjusted for inflation/deflation and by purchasing power parities (PPP)	Procurement price, retail price	Surveys were conducted between 2001 and 2006	Public sector procured generic medicines at prices 1.11 times higher than international reference prices, although purchasing efficiency ranged from 0.09 to 5.37 times international reference prices. In private sector, patients paid 9–25 times international reference prices for lowest-priced generic products and over 20 times international reference prices for originator products across WHO regions.	[11]
Vogler, 2012	How large are the differences between originator and generic prices? Analysis of five molecules in 16 European countries	Article published in *Farmeconomia*	Originator and generics for selected basket of molecules	AT, BE, DK, FI, FR, DE, EL, IE, IT, NL, NO, PT, ES, CH, SE, UK	Ex-factory prices as of November 2011 of five molecules were analysed for 16 European countries	Ex-factory price	2011	Considerable variations among the extent of price differences between originator and generic molecules were identified (gemcitabine: lowest price difference of 1.4% between originator and generic in BE and highest difference of 73.4% in PT; mycophenolate mofetil: 3.4% NO–71.7% NL; olanzapine: 0.1% ES–97.1% SE; risperidone: 0.9% NL–97.3% UK; sumatriptan: 5.8% EL–95.0% DK). Further, no difference at all between originator and generic prices was found for some molecules in a few countries (NO: for 4 of the 5 molecules analysed; ES: 3; BE: 2; in AT, FR and EL for one	[16]

Continued

Table 3.1 Key price studies for different medicine groups—cont'd

Author/year	Title	Publication type	Med. group(s)	Country/ region	Methods/data source	Price type[a]	Year(s)	Key results	References
								molecule respectively). For the five molecules of the sample, EL, ES, IE and NO consistently displayed lower price differences, whereas DK, FI and SE tended to show higher differences between originator and generic prices.	
Jiang et al., 2013	Measuring access to medicines: a survey of prices, availability and affordability in Shaanxi province of China	Article published in *PLoS One*	Medicines included in WHO/HAI survey core lists	CN	Twelve trained data collectors organised in pairs to visit medicine outlets and recorded medicine availability and price using a standardised form.	Procurement price, retail price	2010	Median price ratios of generic medicines and originator brands procured in the public sector were 0.75 and 8.49, respectively, while patients paid 0.97 and 10.16. Final patient prices for lowest-priced generics and originator brands in the private sector were about 1.53 and 8.36 times their international pharmacy retail prices, respectively. In the private sector, originator brands cost on average 390.7% more than their generic equivalents. Generic medicines were priced 17.3% higher in the private sector than in the public sector.	[4]
Yang et al., 2010	Prices, availability and affordability of essential medicines in rural areas of Hubei Province	Article published in *Health Policy and Planning*	Medicines included in WHO/HAI survey core list	CN	Data were collected by trained pharmacy students and supervised by the survey manager and the principal investigator. All the collected and completed forms containing data on medicine prices were checked on a daily basis.	Procurement price, retail price	2007	The medians of all obtained median price ratios (MPR) of procurement prices for innovator brands and lowest-price generics in the public sector were 9.78 and 0.74 times the international reference prices; and the median MPR of pharmacy retail prices to patients for lowest-price generics in the public sector (1.04) were higher than those in the private sector (0.68).	[5]

Dabare et al., 2014	A national survey on availability, price and affordability of selected essential medicines for non-communicable diseases in Sri Lanka	Article published in *BMC Public Health*	Medicines included in WHO/HAI survey core list	LK		Prices were collected from all pharmacies except those in public healthcare facilities. The prices were not obtained from public healthcare facilities as medicines are provided free of charge to patients from these institutions.	Procurement price, retail price	2013	Unit price of 76% of selected individual medicines was less than 10 Sri Lankan rupees (€ 1 ~ LKR 190, US$ 1 ~ LKR 155). Around a quarter of these medicines cost less than one Sri Lanka rupee. For 21 of the surveyed medicines the median price ratio to the international reference price was less than one. For 14 surveyed medicines the prices of originator brands were fivefold that of the lowest price generics	[8]
Senarathna et al., 2011	Medicine prices, availability and affordability in Sri Lanka	Article published in *Indian Journal of Pharmacology*	28 essential medicines with respect to local burden of disease	LK		Data were collected using the standardised medicine price data collection form.	Procurement price, retail price	2003, 2006, 2009	Originator brands were five to six times the international reference price (IRP) at privately owned pharmacies and four to seven times at the public sector pharmacies. The prices of generics were ≤1 the IRP during 6 years in privately owned and public sector pharmacies. Lowest priced generics (LPG) were high in availability (>80%) throughout the study period.	[9]
Balasubramaniam, 2014	A national survey of price and affordability of key essential medicines for children in Sri Lanka	Article published in *Indian Journal of Pediatrics*	25 essential medicines for children	LK		Data were collected using the standardised WHO/HAI medicine price data collection form	Procurement price, retail price	2009	For the originator brands (OB), median MPR of pharmacy retail prices to patients was 3.7 (range 0.23–20), while for the LPG, it was 1.35 (range 0.05–3.75). An MPR >5 was observed for the OB of 5 medicines: ceftriaxone, diazepam, mebendazole and metronidazole, whereas MPR >2.5 was observed only for the LPG of 3 medicines: chlorphenamine, clotrimazole	[7]

Continued

Table 3.1 Key price studies for different medicine groups—cont'd

Author/year	Title	Publication type	Med. group(s)	Country/ region	Methods/data source	Price type[a]	Year(s)	Key results	References
								and paracetamol. Mean percent difference in price between OB and LPG products was 365% (range from −21 to 2,343%)	
Babar et al., 2007	Evaluating drug prices, availability, affordability, and price components: implications for access to drugs in Malaysia	Article published in *PLoS Medicine*	48 essential medicines, of which 28 belonged to the WHO/HAI core list	MY	Data were collected using the standardised WHO/HAI medicine price data collection form. With respect to the selection of geographical regions a systematic sampling method was used to collect data	Procurement price, retail price	2007	In private pharmacies, prices of originator brands (OB) were 16 times higher than the IRPs, while generics were 6.6 times higher. In dispensing doctor clinics the figures were 15 times higher for OB and 7.5 for generics.	[6]
Mansfield, 2014	Generic drug prices and policy in Australia: room for improvement? A comparative analysis with England	Article published in *Australian Health Review*	Generics; 15 generic molecules (representing 45 different drug presentations)	AU, UK	Australian and English reimbursement prices were compared for a range of generic medicines using pricing information obtained from government websites.	Reimbursement price	2012	Analysis of reimbursement prices for 15 generic molecules (representing 45 different pharmaceutical presentations) demonstrated that Australian prices were on average over sevenfold higher than in England. In addition, supply-side (e.g., aspects of pricing policy, the relative size of the generics markets) and demand-side (e.g., generic substitution) policies of both countries were compared.	[12]
Kwon et al., 2015	The impact of South Korea's new drug-pricing policy on market competition among off-patent drugs	Article published in *Expert Review of Pharmacoeconomics & Outcomes Research*	Oral forms of medicines among four major therapeutic classes including antihypertensives, lipid-lowering medicines, antidepressants and antiulcerants	KO	Data used for this study were extracted from the National Health Insurance (NHI) data warehouse, where NHI claims data were reposited without patient information. Monthly cost and	Reimbursement price	2011–2013	The introduced pricing policy did not achieve the expected effects, that is, enhancing competition among off-patent medicines. In fact, price dispersion significantly decreased as opposed to the expected change. After the introduction of the pricing policy a shift towards the utilisation of OB was observed. Utilisation ratio of	[13]

					quantity for each pharmaceutical were included in the data warehouse			OB-to-generics increased 6.12 times ($P = .000$)	
Brick et al., 2013	Ireland: pharmaceutical prices, prescribing practices and usage of generics in a comparative context	Research Paper published by the *Economic and Social Research Institute (ESRI)*	Top 10 single source on-patent and multiple source off-patent pharmaceuticals	EU 28 + 2 EEA countries	Price information was obtained from the EURIPID database; for multiple source off-patent pharmaceutical products the median price was used	Ex-factory and wholesale price	2010–2012	Irish wholesale prices of single source on-patent pharmaceuticals for this period were high in comparison with other EU Members (second highest price). Irish wholesale prices of multiple source off-patent pharmaceuticals showed mixed results: originator medicines were less likely to be among the highest across countries in the reference basket or other countries of comparison. However, generic prices were consistently higher in Ireland than in other reference countries.	[15]
Tuncay, 2015	Generic competition and price regulation in pharmaceuticals: evidence from the European Union	Article published in *International Journal of Industrial Organization*	Generic market for cardiovascular diseases (CVD)	UK, DE, FR, IT, ES	Data used in this study were obtained from IQVIA Health. Data were collected at the level within the pharmaceutical market supply and distribution chain that provides reliable information. IQVIA Health measured for all dosage forms and strengths is the IQVIA standard unit (SU).	Pharmacy retail price	1994–2003	The analysis found that in those EU countries with free pricing for generic medicines, the entry of generics had a price reducing impact, whereas in those EU countries with strict price and reimbursement regulation, generic competition seems ineffective and/or counterproductive. Although regulation is inversely correlated to the price level, low regulated prices for originator products do not necessarily encourage generic entry following patent expiration.	[66]
Dylst and Simoens, 2011	Does the market share of generic medicines influence the price level?	Article published in *Pharmacoeconomics*	Entire off-patent market for 35 substances	AT, BE, DK, DE, FR, IT, NL, ES, SE, UK	Data on medicine volumes and values for 35 active substances were	Ex-factory price	2002–2007	In the survey period the observed developments in the generic market shares in value and volume were attributed to	[67]

Continued

Table 3.1 Key price studies for different medicine groups—cont'd

Author/year	Title	Publication type	Med. group(s)	Country/ region	Methods/data source	Price type[a]	Year(s)	Key results	References
					obtained from IQVIA. Ex-factory prices were used, and the analysis was limited to medicines in immediate-release, oral, solid dosage forms.			the use of generic medicines and a shift of use from originator to generic medicines. While in high generic market share countries, medicine prices dropped by −43.18% and low market share prices decreased by −21.56%.	
Wouters and Kanavos, 2017	A comparison of generic drug prices in seven European countries: a methodological analysis	Article published in *BMC Health Services Research*	110 active ingredients from the off-patent market sold in all examined countries	BE, DK, FR, DE, IT, ES, SE	Data from IQVIA on volumes and sales of 200 off-patent active ingredients in seven countries with similar income levels have been used to calculate commonly used indices.	Ex-factory price and pharmacy retail price	2013	There were large differences in generic medicine prices between countries, but methodological decisions had a major impact. Results varied depending on the choice of index, base country, unit of volume, method of currency conversion and therapeutic category. The results also differed depending on the price type, that is, whether one looked at ex-factory prices or retail prices.	[20]
Gooi and Bell, 2008	Differences in generic drug prices between the US and Canada	Article published in *Applied Health Economics and Health Policy*	19 generic medications available in examined countries based on the IQVIA listing of the most dispensed medications	CA, US	A telephone and Internet survey of pharmacies was conducted for the top 19 dispensed generic medications available in both countries. 12 pharmacies in total were selected: 6 from the US (3 online and 3 'walk-in') and 6 from Canada (3 online and 3 walk-in).	Pharmacy retail price	2007	12 of the 19 (63%) generic medications were less expensive in the US than in Canada, with average savings of 47% per medicine for these 12 medicines. 7 of the 19 (37%) medicines were less expensive in Canada than the US, with average savings of 29% per medicine for these 7 medicines. Overall, there was a sizable variation in prices for the same generic medications within and between the US and Canada.	[10]

Aho et al., 2017	International price comparison of pharmaceuticals 2016 – a volume based analysis of Swedish pharmaceutical prices relative to 19 other European countries	Technical report published by TLV	Most selling prescription pharmaceuticals further differentiated into on-patent and off-patent segments	DE, UK, AT, FI, NL, CH, IE, NO, DK, FR, BE, SK, ES, IT, CZ, HU, EL, PL, PT, SE	Price data obtained from IQVIA for 200 products in the segment 'protected pharmaceuticals', 180 products in the segment 'unprotected originator pharmaceuticals' without competition and 200 substances in the segment 'unprotected pharmaceuticals' with competition with the highest sales, respectively	Wholesale price	March 2015–March 2016	In the segment of pharmaceuticals exposed to competition, SE was found to be among the three countries with the lowest prices in the sample. Between 2014 and 2015, differences in price between the countries fell somewhat. Between 2015 and 2016, however, the differences increased again and in most countries they were higher than they were in 2014.	[19]
Vogler et al., 2015	Analysis of medicine prices in New Zealand and 16 European countries	Article published in *Value in Health*	14 medicines for different therapeutic indications; originators and some generics	AT, BE, CH, DE, DK, EL, ES, FI, FR, IT, IE, NL, NO, NZ, PT, SE, UK	Data provision from PPI service (for European countries), NZ Pharmaceutical Schedule Comparison of 14 specialties (thereof all as originators and additionally 5 as generic versions)	Ex-factory price	2012	EL, PT, UK and ES ranked at the lower end; prices in CH, DE, DK and SE were at the upper end; the results for NZ compared with Europe were variable. Price differences of up to 90% between the originator products and generic versions were found. For 3 out of the 5 generic medicines price differences between highest-priced and lowest-priced country were more than 1000%; for the two other generic versions 305% and 514% respectively, and for the 14 originators between 83% and 637%.	[68]
Danzon/ Furukawa, 2008	International prices and availability of pharmaceuticals in 2005	Article published in *Health Affairs*	No further specifications about medicines analysed in this article	US, FR, DE, IT, ES, UK, CA, AU, JP, BR, MX, CL	Data have been accessed from the IQVIA; calculation of price indices and prices was adjusted	Ex-factory price, pharmacy retail price, and hospital price	2005	The overall generic price indices (including both branded and unbranded generics) showed that the US had the lowest generic prices. In comparison to the US,	[64]

Continued

Table 3.1 Key price studies for different medicine groups—cont'd

Author/year	Title	Publication type	Med. group(s)	Country/ region	Methods/data source	Price type[a]	Year(s)	Key results	References
					by purchasing power parities (instead of exchange rates) and normalised by average income measured as Gross Domestic Product (GDP) per capita			all countries had on average higher generic prices, ranging from 8%–9% higher in FR and ES to 111%–116% higher in JP and MX. The low US generic price index reflected very low US prices of unbranded generics. For unbranded generics, all non-US prices were higher, ranging from 14% higher in CL to threefold higher in AU and fivefold higher in CA. For branded generics, prices were highest in JP, similar in the US, DE and MX.	
Biosimilar medicines									
Rovira et al., 2013	Biosimilars in the European market	Article published in *GaBi Journal*	All biosimilars authorised by EMA until 31 December 2012 and their respective reference product	All EU member states	A quantitative analysis of the EU biosimilar market from 2007 to 2010 was conducted; data were obtained from the European Medicines Agency (EMA) and IQVIA.	Not clear	2010	Differences in biosimilar and originator product prices per DDD appeared across the five main countries (DE, UK, ES, IT, FR) in 2011. Variation ratios between the highest and the lowest country price ranged from 1.4 to 2.7.	[21]
Remuzat et al., 2017	Key drivers for market penetration of biosimilars in Europe	Article published in *Journal of Market Access & Health Policy*	All biosimilars approved by the EMA between 2006 and 2015	BE, FR, DE, EL, HU, IT, PL, ES, SE, UK	Two commercial databases providing data for the 10 selected countries were used: IQVIA MIDAS database and IQVIA Pricing Insights database.	Ex-factory prices and pharmacy retail price	2006–2015	In the regression analysis, average generic price discount over originator and the number of biosimilars showed correlation with biosimilar uptake, but both did not reach the significance threshold. In contrast, the lower price of a biosimilar compared to the prices of the reference biological product, the number of analogues and the distribution channel were not correlated with the biosimilar uptake.	[22]

Merkur/ Mossialos, 2007	A pricing policy towards the sourcing of cheaper drugs in Cyprus	Article in *Health Policy*	50 most expensive products and 50 most sold products by volume in Cyprus	CY, DK, EL, PT, ES, SE, UK	Several data sources were consulted for this study. Data on pharmaceutical prices were collected from two lists in CY; for the comparator countries selected, retail prices were obtained from national price lists that were publicly available or lists used by pharmacists.	Pharmacy retail price	2003	When comparing retail prices of products in CY with other EU countries, CY appears to be a high price country for pharmaceuticals. For the same basket of products (weighted for CY volumes), the index of retail prices for a sample of the most expensive products was higher in CY than in DK (84%), SE (62%), PT (61%), UK (61%), ES (58%) and EL (56%).	[28]
Aho et al., 2017	International price comparison of pharmaceuticals 2016. A volume based analysis of Swedish pharmaceutical prices relative to 19 other European countries	Technical report published by TLV	Top-selling prescription pharmaceuticals further differentiated into on-patent and off-patent segments	DE, UK, AT, FI, NL, CH, IE, NO, DK, FR, BE, SK, ES, IT, CZ, HU, EL, PL, PT, SE	IQVIA was given the task of delivering data for 200 products in the segment protected pharmaceuticals, 180 products in the segment unprotected original pharmaceuticals without competition	Wholesale price	March 2015–March 2016	Since 2014, Swedish prices have declined in relation to prices of other countries. Between 2014 and 2015 the decrease of Swedish relative prices was larger compared to changes between 2015 and 2016. Swedish prices have been marginally lower compared to other countries. Of the 20 countries included in the analysis, Swedish prices for 2016 and 2015 were found among the eight countries with the highest prices. On average, Swedish prices are thus in line with prices in other countries and the cross-section index was 99.6 Q1 2016 for the segment pharmaceuticals not exposed to competition.	[19]
Vogler et al., 2016	Price comparison of high-cost medicines in 2015 among European Union Member States	Technical report published by the Austrian Public Health institute	60 high-cost medicines from the Austrian out-patient and in-patient sectors	EU-28	Price survey and single price comparison of 60 high-cost medicines that accounted for a high share of	Ex-factory, wholesale price, pharmacy retail price	2015	On average Austrian ex-factory prices for all 60 surveyed medicines were 55% above the price displayed in the lowest-priced country, 6% above the average price and 24% below	[26]

Continued

Table 3.1 Key price studies for different medicine groups—cont'd

Author/year	Title	Publication type	Med. group(s)	Country/ region	Methods/data source	Price type[a]	Year(s)	Key results	References
					pharmaceutical expenditure to Austrian public payers.			the price in the highest-priced country. Ex-factory prices of surveyed medicines observed in Austria, ranged among the highest prices in EU context. For the medicines surveyed high ex-factory prices tended to be found in DE, IE, DK and SE, whereas BG, CY and EL were identified as low-priced countries.	
Busse et al., 2016	Preise patentgeschützter Arzneimittel im europäischen Vergleich [Prices of on-patent medicines in European comparison]	Technical report published by the Scientific Institute of the AOK (General Local Health Insurance Funds) and Technical University Berlin	260 pharmaceutical specialties that accounted for 64% of the on-patent segment	DK, DE, FR, UK, NL, AT	From 260 active ingredients that represented 98% of the entire off-patent segment, the most sold specialty was selected. For those pharmaceutical specialties prices have been obtained from publicly available sources in the reference countries; prices were adjusted with PPP and GDP per capita.	Ex-factory prices	2015	DE could be considered as high-price country. PPP-adjusted prices of the reference countries are between 13% (NL) and 30% (FR) below German prices. Further consideration of GDP per capita adjusted prices, yields prices of reference countries that were between 16% (UK) and 27% (DK) below the prices in DE. If German prices were around the average price in the comparison, the cost-containment potential would be between 2.1 and 2.9 billion €. It increases further to 3.5 billion € if German prices were equal to the lowest price in the comparison.	[27]
Orphan medicinal products									
Blankart et al., 2011	Availability of and access to orphan drugs	Article published in *Pharmacoeconomics*	Pulmonary arterial hypertension (PAH), Fabry disease (FD),	AU, CA, UK; FR, DE, HU, NL, PL, SK, CH, US	Indicators of patient access were defined as (1) the outcomes of technology appraisals; (2) the	Pharmacy retail price	2008	The highest prices for the included medicines were found in DE and the US, and the lowest in CA, AU and UK. Although the prices of all of the	[36]

			hereditary angioedema and chronic myeloid leukaemia		extent of coverage provided by healthcare payers and (3) the price of the medicines in each country. Data on the prices of the various orphan medicines were collected by surveying medicine prices for a 30-day treatment period based on retail prices and WHO DDD			included medicines were high compared with those of most non-orphan medicines, it did not have negative impacts on patient access due to higher co-payments. All countries of the study sample provided full coverage for authorised medicines after a certain threshold.	
Picavet et al., 2011	Drugs for rare diseases: influence of orphan designation status on price	Article published in *Applied Health Economics and Health Policy*	All authorised orphan medicines	BE	Prices represent official Belgian hospital prices (n = 37) wherever possible. Missing data were completed with Belgian prices from the website of the Belgian Centre for Pharmacotherapeutic Information (n = 2) or through direct contact with pharmaceutical companies (n = 5).	Hospital price	2010	The median price per DDD was higher for designated orphan medicines (€ 138.56 [interquartile range; IQR € 406.57]) than for non-designated medicines (€ 16.55 [IQR € 28.05]) [$P < .01$]. A sensitivity analysis confirmed that this difference remained statistically significant after excluding from the analysis the three designated orphan medicines that were treated as non-designated medicines. The prevalence of the rare diseases involved did not result in statistically significant differences between prices of designated orphan medicines and non-designated medicines.	[38]
Aballea et al., 2010	Quantitative analysis of the influence of disease and product characteristics on	Abstract presented at ISPOR Conference 2010	Products with orphan designation approved by EMA	FR, IT, DE, ES, UK	Products with orphan designation approved by EMA were identified up to June 2009. Yearly	Not clear, but presumably ex-factory price	2009	51 products were identified of which respectively 37, 35, 28, 36 and 39 were available in FR, DE, IT, ES and UK respectively. Available products	[32]

Continued

Table 3.1 Key price studies for different medicine groups—cont'd

Author/year	Title	Publication type	Med. group(s)	Country/region	Methods/data source	Price type[a]	Year(s)	Key results	References
	orphan drug prices in Europe	and published in *Value in Health*			prices per product were derived from publicly available prices, WHO defined daily dose and treatment duration based on guidelines or summary product characteristics.			did not overlap across countries. Prices were highest in IT and lowest in UK. No significant correlation was found between any of the variables and price. Low prevalence and low number of available treatment alternatives seemed associated with high prices, but these trends were not statistically significant.	
Picavet et al., 2014	Shining a light in the black box of orphan drug pricing	Article published in *Orphanet Journal of Rare Diseases*	59 orphan medicines	BE, NL, CZ, FR, IT, UK	Annual treatment costs per indication per patient were calculated for 59 orphan medicines with a publicly available price in examined countries. A multiple linear regression model was built with 14 medicine- and disease-specific variables.	Reimbursement price, retail price	2013	The regressions showed that repurposed orphan medicinal products (OMP), orally administered OMP or OMP for which an alternative treatment is available are correlated with lower annual treatment costs. OMP with multiple orphan indications, for chronic treatments or for which an improvement in overall survival or quality-of-life has been demonstrated, are associated with higher annual treatment costs. National pricing and reimbursement systems showed no association with annual treatment costs of OMP.	[33]
Medic et al., 2017	Do payers value rarity? An analysis of the relationship between disease rarity and orphan drug prices in Europe	Article published in *Journal of Market Access and Health Policy*	120 approved orphan medicines	FR, DE, IT, NO, ES, SE, UK	Approved orphan medicines and prevalence data were extracted from the European Medicines Agency website. Annual treatment costs were calculated	Ex-factory price	2016	Annual treatment costs per patient ranged from € 755 to € 1,051,956 (mean € 100,000, median € 39,303). Results showed a statistically significant inverse correlation between annual treatment cost and disease prevalence in all countries.	[34]

					using ex-factory price. Simple regression was used to analyse the relationship between costs and prevalence. A specific bivariate analysis was performed for the rarest diseases			When analysis was focused on the rarest diseases, a stronger correlation exists in all countries.	
Schey et al., 2017	Estimating the budget impact of orphan medicines in Europe: 2010–2020	Article published in *Orphanet Journal of Rare Diseases*	Orphan medicines	AT, BE, CY, DE, EE, ES, FI, FR, EL, IE, IT, LU, MT, NL, PT, SK, SI, UK	Estimating the average expenditure for public payers at ex-factory price level across an orphan disease life cycle	Estimated ex-factory price	2000–2020	The estimation predicted annual cost per patient of existing orphan medicines to vary between € 1251 and € 407,631, with the median cost being € 32,242 per year. The share of the total pharmaceutical market represented by orphan medicines is predicted to increase from 3.3% in 2010 to a peak of 4.6% in 2016 after which it is expected to level off through 2020, as growth falls into line with that in the wider pharmaceutical market.	[37]
Simoens et al., 2011	Are some orphan drugs for rare diseases too expensive? A study of purchase versus compounding costs	Article published in *Drugs & Therapy Perspectives*	Six selected orphan medicines	BE	From a list of all reimbursed orphan medicines in Belgium in 2011, a sample of medicines considered to have low costs of R&D and market access procedures was selected	Hospital price	2011	For each OMP, the hospital purchase price exceeded the compounding production costs. The difference between hospital purchase price and compounding production costs ranged from a ≥2.5-fold difference for mercaptamine bitartrate to a 148-fold difference for aminolevulinic acid hydrochloride	[31]
Logviss et al., 2016	Impact of orphan drugs on Latvian budget	Article published in *Orphanet Journal of Rare Diseases*	All approved orphan medicinal products	LV	The study covered a 5-year period, from 2010 to 2014. Impact of orphan	Reimbursement price	2010–2014	In LV, average annual expenditures per patient on OMP varied widely, from € 1534 to € 580,952. The most	[69]

Continued

Table 3.1 Key price studies for different medicine groups—cont'd

Author/year	Title	Publication type	Med. group(s)	Country/region	Methods/data source	Price type[a]	Year(s)	Key results	References
					medicines on Latvian budget was estimated from the National Health Service's perspective. It was calculated in absolute values and relative to total pharmaceutical market and total medicine reimbursement budget.			costly treatment was enzyme replacement therapy (Elaprase) for mucopolysaccharidosis (MPS) II. Glivec had the highest share (34%) of the total orphan medicine expenditure. More than a half of the total OMP expenditures were attributed to oncological medicines, followed by medicines for metabolic and endocrine conditions and medicines for cardiopulmonary diseases.	
Young et al., 2017	A comparative study of orphan drug prices in Europe	Article published in *Journal of Market Access and Health Policy*	120 orphan medicines	FR, DE, IT, NO, ES, SE, UK	Annual treatment costs per medicine were calculated using ex-factory prices from a commercial provider of medicine prices (IHS POLI) and country price databases. The treatment cost in the comparator country was compared to the UK and ratios were analysed. Sub-analyses were done on disease areas and UK cost quartiles.	Ex-factory price	2016	Compared to the UK, the average costs were cheaper in SE (0.99) and NO (0.88) while they were more expensive in FR (1.13), DE (1.11), IT (1.08) and ES (1.07). A focus on average ratios may be a restrictive view, as ratios were greatly heterogeneous (0.26–1.92) which was also seen in the different disease areas. However, in the UK average ratios varied minimally among the cost quartiles which showed that cost differences were similar for the most expensive and least expensive OMP.	[35]
Orofino et al., 2010	Global spending on orphan drugs in France, Germany, the UK, Italy and Spain during 2007	Article published in *Applied Health Economics and Health Policy*	38 orphan medicines authorised by EMA	FR, DE, UK, IT, ES	The analysis was limited solely to costs of orphan medicines with sales data available for 2007. The mean annual cost per patient was	Ex-factory price	2007	The mean annual cost per patient and indication of the 38 OMP on the market ranged widely from € 331 to € 337 501. It appeared that prevalence of the diseases to treat was inversely correlated	[70]

					estimated using recommended regimens for maintenance dose and duration from the summary of product characteristics. Likewise, the ratio between annual costs per patient for treatment of each disease and its prevalence was calculated. The prices of the medicines under consideration were obtained from information provided by IQVIA.			with higher annual per-patient costs.	
HIV/AIDS medicines									
Wirtz et al., 2012	Allocating scarce financial resources for HIV treatment: benchmarking prices of antiretroviral medicines in Latin America	Article published in *Health Policy and Planning*	Antiretroviral (ARV)	Latin American and Caribbean countries	Global Price Reporting Mechanism (GPRM) database.	Procurement price	2008	The study found large price variations for first- and second-line ARV combinations between countries in the Latin American and Caribbean region. If procurement prices were closer to the LPG in the region, most of the surveyed countries in the LAC region could be treating between 1.17 and 3.8 times more patients. With regard to second-line combinations: a price closer to the lowest regional OB or to the global median transaction price for LMIC would also result in treating up to nearly five times more patients.	[44]

Continued

Table 3.1 Key price studies for different medicine groups—cont'd

Author/year	Title	Publication type	Med. group(s)	Country/ region	Methods/data source	Price type[a]	Year(s)	Key results	References
Sagaon-Teyssier et al., 2016	Affordability of adult HIV/AIDS treatment in developing countries: modelling price determinants for a better insight of the market functioning	Article published in the *Journal of the International AIDS Society*	HIV/AIDS med.	LMIC clustered into 6 World Bank developing regions	GPRM from the World Health Organization (WHO).	Procurement price	2003–2015	In the sub-Saharan Africa region, prices of OB are on average to be found the least expensive in the World Bank developing regions, where at the same time, generic medicines are on average most expensive. By contrast, OB are most expensive in Europe and Central Asia, and generic medicines are least expensive there.	[45]
Liu/Galárraga, 2017	Do national drug policies influence antiretroviral drug prices? Evidence from the Southern African Development community	Article published in *Health Policy and Planning*	ARV	South African Development Community (SADC)	GPRM from the WHO	Procurement price	2004–2013	In the regression, generic status of the purchased ARV was found to be the best predictor of an ARV's price —the generic versions of 8 out of 10 ARV medicines were priced lower than branded versions. In contrast, transaction volume, HIV prevalence, national pharmaceutical policies and PEPFAR/CHAI involvement were either not associated with ARV prices or were not consistent predictors of price across different ARV medicines.	[71]
Vasan et al., 2006	The pricing and procurement of antiretroviral drugs: an observational study of data from the Global Fund	Article published in *Bulletin of the World Health Organization*	Antiretrovirals (10 of the most commonly used adult formulation ARV)	Low-income countries (LIC), lower middle-income countries (MIC)	ARV transaction data in the purchase price report	Procurement price	2005	The study found that prices in LIC were broadly consistent or lower than the lowest differential prices quoted by the research and development sector of the pharmaceutical industry. In lower MIC, prices were more varied and in several active ingredients or combinations (lopinavir/ritonavir, didanosine and zidovudine/lamivudine) were very high compared with	[41]

								the per capita income of the country. In all LIC and lower MIC, ARV prices were still significantly high given limited local purchasing power and economic strength	
Seoane-Vazquez/Rodriguez-Monguio, 2006	Negotiating antiretroviral drug prices: the experience of the Andean countries	Article published in *Health Policy and Planning*	ARV	Andean countries	Price information of ARV purchased by public programmes during 2004 was collected from the Ministries of Health	Procurement price	2004	Study results showed that the negotiations did achieve lower prices and higher quality and bioequivalence standards for ARV compared to purchasing without negotiations for public programmes. Prices paid by the Andean countries' public programmes in 2004 were a weighted average of 65% higher than the negotiated prices. The difference between negotiated prices and actual prices would translate into 39.5% of the programmes' ARV expenditures in 2004, or 18 million US$ in ARV expenditures.	[42]
Waning et al., 2009	Global strategies to reduce antiretroviral prices	Article published in the *Bulletin of the World Health Organization*	ARV	Countries that have signed an agreement with the Clinton Foundation HIV/AIDS Initiative (CHAI)	Data on ARV procurement transactions from the Global Fund Price Reporting Mechanism and the WHO Global Price Reporting Mechanism (GPRM) were used to estimate the impact of global strategies (e.g., pooled procurement,	Procurement price	July 2002–October 2007	For the majority of ARV dosage forms (19 out of 24), no association between price and volume purchased was detected. When comparing high-volume purchases with low-volume purchases, for five ARV prices were between 4% and 21% lower for high-volume purchases. CHAI purchased generic ARV (9 out of 13) at prices 6%–36% lower than other initiatives. Another majority of branded ARV (15 out of 18) were priced 23%–498% higher	[43]

Continued

Table 3.1 Key price studies for different medicine groups—cont'd

Author/year	Title	Publication type	Med. group(s)	Country/ region	Methods/data source	Price type[a]	Year(s)	Key results	References
					differential) to reduce prices of ARV.			for differentially priced purchases compared with non-CHAI generic purchases. However, two branded, differentially priced ARV were priced 63% and 73% lower, respectively, than generic non-CHAI equivalents.	
Cancer medicines									
Goldstein et al., 2017	A global comparison of the cost of patented cancer drugs in relation to global differences in wealth	Article published in *Oncotarget*	Cancer med.	AU, CN, IN, IL, ZA, UK, US	Primary data collection from various sources, for example, prices published by MoH, survey with hospital, price registries	Pharmacy retail prices	November 2015–January 2016	Prices of cancer medicines are highest in the US. If patterns of affordability are controlled for by dividing prices by markers of health, India has the least affordable prices. Although in MIC prices are lower compared to US prices, in those countries they are less affordable.	[48]
Vogler et al., 2015	Cancer drugs in 16 European countries, Australia, and New Zealand: a cross-country price comparison study	Article published in *The Lancet Oncology*	Cancer med.	16 European countries, Australia, New Zealand	Primary data collection plus data provision from PPI service for European countries Comparison of 31 defined specialties	Ex-factory price	2013	Variation between highest priced country and lowest priced country ranged from 28% to 388% Prices in CH, DE and SE ranked high in comparison, and prices in EL and UK low.	[14]
Degrassat-Theas et al., 2012	Hospital reimbursement price cap for cancer drugs: the French experience in controlling hospital drug expenditures	Article published in *Pharmacoeconomics*	Cancer med.	France	Intra-country price comparison of procurement prices for hospitals. 487 hospitals were surveyed about purchasing prices	Ex-factory price/hospital price	2004–2007	Results showed a transient price decrease in 2005 before an alignment of patented medicines with regulated prices in the context of a dynamic market with a 22.5% yearly growth rate in value between 2004 and 2007.	[46]

Hepatitis C medicines									
Iyengar et al., 2016	Prices, costs, and affordability of new medicines for hepatitis C in 30 countries: an economic analysis	Article published in *PLoS Medicine*	Hepatitis C	Global, 30 countries (26 OECD countries and 4 LMIC)	Primary data collection from PPI service (European countries), national government or medicine reimbursement authorities, press releases 2 specialties (sofosbuvir and ledipasvir/sofosbuvir) Nominal exchange and weighting by PPP	Ex-factory price, assumption of 23% rebate	2015	The study found high variation between prices (both nominally as well by PPP): median nominal ex-factory price of a 12-week course of sofosbuvir across 26 OECD countries was US$ 42,017, ranging from US$ 37,729 in JP to US$ 64,680 in the US; the nominal price of ledipasvir/sofosbuvir varied between US$ 43,215 (UK) and US$ 72,765 (US) among the OECD countries. With PPPs adjustment, Central and Eastern European countries showed higher prices	[50]
Central nervous system									
Cameron et al., 2012	Mapping the availability, price, and affordability of antiepileptic drugs in 46 countries	Article published in *Epilepsia*	Antiepileptic med. (phenytoin, carbamazepine, valproic acid, phenobarbital, diazepam)	Global; 46 countries; 12 LIC, 22 LMIC, 9 UMIC, 3 HIC	Primary data collection; data were obtained from facility-based surveys; secondary data analysis from the HAI global database of survey results for individual medicines	Pharmacy retail price	2003–2010	Public sector patient prices for generic carbamazepine and phenytoin were 4.95 and 17.50 times higher than IPR, respectively, whereas in the private sector, retail prices were 11.27 and 24.77 times higher, respectively. For both medicines, OB prices were about 30 times higher.	[52]
Suh et al., 2009	International price comparisons of Alzheimer's drugs: a way to close the affordability gap	Article published in *International Psychogeriatrics*	19 medicines to treat neuropsychiatric conditions (e.g., Alzheimer)	21 countries on different continents	Primary data collection through price surveys in the countries. Prices of medicines to treat Alzheimer's disease were compared using the affordability index (i.e., total	Pharmacy retail price	2007	There were large price differences in the examined countries: While in India and Mexico a 5 mg tablet of the OB costs US$ 0.26 and US$ 0.31 respectively, it costs US$ 6.64 in the US. Pricing conditions of rivastigmine, galantamine and memantine appeared to be	[55]

Continued

Table 3.1 Key price studies for different medicine groups—cont'd

Author/year	Title	Publication type	Med. group(s)	Country/ region	Methods/data source	Price type[a]	Year(s)	Key results	References
					number of units purchasable with one's daily income) derived from PPP converted prices as well as raw prices.			similar to that of donepezil. Lowest prices of OB medicines were often found in India or Mexico, but if affordability patterns are considered, prices of medicines in LMIC are much more expensive than in HIC.	
Medicines for further chronic diseases									
Mendis et al., 2007	The availability and affordability of selected essential medicines for chronic diseases in six low- and middle-income countries	Article published in *Bulletin of the World Health Organization*	32 medicines used to treat chronic diseases (e.g., CVD, diabetes, asthma, glaucoma) and to provide palliative cancer care	3 LMIC (Brazil, Pakistan, Sri Lanka) and 3 LIC (Bangladesh, Malawi, Nepal)	Primary data collection through price surveys in the countries. The authors analysed the availability of medicines, the median price vs. the international reference price (expressed as the median price ratio) and affordability in terms of the number of days' wages it would cost the lowest-paid government worker to purchase 1 month of treatment.	Pharmacy retail price	2005	In Malawi and Sri Lanka, the price of OB in the private sector was three times more than generic medicines. Affordability varied among countries and diseases: One month of treatment for/with • coronary heart disease: from 1.5 days' wages in Sri Lanka to 18.4 days' wages in Malawi • asthma: from 1.3 days' wages in Bangladesh to 9.2 days' wages in Malawi. • intermediate-acting insulin: from 2.8 days' wages in Brazil to 19.6 in Malawi.	[60]
Wang et al., 2017	Availability, price, and affordability of selected essential medicines for chronic diseases in 11 countries of the Asia Pacific region: a secondary analysis	Article published in *Asia Pacific Journal of Public Health*	15 medicines used to treat chronic diseases (e.g., CVD, diabetes, asthma)	11 countries in Southeast Asia and Western Pacific Region	Secondary analysis based on data on medicine prices and availability from the HAI global database. Price data were converted into the base year of 2014	Pharmacy retail price	September 2001– November 2013	Countries paid 1.4 times the IRP to procure the LPG and 9.1 times for OB. Patients would have to spend 2.3 and 0.4 day's wages to purchase 1 month's treatment of a chronic disease for innovator brands and LPGs, respectively, in the private sector.	[61]

Babar et al., 2011	The availability, pricing and affordability of three essential asthma medicines in 52 low- and middle-income countries	Article published in *Pharmacoeconomics*	Essential medicines for chronic diseases; asthma medicines	Low- and middle-income countries	Cross-sectional pricing survey. Prices and availability data were collected for salbutamol, beclometasone and budesonide in two private retail pharmacies, the national procurement centre and a main public hospital	Pharmacy retail price and procurement price/CIF price	2011	Considerable variability was found in prices and affordability across countries. When Asthma Drug Facility prices were applied as benchmark, procurement systems appeared largely inefficient. Some countries appear to be subsidising asthma medicines, making them free or less expensive for patients, while other countries applied very high margins. The latter can significantly increase the price for patients unless a reimbursement system exists.	[54]
Cho et al., 2015	The effect of new drug pricing systems and new reimbursement guidelines on pharmaceutical expenditures and prescribing behavior among hypertensive patients in Korea	Article published in *Health Policy*	Medicines for chronic diseases; antihypertensives	KO	Multi-level mixed-effect regression on reimbursement claims	Reimbursement price	2011–2013	The monthly average pharmaceutical expenditures per each patient with the examined conditions were lowered by 1446 South Korean Won (KRW) (€ 1 ~ KRW 1.320, US$ 1 ~ KRW 1080) and also the number of medicines per prescription decreased significantly. The percentage of costs attributed to originators and the number of originator medicines declined.	[53]
Gelders et al., 2008	Price, availability and affordability. An international comparison of chronic disease medicines	Technical report published by WHO	Medicines to treat chronic diseases (asthma, diabetes, hypertension, epilepsy, psychiatric disorders)	Low- and middle-income countries (LMIC)	The survey data available on the HAI website	Median price ratios (MPR)	2001–2005	• Government procurement systems were found to be generally efficient in obtaining prices similar to the IRP when procuring for their own supply systems • Availability of medicines was higher in the private sector, but prices are much higher, ranging from 3 times the IRP to peaks of 100 times the IRP at country level	[58]

Continued

Table 3.1 Key price studies for different medicine groups—cont'd

Author/year	Title	Publication type	Med. group(s)	Country/ region	Methods/data source	Price type[a]	Year(s)	Key results	References
								• Affordability has been determined and expressed as the number of days the lowest paid unskilled government worker would have to work to buy predetermined regimens of treatment for selected chronic conditions • Taxes and duties levied on medicines, as well as the mark-ups applied, frequently contribute more to the final price than the actual manufacturers' price does.	
Garuoliene et al., 2011	European countries with small populations can obtain low prices for drugs: Lithuania as a case history	Article published in *Expert Review of Pharmacoeconomics Outcomes Research*	Medicines from 5 different groups: proton pump inhibitors, statins, ACE inhibitor, angiotensin II receptor blocker, SSRI	LT, AT, FR, DE, IT, PT, SE, ES, UK	In 2009, for each class of medicines the reimbursed expenditure/DDD was calculated and compared with the price level in 2000, when in all groups the originator	Reimbursement price/ reimbursed expenditure	2000 and 2009	There was an appreciable reduction in reimbursed expenditure/DDD for generics in each medicine class in LT, despite appreciably lower utilisation for certain group of medicines (e.g., proton pump inhibitors, statins and antidepressants) in LT vs. Western European countries. Reductions in generic prices were similar to those among a range of European countries. The authors did not find an apparent correlation between the number of competitors and price reductions in practice.	[57]
Khatib et al., 2015	Availability and affordability of cardiovascular disease medicines and their effect on use in	Article published in *Lancet*	4 medicines for secondary prevention of CVD	18 high-, middle- and low-income countries	Information about availability and costs of cardiovascular disease medicines (aspirin, β blockers,	Pharmacy retail price	2003 and 2009	The four CVD medicines were potentially unaffordable for 0.14% of households in HIC (14 of 9934 households), 25% of upper MIC (6299 of 24,776),	[59]

	high-income, middle-income, and low-income countries: an analysis of the PURE study data				angiotensin-converting enzyme inhibitors and statins) in pharmacies gathered from 596 communities in 18 countries. Medicines were considered affordable if their combined cost was less than 20% of household capacity-to-pay.			33% of lower MIC (13,253 of 40,023), 60% of LIC (excluding India; 1976 of 3312), and 59% households in India (9939 of 16,874).	
Van Mourik et al., 2010	Availability, price and affordability of cardiovascular medicines: A comparison across 36 countries using WHO/HAI data	Article published in *BMC Cardiovascular Disorders*	5 medicines to treat CVD	Low- and middle-income countries	Outcome measures were percentage availability, price ratios to international reference prices and number of day's wages needed by the lowest-paid unskilled government worker to purchase 1 month of chronic treatment.	Public sector procurement price and retail prices	2008	Procurement prices were very competitive in some countries, whereas others consistently paid high prices. Patient prices were generally substantially higher than IRP; some countries, however, performed well. Chronic treatment with anti-hypertensive medication cost more than 1 day's wages in many cases. However, when monotherapy is insufficient (e.g., two or more medications) treatment became unaffordable.	[56]
Medicines for further infectious diseases									
Tougher et al., 2012	Effect of the affordable medicines facility—malaria (AMFm) on the availability, price, and market share of quality-assured artemisin-based combination therapies in seven	Article published in *Lancet*	Antimalarial treatments, that is, non-artemisin therapies, artemisin monotherapies and artemisin-based combination therapies (ACT)	8 African countries (Ghana, Kenya, Madagascar, Niger, Nigeria, Tanzania, Uganda, Zanzibar)	Primary data collection through standardised surveys (methods for these surveys were adapted from the ACT watch project). Price data were collected in local currencies and endpoint data were	Pharmacy retail price	2010	Large falls in median price for quality-assured ACT per adult equivalent dose were seen in the private for-profit sector in six pilots, ranging from US$ 1.28 to US$ 4.82. The pilot studies were conducted in Nigeria and Zanzibar, and in both cases the market share of oral artemisin	[51]

Continued

Table 3.1 Key price studies for different medicine groups—cont'd

Author/year	Title	Publication type	Med. group(s)	Country/ region	Methods/data source	Price type[a]	Year(s)	Key results	References
	countries: a before-and-after analysis of outlet survey data				adjusted to 2010 prices using national consumer price indices. Prices were converted to US dollars using the average interbank rate for 2010.			monotherapies decreased from its baseline value at 5%.	
Hospital medicines									
Vogler et al., 2016	European price comparison of high-cost hospital medicines	Abstract based on a technical report published by the Austrian Public Health institute	15 high-cost medicines from the Austrian in-patient sector	28 Member States of the European Union	Price survey and single price comparison of 15 high-cost medicines that accounted for a high share of pharmaceutical expenditures in two Austrian public hospitals	Ex-factory price	2015	Six of the selected medicines had a pack price (median of the 16 countries surveyed) of more than € 1,000, thereof ipilimumab of a median price of € 17,000. When ranking medicine prices, the cross-country comparison showed that SE had most frequently unit ex-factory prices in the fourth quartile (83% of the 15 medicines), followed by DE (73%) and FI (53%). Prices ranking most frequently in the first quartile were observed in HU (90% of the medicines), EL (85%) and UK (67%). For the surveyed medicine sample, Greek prices were most often (74%) to be found the lowest.	[72]
Degrassat-Theas et al., 2012	Hospital reimbursement price cap for cancer drugs: the French experience in controlling hospital drug expenditures	Article published in *Pharmacoeconomics*	Cancer med.	FR	Intra-country price comparison of procurement prices for hospitals. 487 hospitals were surveyed about purchasing prices	Hospital price	2004–2007	Results showed a transient price decrease in 2005 before an alignment of patented medicines with regulated prices in the context of a dynamic market with a 22.5% yearly growth rate in value between 2004 and 2007.	[46]

Prescription medicines									
Roughhead et al., 2007	Prices for innovative pharmaceutical products that provide health gain: a comparison between Australia and the United States	Article published in *Value in Health*	Innovative medicine	Australia, United States	Products identified by the FDA and the Canadian Patented Medicines Price Review Board as likely to confer significant health gains; prices were obtained from the Federal Supply Schedule (FSS)	Ex-factory price	1999–2004	For the sample for which comparisons were possible (22 medicines), Australian prices were in 64% of the products (14 medicines) higher than the US FSS prices. Also when compared with the US average manufacturer prices (AMP), Australian prices were still higher for the remainder of eight products. Overall, Australian prices were higher on average by 4.2% when compared with the FSS and lower by 14.4% when compared with the AMP.	[73]
Hsiao et al., 2010	Price regulation, new entry, and information shock on pharmaceutical market in Taiwan: a nationwide data-based study from 2001 to 2004	Article in *BMC Health Services Research*	Non-steroidal anti-inflammatory drugs (NSAIDs)	Taiwan	All NSAID prescribed in ambulatory visits in the NHI system during study period, data were drawn from NHI databases	Reimbursement price	2001–2004	The study found 'New entry' to be the only variable significantly correlated with changes of expenditures (positive change, $P = .02$) and market structure of the NSAID market in the NHI system. The correlation between price regulation (first price regulation, $P = .62$; second price regulation, $P = .26$) and information shock ($P = .31$) and pharmaceutical expenditure were not statistically significant.	[74]
Martikainen et al., 2005	European prices of newly launched reimbursable pharmaceuticals- a pilot study	Article in *Health Policy*	Newly launched medicines	BE, DK, FI, FR, IE, NL, ES, SE, UK	Price data were collected from eight pharmaceutical products for which marketing authorisation had been granted by the European Commission during the year 2000.	Wholesale price	2000	Prices of newly launched medicines varied considerably between examined countries. Wholesale prices were highest in those countries where manufacturers are free to set the prices of their products. However, distribution remuneration for pharmacist, for example, through regulated	[75]

Continued

Table 3.1 Key price studies for different medicine groups—cont'd

Author/year	Title	Publication type	Med. group(s)	Country/ region	Methods/data source	Price type[a]	Year(s)	Key results	References
								mark-ups/margins and taxes, changes the ranking of the most expensive or the cheapest countries.	
Morel et al., 2011	The level of income appears to have no consistent bearing on pharmaceutical prices across countries	Article in *Health Affairs*	Not clear	DZ, BR, EG, IN, ID, MY, MX, MA, PH, PL, ZA, TH, TN, TR, FR, UK, US	Price data were provided by IQVIA and then Laspeyres and Paasche indices were calculated.	Ex-factory price	1999–2008	Some MIC paid more for pharmaceuticals than HIC – for example, prices in several MIC exceeded those in the UK for some years of the study period. In addition, other MIC paid less than LIC – for example, average prices in India were consistently below prices in western Africa.	[76]
Niens et al., 2010	Quantifying the impoverishing effects of purchasing medicines: a cross-country comparison of the affordability of medicines in the developing world	Article published in *PLoS Medicine*	Essential medicines	KG, ML, NG, PK, TJ, TZ, UG, UZ, YE, SV, ID, JO, MN, PE, PH, TN	Medicine prices were taken from standardised surveys using the WHO/HAI price measurement methodology	Retail price	Not clear	In the countries studied, purchasing these medicines would impoverish large portions of the population (up to 86%). OB products were less affordable than the LPG equivalents. In the Philippines, for example, OB atenolol would push an additional 22% of the population below US$ 1.25 per day, whereas for the LPG equivalent this demographic shift is 7%.	[77]
Kanavos et al., 2013	Higher US branded drug prices and spending compared to other countries may stem partly from quick uptake of new drugs	Article in *Health Affairs*	Branded medicine prices	AU, CA, FR, DE, CH, UK, US	68 brand-name medicines that had the highest combined sales, in US dollars, in 2010. These medicines accounted for 48% of the total expenditure for prescription medicines – that is, spending for both brand-name and	Ex-factory price	2010	Depending on how prices were weighted for volume across the countries, prices of brand-name prescription-only-medicines (POM) were 5%–198% higher in the US than in the other countries in all three study years. A main driver to higher US per capita pharmaceutical spending is faster uptake of new and more expensive POM in the US relative to other countries. In	[78]

					generic prescription medicines – across the study countries.			contrast, other OECD countries employed several mechanisms that slowed down spending: (1) HTA, (2) Restrictions on patients' eligibility for new prescription medicines, (2) Requirement of strict evidence of the value of new medicines.	
Kanavos/ Vandoros, 2011	Determinants of branded prescription medicine prices in OECD countries	Article in *Health Economics, Policy and Law*	Branded POM	US, JP, FR, DE, IT, ES, UK, AU, MX, AT, PT, SE, EL, SK, BE	Price data for 100 branded products were collected from national official sources, whereas sales were acquired from IQVIA	Ex-factory price and retail price	2004–2007	Compared to other OECD countries, US retail prices for branded POM were higher, but not as high as widely thought. Large differences in prices are mainly observed at an ex-factory level, but these were not the prices that consumers and payers pay. A cross-country comparison at retail prices found that differences at this level were actually not as high as expected and, when controlling for exchange rates, these differences could be even smaller. In the regression analysis, product age had a significant effect on prices in all settings after having controlled for other factors. Price convergence was observed across countries for newer POM compared with older medicines. There was no evidence that OB prices fall after generic entry in the US, a phenomenon known as the 'generics paradox'.	[49]
Vogler et al., 2015	Analysis of medicine prices in New Zealand and 16 European Countries	Article published in *Value in Health*	14 medicines	AT, BE, DK, DE, EL, FI, FR, IT, IE, NL, NO, PT, ES, SE, CH, UK, NZ	Data provision from PPI service (for European countries), NZ Pharmaceutical Schedule Comparison of 14	Ex-factory price, wholesale price and pharmacy retail price	2012	Considerable price differences at the ex-factory price level were identified for the 14 medicines surveyed. Prices in EL, PT, UK and ES ranked at the lower end, whereas prices in CH, DE, DK	[68]

Continued

Table 3.1 Key price studies for different medicine groups—cont'd

Author/year	Title	Publication type	Med. group(s)	Country/ region	Methods/data source	Price type[a]	Year(s)	Key results	References
					specialities (thereof all as originators and additionally 5 as generic versions)			and SE were at the upper end. NZ prices were found in the lowest quartile for five medicines and in the highest quartile for seven other products. Price differences between the OB and generic versions ranged from 0% to 90% depending on the medicine and the country.	
Danzon/ Furukawa, 2008	International prices and availability of pharmaceuticals in 2005	Article published in *Health Affairs*	Medicines available on the retail/outpatient market	US, FR, DE, IT, ES, UK, CA, AU, JP, BR, MX, CL	Data have been accessed from IQVIA; calculation of price indices and prices was adjusted by purchasing power parities (instead of exchange rates) and normalised by average income (GDP per capita)	Ex-factory prices, pharmacy retail prices and hospital prices	2005	Prices of medicines - (aggregated on ATC3 level) are in most of the surveyed countries 20%–40% lower than US prices. On the retail price level non-US prices are only 10%–30% lower than the US prices, while on the ex-factory price level this difference is between 20% and 40%. When pharmacy retail prices are used in place of ex-factory prices, France's price index increases from 74 to 91, Germany's increases from 75 to 90, and Italy's increases from 67 to 87. Distribution margins absorbed a larger share of total pharmaceutical spending in several regulated markets than in the US.	[64]
Non-prescription medicines									
Danzon/ Furukawa, 2008	International prices and availability of pharmaceuticals in 2005	Article published in *Health Affairs*	Medicines available on the retail/outpatient market	US, FR, DE, IT, ES, UK, CA, AU, JP, BR, MX, CL	Data have been accessed from IQVIA; calculation of price indices and prices was adjusted by purchasing power	Ex-factory prices, retail prices and hospital prices	2005	Prices of non-prescription medicines (NPM) are at least 80% higher in all surveyed countries than in the US; in some cases (IT, JP, ES and CL) prices can be more than three	[64]

					parities (instead of exchange rates) and normalised by average income (GDP per capita). The price data served as input to a probit regression model that was used to identify factors that increased the likelihood of price changes			times higher. The low NPM prices in the US were attributed to its highly price-competitive retail pharmacy market, dominated by the large chains, many of which produce their own private-label generic medicines. Countries in the survey that regulated prices of POM also tend to regulate NPM prices directly or via retail price maintenance. A prohibition of chain pharmacies would undermine NPM price competition, because single pharmacies have weak leverage on brand-name NPM prices and are unlikely to produce their own alternative to brand-name NPM.	

ACE, angiotensin-converting enzyme; *ACT*, artemisin-base combination therapy; *AIDS*, acquired immune deficiency syndrome; *AMFm*, affordable medicines facility-malaria; *AMP*, average manufacturer price(s); *ARV*, antiretroviral(s); *ATC*, anatomical therapeutic chemical; *CHAI*, Clinton health access initiative; *CVD*, cardiovascular disease(s); *DDD*, defined daily dose; Dev., development (i.e.; the study informs about price developments over time); *EEA*, european economic area; *EG*, egypt; *EMA*, European medicines agency; *EML*, essential medicines list; *ESRI*, economic and social research institute; *EU*, European Union; *FDA*, Food and Drug Administration; *FSS*, Federal Supply Schedule; *GDP*, Gross Domestic Product; *GPRM*, Global price reporting mechanism; *HAI*, Health Action International; *HIC*, high-income country/ies; *HIV*, human immunodeficiency virus; *HTA*, health technology assessment; *IHS POLI*, Information Handling Services PharmOnline International; *IQR*, Interquartile range; *IRP*, International reference price; *ISPOR*, International Society For Pharmacoeconomics and Outcomes Research; *KRW*, South Korean Won; *LAC*, Latina American and Caribbean; *LIC*, low-income country/ies; *LKR*, Sri Lankan rupee; *LMIC*, low- and middle-income country/ies; *LPG*, Lowest price generic; med., medicine(s); MoH, Ministry of Health; *MPR*, Median Price Ratio; *MPS*, Mucopolysaccharidosis; *NHI*, National Health Insurance; *NPM*, non-prescription medicines; *NSAID*, non-steroidal anti-inflammatory drugs; *OB*, originator brand; *OECD*, Organisation for Economic Co-operation and Development, *OMP*, orphan medicinal product(s); *PEPFAR*, President's Emergency Plan for AIDS Relief; *POM*, prescription-only-medicines; *PPI*, Pharma Price Information service of the Austrian Public Health Institute GÖG; *PPPs*, purchasing power parities; *PRP*, pharmacy retail price; R, reimbursement; R&D, Research & Development; Ref., reference; *SADC*, South African Development Community; *SSRI*, selective serotonin reuptake inhibitor; *SU*, standard unit; *TLV*, Tandvårds- och läkemedelsförmånsverket; *UMIC*, upper middle income countries; *US$*, US dollars; *WHO*, World Health Organization; *WP*, wholesale price, Country abbreviations: *AT*, Austria; *AU*, Australia; *BE*, Belgium; *BG*, Bulgaria; *BR*, Brazil; *CA*, Canada; *CH*, Switzerland; *CL*, Chile; *CN*, China; *CY*, Cyprus; *CZ*, Czech Republic; *DE*, Germany; *DK*, Denmark; *DZ*, Algeria; *EE*, Estonia; *EL*, Greece; *ES*, Spain; *FI*, Finland; *FR*, France; *HR*, Croatia; *HU*, Hungary; *ID*, Indonesia; *IE*, Ireland; *IN*, India; *IT*, Italy; *JO*, Jordan; *JP*, Japan; *KG*, Kyrgyzstan; *KO*, South Korea; *LK*, Sri Lanka; *LT*, Lithuania; *LU*, Luxembourg; *LV*, Latvia; *MA*, Morocco; *ML*, Mali; *MN*, Mongolia; *MT*, Malta; *MX*, Mexico; *MY*, Malaysia; *NG*, Nigeria; *NL*, Netherlands; *NO*, Norway; *NZ*, New Zealand; *PE*, Peru; *PH*, Philippines; *PK*, Pakistan; *PL*, Poland; *PT*, Portugal; *SE*, Sweden; *SI*, Slovenia; *SK*, Slovakia; *SV*, El Salvador; *TH*, Thailand; *TJ*, Tajikistan; *TN*, Tunisia; *TZ*, Tanzania; *UG*, Uganda; *UK*, United Kingdom; *US*, United States; *UZ*, Uzbekistan; *YE*, Yemen; *ZA*, South Africa.

[a]All medicine price types are official list prices (i.e., without discounts) unless specified differently.

the suggested classification of medicine groups is not mutually exclusive since a cancer medicine can be high-priced and can also have an orphan designation. The studies were attributed to the most appropriate group, with reference being made to other groups as well.

3.1 GENERIC AND BIOSIMILAR MEDICINES

Generic medicines have been investigated in a large number of price studies. This reflects the importance attributed to generics due to their (perceived) potential to increase affordability and availability of treatments, which is particularly relevant for low- and middle-income countries (LMIC). Price studies that included generic medicines can be classified into three broad groups in terms of the methods and sources applied: (1) use of WHO/HAI survey methodology, (2) use of national administrative databases and (3) use of commercial databases (Chapter 8 on data sources will provide a more detailed description on evaluating different sources).

Price studies conducted in LMIC mainly apply the WHO/HAI survey methodology. It is a reliable methodology of collecting and analysing medicine prices, availability, affordability and medicine price components (cf. Chapters 6.2 and 9.3.3) data across healthcare sectors and regions. Price data are surveyed at the retailers (e.g., pharmacies) by trained data collectors. Price information is entered into a software application in the frame of the WHO/HAI project and is made publicly available [1]. The WHO/HAI survey methodology is explained in a manual [2,3] and will be described in detail in Chapter 6.2. The WHO/HAI surveys were conducted on a country base, as examples from China [4,5], Malaysia [6] or Sri Lanka [7—9] presented and highlighted in previous chapters. Although the method of collecting price information at retailers is predominantly applied in LMIC, it is not limited to these countries. Gooi M and Bell CM [10] conducted a telephone and Internet survey of pharmacies in Canada and the United States (US) to collect price information for the top 19 dispensed generic medicines in both countries. Their comparison revealed that for 12 of the 19 studied generic medicines the lowest price was found in the US with an average saving of 47% for each of these 12 medicines. For the other seven medicines, lowest prices were reported in Canada but the average savings for this group of seven medicines were around 29% per medicine.

Due to the standardised reporting format, results of WHO/HAI surveys of several countries can also be aggregated and used in a secondary analysis. Cameron A, Ewen M, Ross-Degnan D, Ball D and Laing R [11] compared data of 45 surveys performed in 36 countries on prices, affordability and availability of 15 essential medicines included in at least 80% of the surveys.

As the surveys spanned over the period between 2001 (first pilot surveys) and 2006, prices were adjusted for inflation or deflation as well as purchasing power parities (PPP). The authors found that for a basket of 15 medicines examined, the average median government procurement price was around 1.11-fold of the international reference price. However, there was a large variation in prices depending on the group of medicines and the countries. Salbutamol was usually procured at prices lower than its international reference price in all regions except in the Americas, while ciprofloxacin was priced substantially higher than its international reference price in all regions. Across low-income countries (LIC), median government procurement price ratios of lowest-priced generics ranged from 0.09 in Sudan to 5.37 in Nigeria. In the private sector patients paid 9 to 25 times the international reference prices for lowest-priced generics.

The second group of price studies on generics used price information provided by national authorities, international collaborations or public institutions. Mansfield SJ [12] collected price information of generics from publicly available national sources in Australia and England. The author aimed to assess variation in reimbursement prices of generic medicines between Australia and England and to explore possible driving factors of those differences. Her analysis covered around 15 generic molecules (representing 45 different pharmaceutical specialties) out of a list of 50 medicines that accounted for the highest public pharmaceutical expenditures. The analysis showed that Australian prices were on average over sevenfold higher than prices in England. The lower prices of generics in England were attributed to important supply-side differences such as pricing policies or the relative size of the generic markets. The use of reimbursement data was also found in intra-country studies: for instance, Kwon H-Y, Kim H, Godman B and Reich MR [13] used reimbursement prices in South Korea to analyse the impact of a pricing reform related to off-patent medicines on public pharmaceutical expenditures. Overall, international comparisons of reimbursement prices of generics can be challenging: firstly, the information on reimbursement prices may not be publicly accessible, and, secondly, countries may have implemented different reimbursement rules.[1]

[1] Several countries implemented gradations in reimbursement levels to protect vulnerable population groups, for example, pensioners and children. In these so-called 'population-groups based reimbursement schemes', for one population group a larger fraction of the expenditure is covered by the third party payer, resulting in different reimbursement prices across a country.

Price information to conduct price studies of generics could also be provided by international collaborations such as EURIPID (cf. also Chapter 8.2). EURIPID is a database of competent authorities for pharmaceutical pricing and reimbursement that was established in 2009. Participating countries share information about their pharmaceutical prices, and only authorities that have been providing data to EURIPID are granted access. After approval of the board of participants these data can be used for analyses [14]. Brick A, Gorecki P and Nolan A [15] compared prices of pharmaceuticals, prescribing practices and the utilisation of generics in Ireland to comparable European Union (EU) Member States and drew on EURIPID capacities. They found that prices of new (i.e., single source inpatent) medicines were high in Ireland compared to other countries. However, as a tendency, prices of originator medicines were lower in Ireland in those cases when a generic version of that pharmaceutical was available, but Irish prices of generics were consistently higher than in other reference countries.

The Pharma Price Information (PPI) service located at the Austrian Public Health Institute is another reliable and independent source of information of pharmaceutical prices (cf. also Chapter 8.2). The PPI service provides upon request medicine prices of EU Member States plus Norway and Switzerland for all price types. It was established to support, according to the Austrian General Social Insurance Law, the Austrian Pharmaceutical Pricing Committee located at the Austrian Federal Ministry of Labour, Social Affairs, Health and Consumer Protection. Price information on generics from the PPI service was used in reports and publications. Vogler S [16] surveyed price differences between selected originator and generic medicines of five molecules in 16 European countries and analysed similarities and differences with regard to respective national generic policies. Price differences between originator and generic medicines were found to be quite considerable in most of the countries and reached 97.3%. On the other hand, in a few countries no difference was found at all between originator and generic prices. For the five molecules of the sample, Greece, Spain, Ireland and Norway consistently displayed lower price differences, whereas Denmark, Finland and Sweden tended to show higher differences between originator and generic prices.

The last group of studies relies on data provided by commercial providers, among which IQVIA (formerly known as IMS and Quintiles IMS) appeared to be the most frequently used. IQVIA (cf. also Chapter 8.2) collects price data on medicines in the individual countries, usually at different points in the distribution chain. Figures can be collected from manufacturers', importers' or wholesalers' records. It then uses country specific information (discounts, profit regulations, reimbursement prices etc.) collected by their intelligence unit to calculate wholesale and pharmacy margins, and other price types. Some information provided by IQVIA is based on samples of prescriptions from panels of pharmacists and physicians in each country [17]. Frequently, the method of calculating average price levels through indices, most commonly the Laspeyres index (Box 3.1, cf. also Chapter 9 for further indices), is applied on price data obtained from IQVIA.

Aho E, Johansson P and Rönnholm G [19] compared Swedish prices of prescription medicines to 19 European countries. Indices were calculated for pharmaceuticals not exposed to competition (i.e., on-patent medicines) and for pharmaceuticals exposed to competition (i.e., generics). The latter segment accounted for around 19% of total sales in Sweden, and approximately half of the volume. The authors found that Swedish prices of generics are among the lowest ones in the sample. Between 2014 and 2015, the price levels of other countries fell in relation to Swedish prices. Between 2015 and 2016, however, prices in other countries increased more in relation to Swedish prices, resulting in higher price differences between Sweden and most of the examined countries than they were in 2014.

Wouters OJ and Kanavos PG [20] calculated commonly used price indices based on 3,156 generic medicines in seven European countries and found large differences in prices for generics between countries. Denmark and Sweden consistently had the lowest ex-factory and pharmacy retail prices, while prices in France and Italy ranked highest in most of the indices. However, the results showed high uncertainty depending on the method used (e.g., choice of index, base country, unit of volume, method of currency conversion and therapeutic category).

While there is abundant literature on prices of generic medicines, price comparisons of biosimilar medicines are scarce. Rovira J, Lindner L, Giménez E et al. [21] described the development of the biosimilar market and analysed prices of all biosimilars authorised through centralised procedures in relation to originator product prices. The analysis revealed remarkable differences between biosimilar prices. Comparing the variation between the highest and the lowest country price the authors found differences ranging from 1.4 to 2.7. Rémuzat C, Dorey J, Cristeau O et al. [22] aimed to analyse drivers of biosimilar uptake in European countries and found a difference between originator prices and the average prices of respective biosimilar medicines of 0% (Spain) to 32% (Hungary).

Price studies on biosimilars seem to rather focus on the savings potentials for pharmaceutical and total public healthcare budgets, either on an aggregated level [23,24] or in a national context [25]. The relevance and interest in biosimilars appear to grow as an increasing number of publications indicates. This growing interest might be related to the patent expiration of 'blockbuster' medicines such as trastuzumab or rituximab in key markets since 2012 and several other biologicals being on the verge of the 'patent cliff'. Studies on biosimilar medicines mainly relate to interchangeability and substitutability of biosimilars with original medicines.

BOX 3.1 Laspeyres index for price comparison of pharmaceuticals

The Laspeyres price index is a statistic formula in economics to calculate the economy's general price level and its relative changes between two periods. It is assumed that there are two periods (e.g., period '2016' and '2017'), and in each period the same bundle of goods (1, 2, ..., n) is purchased. p_i^t denotes the price of the good i in period t and w_i^t denotes the quantity of the good i in period t. The Laspeyres index is the weighted average of a number of products over time where prices of the different periods act as weights.

$$I_{LP} = \frac{p_1^{2017} w_1^{2016} + p_2^{2017} w_2^{2016} + \cdots + p_n^{2017} w_n^{2016}}{p_1^{2016} w_1^{2016} + p_2^{2016} w_2^{2016} + \cdots + p_n^{2016} w_n^{2016}} \times 100$$

Since the price index is designed to measure change in the average price for a market basket of products in two situations when prices differ between products, it can also be used for the comparison of pharmaceutical prices.

$$I_{LP} = \frac{p_1^{\text{Country2}} w_1^{\text{Country1}} + p_2^{\text{Country2}} w_2^{\text{Country1}} + \cdots + p_n^{\text{Country2}} w_n^{\text{Country1}}}{p_1^{\text{Country1}} w_1^{\text{Country1}} + p_2^{\text{Country1}} w_2^{\text{Country1}} + \cdots + p_n^{\text{Country1}} w_n^{\text{Country1}}} \times 100$$

Time periods can be substituted by countries. In this format the index compares how much more (or less) country 1 would have paid for pharmaceuticals if they had prices of country 2. It is a bilateral index expressing the products of the base country relative to another country.

As a possible limitation, the Laspeyres index is intransitive, for example, the product of the indices for Sweden relative to Germany and Germany relative to France does not yield the index for the Sweden relative to France. Another limitation of indices is that large differences can occur depending on which index (Laspeyres, Paasche or Fischer) is used [18].

Price studies, as described above for generics, have not been conducted on biosimilar medicines so far, but can be expected due to their increasing relevance to public pharmaceutical budgets.

3.2 HIGH-PRICED MEDICINES, INCLUDING ORPHAN MEDICINAL PRODUCTS

In OECD (Organisation of Economic Co-operation and Development) countries, often a few premium-priced medicines constitute a major burden for public pharmaceutical expenditures and push solidarity-based health systems to the edge of financial sustainability. Monitoring the development of prices for those medicines is an important instrument, in line with the principle of prioritisation.[2] As a result, competent authorities and public payers monitor prices of these medicines to ensure affordable access to medicines for patients. Results of such price monitoring are sometimes not accessible at all or, if available, they are usually published in official reports of these institutions (so-called 'grey literature'). Examples of such publications are found in Austria [26], Germany [27] and Sweden [19].

Vogler S, Schneider P and Zimmermann N [26] conducted a price survey and comparison of 60 medicines, which were selected due to their relevance to the Austrian public payers because they accounted for a high share of pharmaceutical expenditures ('high-cost medicines'). Price data from all 28 European Union Member States were collected and compared to Austrian prices at unit price level (i.e., per tablets, per vial). Austrian ex-factory prices of the surveyed medicines ranged among the highest prices in EU comparison. For the medicines surveyed, even higher ex-factory prices tended to be found in Germany, Ireland, Denmark and Sweden; whereas Bulgaria, Cyprus and Greece were identified as low-priced countries. The analysis also showed two particular results: first, in comparison to other European countries, Austrian prices of the surveyed medicines used in the hospital setting were higher than those of the selected out-patient medicines. Second, price levels can differ along the distribution chain. In EU comparison, Austrian pharmacy retail prices of the surveyed

[2] In materials management, the so-called ABC analysis is a technique for inventory categorisation and prioritisation. Products are classified into three categories, A, B and C. For A items there should be very tight controls and accurate records, while the controls can be less tight for items of the other categories. The main criterion for classifying goods is their proportion in terms of the overall value. A items typically account for 70%–80% of the value of all items within a defined period of time.

medicines ranked comparably higher than Austrian ex-factory prices or wholesale prices.

The relevance of monitoring and conducting regular price studies for high-priced medicines was also underlined by Busse R, Panteli D, Schaufler J et al. [27] who identified for the German pharmaceutical market a change in the prescription pattern and (high) prices as main drivers for pharmaceutical expenditures. The authors focused on the price aspect and analysed prices of 260 medicines that accounted for 98% of the entire on-patent market. Results confirmed previous findings of other studies that described Germany as a high-price country. In all examined countries, PPP-adjusted prices were between 13% (Netherlands) and 30% (France) below German prices. If price data were weighted by GDP, price differences were between 16% (UK) and 27% (Denmark) below German prices. If Germany were able to reach the lowest price in the surveyed countries, savings of approximately 2.9 billion Euro would be possible. This would translate into 30% of the total pharmaceutical sales.

In Sweden, the Dental and Pharmaceutical Benefits Agency (Tandvårds- och läkemedelsförmånsverket, TLV) has the mandate to monitor developments in the Swedish pharmaceutical market from an international perspective and conducted three price studies in the last years. In the last report of this kind, Aho E, Johansson P and Rönnholm G [19] compared the price levels of on-patent ('*pharmaceuticals not exposed to competition*') and off-patent ('*pharmaceuticals exposed to competition*') medicines in Sweden to the ones in other 19 European countries. In order to compare average price levels, the authors calculated price indices with price and sales data obtained from IQVIA. Prices taken into account for the comparison were at the wholesale price level (i.e., price type at which medicine prices are set in Sweden). The analysis showed that Swedish prices for on-patent medicines had declined relative to other countries, but were still found among the eight countries with the highest price. In contrast, prices for off-patent medicines were among the three countries with the lowest prices in the sample.

Besides these technical reports, results of price comparisons were also published in peer-reviewed journals. Merkur S and Mossialos E [28] compared pharmaceutical prices of the 50 most expensive and 50 most sold products in Cyprus to other EU countries that had a higher or similar GDP per capita. In comparison to Denmark, Greece, Portugal, Spain, Sweden and UK, pharmacy retail prices of medicines in Cyprus appeared to be high. The volume-weighted index of pharmacy retail prices ('Laspeyres Index') for a sample of the most expensive medicines was higher in Cyprus than in

Denmark (84%), Sweden (62%), Portugal (61%), the UK (61%), Spain (58%) and Greece (56%).

Research on orphan medicinal products (OMP) could also be attributed to the group of studies of high-priced medicines, as the ex-factory prices of these medicines are usually very high. The orphan medicine Eculizumab/Soliris for the treatment of paroxysmal nocturnal haemoglobinuria (PNH) or atypical haemolytic uremic syndrome (AHUS) was reported to be the most expensive medicine in the world with annual treatment costs between US$ 350,000 and US$ 500,000 per patient [29]. The arguments brought forward to justify high prices of OMP are twofold: (1) OMP are intended to have only small sales volume due to small patient groups. According to the EU definition, for instance, orphan medicines are used to treat diseases which are defined as life threatening or chronically debilitation diseases with a prevalence of ≤5 in 10,000 individuals[3]; (2) OMP can be among medicines for which high costs of research and development are claimed for [30]. However, due to the large number of OMP, they can have a large impact on national budgets. In Belgium it was reported that pharmaceutical expenditures made up 5% of the Belgian hospital medicines budget in 2008 (1.9% of total pharmaceutical expenditures), with an estimated increasing tendency for the next 5 years [31].

The relevance of OMP motivated several researchers to explore and explain the driving factors of high prices for OMP. Aballea S, Toumi M, Vataire A, Millier A and Lamure M [32] investigated the determinants of OMP prices in five European countries (France, Italy, Germany, Spain and UK). Their analysis included all products with an orphan designation approved by the European Medicines Agency (EMA) and showed that prices of OMP were highest in Italy and lowest in the UK. A linear regression on prices and several disease-related variables (e.g., prevalence, disease area, prognosis, age and vulnerability of target population) found no correlation between any of the variables and the price. Low prevalence and low number of available treatment alternatives seemed most likely associated with a higher price, but these trends were not statistically significant. Other authors used similar methods. When Picavet E, Morel T, Cassiman D and Simoens S [33] wanted to '*shine a light in the black box of OMP pricing*',

[3] In other regions of the world different definitions are applied: In the US the rare-disease prevalence criterion is set at ≤7.5 per 10,000 inhabitants, in Japan the respective figure is ≤4 per 10,000 inhabitants and in Australia it is fewer than ≤1 per 10,000 inhabitants.

they calculated annual treatment costs per indication per patient in six European countries (Belgium, the Netherlands, Czech Republic, France, Italy and UK) and investigated the possible influence of disease-related and medicine-related factors on those costs. The authors showed that OMP, originated from an established product approved for a common disease ('repurposed'), orally administered OMP, and OMP with availability of alternative treatments were associated with lower treatment costs. In contrast, OMP with multiple (orphan) indications, for chronic treatments or for which an improvement in overall survival or quality of life had been demonstrated, contributed to higher annual treatment costs. Differences in national pricing and reimbursement regulations showed no association with the annual treatment costs of OMP. This last result was used as a starting point for Medic G, Korchagina D, Young KE et al. [34], which aimed to study whether or not price differences for OMP reflect priorities in national health systems. In particular, the authors aimed to investigate how public payers value rarity in pricing decisions. A similar approach as the one applied by Picavet E, Morel T, Cassiman D and Simoens S [33] was used but only diseases-related factors were considered for explaining annual treatment costs of 120 OMP in seven European countries (France, Germany, Italy, Norway, Spain, Sweden and UK). The annual treatment costs per patient ranged from €755 to €1,051,956 in the studied countries. The results of their analysis supported the hypothesis that policy makers value rarity, as there was a statistically significant inverse correlation between annual treatment costs and diseases prevalence in all countries. This relation was even stronger when the analysis focused on the rarest diseases.

The body of literature that is dedicated to a comparison of OMP prices is not as abundant as studies exploring the driving factors of OMP prices. Young KE, Soussi I, Hemels M and Toumi M [35] aimed to assess price differences of 120 OMP between seven European countries (France, Germany, Italy, Norway, Spain, Sweden and UK) by considering annual treatment costs per patient as an approximation for price levels. As base country for the comparisons the authors chose the UK and calculated respective ratios. Compared to the UK, the average annual treatment costs were highest in France (13% above UK costs), Germany (11%), Italy (8%) and Spain (7%). Lower average annual treatment costs were found in Sweden (−2%) and Norway (−12%). However, the authors reasoned that average ratios for treatment costs may not reflect the full picture, since they observed a large variation between price ratios of OMP. Prices of some OMP were 74% lower than UK prices and some were nearly twice the price (+92%) of the UK counterpart. When Blankart CR, Stargardt T and Schreyögg J [36] investigated differences in the availability of OMP and in patient access to them in 11 countries (Australia, Canada, England, France, Germany, Hungary, the Netherlands, Poland, Slovakia, Switzerland and the US) prices were defined as one of the three indicators to measure patient access. Price information for four orphan diseases (pulmonary arterial hypertension, Fabry disease, hereditary angioedema and chronic myeloid leukaemia) was collected from national sources and calculated for a 30-day treatment period based on pharmacy retail prices and defined daily doses (DDD). Prices were found to be highest in Germany and the US and lowest in Canada, Australia and England. Although most of the countries in the sample consider threshold criteria for cost-effectiveness in their coverage decisions for medicines (including OMP), this did not seem to be an impediment to prices since they were high for all included medicines when compared to most non-orphan medicines. Furthermore, there were some cross-country budget impact analyses of OMP, with differing methodological approaches of calculating budget impacts. In a study published in 2011, Schey C, Milanova T and Hutchings A [37] assessed the budget impact of orphan medicines in Europe between 2010 and 2020 by predicting the number of diseases for which new OMP would be approved during that period and estimating the average ex-factory price across an OMP disease life cycle. This data was used to estimate the OMP cost per orphan disease. According to their model, over the period of 10 years the annual cost per patient of existing OMP would vary among the 18 examined European countries between €1251 and €407,631 with the median cost being €32,242 per year. The authors predicted that the share of total pharmaceutical market represented by OMP would increase from 3.3% in 2010 to peak off 4.6% in 2016, after which it was expected to level off through 2020.

Prices for OMP can also be studied in a national context: Simoens S, Cassiman D, Picavet E and Dooms M [31] and Picavet E, Dooms M, Cassiman D and Simoens S [38] examined OMP prices in Belgium. Both studies focused on hospital procurement prices as OMP are often administered in hospital settings and paid out of the hospital budget. While Simoens S, Cassiman D, Picavet E and Dooms M [31] compared hospital prices of OMP to the hospital compounding production costs to estimate possible production costs, Picavet E, Dooms M, Cassiman D and Simoens S [38] compared prices of medicines with an orphan designation approved by EMA to prices of medicines that were used for the treatment of rare disease indications but did not have an orphan designation. The first study showed that the hospital procurement prices for some pharmaceutical specialties exceeded the compounding production cost, ranging from a 2.5-fold difference to a 148-fold difference. In the latter study, Belgian median prices of designated OMP were found to be eight times higher (€138.56, IQR €406.57) than median prices of non-designated OMP (€16.55, IQR €28.05).

3.3 MEDICINES FOR SPECIFIC INDICATIONS

Price studies on medicines for specific indications may reflect the global interest in particular medicine group. Ten years ago studies focused on antiretroviral (ARV) medicines for the treatment of HIV, then they shifted to cancer medicines while in recent years several studies on new Hepatitis C treatments were done.

3.3.1 HIV/AIDS Medicines

The burden of HIV/AIDS has for long been a major concern for policy makers all over the world. It was projected that HIV/AIDS would be the cause of 117 million deaths in the period of 2006–30 and would particularly affect LMIC where coverage of preventive and curative measures is comparably lower [39]. However, treatment developments, particularly the ARV therapy, have changed the face of HIV/AIDS and transformed it from a life-threatening infection to a chronic disease [40]. However, high prices of ARV limiting affordability have been identified as an ongoing barrier to treatment access. Although the entry of generic ARV had resulted in substantial price reductions, regular price comparisons and continuous monitoring are still needed to increase transparency and ensure support to governmental and non-governmental organisations during price negotiations. When the first procurement price report of the Global Fund was released in August 2004, Vasan A, Hoos D, Mukherjee JS et al. [41] analysed the procurement price of 10 most commonly used adult formulation ARV in LMIC to examine the procurement behaviour of principal recipients of Global Fund grants. The authors found that prices in low-income countries (LIC) were consistently lower than prices reported by the research-based pharmaceutical industry. In lower middle-income countries, prices were more varied and in several instances very high in relation to the respective per capita income of the country. In general, ARV prices in LMIC were still significantly high given limited per capita income of the country. Seoane-Vazquez E and Rodriguez-Monguio R [42] did a comparison of procurement prices of ARV in the Andean countries. They collected price information of ARV purchased by public programmes through surveys of ministries of health and compared them to the results of the joint price negotiations that the Andean countries had in 2003 and 2004. The results showed that the joint negotiations did indeed achieve lower prices: prices paid in the public programmes were on average 65% higher than the negotiated prices. These differences in negotiated prices and previously paid prices represented almost 40% of the programmes' ARV expenditures in 2004. The effectiveness in pooled procurement on a global scale was also examined by Waning B, Kaplan W, King AC et al. [43]. The authors compared the impact of strategies, such as pooled procurement arrangements, third-party price negotiation and tiered (or differential) pricing (i.e., pricing considering the economic situation, and thus ability-to-pay of a country) on the price of ARV. For 19 out of 24 ARV, no association between price and purchased volume was detected, and the remainder price reductions related to volume amounted to between 4% and 21%. 9 of 13 generic ARV were priced 6%—36% lower when purchased by a global organisation. The study illustrated that tiered pricing strategies did not deliver the benefits of lower prices (see also Chapter 13.5 on alternative pricing options) compared to other strategies. Pooled procurement had a limited impact on prices and generic competition seemed to be more effective in lowering prices.

The success of price negotiations for ARV — either on national or global scale — depends largely on the availability of reliable benchmarks. Wirtz VJ, Santa-Ana-Tellez Y, Trout CH and Kaplan WA [44] developed several methods for benchmarking the procurement price of ARV in order to provide guidance to procurement agencies. The authors analysed prices of first-line and second-line ARV combinations in 13 Latin American Countries (LAC) in 2008 and found large price variations in the region. Most examined LAC could treat between 1.17 and 3.8 times more patients if procurement prices were closer to the lowest regional generic price. This effect was even more pronounced for second-line combinations where a price closer to the lowest regional originator prices or to the global median transaction price for lower middle-income countries would result in treatment of almost five times more patients.

Overall, there are large differences in the global landscape of ARV prices. When analysing the transactional data on donor-funded ARV procurement between 2003 and 2015, Sagaon-Teyssier L, Singh S, Dongmo-Nguimfack B and Moatti J-P [45] found average prices of originator ARV in the sub-Saharan African region to be lower than the average generic ARV prices. By contrast, originator medicines were found to be most expensive in Europe and Central Asia, and generic medicines were least expensive.

3.3.2 Cancer Medicines

While affordable access to HIV/AIDS medicines is — due to the large burden of disease — more relevant to LMIC, attention in OECD countries has rather shifted towards other indications. The increasing fraction of pharmaceutical expenditure attributed to cancer medicines has become a challenge and a major concern in those countries. Degrassat-Theas A, Bensadon M, Rieu C et al. [46] assessed the bargaining power of French hospitals in their negotiation with pharmaceutical companies in the monopoly market of innovative cancer medicines after the implementation of policy changes. The authors calculated indices to compare the change in the total purchase costs for the same bundle of medicines between the year prior (2004) and 3 years after (2005—07) to the implementation of policy changes. Although the results showed price decreases from 2004 to 2005, they did not seem to be lasting for a longer period as between the entire period from 2004 to 2007, expenditures on value for all cancer medicines rose annually by 22.5%. The authors conjectured that the large increases were related to the provisions of the new regulation extending access to all new cancer medicines for all eligible patients. Prior to the regulation, hospitals had received fixed annual budgets for their overall expenses which seemed to had incentivised restricted access in French hospital settings. Differences in prices were shown to be even more pronounced at the global scale. Vogler S, Vitry A and Babar Z-U-D [47] conducted a cross-country price comparison in 16 European countries plus Australia and New Zealand. The authors compared the unit prices of 31 originator cancer medicines at the ex-factory price level and their results showed large variations between countries. The difference of a medicine price between the highest priced country and the lowest priced country ranged from 28% to 388%. In the analysis, prices in Greece were often identified as lowest prices, whereas Sweden, Switzerland and Germany showed price data in similarly high ranges. Goldstein DA, Clark J, Tu Y et al. [48] compared patterns of affordability of cancer medicines in Australia, China, India, Israel, South Africa, UK and the US, thus selecting countries of large variability in national per capita income. To account for difference in wealth the authors applied weights in the form of GDP per capita and average salary per month. Results confirmed results of several previous price studies [18,49] that indicated the highest prices in the US.

Despite lower prices in MIC than in the US, cancer medicines are less affordable in MIC than in HIC, with India ranking last in terms of affordability.

3.3.3 Hepatitis C Medicines

The market launch of the latest class of hepatitis C virus (HCV) treatments opened the next chapter that attracted global attention. Until recently, the standard treatment recommendation of HCV (pegylated interferon and ribavirin) resulted in sustained virological response (SVR) of 54%–63% in clinical trials while showing severe side effects. The development of direct-acting antivirals (DAAs) has been a turning point in improving treatment efficacy and administration, with SVR up to 93% of trial participants with a once-daily orally administered therapy. Since then, other DAA regimes have gained regulatory approval. They all have in common high prices that would have brought solidarity-based health systems at the verge of sustainability if all patients had been granted access to those medicines at the same time. The increased interest went along with several studies on consequences of high prices. Iyengar S, Tay-Teo K, Vogler S et al. [50] compared prices and affordability of two treatment regimens across 30 countries to assess affordability to health systems and patients. The median nominal ex-factory price of a 12-week course of sofosbuvir was US$ 42,017, ranging from US$ 37,729 in Japan to US$ 64,680 in the US. However, when prices were adjusted for PPPs, Poland and Turkey had higher prices than the US. Treating the entire viraemic population with PPP-adjusted prices and an assumed 23% price reduction would amount to 10.5% of the total pharmaceutical expenditure in the Netherlands, up to 190.5% in Poland.

3.3.4 Further Indications

Price studies were also conducted for other medicine groups including antimalarials [51], antiepileptics [52], antihypertensives [53], medicines to treat asthma [54], Alzheimer's disease [55], cardiovascular diseases [56], and common chronic conditions such as diabetes, psychiatric disorders, gastroesophageal reflux [57–59] and medicines that have been included in the WHO model list of essential medicines [60,61].

3.4 HOSPITAL MEDICINES

Price studies on hospital medicines are rather scarce. This may be attributed to three mutually reinforcing factors: (1) Depending on the organisation of national healthcare systems with regard to the provision of (pharmaceutical) services and their financing, the definition and classification of hospital medicines vary between countries. Medicines that are mainly administered in the outpatient sector in one country could be assigned to the inpatient sector in another country [26]. (2) Certain groups of medicines are exclusively distributed through hospitals (e.g., OMP, cancer medicines) [62], and in these cases studies are rather related to these groups (e.g., medicines with an orphan designation approval by EMA) than to the point of administration. (3) Due to the fragmentation in the hospital sector, prices of medicines used in the inpatient sector may differ between hospitals in a country, and they are not published in national price databases in several countries. This is especially the case for 'actual' discounted prices agreed in negotiations between hospitals and pharmaceutical companies [47]. Because of these reasons prices of hospital medicines were rather compared in the national context, particularly if no centralised procurement unit existed and hospitals procured medicines individually [46]. An example of a European price comparison of high-cost hospital medicines is provided by Vogler S, Schneider P and Zimmermann N [26], with the classification of 'hospital medicines' referring to the sector where those medicines were mainly administered in Austria. The cross-country comparison showed that Sweden had most frequently ex-factory prices in the highest price quartile (83% of the 15 medicines) followed by Germany (73%) and Finland (53%). The authors identified Hungary and Greece as low-price countries, with Greece displaying the lowest prices in 74% of the medicines in the sample.

3.5 NON-PRESCRIPTION MEDICINES

There are rather few price studies related to non-prescription medicines (NPM). A possible explanation of the rarity of these price studies is the fact that NPM tend to be not price-regulated in most countries, and price data are often not available [63]. Two notable exemptions are Danzon PM and Furukawa MF [64] and Stargardt T, Schreyogg J and Busse R [65], both using different methodological approaches. Danzon PM and Furukawa MF [64] used IQVIA data for 12 OECD countries and applied the concept of index calculation to examine how quantity of services, mix of compounds, prices and other factors contribute to differences in pharmaceutical spending, including spending on NPM. In all countries prices of NPM were found to be at least 80% higher than in the US. In Italy, Japan, Spain and Chile prices indices of NMP were even three times higher than prices in the US. High NPM consumption and low NPM prices in the US were attributed to its highly price-competitive retail pharmacy market, dominated by large chains, many of which produce their own private-labelled generic medicines. According to the authors, a contributing factor to the observed price differences may be the fact that most of the other countries in the survey, which regulated prescription prices, also tend to regulate NPM prices directly or via retail price maintenance. A different approach was chosen by Stargardt T, Schreyogg J and Busse R [65] who surveyed pharmacy retail prices of five selected NPM in 256 community pharmacies in Germany. The authors found that 2 years after a price deregulation at wholesale and pharmacy level took place in Germany, 7.5% of the prices for NPM differed from their pre-deregulation level. Population density and geographic concentration of pharmacies were identified as the most likely factors associated with price changes, although coefficient of geographic concentration of pharmacies was negative.

3.6 CONCLUSION

The aim of this chapter was to provide an overview about the 'landscape' of pricing studies for certain groups of medicines and to investigate whether, or not, research interest with regard to price studies varies between medicine groups. The review found large variation in the number of studies per medicine group: with regard to therapeutic groups, HIV/AIDS and cancer medicines were the scope of many price studies, and prices of OMP, other high-priced medicines as well as generics were also frequently analysed. The studies were based on different methodological approaches depending on the investigated medicine groups. Studies on generic medicines tended to include a large number of medicines – in some cases the entire off-patent market of one or more countries – and to calculate average price levels. On the other hand, none of the studies on OMP examined average price levels but these studies were rather interested in explaining driving factors of their high prices. The chosen approach in the examined price studies reflects the research interest. There is no 'one-method-fits-all' but a plurality of approaches; each of them can be justified in the light of the study purpose. While there is abundant literature on prices of certain medicine groups, price studies on other groups are scarce. For instance, prices of biosimilar medicines were analysed in only a few cases, and those studies seemed to rather focus on their savings potential within national healthcare system than price analysis or comparison. Due to the recent patent expiration of some biological medicines and further biologicals being on the verge of the 'patent cliff', comprehensive price studies on biosimilars – as regularly conducted for generics – are interesting candidates for future research.

REFERENCES

[1] Health Action International (HAI). Collecting evidence on medicine prices & availability. Update to the manual 2016. Available from: http://haiweb.org/what-we-do/price-availability-affordability/collecting-evidence-on-medicine-prices-availability/. 2016 Available from: Update to the manual 2016. Available from: http://haiweb.org/what-we-do/price-availability-affordability/collecting-evidence-on-medicine-prices-availability/.

[2] World Health Organization (WHO). Measuring medicine prices, availability, affordability and price components. 2nd ed. Geneva: Health Action International (HAI); 2008.

[3] World Health Organziation (WHO), Health Action International (HAI). Medicine Prices. A new approach to measurement. Working draft for field testing and revision. World Health Origanization, Health Action International; 2003.

[4] Jiang M, Yang S, Yan K, Liu J, Zhao J, Fang Y. Measuring access to medicines: a survey of prices, availability and affordability in Shaanxi Province of China. PLoS One 2013;8(8):e70836.

[5] Yang H, Dib HH, Zhu M, Qi G, Zhang X. Prices, availability and affordability of essential medicines in rural areas of Hubei Province, China. Health Policy and Planning 2009;25(3):219–29.

[6] Babar ZUD, Ibrahim MIM, Singh H, Bukahri NI, Creese A. Evaluating drug prices, availability, affordability, and price components: implications for access to drugs in Malaysia. PLoS Medicine 2007;4(3):e82. https://doi.org/10.1371/journal.pmed.0040082.

[7] Balasubramaniam R, Benaragama B, Ranganathan SS. A national survey of price and affordability of key essential medicines for children in Sri Lanka. The Indian Journal of Pediatrics 2014;81(4):362–7.

[8] Dabare PRL, Wanigatunge CA, Beneragama BH. A national survey on availability, price and affordability of selected essential medicines for non communicable diseases in Sri Lanka. BMC Public Health 2014;14(1):817.

[9] Senarathna SG, Mannapperuma U, Fernandopulle BR. Medicine prices, availability and affordability in Sri Lanka. Indian Journal of Pharmacology 2011;43(1):60.

[10] Gooi M, Bell CM. Differences in generic drug prices between the US and Canada. Applied Health Economics and Health Policy 2008;6(1):19–26.

[11] Cameron A, Ewen M, Ross-Degnan D, Ball D, Laing R. Medicine prices, availability, and affordability in 36 developing and middle-income countries: a secondary analysis. The Lancet 2009;373(9659):240–9.

[12] Mansfield SJ. Generic drug prices and policy in Australia: room for improvement? A comparative analysis with England. Australian Health Review 2014;38(1):6–15.

[13] Kwon H-Y, Kim H, Godman B, Reich MR. The impact of South Korea's new drug-pricing policy on market competition among off-patent drugs. Expert Review of Pharmacoeconomics and Outcomes Research 2015;15(6):1007–14.

[14] Vogler S, Lepuschütz L, Schneider P, Stühlinger V. Study on enhanced cross-country coordination in the area of pharmaceutical product pricing. In: European commission, directorate-general for health and food safety. Brussels: Publications Office of the European Union; 2016.

[15] Brick A, Gorecki P, Nolan A. Ireland: pharmaceutical prices, prescribing practices and usage of generics in a comparative context. Dublin: Economic Social Research Institute Research Series; 2013.
[16] Vogler S. How large are the differences between originator and generic prices? Analysis of five molecules in 16 European countries. Farmeconomia Health Economics and Therapeutic Pathways 2012;13(Suppl. 3):29–41.
[17] Dukes MNG. Drugs and money: prices, affordability and cost containment. IOS Press; 2003.
[18] Danzon PM, Kim JD. International price comparisons for pharmaceuticals. Pharmacoeconomics 1998;14(1):115–28.
[19] Aho E, Johansson P, Rönnholm G. International price comparison of pharmaceuticals 2016 – a volume based analysis of Swedish pharmaceutical prices relative to 19 other European countries. Stockholm: Agency DaPB; 2017.
[20] Wouters OJ, Kanavos PG. A comparison of generic drug prices in seven European countries: a methodological analysis. BMC Health Services Research 2017;17(1):242.
[21] Rovira J, Lindner L, Giménez E, Espín J, de Labry AO, García L. Biosimilars in the European market. GaBI Journal 2013;2(1):30–5.
[22] Rémuzat C, Dorey J, Cristeau O, Ionescu D, Radière G, Toumi M. Key drivers for market penetration of biosimilars in Europe. Journal of Market Access and Health Policy 2017;5(1):1272308.
[23] Kawalec P, Stawowczyk E, Tesar T, Skoupa J, Turcu-Stiolica A, Dimitrova M, et al. Pricing and reimbursement of biosimilars in central and Eastern European countries. Frontiers in Pharmacology 2017;8(288).
[24] Haustein R, de Millas C, Höer A, Häussler B. Saving money in the European healthcare systems with biosimilars. GaBI Journal 2012;1(3–4):120–6.
[25] Mack A. Norway, biosimilars in different funding systems. What works? GaBI Journal 2015;4(2):90–2.
[26] Vogler S, Schneider P, Zimmermann N. Preisvergleich kostenintensiver Arzneimittel 2015 (Wissenschaftlicher Endbericht). Wien: Gesundheit Österreich GmbH; 2016.
[27] Busse R, Panteli D, Schaufler J, Schröder H, Telschow C, Weiss J. Preise patentgeschützter Arzneimittel im europäischen Vergleich. In: Die deutschen Arzneimittelpreise im Vergleich zu den Listenpreisen in fünf ausgewählten europäischen Ländern Wissenschaftliches Institut der AOK (WIdO) und TU Berlin Unter; 2016. http://www.wido.de/arz_arzneimittelmark/EU-Preisvergleich_2016.html. Berlin.
[28] Merkur S, Mossialos E. A pricing policy towards the sourcing of cheaper drugs in Cyprus. Health Policy 2007;81(2–3):368–75.
[29] Meekings KN, Williams CS, Arrowsmith JE. Orphan drug development: an economically viable strategy for biopharma R&D. Drug Discovery Today 2012;17(13):660–4.
[30] Drummond MF, Wilson DA, Kanavos P, Ubel P, Rovira J. Assessing the economic challenges posed by orphan drugs. International Journal of Technology Assessment in Health Care 2007;23(1):36–42.
[31] Simoens S, Cassiman D, Picavet E, Dooms M. Are some orphan drugs for rare diseases too expensive? A study of purchase versus compounding costs. Drugs and Therapy Perspectives 2011;27(10):24–6.
[32] Aballea S, Toumi M, Vataire A, Millier A, Lamure M. PHP6 Quantitative Analysis of the influence of disease and product characteristics on Orphan drug prices in Europe. Value in Health 2010;13(3):A82.
[33] Picavet E, Morel T, Cassiman D, Simoens S. Shining a light in the black box of orphan drug pricing. Orphanet Journal of Rare Diseases 2014;9(1):62.

[34] Medic G, Korchagina D, Young KE, Toumi M, Postma MJ, Wille M, et al. Do payers value rarity? An analysis of the relationship between disease rarity and orphan drug prices in Europe. Journal of Market Access and Health Policy 2017;5(1):1299665.
[35] Young KE, Soussi I, Hemels M, Toumi M. A comparative study of orphan drug prices in Europe. Journal of Market Access and Health Policy 2017;5(1):1297886.
[36] Blankart CR, Stargardt T, Schreyögg J. Availability of and access to orphan drugs. Pharmacoeconomics 2011;29(1):63–82.
[37] Schey C, Milanova T, Hutchings A. Estimating the budget impact of orphan medicines in Europe: 2010-2020. Orphanet Journal of Rare Diseases 2011;6(1):62.
[38] Picavet E, Dooms M, Cassiman D, Simoens S. Drugs for rare diseases: influence of orphan designation status on price. Applied Health Economics and Health Policy 2011;9(4):275–9.
[39] Mathers CD, Loncar D. Projections of global mortality and burden of disease from 2002 to 2030. PLoS Medicine 2006;3(11):e442.
[40] Deeks SG, Lewin SR, Havlir DV. The end of AIDS: HIV infection as a chronic disease. The Lancet 2013;382(9903):1525–33.
[41] Vasan A, Hoos D, Mukherjee JS, Farmer PE, Rosenfield AG, Perriëns JH. The pricing and procurement of antiretroviral drugs: an observational study of data from the Global Fund. Bulletin of the World Health Organization 2006;84(5):393–8.
[42] Seoane-Vazquez E, Rodriguez-Monguio R. Negotiating antiretroviral drug prices: the experience of the Andean countries. Health Policy and Planning 2007;22(2):63–72.
[43] Waning B, Kaplan W, King AC, Lawrence DA, Leufkens HG, Fox MP. Global strategies to reduce the price of antiretroviral medicines: evidence from transactional databases. Bulletin of the World Health Organization 2009;87(7):520–8.
[44] Wirtz VJ, Santa-Ana-Tellez Y, Trout CH, Kaplan WA. Allocating scarce financial resources for HIV treatment: benchmarking prices of antiretroviral medicines in Latin America. Health Policy and Planning 2012;27(8):638–48.
[45] Sagaon-Teyssier L, Singh S, Dongmo-Nguimfack B, Moatti J-P. Affordability of adult HIV/AIDS treatment in developing countries: modelling price determinants for a better insight of the market functioning. Journal of the International AIDS Society 2016;19(1).
[46] Degrassat-Theas A, Bensadon M, Rieu C, Angalakuditi M, Le Pen C, Paubel P. Hospital reimbursement price cap for cancer drugs: the French experience in controlling hospital drug expenditures. Pharmacoeconomics 2012;30(7):565–73.
[47] Vogler S, Vitry A, Babar Z-U-D. Cancer drugs in 16 European countries, Australia, and New Zealand: a cross-country price comparison study. The Lancet Oncology 2016;17(1):39–47.
[48] Goldstein DA, Clark J, Tu Y, Zhang J, Fang F, Goldstein R, et al. A global comparison of the cost of patented cancer drugs in relation to global differences in wealth. Oncotarget 2017;8(42).
[49] Kanavos PG, Vandoros S. Determinants of branded prescription medicine prices in OECD countries. Health Economics, Policy and Law 2011;6(3):337–67.
[50] Iyengar S, Tay-Teo K, Vogler S, Beyer P, Wiktor S, de Joncheere K, et al. Prices, costs, and affordability of new medicines for hepatitis C in 30 countries: an economic analysis. PLoS Medicine 2016;13(5):e1002032.
[51] Tougher S, Ye Y, Amuasi JH, Kourgueni IA, Thomson R, Goodman C, et al. Effect of the Affordable Medicines Facility—malaria (AMFm) on the availability, price, and market share of quality-assured artemisinin-based combination therapies in seven countries: a before-and-after analysis of outlet survey data. The Lancet 2012;380(9857): 1916–26.

[52] Cameron A, Bansal A, Dua T, Hill SR, Moshe SL, Mantel-Teeuwisse AK, et al. Mapping the availability, price, and affordability of antiepileptic drugs in 46 countries. Epilepsia 2012;53(6):962–9.
[53] Cho MH, Yoo KB, Lee HY, Lee KS, Kwon JA, Han KT, et al. The effect of new drug pricing systems and new reimbursement guidelines on pharmaceutical expenditures and prescribing behavior among hypertensive patients in Korea. Health Policy 2015;119(5):604–11.
[54] Babar ZU, Lessing C, Mace C, Bissell K. The availability, pricing and affordability of three essential asthma medicines in 52 low- and middle-income countries. Pharmacoeconomics 2013;31(11):1063–82.
[55] Suh G-H, Wimo A, Gauthier S, O'Connor D, Ikeda M, Homma A, et al. International price comparisons of Alzheimer's drugs: a way to close the affordability gap. International Psychogeriatrics 2009;21(6):1116–26.
[56] van Mourik MS, Cameron A, Ewen M, Laing RO. Availability, price and affordability of cardiovascular medicines: a comparison across 36 countries using WHO/HAI data. BMC Cardiovascular Disorders 2010;10(1):25.
[57] Garuoliene K, Godman B, Gulbinovič J, Wettermark B, Haycox A. European countries with small populations can obtain low prices for drugs: Lithuania as a case history. Expert Review of Pharmacoeconomics and Outcomes Research 2011;11(3):343–9.
[58] World Health Organization. Price, availability and affordability: an international comparison of chronic disease medicines. 2006.
[59] Khatib R, McKee M, Shannon H, Chow C, Rangarajan S, Teo K, et al. Availability and affordability of cardiovascular disease medicines and their effect on use in high-income, middle-income, and low-income countries: an analysis of the PURE study data. The Lancet 2016;387(10013):61–9.
[60] Mendis S, Fukino K, Cameron A, Laing R, Filipe Jr A, Khatib O, et al. The availability and affordability of selected essential medicines for chronic diseases in six low-and middle-income countries. Bulletin of the World Health Organization 2007;85(4):279–88.
[61] Wang H, Sun Q, Vitry A, Nguyen TA. Availability, price, and affordability of selected essential medicines for chronic diseases in 11 countries of the Asia Pacific region: a secondary analysis. Asia-Pacific Journal of Public Health 2017;29(4). https://doi.org/10.1177/1010539517700472.
[62] Gammie T, Lu CY, Babar ZU. Access to orphan drugs: a comprehensive review of legislations, regulations and policies in 35 countries. PLoS ONE [Electronic Resource] 2015;10(10):e0140002.
[63] Vogler S, Arts D, Sandberger K. Impact of pharmacy deregulation and regulation in European countries. Vienna: Gesundheit Österreich Forschungs- und Planungs GmbH; 2012.
[64] Danzon PM, Furukawa MF. International prices and availability of pharmaceuticals in 2005. Health Affairs 2008;27(1):221–33.
[65] Stargardt T, Schreyogg J, Busse R. Pricing behaviour of pharmacies after market deregulation for OTC drugs: the case of Germany. Health Policy 2007;84(1):30–8. Epub 2007/06/08.
[66] Tuncay B. Generic competition and price regulation in pharmaceuticals: evidence from the European Union. International Journal of Industrial Organization; 2015.
[67] Dylst P, Simoens S. Does the market share of generic medicines influence the price Level?: a European analysis. Pharmacoeconomics 2011;29(10):875–82.
[68] Vogler S, Kilpatrick K, Babar Z-U-D. Analysis of medicine prices in New Zealand and 16 European countries. Value in Health 2015;18(4):484–92.

[69] Logviss K, Krievins D, Purvina S. Impact of orphan drugs on Latvian budget. Orphanet Journal of Rare Diseases 2016;11(1):59.
[70] Orofino J, Soto J, Casado MA, Oyagüez I. Global spending on orphan drugs in France, Germany, the UK, Italy and Spain during 2007. Applied Health Economics and Health Policy 2010;8(5):301–15.
[71] Liu Y, Galárraga O. Do national drug policies influence antiretroviral drug prices? Evidence from the Southern African Development community. Health Policy and Planning 2017;32(2):170–7.
[72] Vogler S, Schneider P, Zimmermann N. European price comparison of high cost hospital medicines. European Journal of Hospital Pharmacy 2016;23(Suppl. 1):A163–4.
[73] Roughead EE, Lopert R, Sansom LN. Prices for innovative pharmaceutical products that provide health gain: a comparison between Australia and the United States. Value in Health 2007;10(6):514–20.
[74] Hsiao F-Y, Tsai Y-W, Huang W-F. Price regulation, new entry, and information shock on pharmaceutical market in Taiwan: a nationwide data-based study from 2001 to 2004. BMC Health Services Research 2010;10(1):218.
[75] Martikainen J, Kivi I, Linnosmaa I. European prices of newly launched reimbursable pharmaceuticals – a pilot study. Health Policy 2005;74(3):235–46.
[76] Morel CM, McGuire A, Mossialos E. The level of income appears to have no consistent bearing on pharmaceutical prices across countries. Health Affairs 2011;30(8):1545–52.
[77] Niëns LM, Cameron A, Van de Poel E, Ewen M, Brouwer WB, Laing R. Quantifying the impoverishing effects of purchasing medicines: a cross-country comparison of the affordability of medicines in the developing world. PLoS Medicine 2010;7(8): e1000333.
[78] Kanavos P, Ferrario A, Vandoros S, Anderson GF. Higher US branded drug prices and spending compared to other countries may stem partly from quick uptake of new drugs. Health Affairs 2013;32(4):753–61.

CHAPTER 4

Studies of Medicine Price Developments

Peter Schneider, Sabine Vogler
WHO Collaborating Centre for Pharmaceutical Pricing and Reimbursement Policies, Pharmacoeconomics Department, Gesundheit Österreich GmbH (GÖG/Austrian Public Health Institute), Vienna, Austria

LIST OF ABBREVIATIONS

ACE	Angiotensin-converting enzyme
ATC	Anatomical Therapeutic Chemical classification of the World Health Organization
EPR	External price referencing
EU	European Union
OECD	Organisation for Economic Co-operation and Development
OMP	Orphan medicinal product
US	United States

4.1 IMPACT ASSESSMENT

This chapter aims to present existing evidence on medicine price studies that investigated medicine prices over time. Table 4.1 provides an overview of major studies in this area. Although the number of studies presented is not particularly high, it points to the variation in their methodological design. First – and most obvious – there were differences with regard to the price type whose developments were examined. Some studies focused on ex-factory prices [1–3], some on wholesale or pharmacy purchasing prices [4,5] and some on retail prices [6–8]. In addition, developments in procurement prices were also of research interest, and one example of such a study [9] is included in Table 4.1. Studies on medicine price developments also show variations with regard to other methodological choices and the framework (national vs. international).

The aim of an impact assessment is to analyse the effects (outcomes) of an initiative such as a policy measure. In the area of pharmaceutical policy it can be challenging to identify effects and demonstrate the impact of an

Medicine Price Surveys, Analyses, and Comparisons
ISBN 978-0-12-813166-4
https://doi.org/10.1016/B978-0-12-813166-4.00009-7

Table 4.1 Key studies that analysed medicine prices over time

Author/ year	Title	Publication type	Years of survey/ analysis	Country/ region	Med. group(s)	Price type[a]	Methods/ data source	Key results	References
Benda et al., 2004	An econometric estimation of pricing of brand-name drugs	Article in *Applied Health Economics and Health Policy*	February 1997 —June 2003	CA	Products used in treatment of hypertension; angiotensin-converting enzyme (ACE) inhibitors and angiotensin II receptor blockers (ARBs)	Pharmacy purchasing price	Prices were obtained from IQVIA Canadian Drugstore and Hospital for a regression analysis	Prices decreased when the number of products within the same sub-therapeutic class (i.e., ATC-4 group) increased. However, when competitor products were classified in a different ATC-4 group, then prices increased. In general, the average price of medicines within the therapeutic class increased over time, and it was identified as a main driver of pharmaceutical expenditure.	[4]
Danzon/ Taylor 2010	Drug Pricing and Value in Oncology	Article in *The Oncologist*	May 2004 —May 2009	CA, US	10 cancer medicines and 108 non-cancer medicines	Wholesale price	Prices were obtained from official databases and used to calculate cost/ QALY	Comparing cancer with non-cancer medicines, the overall mean, median and minimum were all higher for cancer medicines. While the mean and median cost/QALYs were 7% and 12% higher, the minimum cost/QALY of cancer medicines was the fourfold of non-cancer	[5]

								medicines' minimum QALY. The structure of the reimbursement system may incentivise manufacturers to set relatively high prices.	
Dylst/ Simoens 2011	Does the Market Share of Generic Medicines Influence the Price Level?	Article in *Pharmacoeconomics*	June 2002 —March 2007	DE, DK, NL, SE, UK	35 medicines based on the top 35 best-selling active substances	Ex-factory prices	Data were obtained from IQVIA and used for a descriptive analysis	Comparing the prices of originator (i.e., non-generic) and generic medicines both dropped over time independent of the generic market share. However, the decrease in countries with a high generic market share was twice the size of the price decrease in countries with low generic market share (−43.18% and −21.6% respectively). This trend was not limited to the aggregated level, but could also be observed at the single country level.	[1]
Håkonsen et al., 2009	Price control as a strategy for pharmaceutical cost containment—What has been achieved in Norway in the period 1994—2004?	Article in *Health Policy*	1994 —2004	NO	POM	Retail prices	Data were obtained from official statistics of the Norwegian Association of Pharmaceutical Manufacturers	Price regulation of POM in combination with a regular revision of price information resulted in substantial price reductions. Regulatory approaches to introduce a more	[10]

Continued

Table 4.1 Key studies that analysed medicine prices over time—cont'd

Author/ year	Title	Publication type	Years of survey/ analysis	Country/ region	Med. group(s)	Price type[a]	Methods/ data source	Key results	References
								competitive environment in the off-patent market did not deliver the expected price reductions, but rather out-of-pocket payments increased.	
Kanavos/ Vandoros 2010	Determinants of branded prescription medicine prices in OECD countries	Article in *Health Economics, Policy and Law*	2004, 2007	AT, AU, BE, DE, EL, ES, FR, IT, JP, MX, PT, SE, SK, UK, US	50 originator branded POM	Ex-factory price and retail price	Data were obtained from IQVIA and used for a regression analysis	The study showed some sort of 'upward convergence' in the two surveyed years. The lowest prices appeared to be increasing for newer medicines, and, at the same time, price differences for those medicines decreased across countries. Furthermore, in five EU countries (DE, ES, FR, IT, UK) there seemed to be some price convergence over time.	[18]

Kanavos et al., 2013	Higher US Branded Drug Prices And Spending Compared To Other Countries May Stem Partly From Quick Uptake Of New Drugs	Article in *Health Affairs*	2005, 2007, 2010	AU, CA, CH, DE, FR, UK, US	68 originator branded POM which accounted for the highest combined sales in USD in 2010	Ex-factory price	Data were obtained from IQVIA Midas database and included prices, volume and sales at the product level	Applying different weights to price information (e.g., Laspeyres or Paasche Index), prices of brand name originator were found to be between 5% and 198% higher in the United States than in other countries in all three study years. Independent of weights, US prices increased more in relation to prices of the other surveyed countries.	[2]
Kaplan et al., 2013	The Market Dynamics of Generic Medicines in the Private Sector of 19 Low and Middle Income Countries between 2001 and 2011: A Descriptive Time Series Analysis	Article in *PLOS*	2001–11	AR, BD, BR, CL, CO, DO, EC, EG, JO, MA, MX, PE, PH, PK, TH, TN, US, UY, ZA	In total 5131 different pharmaceutical substances (molecules or combination of molecules) were analysed. For the top ranked 30 originator medicines in each country, further analysis on price development was done.	Retail prices	Data were obtained from IQVIA database on an aggregated level and regrouped into different categories (originator medicines, unbranded generic medicines, branded generic medicines and patent products)	For 30 top-selling products in each country the effects of the originator's loss in market share were analysed by comparing the change of an originator's market share with the change in market share of the exact counterpart unbranded and branded pharmaceutical substances. In all examined countries, the branded generic market was higher than unbranded generic market share. With regard to price data it	[6]

Continued

Table 4.1 Key studies that analysed medicine prices over time—cont'd

Author/ year	Title	Publication type	Years of survey/ analysis	Country/ region	Med. group(s)	Price type[a]	Methods/ data source	Key results	References
								was noted that there is too little data to make meaningful price comparison between branded and unbranded generic medicines.	
Kohler et al., 2015	Does Pharmaceutical Pricing Transparency Matter? Examining Brazil's Public Procurement System	Article in *Globalization and Health*	2005–13	BR	19 medicines from the Brazilian positive list that were – due to their wide utilisation – of high relevance	Procurement prices	Data were obtained from the 'Banco de Preços em Saúde', and a regression analysis was done	The results from the simple linear regression model showed that only 4 out of 19 medicine prices decreased in all examined states significantly over the time period, while the price of one medicine increased significantly over time. Different results were obtained when using the mixed effects model, which suggests that there is no pattern of consistent price decreases during the period.	[9]

Kyle et al., 2008	Does Reimportation Reduce Price Differences for Prescription Drugs? Lessons from the European Union	Article in *Health Services Research*	1993 –2004	AR, AU, AT, BE, BR, CA, CH, CN, CO, CZ, DE, DK, EL, ES, FI, FR, IE, IT, JP, KO, LU, MX, NL, PL, PT, SE, TR, UK, US, ZA	1023 medicines of 36 therapeutic classes	Ex-factory price, wholesale price and retail price	Longitudinal data obtained from IQVIA were used for a regression analysis	Parallel trade had no significant impact on reducing price dispersion in EU countries. In these countries no substantial reduction was observed when they adopted parallel trade. However, in contrast to the other surveyed countries, price differentials in European countries decreased less.	[21]
Leopold et al., 2013	Is Europe still heading to a common price level for on-patent medicines? An exploratory study among 15 Western European Countries	Article in *Health Policy*	2007, 2008, 2010, 2011, 2012	AT, BE, DE, DK, EL, FI, FR, IE, IT, NL, NO, PT, ES, SE, CH	10 on-patent medicines from 5 different therapeutic classes which were reimbursed	Ex-factory price	Data provision from Pharmaceutical Price Information (PPI) service of the Austrian Public Health Institute	In the surveyed period a price divergence was observed that was mainly driven by Germany and Greece. While German prices were up to 27% more expensive than the average, Greek prices were up to 32% cheaper than the average. The remaining 13 countries had stable prices and centred around the average. In the surveyed period there was no large variation in prices as they remained relatively stable independent of a medicine's price.	[3]

Continued

Table 4.1 Key studies that analysed medicine prices over time—cont'd

Author/year	Title	Publication type	Years of survey/analysis	Country/region	Med. group(s)	Price type[a]	Methods/data source	Key results	References
Puig-Junoy/Lopez-Valcarcel, 2014	Launch prices for new pharmaceuticals in the heavily regulated and subsidised Spanish market, 1997–2005	Article in *Health Policy*	1997–2005	ES	114 pharmaceuticals approved by the Spanish Ministry of Health in the surveyed period	Retail price	Data were obtained from the Directorate General of Pharmacy and Health Products of the Ministry of Health	The regression analysis showed that in Spain therapeutically innovative products were not overpriced in relation to so-called me-too products. This was probably attributed to the national price setting mechanism, which was mainly used to adjust for inflation and did not account for innovation. In contrast, pharmaceuticals with a centralised EMA approval were rather overpriced.	[7]

Von Schulenberg et al., 2011	The effects of drug market regulation on pharmaceutical prices in Europe: overview and evidence from the market of ACE inhibitors	Article in *Health Economics Review*	1991 –2006	DE, DK, FR, NL, SE, UK	Angiotensin-converting enzyme (ACE) inhibitors	Retail prices	Data were obtained from IQVIA Midas database	The regression analysis showed that some measures targeting pharmaceutical expenditure in European countries appeared to be effective in reducing prices, while others had an insignificant effect. Supply-side measures like mandatory generic substitution, regressive pharmacy mark-ups and claw backs were found to be effective in reducing prices.	[8]

ACE, angiotensin-converting enzyme; *ARB*, angiotensin II receptor blockers; *ATC*, anatomical therapeutic chemical code of the World Health Organization; *EMA*, European medicines agency; *EU*, European Union; *OECD*, Organisation for Economic Co-operation and Development; *POM*, prescription-only medicines; *PPI*, pharma price information service of the Austrian Public Health Institute GÖG; *QALY*, quality-adjusted life years, Country abbreviations: *AR*, Argentina; *AT*, Austria; *AU*, Australia; *BD*, Bangladesh; *BE*, Belgium; *BR*, Brazil; *CA*, Canada; *CH*, Switzerland; *CL*, Chile; *CN*, China; *CO*, Colombia; *CZ*, Czech Republic; *DE*, Germany; *DK*, Denmark; *DO*, Dominican Republic; *EC*, Ecuador; *EG*, Egypt; *EL*, Greece; *ES*, Spain; *FI*, Finland; *FR*, France; *IE*, Ireland; *IT*, Italy; *JO*, Jordan; *JP*, Japan; *KO*, South Korea; *L*, Poland; *LU*, Luxembourg; MA, Morocco; *MX*, Mexico; *NL*, Netherlands; *NO*, Norway; *PE*, Peru; *PH*, Philippines; *PK*, Pakistan; *PPT*, Portugal; *SE*, Sweden; *SK*, Slovakia; *TH*, Thailand; *TN*, Tunisia; *TR*, Turkey; *UK*, United Kingdom; *US*, United States; *UY*, Uruguay; *ZA*, South Africa.

[a]All medicine price types are official list prices (i.e., without discounts).

intervention because of the multi-component nature of policy interventions. One outcome parameter is the development of medicine prices. Researchers who did such impact assessments used different methods, including descriptive analysis, time-series analysis and regression analysis.

To investigate the effect of interventions on medicine prices, different approaches have been reported in literature. Håkonsen H, Horn AM and Toverud E-L [10] observed the developments in medicine prices in Norway over a decade and attributed them to the implementation of pharmaceutical policies (descriptive analysis). Between 1994 and 2004 the general price level of medicines in Norway experienced on average an annual decrease of around 1%. The highest decreases in the general price level occurred in the years after the introduction of external price referencing (EPR) and annual revisions of the top-selling products. Another descriptive (time-series) analysis was conducted by Kaplan WA, Wirtz VJ and Stephens P [6] who examined market dynamics — including prices, volume and expenditures — for off-patent medicines in 19 countries in the period from 2001 until 2011. The authors analysed the impact of possible factors (e.g., prices) that could influence the market shares of branded and unbranded generic medicines. Dylst P and Simoens S [1] looked at the same variables but they investigated whether, or how, the penetration of generics in a market can impact the medicine price level in European off-patent markets. Another common approach to examine presumed linkages between interventions and outcomes is a regression analysis.[1] Depending on the context and the research question, there are different methodological techniques (e.g., linear regression, generalised regression) that can be applied in a regression analysis. One example for impact assessment is the study by Von der Schulenburg F, Vandoros S and Kanavos P [8] that aimed to analyse the impact of measures to increase generic uptake (e.g., generic substitution, distribution remuneration) on the prices of angiotensin-converting enzyme (ACE) inhibitors.

[1] A regression analysis is a statistical modelling approach that includes several different techniques. The rationale of all techniques subsumed under a regression analysis is to examine whether, or not, there is a relationship between one variable ('dependent variable') and another or more variables ('independent variable(s)'), and how good the latter can predict the result of the first one ('significance').

4.2 NATIONAL STUDIES

A medicine passes through several different stages; this is known as a 'product life cycle'. Some of the stages may bring changes in the regulatory and policy environment of pharmaceuticals that require an adaption of prices and induce different marketing strategies by the pharmaceutical industry [11]. Two key stages are the period under patent exclusivity, when the pharmaceutical product is on-patent, and the period when patents on the medicines expired and competitors enter the market. Economic theory suggests that dynamics during those both stages is determined through different forces [12]. Benda M-C, Mallory C and Lu H [4] found evidence for such developments during a product life cycle in Canada. The price of a medicine decreased during its life cycle when the number of products within the same sub-therapeutic class, i.e., at level 4 within the Anatomical Therapeutic Chemical (ATC) classification system increased. A reverse effect – increasing prices – was observed when competitor products were classified into a by-near but different ATC-4 group.

Another research question in this field is the development of the general price level at launch of pharmaceuticals and determinants of prices. Puig-Junoy J and López-Valcárcel BG [7] compared 114 pharmaceuticals that were approved by the Spanish Ministry of Health between 1997 and 2005. The authors developed an empirical model to examine determinants of launch prices for medicines over time. The results did not support the assumption that launch prices reflect the degree of innovation, but rather the pricing mechanism acts as an adjustment for inflation independently of the degree of innovation. The findings need to be interpreted in the context of the pharmaceutical policy environment in Spain, but the focus on determinants of launch prices could vary with national contexts. Other researchers, for instance, were rather interested in the link between transparency and price decreases for medicines [9].

4.3 CROSS-NATIONAL STUDIES

Analysing price developments of pharmaceuticals in different countries can be very challenging. Countries differ in several aspects – of which structure of the health system and economic indicators are among the most important ones – and available information on prices may not be as complete as needed for this kind of analysis. However, it was argued that even a comparison of countries with different levels of income is possible and can be done if it helps to answer the research question [13].

Cross-national studies of medicine price developments may contribute to determine whether, or not, prices of pharmaceuticals after launch had higher increase rates than other goods. The recent years have been characterised by the advent of several medicines, for which marketing authorisation holders demanded launch prices that were considered to jeopardise the financial sustainability of health system. While the case of sofosbuvir (Sovaldi) attracted most of public attention [14,15], it was just adding to concerns of payers related to the prices of some cancer medicines and orphan medicinal products (OMPs) [16,17]. Increasing prices were not only observed for individual medicines, but research findings also reported increases in medicine prices in general. Kanavos PG and Vandoros S [18] compared prices of 50 originator prescription-only medicines (POM) and found that the lowest price of newer medicines among the surveyed countries appeared to be increasing. A tendency towards increasing prices in seven OECD countries (Australia, Canada, Switzerland, Germany, France, United Kingdom and United States) was also found with regard to the general price level. In addition, the comparison showed that US prices increased more in relation to prices of the other surveyed countries [2]. Other authors suggested that this could be related to the health system that is not well designed and could incentivise manufacturers to set relatively high prices [5].

Another aim of cross-national studies can be to examine the existence of price divergence or price convergence. It has been argued that due to the current widespread use of EPR [19] there will be a tendency for price convergence for patented medicines [20]. Kanavos PG and Vandoros S [18] found some sort of price convergence in the five major European countries (Germany, Spain, France, Italy and United Kingdom). On the other hand, Leopold C, Mantel-Teeuwisse AK, Vogler S et al. [3] observed a divergence of medicine prices in the surveyed period from 2007 until 2012. However, this divergence was driven by two outliers — Germany in the upper part of the price scale and Greece in the lower end of the price scale — while the remaining 13 countries centred around the average.

A contributing factor to price convergence may be parallel trade of pharmaceuticals, which plays a role for countries in the European Union. According to the Treaty on the Functioning of the EU, a cornerstone of the European integration is the internal market and the free movement of goods, and this principle also applies to pharmaceuticals. Since the main reason of parallel trade is arbitrage of exporting countries (usually countries with lower prices) and importing countries (usually high-priced countries), economic theory suggests that prices between countries which engage in trade converge and arbitrages diminish over time. This effect was not observed for pharmaceuticals. Kyle MK, Allsbrook JS and Schulman KA [21] analysed 1023 medicines of 36 therapeutic classes in 30 countries and found that parallel trade had no significant impact on reducing price dispersion in EU countries. In these countries no substantial reduction in price differences was observed when they adopted parallel trade.

REFERENCES

[1] Dylst P, Simoens S. Does the market share of generic medicines influence the price Level?: a European analysis. Pharmacoeconomics 2011;29(10):875–82.
[2] Kanavos P, Ferrario A, Vandoros S, Anderson GF. Higher US branded drug prices and spending compared to other countries may stem partly from quick uptake of new drugs. Health Affairs 2013;32(4):753–61.
[3] Leopold C, Mantel-Teeuwisse AK, Vogler S, de Joncheere K, Laing RO, Leufkens HGM. Is Europe still heading to a common price level for on-patent medicines? An exploratory study among 15 Western European countries. Health Policy 2013;112:209–16.
[4] Benda M-C, Mallory C, Lu H. An econometric estimation of pricing of brand-name drugs. Applied Health Economics and Health Policy 2004;3(1 Suppl.):S12.
[5] Danzon PM, Taylor E. Drug pricing and value in oncology. The Oncologist 2010;15(Suppl. 1):24–31.
[6] Kaplan WA, Wirtz VJ, Stephens P. The market dynamics of generic medicines in the private sector of 19 low and middle income countries between 2001 and 2011: a descriptive time series analysis. PLoS One 2013;8(9):e74399.
[7] Puig-Junoy J, López-Valcárcel BG. Launch prices for new pharmaceuticals in the heavily regulated and subsidized Spanish market, 1995–2007. Health Policy 2014;116(2):170–81.
[8] Von der Schulenburg F, Vandoros S, Kanavos P. The effects of drug market regulation on pharmaceutical prices in Europe: overview and evidence from the market of ACE inhibitors. Health Economics Review 2011;1(1):18.
[9] Kohler JC, Mitsakakis N, Saadat F, Byng D, Martinez MG. Does pharmaceutical pricing transparency Matter? Examining Brazil's public procurement system. Globalization and Health 2015;11(1):34.
[10] Håkonsen H, Horn AM, Toverud E-L. Price control as a strategy for pharmaceutical cost containment—what has been achieved in Norway in the period 1994–2004? Health Policy 2009;90(2):277–85.
[11] Kesselheim AS. Rising health care costs and life-cycle management in the pharmaceutical market. PLoS Medicine 2013;10(6):e1001461.
[12] Kvesic DZ. Product lifecycle management: marketing strategies for the pharmaceutical industry. Journal of Medical Marketing 2008;8(4):293–301.
[13] World Health Organization (WHO). Measuring medicine prices, availability, affordability and price components. 2nd ed. Geneva: Health Action International (HAI); 2008.

[14] McCarthy M. Hepatitis C drug maker puts profit ahead of patients, US Senate report charges. BMJ British Medical Journal 2015;351.
[15] Gentile I, Maraolo AE, Niola M, Graziano V, Borgia G, Paternoster M. Limiting the access to direct-acting antivirals against HCV: an ethical dilemma. Expert Review of Gastroenterology and Hepatology 2016;10(11):1227–34.
[16] World Health Organization Regional Office for Europe. Access to new medicines in Europe: technical review of policy initiatives and opportunities for collaboration and research. Copenhagen. 2015.
[17] Gonçalves A, Maraninchi D, Vernant J-P. Challenging the soaring price of cancer medicines: a call for equity and transparency. Annals of Oncology 2016;27(9):1812–3.
[18] Kanavos PG, Vandoros S. Determinants of branded prescription medicine prices in OECD countries. Health Economics, Policy and Law 2011;6(3):337–67.
[19] World Health Organization (WHO). WHO guideline on country pharmaceutical pricing policies. Geneva. 2013.
[20] Seiter A. A practical approach to pharmaceutical policy. World Bank Publications; 2010. Report No.: 0821383876.
[21] Kyle MK, Allsbrook JS, Schulman KA. Does reimportation reduce price differences for prescription drugs? Lessons from the European Union. Health Services Research 2008;43(4):1308–24. Epub 2008/03/22.

CHAPTER 5

Discussion and Summary

Sabine Vogler
WHO Collaborating Centre for Pharmaceutical Pricing and Reimbursement Policies, Pharmacoeconomics Department, Gesundheit Österreich GmbH (GÖG/Austrian Public Health Institute), Vienna, Austria

LIST OF ABBREVIATIONS

AIDS	Acquired Immune Deficiency Syndrome
HAI	Health Action International
HIV	Human immunodeficiency virus
LMIC	Low- and middle-income country/ies
UHC	Universal Health Coverage
WHO	World Health Organization

Chapters 2 to 4 provide an overview of available evidence of medicine price information. Medicine price studies were presented for different regions of the world, and they were also analysed with regard to medicine groups investigated (e.g., therapeutic groups as well as groups classified per prescription, patent and reimbursement status).

The review points to some characteristics of Medicine Price Studies:

Methodology applied: Identified medicine price studies can be grouped into two major types with regard to their methodological design. Some medicine price surveys collected price data of defined medicines in the public and private sectors of a certain country, using the World Health Organization/Health Action International (WHO/HAI) methodology to measure medicine prices, availability, affordability and price components [1]. Findings usually related solely to the studied country, and as follow-up they were fed into the global HAI database and thus made publicly accessible. Some researchers (mainly affiliated to or cooperating with WHO and HAI) used the price data generated for secondary cross-country analyses [2,3]. The second group of studies includes analyses of medicine price data retrieved from (national) databases or using comprehensive data sets received from (commercial) service providers. Most of these studies were cross-country comparisons, and a few provided evaluations of policy measures. These studies did not rely on a generally defined methodology,

Medicine Price Surveys, Analyses, and Comparisons
ISBN 978-0-12-813166-4
https://doi.org/10.1016/B978-0-12-813166-4.00010-3

and they varied in their methodological design as a result of different study objectives. Some of them analysed the average medicine price levels of a country, or a market within a country in comparison to other countries by determining price indices. Such methodology requires further data (e.g., volume data) to weight the price data to account for the relative relevance in the national markets. A few of these studies highlighted differences in the findings based on different methodologies (e.g., unweighted data vs. weighted data, using different price indices). Given the lack of a nomenclature, the studies not based on the WHO/HAI methodology will be referred to 'the other group of studies' in the following.

Policy framework, study perspective and commissioners: Surveys using the WHO/HAI methodology tend to be conducted in countries (and settings) without price regulation, usually (but not exclusively) low- and middle-income countries (LMICs). These studies contained a comparison of prices in the public and private sectors. In contrast, a comparison of prices of reimbursable medicines (i.e., those covered by public funding) and non-reimbursable medicines was not the objective of price studies conducted in countries with universal health coverage (UHC) and price regulation. Such comparison would require a mixed survey approach (use of secondary data for the reimbursement sector and primary data collection for the non-reimbursement sector) and would be more resource-intensive than secondary data analysis. There appears to be less public health (and research) interest in non-reimbursable medicines in countries with advanced UHC where this sector is rather small and many essential medicines tend to be included in reimbursement formularies. A major concern in countries without price regulation is limited access to medicines due to their non-affordability for patients; this is also reflected in price studies that frequently assess affordability (as part of the WHO/HAI methodology). For the other group of studies, many of them were focused on prices and did not address affordability issues. In recent times, however, in the light of the emergence of premium-priced medicines (e.g., cancer medicines, hepatitis C treatments), a few studies assessed affordability for public payers. Studies pertaining to this second group were performed from patient, government (payer's) and industry perspectives. These studies were, to a large extent, conducted by researchers (academia or public health institutes) that did these pieces of research based on funding received from public research grants (not necessarily linked to health) or pharmaceutical industry. Surveys using the WHO/HAI methodology, on the other hand, were usually conducted as government activities.

Countries: Surveys using the WHO/HAI methodology were predominantly conducted in LMICs since they aim at collecting primary data. In principle, this method could also be used in other countries, or settings, where due to price variation between dispensaries primary data need to be collected (the method was, for instance, applied for evaluating availability and prices of essential medicines in the Boston area in the United States [4]). For several LMICs, the WHO/HAI survey was the sole medicine price study available, and updates after some years were made in some but not all cases. The majority of studies that included prices of African countries and of LMICs in the Asia–Pacific region were conducted using the WHO/HAI methodology. Studies of Latin-American countries used less frequently this methodology since some of these countries have established price information systems. The other group of studies mainly included high-income countries, particularly North American and European countries, but also Australia and New Zealand. A few medicine price comparisons had large baskets of 12 and more countries, but most publications tended to include a limited number of countries (maximum five to seven), thereof large economies such as the United States, United Kingdom, France, Germany and also Canada, Italy and Sweden. The focus on big pharmaceutical markets was particularly identified in studies that were based on data sets of commercial providers (e.g., IQVIA) and that also performed price index analyses (for which volume data are needed). The review of price studies has also shown that a few research groups in Europe, North America, Australia and New Zealand authored a relatively high share of medicine price studies. Several price studies related to countries that are usually not scope of research (e.g., Cyprus, Norway); this can be attributed to researchers affiliated in these countries.

Medicine groups and sectors: Some medicine groups are more frequently included in price studies, and this might be attributable to three reasons. First, the WHO/HAI manual provides guidance about the choice of medicines and determines a set of medicines to be covered. Second, there is probably increased public health interest in certain medicines: Around the millennium, with civil society demanding access to antiretroviral therapy, several studies investigated prices of HIV/AIDS medicines and analysed the impact of policy changes and competition over time. In general, there seems to be high interest in the impacts of generic competition: Several studies investigated developments in the prices of medicines that went off-patent and of their comparators. Price studies of biosimilar medicines are, however, few. In recent times, a comparably high share of studies surveyed prices of orphan medicines and other high-priced medicines (e.g., cancer medicines, medicines to treat hepatitis C). Third, data availability seems to play a role: Some price studies were based on 'convenience' product samples, and others included prices from sectors (e.g., reimbursable medicines, prescription-only medicines, outpatient medicines) for which data were accessible in databases or price lists. Still, a few studies not using the WHO/HAI methodology aimed to survey primary data from settings with unknown medicine prices, including data of confidential character (e.g., hospital sector, discounted prices following negotiations between the payer and the manufacturer).

Price types and price components: While studies using the WHO/HAI methodology surveyed price data at different stages along the supply chain and analysed different price types, as defined by the manual, many pieces of research pertaining to the other group of studies rather focused on solely one price type. Frequently, price studies were conducted for ex-factory prices. In addition, some studies (e.g., about the United States, Australia) surveyed pharmacy retail prices, applying the perspective of patients who pay or co-pay for medicines. A few cross-country analyses in the European context compared pharmacy purchasing prices (wholesale prices); in most of these studies, the government in the 'base' country of the comparison sets medicine prices at the pharmacy retail price level. Additionally, some price studies investigated (public) procurement prices (e.g., in Latin America). While the WHO/HAI methodology recommends an analysis of different price components, this was only rarely done in studies not using this methodology. A few comparative studies in the European context showed how countries with average ex-factory prices ended up with high pharmacy retail prices in comparison and vice versa due to add-ons in the supply chain.

Availability of medicines: The WHO/HAI methodology includes a survey of the availability of medicines in pharmacies and outlets as an integral part of the study. While availability limitations have become an increasing concern globally [5], research on availability appears to be conducted as a separate topic and not as part of price studies. Availability issues have been addressed in only a few price studies not using the WHO/HAI methodology. In these pieces of research, availability of medicines was usually discussed from a methodological perspective with the aim to ensure comparability in cross-country studies given the lack of comparator data.

Several medicine price studies offered recommendations for research and policy-making. Some studies identified 'black boxes' which would require further data collection and analysis. This concerned countries not yet covered in price surveys as well as specific sectors (e.g., non-funded medicines, hospital sector, non-prescription medicines). The increasing use of confidential discounts that distort price information has been critically discussed in recent literature. While a few researchers see value in confidential price components [6,7], most publications called for more price transparency at all supply chain stages. Concern has been expressed about possible limitations of price databases (e.g., delays in updates of some sources in Latin America). Numerous studies called for regular monitoring of medicine price developments. Overall, the review suggests that more medicine price information needs to be surveyed and analysed. In addition, there appears to be paucity in methodological guidance since no comprehensive standard has been developed and agreed upon for medicine price analyses and comparisons apart from the WHO/HAI methodology.

REFERENCES

[1] WHO, HAI. Measuring medicine prices, availability, affordability and price components. 2nd ed. Geneva: World Health Organization, Health Action International; 2008. Available from: http://www.who.int/medicines/areas/access/OMS_Medicine_prices.pdf.

[2] Cameron A, Ewen M, Ross-Degnan D, Ball D, Laing R. Medicine prices, availability, and affordability in 36 developing and middle-income countries: a secondary analysis. The Lancet 2009;373(9659):240–9.

[3] Ewen M, Zweekhorst M, Regeer B, Laing R. Baseline assessment of WHO's target for both availability and affordability of essential medicines to treat non-communicable diseases. PLoS One 2017;12(2):e0171284.

[4] Sharma A, Rorden L, Ewen M, Laing R. Evaluating availability and price of essential medicines in Boston area (Massachusetts, USA) using WHO/HAI methodology. Journal of Pharmaceutical Policy and Practice 2016;9(1):12.

[5] Gray A, Manasse Jr HR. Shortages of medicines: a complex global challenge. Bulletin of the World Health Organization 2012;90(3):158.

[6] Towse A, Pistollato M, Mestre-Ferrandiz J, Khan Z, Kaura S, Garrison L. European union pharmaceutical markets: a case for differential pricing? International Journal of the Economics of Business 2015;22(2):263–75.

[7] Kaló Z, Annemans L, Garrison LP. Differential pricing of new pharmaceuticals in lower income European countries. Expert Review of Pharmacoeconomics and Outcomes Research 2013;13(6):735–41.

Further medicine price surveys, analyses and comparisons are listed in the references of Chapters 2 to 4.

PART 2

Training — How to Conduct Medicine Price Surveys, Analyses and Comparisons?

CHAPTER 6

Review of Methodologies to Conduct Price Studies

LIST OF ABBREVIATIONS

ATC	Anatomical therapeutic classification
CIF	Cost, Insurance and freight
DDD	Defined daily dose
EPR	External price referencing
GAP	Global action plan
GST	Goods and services tax
HAI	Health Action International
INN	International Nonproprietary Name
LMIC	Low- and middle-income country/ies
LPG	Lowest-priced generic(s)
MPR	Medicine price ratio
MSH	Management Sciences for Health
MSP	Manufacturer's selling price
NCD	Noncommunicable disease
NGO	Nongovernmental organization
PPP	Purchasing power parity/ies
UHC	Universal Health Coverage
USA	United States of America
VAT	Value added tax
WHO	World Health Organization

Medicine Price Surveys, Analyses, and Comparisons
ISBN 978-0-12-813166-4
https://doi.org/10.1016/B978-0-12-813166-4.00011-5

CHAPTER 6.1

Overview of Existing Methodologies

Sabine Vogler

WHO Collaborating Centre for Pharmaceutical Pricing and Reimbursement Policies, Pharmacoeconomics Department, Gesundheit Österreich GmbH (GÖG/Austrian Public Health Institute), Vienna, Austria

"People who may be exposed and criticized by the study's findings may prefer to attack the methods used in the study rather than address the results." [1]. This quote taken from the World Health Organization (WHO)/Health Action International (HAI) manual for measuring medicine prices, availability and availability, and price components highlights the importance of a robust methodological design. The statement is valid for any piece of research, including medicine price studies.

What is a medicine price study? For the purpose of this book (see also Chapter 7 on terminology), it is defined as any research that investigates prices, or price components, of medicines in a single country or across countries at a specific date or over time. A medicine price study can take the form of a survey, an analysis or a (cross-country) comparison, or a combination:

- A *medicine price survey* aims to access data of medicine prices according to a predefined methodology.
- A *medicine price analysis* aims to interpret medicine price data. It can address specific therapeutic groups of medicines, different types of prices (such as government procurement prices and consumer prices) or several countries, for instance. Data can be collected and analyzed over a long period (time series analysis) or at one point in time. A price analysis can also be used to determine other indicators, e.g., to assess the affordability of a medicine.
- A (cross-country or cross-national) *medicine price comparison* aims to survey and analyze data of medicine prices in more than one country. Within a country, further comparisons can be made, such as across sectors (e.g., public vs. private sectors) or between groups of medicines (e.g., originator vs. generic medicines).

Findings of medicine price studies are essential for policy-making. Developing knowledge about medicine prices in the own country and in comparison with other countries, as well as about price developments, is key for policy-makers who aim to improve their health-care system to advance Universal Health Coverage (UHC) and to ensure access to quality-assured essential medicines [2]. In any health-care system, price monitoring and analysis are crucial to understand the drivers of pharmaceutical expenditure (both in the public and private sectors) [3]. Furthermore, policy-makers require price information to review whether medicine prices are in line with the country's health priorities set [1,2].

According to Danzon and Kim [4], international medicine price comparisons serve, in principle, two purposes: (1) to draw conclusions about differences in the average price levels across countries and (2) to provide a basis for setting domestic prices. The latter is referred to as the policy of "external price referencing" (EPR) (also called "external reference pricing" or "international price benchmark"). Part 3 of this book is devoted to present and discuss the EPR policy. Cross-national medicine price comparisons could also serve further purposes, such as learning about the price of selected medicines in other countries or understanding price developments for specific therapeutic groups or submarkets (cf. Chapter 3). Price analyses (and comparisons) could also aim to explore the causes of price developments, to assess the impact of policy measures on medicine prices, or to investigate differences between price types or between different kinds of medicines (originator and generic equivalents).

Depending on the purpose of a price study, an appropriate methodological design has to be chosen. A methodology for a price study comprises several elements, including the choice of medicines, price types, dispensaries, regions and countries studied, the data collection (on-site survey vs. existing price lists or databases), the challenge of making identified medicines comparable, weighting and indexing data, exchange rate issues, interpretation, and dealing with limitations.

Despite the importance of the methodological framework, there is paucity in publications related to the methodology of how to conduct price studies.[1] As also shown in Part 1, most price studies in low- and middle-income countries (LMIC) are based on the methodology developed by the WHO and HAI [1,5] that provides a standardized approach to survey availability and prices of medicines, to investigate the price components, and to assess the affordability of treatments. No other manual to guide academics, staff in competent authorities, and other people interested in conducting price surveys, analyses, and comparisons was identified.

Table 6.1 provides a summary of relevant publications that address methodological approaches of price studies. With one exemption, all

[1] A focused literature review was performed, based on searches in PubMed and Google Scholar, reviewing reference lists and hand-searching.

Table 6.1 Key publications on the methodology for performing medicine price surveys, analyses, and comparisons

Authors	Title	Year	Publication	Price			Countries	Content	Ref.
				S	A	C			
Andersson	Methodological Aspects of International Drug Price Comparisons	1993	Article published in Pharmacoeconomics	—	—	✓	Mentioned examples refer to European countries, Canada, and USA	Definition of six principles for medicine price comparisons: **1.** *Selection of similar countries*: in terms of disease patterns, therapeutic tradition, level of pharmaceutical consumption, distribution and reimbursement, distribution of income, age and gender **2.** *Selection of a representative sample of medicines*: either randomly selected (though still large enough to be representative) or top 100–200 medicines by sales in the countries of interest **3.** *Selection of price type*: comparisons can be done	[6]

								at manufacturer, wholesale, or retail price level, and all three have limitations; discounts are another confounding factor **4.** *Ensuring comparability*: developing a common basis for medicines given the fact that available pack sizes, forms, strengths, indications, and ways of dispensing vary between countries; suggestion to adjust the price of all sizes of packs into the price equivalent of an arbitrary standard pack size, or disaggregate the medicine price into packaging cost plus the cost of the substance **5.** *Weighting prices*: suggestion of using a weighted price index to weight the price with the

Continued

Table 6.1 Key publications on the methodology for performing medicine price surveys, analyses, and comparisons—cont'd

Authors	Title	Year	Publication	Price S	Price A	Price C	Countries	Content	Ref.
								shares of sales in a country; despite the limitations of Laspeyres', Paasche's, and Fisher's indexes, it is recommended to use all of them; use of "real income approach" (e.g., examining how long an individual has to work in paid employment to pay for his or her sample of medicines or an average pack, or PPP) is not recommended because of variations in the definitions of salary, technology levels, and distribution of labor forces in different countries. **6.** Conversion of medicine price data into a common currency: through official exchange rates or PPP	

Danzon and Kim	International Price Comparison. Measurement and Policy Issues	1998	Article published in Pharmacoeconomics[1]	—	—	✓	USA, Canada, Germany, France, Italy, Japan, UK, Switzerland, Sweden	Examination of methodological issues raised by medicine price comparisons and suggestions of principles: **1.** *Price indexes*: recommendation to do price comparisons based on price indexes, Laspeyre's index is considered as the most appropriate one **2.** *Sample selection*: comparison should be done for "international" medicines that are available in both[2] countries under comparison; imputations in case of nonmatching medicines are not recommended, restrictions of samples are not recommended (e.g., generics and over-the-counter medicines should	[4]

Continued

Table 6.1 Key publications on the methodology for performing medicine price surveys, analyses, and comparisons—cont'd

Authors	Title	Year	Publication	Price S	Price A	Price C	Countries	Content	Ref.
								be included), and a quality-constant course of therapy is recommended as unit for comparison **3.** *Price types*: comparison of manufacturer prices is preferred to a comparison of retail prices because it is considered as very inaccurate Methodological guidelines for the comparison of individual products (also seen in connection with setting domestic prices): **1.** *Similar countries*: recommendation to limit the comparison to similar countries	

								2. *Full portfolio*: recommendation to base the comparison on the full portfolio of the manufacturer's products, taking into account life cycle price profiles 3. *Exchange rates*: recommendation to use exchange rates for currency conversion (not PPP because this may create opportunities for parallel trade)	
WHO/ HAI	Medicine Prices. A new approach to measurement Measuring medicine prices,	2003 2008	Manuals (1st and updated 2nd edition) with accompanying workbooks	✓	✓	✓	Any country, including and particularly countries and setting where access to medicine price information	Detailed and practical manual of how to do price surveys in the field and analyze price data; provision of data collection forms and workbooks for data entry and analysis. Manual provides guidance for the presurvey and	[1,5]

Continued

Table 6.1 Key publications on the methodology for performing medicine price surveys, analyses, and comparisons—cont'd

Authors	Title	Year	Publication	Price S	Price A	Price C	Countries	Content	Ref.
	availability, affordability and price components						is not available at central level (e.g., LMIC)	preparation phases, data collection, data entry and analysis, and follow-up activities (dissemination of results, exploring policy options). See Chapter 6.2 for more in-depth descriptions. Methodological issues addressed in the manual: **1.** *Country, area and outlet selection:* Recommended to survey the capital and five other survey areas within a country (or province for subnational surveys), randomly selected within 1 day's travel reach of the capital. Up to four sectors can be surveyed. It is recommended to collect data in at least five outlets per sector per survey area. Government	

								procurement prices collected from the Ministry of Health or Central Medical Store (central tenders) or regional stores/public sector outlets where procurement is decentralized. **2.** *Product selection:* 14 medicines from a defined global core list, and 36 medicines decided nationally[3]; survey medicines are strength and dose form specific. For each medicine, data are collected for the originator brand (product identified centrally) and the lowest price generic equivalent in the outlet. For international comparisons to other surveys undertaken using the WHO/HAI methodology: choice of	

Continued

Table 6.1 Key publications on the methodology for performing medicine price surveys, analyses, and comparisons—cont'd

Authors	Title	Year	Publication	Price S	Price A	Price C	Countries	Content	Ref.
								medicines with one major indication and used in a similar manner across countries is preferred; preference to a comparison of individual medicines (option of performing a composite price comparison, with methodological challenges is referred to but not scope of the manual) **3.** *Price analysis*: prices are expressed as a ratio to the MSH International Product Price Guide **4.** *Availability and affordability:* The availability of the survey medicines in outlets is measured. Affordability is assessed based on median patient prices and standard treatment regimens and expressed	

								as the number of days the lowest-paid unskilled government worker has to work to buy 7 days supply of a medicine to treat an acute condition, and 30 days' medicine for a chronic condition. **5.** *Weighting price data (in international comparison of data from other surveys undertaken using the WHO/HAI methodology):* adjustments for deflation/inflation in case of data from different years; weighting PPP for private sector patient prices; acknowledgment of the need for weighting (e.g., to account for different market power and discount strategies) in price indexes but price indexes are beyond the scope of the manual (the

Continued

Table 6.1 Key publications on the methodology for performing medicine price surveys, analyses, and comparisons—cont'd

Authors	Title	Year	Publication	Price S	Price A	Price C	Countries	Content	Ref.
								method of comparing individual prices is considered as the most robust one and is recommended to the users of the WHO/HAI methodology).	
EURO-MED-STAT Working Group	The EurMedStat proposals on indicators for price and utilisation	2006	Italian Journal of Public Health	—	—	✓	No country defined (illustrative comparisons targeting European countries)	Development of indicators for indicators for cross-country price comparisons, in addition to the development of indicators for cross-country comparisons of pharmaceutical expenditure and utilization. The paper addresses the following methodological aspects of international price comparisons: **1.** *Price types*: Perspective ("price interest") determines the choice of the price type examined; the authors tend to consider the pharmacy retail price as preferred	[9]

								2. *PPP*: Weighting by PPP can help address the challenge of exchange rate fluctuations **3.** *Comparability of medicines*: comparison of individual medicines of the same "preparation" (same strength and pack size) is seen as the ideal approach; it is suggested to standardize in DDD	
Machado et al.	International drug price comparisons: quality assessment	2011	Revista Panamericana de Salud Publica	–	–	✓	Not mentioned	Assessment of medicine price comparisons of whether, or not, they comply with the principles set by Andersson [6]: one of 21 identified studies was found to address all quality aspects. Machado et al. comment on the Andersson's six principles and developed two further principles: **1.** *Selection of similar countries*: this criterion should be applied in comparisons	[7]

Continued

Table 6.1 Key publications on the methodology for performing medicine price surveys, analyses, and comparisons—cont'd

Authors	Title	Year	Publication	Price S	Price A	Price C	Countries	Content	Ref.
								that are done for price setting, but it is considered unnecessary for studies that aim to gather information on countries of different income levels or that aim to assess affordability **2.** *Selection of a representative sample of medicines*: endorsement of the recommendation to select a sample of top 100–200 medicines by sales in the countries of the comparison **3.** *Selection of price type*: recommendation against a price comparison at retail price level **4.** *Ensuring comparability*: endorsement of Andersson's principle, it	

								is suggested to standardize into DDD **5.** *Weighting prices*: endorsement of Andersson's principle of weighting price data by building indexes (Laspeyres', Paasche's, and Fisher's indexes) **6.** *Conversion of medicine price data into a common currency*: the authors acknowledge Andersson's principle of conversion into exchange rates or PPP; PPP appear to be recommended **7.** *Weighting of price data by average income*: a newly proposed principle to reveal the burden of medicine prices on an average person; alternative approach: twice-weighting of the average income and the

Continued

Table 6.1 Key publications on the methodology for performing medicine price surveys, analyses, and comparisons—cont'd

Authors	Title	Year	Publication	Price S	Price A	Price C	Countries	Content	Ref.
								inverse of the Gini coefficient **8.** *Weighting of price data by inflation*: a newly proposed principle (particularly relevant for analyses over time)	
WHO	WHO Guideline on Country Pharmaceutical Pricing Policies	2013	WHO guideline related to medicine price policy	—	—	✓	Not mentioned	Not a methodology paper for price studies, but guidance on price comparisons used for EPR, with a recommendation to the selection of countries (for details see Chapter 14 in Part 3): The selection of comparator countries to be used in EPR is recommended to be "based on economic status, pharmaceutical pricing systems in place, published actual versus negotiated or concealed prices, exact	[19]

								comparator products supplied, and similar burden of disease."	

A, analysis; *C*, cross-national comparison; *DDD*, defined daily dose(s); *EPR*, external price referencing; *HAI*, Health Action International; *LMIC*, low- and middle-income country/ies; *MSH*, Management Sciences for Health; *PPP*, purchasing power parities; *Ref.*, reference; *S*, survey; *US*, United States; *WHO*, World Health Organization.

[1]Danzon and colleagues also addressed methodological aspects of price comparisons in further publications.

[2]Bilateral comparisons.

[3]A change in methodology in 2016: Before, 16 medicines were selected from a regional list and 20 medicines were decided nationally. In 2016, the regional lists were abolished [13].

Compilation done by the author.

publications relate to international price comparisons. Solely the WHO/HAI methodology [1,5] also addressed the challenge of sourcing and accessing medicine price data (price surveys).

Some of the methodology documents quoted the work of Andersson [6]. More than 20 years ago, he defined some basic principles for performing medicine price comparisons in the following six areas:

- Country basket
- Product basket
- Price type
- Comparability of medicines
- Weighting price data
- Conversion of medicine prices into a common currency

Machado et al. [7] reviewed price studies in the light of their compliance with Andersson's principles and developed two further principles. They suggested weighting of the price data by income and by inflation.

Although the EURO-MED-STAT Working Group was focused on identifying data sources (see also Chapter 8) and made recommendations on indicators that relate to pharmaceutical expenditure and utilization [8], it also published methodology reflections related to cross-country price comparisons and discussed strengths and weaknesses of different price indicators [9]. The authors concluded that there is "no ideal way of measuring prices and no ideal price indicator" [9].

Some authors showed how different methodologies (e.g., related to the selected survey medicines, use of price indexes, "inflated" list prices, weighting by income of the countries) can impact the results of price studies [4,11,12]. Therefore, the methodology of a price study has to be carefully designed.

Although there is a need for a robust methodology for of a medicine price study, guidance of how to design the study (particularly with regard to aspects of surveying and analyzing data) is scarce. In response of this perceived lack, Part 2 of this book is devoted to discuss key elements that should be considered when the methodology of a medicine price survey, analysis, and/or comparison is developed. It starts off by providing definitions of key terms in Chapter 7, to ensure clarity and understanding. Chapter 8 provides guidance on how to identify medicine price data and assess their quality and usefulness for studies. Chapter 9 elaborates on different methodological choices that need to be made in the setup of the medicine price study, with regard to selection and adjustment criteria and processes (e.g., the choice of price types for the analysis, making selected medicines comparable, exchange rates vs. purchasing power parity/PPP, and price indexes). Chapter 10 offers training exercises.

Given its relevance, the WHO/HAI methodology [1,5] that offers advice on how to do facility-based price surveys and guidance for analyzing and interpreting price data in the context of a single country, as well as internationally, is presented in detail in Chapter 6.2.

CHAPTER 6.2

WHO/HAI Methodology for Measuring Medicine Prices, Availability and Affordability, and Price Components

Priyanka Konduru Subramani Raju
Boston University, Boston, United States

6.2.1 BACKGROUND AND HISTORY

Access to essential medicines is part of the right to the highest attainable standard of health ("the right to health") and is well-founded in international law [10]. However, approximately two billion people were estimated to lack access to essential medicines globally [11]. Among others, the 2016 report "Essential medicines for universal health coverage" of the Lancet Commission on Essential Medicines and Policies noted that "the lack of medicine pricing information makes it difficult for consumers – both individuals and health systems – to make informed decisions about purchasing medicines." [12]. To make medicines affordable, recommendations were made to maintain a database of information concerning price and availability in the public and private sectors [12]. This statement refers to the work of the World Health Organization (WHO) and Health Action International (HAI) on measuring availability, affordability, and price components of medicines.

In 2001, the World Health Assembly passed a resolution (No. 54.11) that called for exploring the feasibility and effectiveness of implementing systems in coordination with organizations and partners around the world. This included voluntary monitoring of medicine prices and reporting global medicine pricing information with the aim to improve equity in access to essential medicines in health systems.

In response to the resolution, experts from WHO and HAI established a project on medicine prices and availability in 2001. Its objectives were as follows:

Medicine Price Surveys, Analyses, and Comparisons
ISBN 978-0-12-813166-4
https://doi.org/10.1016/B978-0-12-813166-4.00012-7

- To develop a reliable methodology for collecting and analyzing medicine prices and their components, availability, affordability across healthcare sectors and regions in a country;
- To publish survey data on a publicly accessible website to improve price transparency;
- To advocate for appropriate national policies and monitor their impact.

In 2003 a first edition [5] was produced as a draft manual for field testing. Prior to its publication, pilot testing of the methodology was conducted in nine countries. A second edition [1] was published in 2008 that incorporated the wealth of practical experience gained through conducting surveys around the world. As a result, slight modifications to the survey methodology were made to increase the reliability of the data obtained.

6.2.2 OBJECTIVE OF THE WORLD HEALTH ORGANIZATION/ HEALTH ACTION INTERNATIONAL METHODOLOGY

The main objective of the WHO/HAI methodology is to generate reliable information of the price, availability, and affordability of selected essential medicines and their price components in the supply chain. The method is intended to support work toward the ultimate goal of improving access to affordable medicines for all.

The method offers a data collection tool to obtain medicine price and availability information in countries and/or settings (e.g., in low- and middle-income countries [LMIC]) where access to price information is not available at a central level (Box 6.2.1).

6.2.3 STEPS OF A SURVEY USING THE WORLD HEALTH ORGANIZATION/HEALTH ACTION INTERNATIONAL METHODOLOGY

The WHO/HAI methodology suggests following a number of steps for undertaking a survey, including presurvey planning and follow-up activities. These include the following:

- Presurvey planning
- Preparation
- Training area supervisors, data collectors, and data entry personnel
- Preparing for data collection in the field
- Fieldwork data collection

Box 6.2.1 Questions to be answered by conducting a survey using the World Health Organization (WHO)/Health Action International (HAI) methodology

- What price do people pay for key medicines to treat acute and chronic conditions?
- Do prices and availability of the same medicine vary across different sectors and regions of the country?
- What is the difference in prices and availability of originator brands and lowest price generic equivalents?
- What price does the government pay for medicines and how are public sector patient prices compared to procurement prices?
- How are national prices compared to international reference prices?
- How affordable are standard treatments for low-paid people?
- How do the manufacturer's price, duties, taxes, markups, and other charges contribute to the final patient price?

WHO, HAI. Measuring medicine prices, availability, affordability and price components. 2nd ed. Geneva: World Health Organization, Health Action International; 2008. Available from: http://www.who.int/medicines/areas/access/OMS_Medicine_prices.pdf.

- Data entry
- Data analysis and interpretations
- Measurement of price components
- Conducting international comparisons
- Exploring policy options
- Reporting

These activities will be described in the following.

6.2.3.1 Presurvey Planning

The WHO/HAI methodology stresses the importance of good planning in the presurvey phase—both in terms of developing the method and of practical organizational issues. It is suggested considering and setting the following steps in the presurvey planning.

Establishing an advisory committee: An advisory committee can help in the planning of the survey, and it can further support and promote its findings. The advisory committee should complement the survey manager's skills. It is suggested involving a medical doctor, a pharmacist, a health economist (where possible), and other stakeholders such as policy-makers and public health institutions.

Clarifying the survey objective: A specific research and policy objective may vary from one survey to another. For example: a country may want to survey prices and availability in a particular region and/or in a particular therapeutic group (such as antidiabetic medicines). A well-defined survey objective will help guide the data analysis and interpretation, as well as communication and advocacy activities.

Obtaining health system and pharmaceutical sector information: It is recommended collecting information on the structure of the health-care system and pharmaceutical sector of the country where the survey will be carried out. These pieces of information provide an understanding of how pharmaceutical services are organized, and they help identify countries with similar characteristics for international comparisons.

Selecting and training the survey personnel: The WHO/HAI methodology suggests the involvement of a survey manager, area supervisors (i.e., responsible for overseeing all aspects of data collection in their defined survey area or areas), data collectors, and data entry personnel. Their specific roles are detailed in the WHO/HAI manual.

Ensuring required technical and financial resources: A realistic budget is needed for the survey (helped by a budget template provided in the manual) and technical requirements, such as a personal computer for performing the data entry. It is also suggested to seek endorsement of the survey (e.g., through an official letter of the Ministry of Health or the national pharmacy association); this might help when asking further funding or performing data collection in the field.

Preparing a survey schedule: Another important aspect of the pre-survey planning is to develop the survey schedule where time is allotted to each activity throughout the process. The WHO/HAI methodology recommends 14 weeks for the survey (including data collection, data entry, data analysis, and report writing) to ensure that the data do not get outdated. Table 6.2.1 informs about the time periods foreseen for the different steps of the survey.

6.2.3.2 Preparation of the Survey

In preparing for the survey, different choices have to be taken. The WHO/HAI methodology provides guidance as described below.[1]

[1] It should be noted that the description is relevant for a national survey, but within a country regional price surveys can also be conducted.

Table 6.2.1 Overview of steps, activities, and timelines when conducting a survey using the World Health Organization (WHO)/Health Action International (HAI) methodology

Tasks	Individual activities	Time schedule
Presurvey preparation	Establishment of an advisory committee, collection of background information on pharmaceutical sector, selection of survey personnel, securement of funds, endorsement (e.g., Ministry of Health), preparation of work schedule	2–3 weeks
Planning	Sampling of survey areas and selection of medicine outlets for the survey, finalizing the medicines to be surveyed, preparation of data collection forms, planning and conduct of training sessions (including pilot)	2–3 weeks
Preparation for fieldwork	Preparation of introduction letters, scheduling visits, arrangement of transport, accommodation and communications, arrangement of survey tools and materials (forms, information sheets) for data collectors	1 week
Data collection	Collection of government procurement prices, visiting outlets and collection of availability and price data, daily check of completed data collection forms, validation of data, copying and storing of forms	2–3 weeks
Data entry and analysis	Entering data twice into the "workbook" (electronic data collection instrument), running data checker, workbook sent to HAI for checking, meeting the advisory group to analyze data	3 weeks
Price components survey	Sampling medicines to be surveyed, collection of data, entering of data into the workbook, performing data analysis	3 weeks
Use the information	Deciding on recommendations, drafting the survey report, sharing findings with stakeholders, planning and implementation of advocacy activities	1–2 weeks

Note: Some of the steps described in the chapter have been combined in this table.

First, the sectors have to be identified. Patient price and availability data can be collected from the public sector (or availability only if medicines are provided free of charge), the private sector, and up to two "other" sectors (e.g., health facilities run by NGOs, such as charitable organizations, or by religious institutions, such as church missions). In these sectors, prices to patients as well as availability are measured, and affordability is assessed. In addition, government procurement prices are collected from the Ministry of Health or Central Medical Store, or regional stores/public sector outlets in countries with decentralized medicine procurement. Table 6.2.2 provides an overview of the different price types per sector and suggests approaches to collect them.

Table 6.2.2 Sectors and price types to be measured using the World Health Organization (WHO)/Health Action International (HAI) methodology

Price type per sector	Mode of collection
Public sector procurement prices (i.e., prices that the government pays) and availability	It is suggested to collect the procurement price information from the ministry of health (tender/other documents) or from a regional or central medical store. In case of decentralized procurement or a mix of centralized and decentralized procurement, public health facilities procurement data are collected.
Public sector patient prices and availability	The survey includes data collection from government, municipality, or other local authority facilities where patients receive medicines in hospitals (outpatients), clinics, and health centers.
Private sector patient prices and availability	Data are collected from licensed retail pharmacies (i.e., a legally authorized pharmacy allowed to dispense medicines) and licensed medicine-dispensing outlets.
"Other" sector patient prices and availability	A sector other than the public and private sector that supplies medicines is considered an "other" sector, such as health facilities run by nongovernmental organizations, church missions, private hospitals, or private dispensing doctors. Up to two "other" sectors can be included in the survey.

Note: Price components, which are "add-on" costs of medicines as they move through the supply chain from manufacturer to patient (such as markups, taxes, tariffs, and other charges), are also collected as part of WHO/HAI methodology.

Second, the survey areas need to be identified. It is recommended collecting data in the capital (or major urban areas) plus five other areas in the country. As a guide, the selected surveys areas should cover a population of about 100,000 to 250,000 (at least in large countries) each to be large enough to be a representative and, for pragmatic reasons, they should be reachable within 1 day's travel from the country's capital (or main urban center). Stratification by urban and rural areas should also be considered.

Third, the sample of medicine outlets that is surveyed in each sector has to be identified.

For each survey area, it is advised:

- To choose the main public hospital;
- To randomly select four public sector outlets within 3 hours' travel of the main hospital and four back-up outlets (nearest outlet to the originally selected outlet);
- To select the private pharmacy closest to each public sector outlet selected and four back-up private pharmacies;
- To select five outlets for each other sector, plus back-up outlets, closest to the public-sector outlet.

Fourth, the list of medicines to be surveyed has to be finalized.

The WHO/HAI methodology suggests to survey 50 medicines (each strength and pharmaceutical form specific):

- Fourteen medicines that have been predetermined by WHO/HAI to enable international comparisons ([14] global medicines, see Table 6.2.3).
- Thirty-six supplementary medicines selected nationally for local importance: criteria for selection can be the national burden of disease, national priorities, and problems in terms of availability and/or price in some or all sectors.

This current suggestion for the selection of medicines to be surveyed is based on a change in the manual in May 2016. Before, the 2008 manual suggested including 14 medicines of the global core medicine list, 16 of a regional list developed by WHO/HAI, and it was recommended choosing the remaining medicines on a national basis. In May 2016, the regional lists were abolished [13].

Local prices are expressed as a ratio to an external benchmark (termed an international reference price in the manual, see below). The WHO/HAI methodology recommends using median supplier prices in the International Medical Products Price Guide of Management Sciences for Health (MSH) as the source of the reference prices. So the surveyed medicines need to be included in the Guide.

Table 6.2.3 World Health Organization (WHO)/Health Action International (HAI)'s global core medicines list (2018)

No.	Disease	Active ingredient	Strength	Pharmaceutical form
1	Asthma	Salbutamol	0.1 mg/dose	Inhaler
2	Diabetes	Metformin	500 mg	Cap/tab
3	Cardiovascular disease	Bisoprolol	5 mg	Cap/tab
4	Cardiovascular disease	Captopril	25 mg	Cap/tab
5	Cardiovascular disease	Simvastatin	20 mg	Cap/tab
6	Depression	Amitriptyline	25 mg	Cap/tab
7	Infectious disease	Ciprofloxacin	500 mg	Cap/tab
8	Infectious disease	Co-trimoxazole	8 + 40 mg/mL	Suspension
9	Infectious disease	Amoxicillin	500 mg	Cap/tab
10	Infectious disease	Ceftriaxone	1 g/vial	Injection
11	Central nervous system	Diazepam	5 mg	Cap/tab
12	Pain/inflammation	Diclofenac	50 mg	Cap/tab
13	Pain/inflammation	Paracetamol	120 mg/5 mL	Suspension
14	Ulcer	Omeprazole	20 mg	Cap/tab

WHO, HAI. Measuring medicine prices, availability, affordability and price components. 2nd ed. Geneva: World Health Organization, Health Action International; 2008. Available from: http://www.who.int/medicines/areas/access/OMS_Medicine_prices.pdf; Health Action International (HAI). Collecting evidence on medicine prices & availability. Update to the manual 2016. Available from: http://haiweb.org/what-we-do/price-availability-affordability/collecting-evidence-on-medicine-prices-availability/.

For each medicine, the WHO/HAI methodology recommends collecting data for two product types:

- **Originator brand**: It is defined as an original medicine that was first authorized for marketing, normally as a patented product. The selected originator brand should have a brand name that does not vary from outlet to outlet within a country. The originator brand product of each survey medicine is identified centrally before data collection. However, it might not be identifiable in case of very old medicines.
- **Lowest-priced generic (LPG) equivalent:** It is a product other than the originator brand that contains the same active ingredient whether marketed under another brand name or generic name (international nonproprietary name/INN). For LPG, data collectors identify the

generic with the lowest unit price at each outlet. The product can vary from outlet to outlet.

6.2.3.3 Training of Area Supervisors, Data Collectors, and Data Entry Personnel

The manual stresses the importance of training all survey personnel to ensure accuracy, completeness, and consistency especially in data collection but also in data entry.

The WHO/HAI methodology recommends conducting comprehensive trainings prior to initiating fieldwork in form of workshops that include piloting data collection in the public and private sectors. The manual provides detailed information to assist survey managers in conducting training workshops for their survey personnel.

6.2.3.4 Preparing for Data Collection

The WHO/HAI methodology gives practical instructions to data collectors and area supervisors. For instance, the latter are advised to:

- schedule data collection visits (up to 2 hours each in the private sector but less in the public sector),
- prepare the medicine data collection forms needed for field visits,
- prepare information materials for data collectors, and
- arrange for regular communications between them and data collectors.

6.2.3.5 Data Collection in the Field

The workbook generates the data collection forms for use in the field. Prices are only entered if the medicine was physically available in the outlet on the day of the visit (see a sample in Fig. 6.2.1).

The WHO/HAI manual defines the following specifications (relevant for the originator brand as well as the LPG):

- Related to availability:

    If the medicine is in stock but the pharmaceutical form or strength differs from the one indicated on the data collection form, it is considered unavailable. If a medicine is unavailable, other products (of different strengths and pharmaceutical forms) are not substituted.

    If the recommended pack size is available, the size of that particular pack is entered onto the data collection form. If not available, the closest, larger pack size identified is entered.

A	B	C	D	E	F	G	H	I	J
Generic name, dosage form, strength	**Medicine type**	**Brand or product name(s)**	**Manufacturer**	**Available: "yes" or "no"**	**Pack size recom-mended**	**Pack size found**	**Price of pack found**	**Unit price (4 digits)**	**Comments**
Amitriptyline cap/tab 25 mg	Originator brand	Tryptizol	MSD		100			/tab	
	Lowest-priced generic				100			/tab	
Amoxicillin cap/tab 500 mg	Originator brand	Amoxil	GSK		21			/tab	
	Lowest-priced generic				21			/tab	

Note: In the WHO/HAI methodology, the term 'dosage form' is used to describe the way in which a medicine is presented, e.g., a film coated tablet, an ointment, a vial, or a spray. In the remainder of this book, the synonym 'pharmaceutical form' is used as synonym.

Figure 6.2.1 Example of the data collection form of the World Health Organization (WHO)/Health Action International (HAI) methodology. *(WHO, HAI. Measuring medicine prices, availability, affordability and price components. 2nd ed. Geneva: World Health Organization, Health Action International; 2008. Available from: http://www.who.int/medicines/areas/access/OMS_Medicine_prices.pdf.)*

Data collectors are also advised to ask to see a pack of the product and only record that it is available if they actually saw it.

- Related to the price:
  The full price of the medicine pack and the pack size are entered onto the data collection form. If part of the price is paid by an insurance or other means (e.g., the insurance pays 80% and the patient pays 20%), the full price (100%) is noted. If a medicine is available and provided free of charge to all, "free" is entered onto the form and entered into the workbook.
  No discounts to specific groups of patients should be recorded but the manual advises entering discounted prices in case that they apply for all patients.
  Once the pack price and pack size are entered, the unit price is calculated (price per tablet or capsule, milliliter for liquids, gram for creams, dose for inhalers, etc.).

6.2.3.6 Data Entry

At the end of each day, area supervisors check the data collection forms. Any queries are checked with the data collector and, if need be, the outlet. Then the survey manager checks the data collection forms, and trained data entry personnel centrally enter the unit prices into the workbook. Data are double entered by a second person to reduce errors.

6.2.3.7 Data Analysis and Interpretation

6.2.3.7.1 Availability

In the WHO/HAI methodology, availability is defined as the percentage of outlets where an individual medicine was found on the day of data collection.

Based on this definition, summary data related to availability can be analyzed, such as the average (mean) percentage availability across the medicines (for originator brands and generics).

6.2.3.7.2 Prices

The methodology expresses prices as median price ratios (MPR). Median local prices are expressed as relative ratios to international reference prices. Thus, the MPR is calculated by dividing the median local unit price by the median international reference unit price.

This ratio informs about the relation of the local medicine price in comparison to the international reference price. For instance, an MPR of 2

Box 6.2.2 Management Sciences for Health (MSH) reference prices

MSH is a global nonprofit health organization that works to improve health service management systems.

Since 1986, MSH has been publishing an annual guide of supplier and buyer prices for medicines: the "International Drug Price Indicator Guide" (today renamed into "International Medical Products Price Guide"). Since 2000, the MSH has been publishing this guide in collaboration with World Health Organization (WHO).

The MSH price guide offers a spectrum of most recent price information provided by both buyers and suppliers (e.g., international organizations, government agencies, international development agencies). It acts as a reference for comparing prices of several medicines.

The MSH price guide is used for various purposes: (1) to compare latest prices paid and prices available on the international market, (2) to help plan budgets, (3) to assess the financial impact of changes to the existing medicines list of a specific country, and (4) to support the rational use of medicines through education. The MSH price guide includes the price sources, i.e., from where the medicine prices were collected and how they differ from suppliers to buyers.

Management Sciences for Health (MSH). International Drug price indicator guide; 2017. Available from: https://www.msh.org/resources/international-drug-price-indicator-guide; Management Sciences for Health (MSH), World Health Organisation (WHO). International medical products price indicator guide. 2015 ed. Arlington; 2016.

would mean that the local medicine price is twice the international reference price.

MSH prices [14,15] are recommended as most useful standard. These are prices offered by mostly not-for-profit suppliers to LMIC for multisource products, and, in general, they do not include insurance or transportation charges (see Box 6.2.2 for further information on MSH reference prices).

6.2.3.7.3 Affordability

Affordability is assessed as the number of days' wages required by the lowest-paid unskilled government worker to purchase 7 days' supply of a medicine to treat an acute condition, and 30 days for a chronic condition, based on standard treatment regimens.

The affordability analysis expresses the survey results in a slightly different way. The cost of a course therapy for important conditions is compared with the daily wage of the lowest-paid unskilled government worker, instead of comparing medicine prices with an index price. It serves as an advocacy tool because it expresses prices in relation to an individual's ability to pay for medicines. It allows explaining to policy-makers that the cost of a month's treatment for a specific condition with medicine x would require 10.5 days of wages with originator brands and 6.3 days of wages for generic medicines.

6.2.3.8 Measuring Price Components

Price components that are commonly found in the medicine supply chain are the manufacturer's selling price (MSP), insurance and freight, port and inspection charges, pharmaceutical import duties, markups (i.e., a charge added to the purchasing tax) by importers, wholesalers and retailers, tax (value added tax/VAT or goods and service tax/GST), and dispensing fees. These price components, that vary from country to country, impact patient prices.

Markups and other price components are identified by backtracking in the supply chain, starting with the retailer and looking at buying and selling prices and all that contributes to the price. To examine the contribution of price components to final prices, the WHO/HAI methodology divides the supply chain into five stages as medicines move from the manufacturer to the patient:

STAGE 1: MSP plus insurance and freight. For locally produced medicines, the Stage 1 cost is the MSP for the recommended or surveyed pack size, plus (possibly) domestic transport to the purchasing entity. For imported medicines, the Stage 1 cost is the MSP plus insurance and international freight (CIF).

STAGE 2: Landed price. The landed price includes all other price components that arise during medicine procurement and delivery to the procurement office. This includes banking fees for foreign currency purchases, inspection charges (either pre- or postshipment), port fees (docking, storage, handling, insurance in port), customs clearing, import tariff, and importer's markup. Any fees collected centrally are listed here, e.g., the Pharmacy Board fee. The landed price also includes local transport charges to the central warehouse, the importer, or the wholesaler but does not include domestic storage and distribution costs after the medicines leave the purchasing warehouse.

STAGE 3: Wholesale selling price (private) or Central Medical Stores price (public). The wholesale selling price or Central Medical Stores price is based on the landed price and includes either the wholesaler's additional expenses or the central warehouse's overhead costs, e.g., quality control, storage, handling, overhead expenses (such as salaries, security, and rent), and profit margin as well as local transport to the retailer/health facility. Many of these might be included in the wholesale markup; it is important not to count them twice.
STAGE 4: Retail price (private) or dispensary price (public). The retail (pharmacy) selling price is based on the wholesale selling price, and it includes the retailer's/dispensary's additional expenses, e.g., storage, handling, overhead expenses, and profit margin. Many of these expenses might be included in the retailer's markup; it is important not to count them twice.
STAGE 5: Dispensed price. The dispensed medicine price includes the Stage 4 price plus any dispensing fees and any sales taxes (VAT or GST), if applicable. Where there is no dispensing fee or sales tax applied, there are no Stage 5 costs and the price at the end of Stage 4 is the dispensed price. Furthermore, in many public sector programs the patient does not pay; the cost at the end of Stage 5 is intended to reflect the cost at the point of delivery, whether to the health system, insurance group, or patient. [1].

The manual suggests collecting price components for 5–7 products (mix of originator brands, LPGs, locally produced and imported products) as a case study.

6.2.3.9 International Comparisons of Data from Surveys Undertaken Using the World Health Organization/Health Action International Methodology

Data collected through surveys undertaken using the WHO/HAI methodology enable international comparisons of:

- the availability and prices of originator brands and LPG, in the public and private sectors, for global core list medicines and other medicines common to surveys,
- the "brand premium", i.e., the difference in price between an originator brand compared to the LPG equivalent,
- the affordability of selected courses of treatment, and
- the way in which the retail price of the medicine is composed in different countries.

The WHO/HAI methodology provides some guidance of how to perform international comparisons: The manual notes that the selection of countries will vary, depending on the purpose of the comparison. It is argued that the usual rationale of international comparisons, such as comparability in terms of economic wealth and development, similar population size, and similar health system structure, might not be the appropriate choice in any case. Even a comparison of very poor and very rich countries might be meaningful when, for advocacy purposes, it is shown that prices in a poor country are more or less the same as in a rich country. It is advised that the medicines included in an international comparison target a major indication and they are used in a similar manner across countries. The manual lists medicines for chronic diseases, such as diabetes medicines (e.g., metformin) and asthma medication (e.g., salbutamol inhaler), as examples.

With regard to key indicators of availability, prices, and affordability, the WHO/HAI methodology proposes the following approaches:

- Availability of medicines is compared in a similar manner to their price data. It can be done for individual products or for selected baskets of medicines.
- Prices of individual medicines: The comparison of the prices of individual medicines is considered as the most robust methodology, and it is recommended to the users of the WHO/HAI methodology. It is suggested to compare the ratio of the local price to the international reference price MPR between countries and against a reference price (a focus on a sector and/or on originator brand price ratios or LPG price ratios is possible). It is urged to use the same set of reference prices for all studies, and the MSH international reference prices are recommended (cf. also Chapter 6.2.3.7). The option of making composite price comparisons (for a large basket of medicines, such as of a disease group) is referred to in the WHO/HAI manual but is not discussed in further detail. Challenges of this type of comparisons (e.g., not comparing the exact medicine of the same pharmaceutical form and strength, the need for further data, e.g., volume data for adjusting for market power, etc.) are briefly outlined.
- Price components: The manual also invites making international comparisons at different stages of the medicine prices. It is suggested to compare the contribution of each stage of the supply chain to the final medicine price or to examine the contribution of the MSP between countries.

- Affordability: The international comparisons of affordability are made by transferring the data on the number of days' wages required to pay for a course of treatment to a cross-country comparison chart.

Adjustments for deflation/inflation are suggested in case of data comparison from different years. It is advised to consider weighting data by purchasing power parities (PPP) for the private sector (not for public sector procurement or patient prices) in case of different income levels of countries.

6.2.3.10 Exploring Policy Options

Although the WHO/HAI methodology provides a survey instrument for measuring medicines' availability and prices, the manual also addresses policy issues. It elaborates on the importance of understanding and identifying causes of high prices and price variations. It is stressed that collecting evidence is the first step to the ultimate goal of improving the availability and affordability of medicines for patients, and price reductions for governments. The manual also highlights the necessity to monitor the impact of a policy change to detect unintended consequences, whenever a policy has been introduced.

The manual also discusses possible factors that may be responsible for high medicine prices and/or low availability. These include lack of resources or underbudgeting, inefficient procurement/distribution and products of low demand as possible explanations for low public sector availability and high MSPs, and high import costs, taxes and tariffs, and high markups as possible components for high private sector prices.

The manual presents policy options to address low availability and high prices (see Box 6.2.3).

6.2.3.11 Reporting

The WHO/HAI methodology stresses the importance of producing a report, disseminating the findings and using them for advocacy to bring change. This is the ultimate goal of the price survey (cf. Chapter 6.2.3.10) because otherwise the study would be considered an interesting but futile exercise.

The manual provides practical guidance of how to write the report (including the provision of a standard report template) and which audiences to consider for dissemination.

In addition, survey managers are encouraged to submit their survey findings to HAI for inclusion in the WHO/HAI price database on HAI's

Box 6.2.3 Possible interventions and policy recommendations

Improvement of Procurement Efficiency

- For example, procurement by generic name, encouraging suppliers of quality-assured lower-cost generics to bid

Ensuring Adequate, Equitable, and Sustainable Financing

- For example, health insurance systems that cover essential medicines
- For example, schemes to make NCD medicines available in the private sector at public sector prices

Prioritized Medicine Budget

- Aiming to target widespread access to a reduced number of essential generic medicines rather than attempting to supply a larger number of both originator brand and generic medicine

Promoting the Use of Generic Medicines

- Preferential registration procedures, e.g., fast-tracking, lower fees
- Ensuring products are quality-assured
- Permitting generic substitution and providing incentives for dispensing of generics
- Educating doctors/consumers on availability and acceptability of generics

WHO, HAI. Measuring medicine prices, availability, affordability and price components. 2nd ed. Geneva: World Health Organization, Health Action International; 2008. Available from: http://www.who.int/medicines/areas/access/OMS_Medicine_prices.pdf.

website (http://haiweb.org/what-we-do/price-availability-affordability/price-availability-data/). This allows for comparisons of findings across countries and also secondary analyses as described above.

6.2.4 USE OF THE WORLD HEALTH ORGANIZATION/HEALTH ACTION INTERNATIONAL METHODOLOGY IN PRACTICE

Since the first publication of WHO/HAI methodology in 2003, more than a 100 medicine price and availability surveys have been conducted using this method. The surveys exposed poor access to medicines due to high prices and low availability.

One flagship example is a secondary analysis by Cameron et al. of data from 36 developing and middle-income countries collected using the WHO/HAI methodology [16]. The research found that generic medicine availability in the public sector was between 29.4% and 54.4%. In addition, median government procurement prices for 15 selected generic medicines were 1.11 times the international reference prices. Private sector patients paid 9—25 times the international reference price for LPGs and more than 20 times the international reference price for originator brand products across the countries. The study found that low procurement prices do not necessarily mean lower patient prices in the public sector. For acute and chronic illness, markups were up to 380% and 552%, for wholesale and retail respectively. The authors concluded that policies to increase availability and affordability, such as generic promotion, as well as the development of alternative financing mechanisms are imperative to improve access.

In 2016, Ewen et al. performed another secondary analysis of data from 30 surveys in LMIC looking at availability and affordability in combination [17]. That research was aimed as a baseline for WHO's Global Action Plan for the Prevention and Control of noncommunicable diseases 2013— 2020 (GAP) voluntary target of 80% availability of affordable essential medicines to treat noncommunicable disease (NCD) by 2025. The findings demonstrated that few NCD medicines were both available and affordable in LMIC. The authors concluded that increased commitments from governments are needed to improve the situation through the development of evidence-informed, nationally contextualized interventions, with regular monitoring of availability, patient prices, and affordability of NCD medicines. This analysis illustrates the importance of conducting surveys, making the findings public, and developing evidence-based policy recommendations.

Although the WHO/HAI methodology was originally intended to help LMIC to collect medicine price and availability information, its use has not been limited to these countries. Surveys have been conducted in high-income countries as far afield as Saudi Arabia and the Boston area in Massachusetts, USA [18].

All the price surveys undertaken using the WHO/HAI methodology have contributed to greater price transparency. However, price transparency is not the sole aim. The ultimate goal is to contribute to making medicines available and affordable, thereby improving health outcomes for the entire population.

REFERENCES

[1] WHO, HAI. Measuring medicine prices, availability, affordability and price components. 2nd ed. Geneva: World Health Organization. Health Action International; 2008 Available from: http://www.who.int/medicines/areas/access/OMS_Medicine_prices.pdf.
[2] Seiter A. A practical approach to pharmaceutical policy. Washington, DC: World Bank Publications; 2010.
[3] Morgan SG, Leopold C, Wagner AK. Drivers of expenditure on primary care prescription drugs in 10 high-income countries with universal health coverage. Canadian Medical Association Journal 2017;189(23):E794–9.
[4] Danzon PM, Kim JD. International price comparisons for pharmaceuticals. PharmacoEconomics 1998;14(1):115–28.
[5] WHO, HAI. Medicine Prices. A new approach to measurement. Working draft for field testing and revision. World Health Organization, Health Action International; 2003. Available from: http://www.haiweb.org/medicineprices/manual/manuals/MedicinePrices.pdf.
[6] Andersson F. Methodological aspects of international drug price comparisons. PharmacoEconomics 1993;4(4):247–56.
[7] Machado M, O'Brodovich R, Krahn M, Einarson TR. International drug price comparisons: quality assessment. Revista Panamericana de Salud Públic 2011;29(1):46–51.
[8] Rosian I, Vogler S, Vander Stichele R, Larsen L, Odegaard B, Brahm AK, et al. EURO-MED-STAT–Monitoring expenditure and utilization of medicinal products in the European Union countries: a Public Health approach. The European Journal of Public Health 2003;13(Suppl. 3):95–100.
[9] Walley T, Folino-Gallo P, Barry M, Bruzzone M, DeJoncheere K, Rosian I, et al. The EurMedStat proposals on indicators for price and utilisation. Italian Journal of Public Health 2006;3:15–21.
[10] Hogerzeil HV, Samson M, Casanovas JV, Rahmani-Ocora L. Is access to essential medicines as part of the fulfilment of the right to health enforceable through the courts? The Lancet 2006;368(9532):305–11.
[11] World Health Organization (WHO). The world medicines situation. Geneva. 2004.
[12] Wirtz VJ, Hogerzeil HV, Gray AL, Bigdeli M, de Joncheere CP, Ewen MA, et al. Essential medicines for universal health coverage. The Lancet 2017;389(10067): 403–76.
[13] Health Action International (HAI). Collecting evidence on medicine prices & availability. Update to the manual. 2016. Available from: http://haiweb.org/what-we-do/price-availability-affordability/collecting-evidence-on-medicine-prices-availability/.
[14] Management Sciences for Health (MSH). International drug price indicator guide. 2017. Available from: https://www.msh.org/resources/international-drug-price-indicator-guide.
[15] Management Sciences for Health (MSH), World Health Organisation (WHO). International medical products price indicator guide. 2016. 2015 edition. Arlington.
[16] Cameron A, Ewen M, Ross-Degnan D, Ball D, Laing R. Medicine prices, availability, and affordability in 36 developing and middle-income countries: a secondary analysis. The Lancet 2009;373(9659):240–9.
[17] Ewen M, Zweekhorst M, Regeer B, Laing R. Baseline assessment of WHO's target for both availability and affordability of essential medicines to treat non-communicable diseases. PLoS One 2017;12(2):e0171284.

[18] Sharma A, Rorden L, Ewen M, Laing R. Evaluating availability and price of essential medicines in Boston area (Massachusetts, USA) using WHO/HAI methodology. Journal of pharmaceutical policy and practice 2016;9(1):12.
[19] World Health Organization. WHO guideline on country pharmaceutical pricing policies. Geneva. 2013.

CHAPTER 7

Terminology – Is Talking About Definitions Boring, or Is It the Starting Point?

Nina Zimmermann
WHO Collaborating Centre for Pharmaceutical Pricing and Reimbursement Policies, Pharmacoeconomics Department, Gesundheit Österreich GmbH (GÖG/Austrian Public Health Institute), Vienna, Austria

LIST OF ABBREVIATIONS

ADR	Adverse Drug Reaction
ATC	Anatomical Therapeutic Chemical Classification System
DDD	Defined Daily Dose
EU	European Union
HTA	Health Technology Assessment
ID	Identification Code
NHS	National Health Service
PPRI	Pharmaceutical Pricing and Reimbursement Information
PRP	Pharmacy Retail Price
SU	Standard Unit
VAT	Value-Added Tax
WHO	World Health Organization

7.1 PURPOSE

When preparing a medicine price survey it is crucial to define some cornerstones of the piece of research:

- which products do you want to look at,
- which price type will be surveyed (ex-factory price, wholesale price, etc.),
- which data sources will be consulted (international databases, national data sources etc.),
- how are the prices calculated (incl. margins, mark-ups, taxes, discounts etc.) and
- further elements (cf. Chapter 9).

Medicine Price Surveys, Analyses, and Comparisons
ISBN 978-0-12-813166-4
https://doi.org/10.1016/B978-0-12-813166-4.00013-9

For the correct interpretation of medicine prices and the correct development of an appropriate methodological design of a price study, researchers are required to understand how prices are set in their national contexts, which components they include and which incentives are behind the policies used. Misunderstandings and misinterpretations may occur when definitions of terms used in a survey are missing or vague, or when researchers are not fully aware of key methodological concepts of medicine price research. Researchers may easily challenge the level of terminology knowledge about medicine price in their group by asking questions as follows: Does everybody in our team understand the difference between discount and rebate, or between mark-up or margin, for instance? Can the ex-factory price, the manufacturer price and the list price be considered as synonyms?

Common understanding is of major importance in any field. Therefore development and communication of ambiguous definitions as part of a comprehensive terminology strategy is one of the major actions in the methodology design of a medicine price study. This helps contribute to a situation in which all people involved in providing information and/or using the findings – no matter whether they are experts or lay persons – understand the underlying concepts and notions in that specific field. It is often a matter of details to ensure correct approaches in medicine price surveys, analyses and comparisons. Specifications related to medicine prices (in terms of the selected price types and units of comparison, for instance, cf. also Chapter 9) are required to achieve comparability. The importance of definitions might not seem to be obvious at the start of a project but uncertainties about details can arise in the course of time, e.g., when trying to interpret the results of a price survey. It is thus strongly advised to define variables, concepts and terms at an early stage of the research.

The need for clarity and a basis of common understanding was also a major lesson learned in the PPRI (Pharmaceutical Pricing and Reimbursement Information) project (for further information on PPRI see http://whocc.goeg.at) in which a network of competent authorities working in the field of pricing and reimbursement policies was built. Based on observations about misunderstandings among the PPRI network members, all of them experts in the pharmaceutical field, it was decided in 2006 to establish a glossary of pharmaceutical terms, which includes definitions and descriptions [2].

This Glossary [1] has regularly been updated and meanwhile contains more than 350 terms. It is accessible at the website of the Vienna WHO

Collaborating Centre for Pharmaceutical Pricing and Reimbursement Policies, http://whocc.goeg.at — translations of key terms exist in German and Spanish.

If not stated otherwise, the terms used in this book refer to the definitions as provided in this chapter.

7.2 KEY TERMS

In this section relevant terms related to medicine price surveys are defined. The majority of the definitions were taken or adapted from the above-mentioned Glossary of the WHO Collaborating Centre for Pharmaceutical Pricing and Reimbursement Policies: Glossary of pharmaceutical terms. Update July 2016. Accessible at http://whocc.goeg.at/Glossary (short: WHO CC Glossary).

Key term	Definition/description	Source
	Product-related terms	
Medicine (synonyms: pharmaceutical, pharmaceutical product, medication, medicinal product)	Any substance or combination of substances which may be used in or administered to human beings either with a view to restoring, correcting or modifying physiological functions by exerting a pharmacological, immunological or metabolic action, or to making a medical diagnosis. Terms to be avoided: drug unless in well-established terms such as adverse drug reaction (ADR).	Adapted from Ref. [1]
Pharmaceutical form (dosage form, dose form)	Way in which a medicine is presented, e.g., a film-coated tablet, an ointment, a vial or a spray. In the WHO/HAI methodology to measure medicine prices and availability, the term 'dosage form' is used [9].	[1]
Dosage (synonym: strength)	The content of an active ingredient expressed quantitatively per dosage unit, per unit of volume or per unit of weight, according to the pharmaceutical dose form (e.g., 200 mg/mL, 4 g).	[1]

Continued

Key term	Definition/description	Source
	Product-related terms	
Presentation	A medicine defined by its dosage (strength), pharmaceutical form, pack size and also, if applicable, container and/or supplements (e.g., needles); it is uniquely identifiable due to an ID (identification) code granted during marketing authorization.	[1]
Pack size	The amount of separate items bound together in one package and offered together as a single or inclusive unit (e.g., a pack may contain 28 tablets) for a specific price.	[1]
Price-related terms		
Medicine price	Value component of pharmaceutical expenditure. Typically, it is indicated per pack, but it can also refer to items in a pack or to standard units. It can be indicated for different ➲ price types.	Adapted from Ref. [1]
Price type	The level at which the price of a medicine is set. Common price types include: • ex-factory price • pharmacy purchasing price • pharmacy retail price	Adapted from Ref. [1]
Ex-factory price (synonyms: manufacturer price, ex-manufacturer price, manufacturer's selling price)	The price at the level of industry, charged by a pharmaceutical manufacturer. Official ex-factory prices can be lowered by discounts or other arrangements offered by manufacturers (➲ actual price).	Adapted from Ref. [1]
Pharmacy purchasing price (synonyms: wholesale price, pharmacy purchase price)	The price charged by wholesalers to the retailers (usually community pharmacies). It is based on the ex-factory price and additionally includes any remuneration for pharmaceutical wholesale (e.g., in the form of a wholesale ➲ mark-up or a wholesale ➲ margin).	Adapted from Ref. [1]
Pharmacy retail price (abbreviated as	The price charged by community pharmacies to the general public. It is based on the pharmacy purchasing price	Adapted from Ref. [1]

Key term	Definition/description Product-related terms	Source
PRP; synonyms: public price, consumer price)	and additionally includes any pharmacy remuneration (such as a pharmacy ➲ mark-up, a pharmacy ➲ margin or dispensing fee). It can be a gross PRP (including value-added tax/VAT) or a net PRP (excluding VAT).	
List price	The price that purchasers display as the price at which they are prepared to sell their product and/or regulated by legislation. A list price is quoted and/or indicated in a purchaser's price list, a catalogue, on an internet site, in advertisements, in a national price list/formulary or similar. A list price may differ from the actual transaction price. Depending on the country and/or the product, they may or may not include delivery and installation costs, ➲ value-added tax/VAT and other indirect taxes on products, ➲ discounts, surcharges and ➲ rebates, invoiced service charges and voluntary gratuities.	[1]
Tendered/ procured price	The price stated as the outcome of a ➲ procurement or ➲ tendering procedure. The tenderer who offered the most advantageous bid (with price as one key award criterion) is awarded.	[1]
Hospital price	The price or amount paid by a purchaser in the hospital setting (e.g., a hospital pharmacy) in order to take delivery of certain unit of medicines. Often, the hospital list price corresponds to the ➲ ex-factory price, in some cases to the ➲ pharmacy purchasing price. It may or may not include ➲ value-added tax/VAT. In addition, ➲ discounts and/or ➲ rebates may be granted to the hospitals by the suppliers.	Adapted from Ref. [1]

Continued

Key term	Definition/description Product-related terms	Source
Maximum price (synonym: price ceiling)	An upper threshold provided for by regulation or by tender specifications. Purchasers are not allowed to price above this threshold but have flexibility to set a price below this ceiling, thus making use of a competitive setting. Maximum prices can be set at all ➲ price types.	Adapted from Ref. [1]
Price per unit (synonym: unit price)	The price of a single item in one package (calculated as the price divided by the pack size).	[1]
Standard Unit (SU)	An SU is measured differently depending on the formulation of the medicine. By and large, one SU usually equals one tablet, one capsule, one suppository or pessary, one pre-filled syringe/cartridge, pen, vial or ampoule, one dose of an inhaled medicine or 5 mL of an oral syrup or suspension. SUs of topical treatments, granules, powders, pellets, eye and ear preparations vary depending on the exact composition of the product but can be based on millilitres or grams. In addition, in some countries an SU of a reconstituted product will treated as mg.	[3]
Actual price (synonyms: real price, transaction price)	The price that is actually paid by the purchaser taking into account any granted discounts and/or rebates. The actual price may correspond to the ➲ list price, ➲ ex-factory price or ➲ pharmacy purchase price if no price lowering agreements are in place. Actual prices are often kept confidential.	[1]
Reimbursement price	The reimbursement price is the maximum amount paid for by a third party payer. Few countries explicitly publish official reimbursement prices (e.g., Austria — the so-called 'sickness fund price'), and in some countries the reimbursement price is set at a defined percentage share of the pharmacy retail price. Under a reference price system, the reimbursement price may correspond to the reference price.	Adapted from Ref. [1]

Key term	Definition/description Product-related terms	Source
Reference price	Price that is set in a reference price system, where the third party payer funds a maximum amount (= reference price), while the patient must pay the difference between the reference price and the ➲ pharmacy retail price of the medicine, in addition to any further co-payments (e.g., prescription fees, or percentage co-payment rates).	Adapted from Ref. [1]
Price components	Elements in which a (medicine) price is composed of. They include, for instance, ➲ margins, ➲ mark-ups, ➲ taxes and ➲ duties.	[1]
Margin	The percentage of the selling price that is profit. In the case of the pharmaceutical distribution, a wholesale or pharmacy margin is a price-dependent type of remuneration awarded to distribution actors such as wholesalers and pharmacies for handling their services. The wholesale margin is the gross profit of wholesalers, expressed as a percentage of the ➲ pharmacy purchasing price (wholesale price). The pharmacy margin is the gross profit of pharmacies expressed as a percentage of the ➲ pharmacy retail price.	[1]
Mark-up (synonym: distribution mark-up)	The mark-up is the percentage of the purchasing price added on to get the selling price. A mark-up is added on to the total cost incurred by the producer of a good in order to create a profit. The wholesale mark-up is the gross profit of wholesalers, expressed as a percentage add-on to the ➲ ex-factory price. The pharmacy mark-up is the gross profit of pharmacies expressed as a percentage add-on to the ➲ pharmacy purchasing price (wholesale price).	[1]

Continued

Key term	Definition/description	Source
	Product-related terms	
Value-added tax (VAT)	A sales tax on products collected in stages by enterprises. It is a wide-ranging tax usually designed to cover most or all goods and services, including medicines. The VAT rate of medicines in European Union Member States is often lower than the standard VAT rate.	[1]
Duty (synonym: customs duty)	A tax levied on imports (goods that are imported from another country where they had been manufactured) and, in some cases, on exports by the customs authorities to raise state revenue, and/or to protect domestic industries.	[4]
Defined daily dose (DDD)	A unit of measurement to specify the assumed average maintenance dose per day for a medicine used for its main indication in the adult. A DDD will normally be only assigned for a substance after a product has been approved and marketed in at least one country. The basic principle is to assign only one DDD per route of administration within an ATC code. DDDs for plain substances are normally based on monotherapy. Doses for individual patients and patients groups will often differ from the DDD. A DDD does not necessarily reflect the recommended or prescribed daily dose. DDDs are not established for topical products, sera, vaccines, antineoplastic agents, allergen extracts, general and local anaesthetics and contrast media.	Adapted from Ref. [1]
Pricing policies		
Pricing policies	Regulations and actions taken by government authorities to set the price of medicine as part of exercising price control. Strategies by industry and supply chain actors to determine and set a medicine price are not subsumed under the term 'policy'.	Adapted from Ref. [1]

Key term	Definition/description	Source
	Product-related terms	
Statutory pricing	Pricing procedure, where medicine prices are set on a regulatory basis (e.g., law, enactment, decree).	Adapted from Ref. [1]
Price control (price regulation)	Action by a government authority to set the price of a medicine and/or indirectly influence it (e.g., through statutory pricing, price negotiations, public procurement). Contrary to free pricing. Criteria for setting prices may be prices in the same country or other countries, (production) costs, return on investment, mark-ups etc.	Adapted from Ref. [1]
Pricing procedure	There are several methods how government authorities can set the price of a medicine: internal price referencing, external price referencing, cost-plus pricing and profit control. Sometimes pricing procedures and pricing policies are used as synonyms.	[1]
External price referencing (synonyms: international price comparison, external reference pricing)	The practice of using the price(s) of a medicine in one or several countries in order to derive a benchmark or reference price for the purposes of setting or negotiating the price of the product in a given country.	[1]
Value-based pricing (VBP)	Through this policy authorities set the prices of a new medicine and/or decide on reimbursement based on the therapeutic value that a medicine offers, usually assessed through health technology assessment (HTA) or economic evaluation. In a fully fledged VBP, the pricing and reimbursement systems are integrated.	[1]
Health technology assessment (HTA)	A multidisciplinary process that summarises information about the medical, social, economic and ethical issues related to the use of a health technology in a systematic, transparent, unbiased, robust manner. Its aim is to inform the formulation of safe, effective, health policies that are patient focused and seek to achieve best value.	[5]

Continued

Key term	Definition/description Product-related terms	Source
Conditional pricing	Pricing policy that links the price of a medicine to specific criteria (e.g., health outcomes, minimum purchases). Conditional pricing falls under a variety of terms and taxonomies (e.g., managed-entry agreements, risk-sharing, pay-for-performance).	[1]
Managed entry agreement (MEA)	An arrangement between a manufacturer and payer/provider that enables access to (coverage/reimbursement of) a health technology subject to specified conditions. These arrangements can use a variety of mechanisms to address uncertainty about the performance of technologies or to manage the adoption of technologies in order to maximize their effective use, or limit their budget impact.	[6]
Internal price referencing	The practice of using the price(s) of identical medicines (ATC 5 level) or similar products (ATC 4 level) or even with therapeutic equivalent treatment (not necessarily a medicine) in a country in order to derive a benchmark or reference price for the purposes of setting or negotiating the price or reimbursement of the product in a given country.	[1]
Differential pricing	Cross-country approach of setting the price of medicine in accordance with the ability-to-pay, and/or the economic situation of the involved countries. The pricing decision would be taken in a collaborative approach by the governments of the involved countries or an international organization. There is a difference to 'price discrimination' ('market discrimination', 'Ramsey pricing') that describes a business strategy of economic actors to segment the market according to the observed demand-elasticity of consumers.	Adapted from Ref. [7]

Key term	Definition/description	Source
	Product-related terms	
Free pricing	Pricing policy, in which pharmaceutical companies determine the price of the medicine they launch	[1]
Tendering	Any formal and competitive procurement procedure through which tenders (offers) are requested, received and evaluated for the procurement of goods, works or services, and as a consequence of which an award is made to the tenderer whose tender/offer is the most advantageous.	[1]
Procurement	A process to purchase goods and services (e.g., medicines) that involves many steps and many stakeholders based on national, or supranational, regulation, policies, structures and procedures. An efficient procurement process must ensure that four strategic objectives are achieved: • the procurement of the most cost-effective medicines in the right quantities, • the selection of reliable suppliers of high-quality products, • procurement and distribution systems that ensure timely and undisturbed deliveries, • processes that ensure the lowest possible total costs of procurement.	Adapted from Ref. [1]
Price negotiation	A pricing procedure, in which medicine prices are discussed and agreed (e.g., between manufacturer and third party payer).	[1]
Price review	Evaluation of the price of all, or groups of, medicines, typically in comparison to the prices of the same medicines in other countries, in order to account for developments such as the market entry of medicines and price changes in other countries and exchange rate evolutions. Price reviews can be done systematically (e.g., once a year) or out-of-schedule.	[1]

Continued

Key term	Definition/description	Source
	Product-related terms	
Price notification	A form of pricing procedure where pharmaceutical companies can freely set the price of a medicine (free pricing) but have to officially inform the authorities about the price of the medicine.	[1]
Cost-plus pricing	Pricing policy that determines a medicine price by taking into account production costs, promotional expenses, research & development, administration costs, overheads and profit.	Adapted from Ref. [1]
Price studies		
Price study	Any research that investigates prices, or price components, of medicines in a single country or across countries at a specific date or over time. A medicine price study can take the form of a survey, an analysis and/or a (cross-country) comparison or a combination.	[1]
Price survey	Price study that aims to access and collect medicine price data according to a predefined methodology.	[1]
Price analysis	A medicine price analysis aims to interpret medicine price data. It can address specific therapeutic groups of medicines, different types of prices (such as government procurement prices and consumer prices) or several countries, for instance. Data can be collected and analysed over a long period (time-series analysis) or one point in time. A price analysis can also be used to determine other indicators, e.g., to assess the affordability of a medicine.	[1]
Price comparison	A cross-country (or cross-national) medicine price comparison aims to survey and analyse data of medicine prices in more than one country. Within a country, further comparisons can be made, such as across sectors (e.g., public vs. private sector) or between groups of medicines (e.g., originator vs. generic medicines).	[1]

Key term	Definition/description	Source
	Product-related terms	
Index	A figure in a system or scale representing the average value of specified prices, shares or other items as compared with some reference figure (e.g., of a specific country or year).	Adapted from Ref. [8]
Other pricing-related terms		
Discount	A price reduction granted to specified purchasers under specific conditions prior to purchase.	[1]
Rebate	Rebate is a payment made to the purchaser after the transaction has occurred. Purchasers (either hospitals or pharmacies) receive a bulk refund from a wholesaler, based on sales of a particular product or total purchases from that wholesaler or manufacturer over a particular period of time.	[1]
Clawback	A system allowing third party payers to recoup (part of the) discounts/rebates granted in a reimbursement system between various stakeholders, e.g., wholesalers and pharmacists Or A system by which money already paid by public payers to pharmaceutical companies, wholesalers or pharmacists must be paid back under certain conditions.	Adapted from Ref. [1]

7.3 TRAINING MATERIAL: EXERCISES

7.3.1 Definitions – Multiple Choice Questions

1. Medicine prices can be determined by
   - **a.** the manufacturer
   - **b.** the wholesalers
   - **c.** the pharmacists
   - **d.** the state (legislation)
   - **e.** the public payer

2. Which price types can be regulated?
   a. Only ex-factory prices (manufacturer prices)
   b. Only pharmacy purchasing prices (wholesale prices)
   c. Only pharmacy retail prices (consumer prices)
   d. In principle, all three prices types
   e. In principle, all three prices types in the out-patient sector
3. External price referencing is
   a. building clusters of identical medicines in your country for the purposes of setting or negotiating the price of the product in your country
   b. comparing price(s) of a medicine in one or several countries in order to derive a benchmark or reference price for the purposes of setting or negotiating the price of the product in a given country
   c. first comparing price(s) of a medicine in one or several countries and then building clusters of similar medicines in your country for the purposes of setting or negotiating the price of the product in your country
4. Discounts and rebates
   a. are only granted in the hospital sector
   b. are always confidential between the manufacturer and the hospital/public payer
   c. help purchasers achieve the best price
5. What's the difference between a margin and a mark-up?
   a. there is no difference, these terms are used synonymously
   b. margins are calculated on the basis of the purchasing price added on to get the selling price and mark-ups are added to reach the final consumer price
   c. mark-ups are added on the purchasing price whereas margins are deducted from the selling price to reach the purchasing price

7.3.2 Cloze test - Please Fill Out This Cloze Test by Adding the Missing Words

Term	Definition
.... pricing	Pricing policy that determines a medicine price by taking into account production costs, promotional expenses, research & ...., administration costs, overheads and ....
Pharmacy .... price (synonym:	The price charged by .... to the retailers (usually community pharmacies). It is based on the

Term	Definition
.... price, pharmacy purchase price)	ex-factory price and additionally includes any .... for pharmaceutical wholesale (e.g., in the form of a wholesale .... or a wholesale margin).
Discounts	A .... (2 words) granted to specified purchasers under specific conditions prior to ....
.... pricing	Pricing procedure, where medicine prices are set on a .... (2 words) (e.g., law, enactment, decree).
Hospital price	The price or amount paid by a purchaser in the .... setting (e.g., a hospital pharmacy) in order to take delivery of certain unit of medicines. Often, the hospital list price corresponds to the .... (2 words), in some cases to the pharmacy purchasing price. It may or may not include value-added tax/VAT. In addition, ... and/or rebates may be granted to the hospitals by the suppliers.

7.3.3 Crossword Puzzle

1 Tablets, vials or syringes are pharmaceutical....
2 The price a pharmaceutical supplier charges a hospital pharmacy. (2 words)
3 An entity or a person who sells goods to consumers/patients.
4 What does the E in EPR stand for?
5 A system by which money already paid by public payers to pharmaceutical companies, wholesalers or pharmacists must be paid back under certain conditions.
6 Pharmaceutical companies determine the prices of the products they launch. (2 words)
7 A price reduction granted to specified purchasers of a pharmaceutical product under specific conditions.
8 Contrary to free pricing – price .....
9 .... evaluation used in value-based pricing
10 Synonym for Pharmacy Retail Price (2 words)
11 Companies have to officially inform the authorities about the price of the medicine. (2 words)
12 What does the T in HTA stand for?

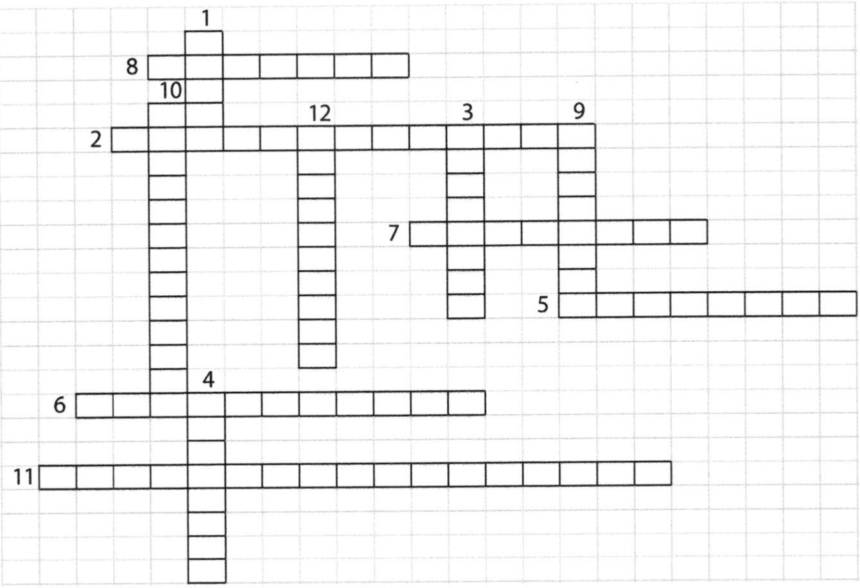

Solutions of the training exercises are found in the Annex at the end of the book.

REFERENCES

[1] WHO Collaborating Centre for Pharmaceutical Pricing and Reimbursement Policies: Glossary of Pharmaceutical Terms. Update 2018. Available from: http://whocc.goeg.at/Glossary/Search.

[2] Vogler S, Leopold C, Zimmermann N, Habl C, de Joncheere K. The Pharmaceutical pricing and reimbursement information (PPRI) initiative-experiences from engaging with pharmaceutical policy makers. Health Policy and Technology 2014;3:139–48.

[3] Laing R, Stephens P. Indicators for tracking the effect of the economic crisis on pharmaceutical consumption, expenditures and unit prices. IMS and WHO; 2009. Available from: http://www.who.int/medicines/areas/policy/WHO_IMSreportonglobaldrugconsumption.pdf.

[4] Business dictionary: customs duty. Adapted. Available from: http://www.businessdictionary.com/definition/customs-duty.html.

[5] EunetHTA. What is health technology assessement. 2018. Available from: http://www.eunethta.eu/faq/Category%201-0#t287n73.

[6] Klemp M, Frønsdal KB, Facey K. What principles should govern the use of managed entry agreements? International Journal of Technology Assessment in Health Care January 2011;27(1):77–83.

[7] Vogler S, Lepuschütz L, Schneider P, Stühlinger V. Study on enhanced cross-country coordination in the area of pharmaceutical product pricing. Vienna: Funded by the Health Programme of the European Union; 2016. Available from: https://ec.europa.eu/health//sites/health/files/systems_performance_assessment/docs/pharmaproductpricing_frep_en.pdf.

[8] English Oxford Dictionary. Definition of index. Available from: https://en.oxforddictionaries.com/definition/index.
[9] WHO, HAI. Measuring medicine prices, availability, affordability and price components, 2nd ed. Geneva: World Health Organization, Health Action International; 2008. Available from: http://www.who.int/medicines/areas/access/OMS_Medicine_prices.pdf.

CHAPTER 8

Medicine Price Data Sources

Sabine Vogler, Peter Schneider
WHO Collaborating Centre for Pharmaceutical Pricing and Reimbursement Policies, Pharmacoeconomics Department, Gesundheit Österreich GmbH (GÖG/Austrian Public Health Institute), Vienna, Austria

LIST OF ABBREVIATIONS

AMDS	AIDS Medicines and Diagnostics Service
ARV	Antiretroviral
ATC	Anatomical therapeutic classification
CEDD	Common European Drug Database
DDD	Defined daily dose(s)
DIME	Decisiones Informadas en Medicamentos
EC	European Commission
ECPHIN	European Community Pharmaceutical Information Network
EPR	External price referencing
EU	European Union
Euripid	European Integrated Price Information Database
GPRM	Global Price Reporting Mechanism
HAI	Health Action International
HIV	Human immunodeficiency virus
INN	International Nonproprietary Name
LMIC	Low- and middle-income country/ies
MSH	Management Sciences for Health
PAHO	Pan American Health Organization
PIEMEDS	Price Information Exchange for Essential Medicines
PPI	Pharma Price Information
SAGE	Strategic Advisory Group of Experts on Immunization
TED	Tenders Electronic Daily
UNICEF	United Nations Children's Fund
V3P	Vaccine Product, Price, and Procurement
WHO	World Health Organization

"Where do I get price data?" This question has been regularly addressed to the authors of this chapter by researchers who aim to conduct price studies. It was also raised by technical experts in pricing authorities who wanted to review medicine prices in their country in comparison to other countries. Some researchers insisted on applying a specific method regarding the inclusion of medicines, countries, and price types because

Medicine Price Surveys, Analyses, and Comparisons
ISBN 978-0-12-813166-4
https://doi.org/10.1016/B978-0-12-813166-4.00014-0

they had a price data set at hand, and they wanted to use these data. As a result, they adjusted the methods to their "convenience sample".

The choice of the data source is crucial. The level of completeness and the organization of data in a source can have important implications on the findings. Thus, sufficient attention and time resources should be dedicated to the data source selection process during the planning phase of a price study.

The objective of this chapter is to provide guidance to researchers and other experts, who are interested in performing a price survey, analysis, or cross-national comparison, about the identification of possible data sources, assessment of their feasibility, and selection of the most appropriate one(s) in accordance with the purpose of their study. In addition to the provision of practical support, the authors aim to raise awareness for the sensitiveness of this methodological decision.

The considerations discussed below are also of relevance for policy-makers when they decide on reference countries for external price referencing (EPR) because access to appropriate data sources is a key element [1]. Additional aspects need to be considered in the selection of reference countries for EPR, which will be discussed later in Part 3 (chapters 11-15) of this book.

8.1 SELECTION OF MEDICINE PRICE DATA SOURCES

8.1.1 Taxonomy of Data Sources

Conducting price research can, in principle, be based on three possible data sources:

1. Availability of a convenience sample,
2. Receipt of data in a customized, possibly aggregated way (from a price data service, for instance), or
3. Collection of price data by accessing identified data sources.

This chapter refers, in principle, to the third-mentioned option of data collection. Nonetheless, some key questions to assess the feasibility of the data (as outlined in Table 8.1) should always be considered. Research using a convenience sample or data of a customized query might, in some cases, still require the survey of further data.

Sources for data collection include:

a. (national) medicine price lists, registers, and databases,
b. literature, and
c. (on-site) surveys from pricing and procurement authorities or from supply chain actors.

Table 8.1 Catalog to assess the feasibility of medicine price data sources

Criteria	Questions	Checklist: recommendations of how to proceed
Mandatory criteria		
Date	• Do you know which dates the price data refer to? • How frequently is the data source updated? • Does the data source also provide historic data (at which intervals) that are presented in the same format?	It is absolutely crucial that researchers know the date which the price data refer to. Otherwise no correct standardization of data (e.g., inflation adjustment for time series analyses) can be made. Also, if you apply exchange rates, they have to refer to the appropriate date or period. Do not use price data for any research if you do not know the date of the data! The database might be out-dated (see, for instance, the comments made on the EURO-MED-STAT database set up for research purposes, cf. Chapter 8.2.2). Knowledge about the frequency of the updates is appreciated. This is particularly needed if time series analyses are conducted. Researchers must be sure that included data really represent updates and are not simply extrapolated. Ideally, price data should be consistently presented in the same format. Otherwise, changes in the way in which they are presented should be clearly indicated. In case of breaks in the presentation of the price data, it should be explored whether, or not, these changes are considerable. This could justify the exclusion of the data source. Practical advice: Some databases are regularly updated (even at a daily basis). But the historic price information is no longer provided to the users. Unless other solutions can be found (e.g., agreements with data source providers), data over time from these sources can only be used in prospective study design. However, in such cases, researchers need to follow up the changes in the data sources on a regular basis (in accordance with the frequency of changes in the source).

Continued

Table 8.1 Catalog to assess the feasibility of medicine price data sources—cont'd

Criteria	Questions	Checklist: recommendations of how to proceed
Geographic scope	• Does the data source offer information that is valid for the whole country (or other defined geographic area)? • If this is not the case: Does it specify the gaps?	If there is no price regulation or no central procurement for a whole country (or any other defined geographic area), prices may vary between regions, and between pharmacies, dispensaries, and retailers of medicines. Researchers are advised to check in advance whether this is the case for their selected medicines at the defined price type (e.g., exfactory prices might be uniform throughout a country, but the final pharmacy retail prices of a medicines group, such as nonprescription medicines, may differ between pharmacies). In case of such possible variation, it should be checked whether, or not, price information covers a number of data points that are considered comparable for the studied area. <u>Practical advice:</u> Even in high-income countries with price regulation, prices of some medicines (particularly nonreimbursed medicines and nonprescription medicines) are not controlled and can vary across the country. It is advised to assess the legal framework of price regulation in a country included in the study, and check to which medicine regulations apply.
Medicines	• Does the data source offer price information for the required groups of medicines? • Does the data source specify which medicines (e.g., nonprescription, nonfunded medicines, hospital-only medicines, those not marketed) are included/not included?	Experience has shown that a considerable share of data sources focus on specific parts of the pharmaceutical market. Price lists and databases provided by public funders usually include only medicines that they (co-)fund. Because nonprescription medicines tend not to be funded in many countries, they likely are not included in these sources. Because of the fragmentation of the pharmaceutical system in many countries, with different payers and payment mechanisms for the outpatient and inpatient sectors, data sources provided by public payers responsible for the outpatient sector usually do not provide price information for medicines applied in hospitals.

	• Does the source fail to provide price data for some of the medicines included? • Are price data offered for single presentations? • Is it explained why price information has not been included in the data source?	During the selection process of the data source(s), researchers and other users are strongly advised to check the coverage of the source. If no information about the scope of medicines included is made available, further inquiries are recommended: you may address the owners/managers of the data source and/or test the source by searching for selected medicines you are interested in. Should the data source not be publicly accessible, ask the owners/managers to provide access to a demo version or to share with you a results sample. Reviewing a demo version also allows checking if the price data are provided at the level of the individual presentation (i.e., a medicine in a defined dosage, pharmaceutical form, and pack size, as specified by the marketing authorization ID code). Given the limited coverage of several existing medicine price sources, data collection from more than one source might be needed. In such cases, special attention should be given to ensuring comparability of the data retrieved from different sources, with regard to possible variation in date, price type, and other characteristics of the data. Practical advice: In some data sources price information is only available for some medicines. Other medicines might be listed, but without price information. To avoid unexpected difficulties during the price survey, it is recommended to carefully check the actual content of the database in advance.

Continued

Table 8.1 Catalog to assess the feasibility of medicine price data sources—cont'd

Criteria	Questions	Checklist: recommendations of how to proceed
Price data	• Does the source offer price, expenditure, or cost data? • At which price type, or types, does the source provide the data? • Does the data source offer price information for the price type that was selected for the analysis? • Is the format of how data are presented clear? • Can price information be standardized?	A study can be performed for different price types. Although some authors have been arguing for, and against, the use of specific price types (cf. Chapter 6.1), any of these price types can be relevant for a price survey (cf. Chapter 9). It is important to select the price type in line with the research question. The availability of a specific price type in a source should not impact the methodological decision of the choice of the price type. Having said this, it is advised to check in advance whether, or not, the data source provides data for the relevant price type(s) of the study. Alternatively, it could be explored whether, or not, the selected price type might be derived from information provided in the source, e.g., calculating the pharmacy retail price based on the exfactory price plus the application of statutory mark-ups for pharmaceutical wholesale and community pharmacy. Cross-country comparisons must be done for the same price type. Therefore, it has to be checked in advance whether data sources of different countries offer the selected price type, or another price type that allows determining the selected price type. Also, the format of how price data are presented (e.g., per pack, per standard unit per defined daily dose (DDD), per treatment course) must be clear, and the information required (such as the pack size, the DDD used) to do a standardization of price data retrieved from different sources must be available. Make sure that price data (and not expenditure or sales data) are included in the data source! In practice, it has been observed that the terms "price," "expenditure," and "costs" are sometimes used as synonyms but this is not correct.

		<u>Practical information:</u> Check, or ask the data source owners/managers about the original source of the data. Are the data administrative data, as published by law, or were they collected from points of sale? Are the prices secondary data derived from other primary data sources? These questions help identify whether the source offers price data, or solely estimates of prices.
Accessibility	• Is the data freely accessible? Do you have to register? • Is it password protected? • For how long will you be granted access to the protected source (one point in time or for a longer period)? • Is it a price service that offers customized findings? How long do you have to wait for the delivery of the data? • Is data provision free of charge? Do you know the total cost that you will have to pay (e.g., are there additional costs per query, or for accessing supplementary background data)?	In principle, there are three options of how data can be accessed: 1) they are freely accessible (e.g., no registration, no password, no costs); 2) accessible after having been granted access (after a check of your eligibility status, or against payment); and 3) no access to the primary data source but a provision of defined results (through a price service). All three approaches have advantages and limitations. Option 1 offers the benefit of being immediately able to check the appropriateness of the source for the study's purpose (no demo version needs to be requested), and so it allows getting started with the data collection without any delay. Furthermore, it does not require ensuring funding. Still, freely accessible data sources should be critically assessed with regard to the other criteria, in particular the "reliability" criterion (see below). Major barriers to access sources under options 2 and 3 are the time it takes until you get the data and the costs. There is the risk that time to discuss the request with the owners/managers of the source is invested in vain because eventually data from this source will not be used. A medicine price service has the advantage that in return for investments (costs and negotiation time) substantial time can be saved because the collection of the primary price data is delegated. This is especially an advantage for large amounts of data. Using a medicine price service may provide the benefit of receiving additional information required for the analysis.

Continued

Table 8.1 Catalog to assess the feasibility of medicine price data sources—cont'd

Criteria	Questions	Checklist: recommendations of how to proceed
		Practical advice: Researchers who are interested in performing a price study are recommended to provide for some budget to purchase price data that would otherwise not be accessible. Researchers may be able to get access to the price data at lower costs because some providers offer discounts if data are used for research, or by research institutions.
Reliability	• Do you know who owns/manages the data source? • Are contact details indicated? Were requests responded in due time? • Is it a new data source, or has it been established for a long period of time? • Have scientific papers been published that used data from the source? • Do you know researchers who worked with data of the identified source? What were their experiences?	Unpleasant experiences that researchers may encounter during a price study include: 1) the data source is no longer accessible (e.g., a website is shut down), 2) no delivery of the ordered price data (or requested access is not granted) despite payments having been made, and 3) no contact person of the data source can be reached. This may happen in cases of fraudulent "fake providers", but when reliable experts have set up a price data source as part of their research but no resources were available for follow up for maintenance after the end of the project. Therefore, researchers are urged to identify the owners/managers of the data source before they immerge into the data collection. Full contacts should be clearly indicated. Using data received from an official body (e.g., public authority maintaining a data source in accordance with legal provisions) or a well-known provider helps being on the safe side. Learning about experiences from peers who worked with data of identified sources is also helpful. Practical advice: Before starting collecting data from an unknown data source, researchers should get into contact with the providers of the data source, ideally both in writing and through a telephone call.

Indicative criteria		
Easy handling	• Is the source electronically available? • Can the data be easily retrieved and transferred into a format required for further analyses? • Does the source allow the collection of several data points at one point in time, or do you have to retrieve each single data point separately? • How are data stored in the source, and how are stored data made accessible to the collectors?	Sources can offer their data in different formats, ranging from paper lists to the information provision in a query format that easily allows further data manipulation. The way of how data are presented in a source may considerably impact the time resources required for the data collection. Even data collection from a website can be time-intensive: this is, for instance, the case if each medicine has to be accessed separately, if price data are to be retrieved one by one and no download function has been made available. Some sources require opening several webpages (headers) for each medicine to access additional information. Another aspect to consider is the storage of data provided by the source. It is suggested checking whether retrieved data points can be accessed at a later stage as well, or, at least, be saved without difficulty. During the data manipulation or the analysis, researchers might need to go back to the data to check or search for additional information, and the nonavailability of originally retrieved data at this stage could cause major problems. Furthermore, it is advised to investigate how searches are set up in the data source. Some sources allow searching by the International Nonproprietary Name (INN) or by ATC code, whereas others require a search by trade name. The latter is a challenge in a cross-country comparison because trade names can vary between countries. Thus national trade names might need to be first identified through other searches (e.g., in a register that contains all medicines with a marketing authorization). In case that the aim of the research is to compare price differences between the originator and the lowest-priced generic (as suggested by the WHO/HAI methodology), a source that lists all

Continued

Table 8.1 Catalog to assess the feasibility of medicine price data sources—cont'd

Criteria	Questions	Checklist: recommendations of how to proceed
		available generic versions but does not offer a possibility to rank them may require time-intensive data collection work: First, researchers have to retrieve the prices for dozens of generic versions to sort them and identify the lowest one. Similarly, the implementation of methodological choices made (e.g., exclusion of nonreimbursed, nonprescription, or nonmarketed medicines) could be time-consuming in cases when these additional features have to be collected manually. A quick automated query based on filtering is preferred.
Additional information	• Which additional (not price-related) information is provided by the source? • Are pieces of additional information essential for the research question?	For a price study, further information about medicines might be helpful and, in some cases, even essential. This is, for instance, the case if research will be focused on specific market segments such as the reimbursement, outpatient, or prescription-only medicines sectors, or if these sectors should be compared to their mirroring segments (prescription vs. nonprescription market). Easy accessibility of such information in a source could be considered as a benefit and might contribute to the positive decision for the selection of a specific source. Furthermore, the existence of a manual to the data source is another added value. In this context, it could also be beneficial if the same data source, or the provider of the selected data source, could also offer volume data for the surveyed medicines in case that volume data are needed (e.g., if indexes are calculated). Should price data not be provided in national currency units, information about the exchange rate applied should be provided in the data source.

Source: The authors.

Ad a) Searching national data sources appears to be the most feasible approach in the context of price research in high-income countries because national medicine price lists and databases likely exist in countries and sectors with regulated medicine prices (cf. also Chapter 8.2.1).

Ad b) In general, literature does not qualify as appropriate data source for price surveys, analyses, and comparisons. As the price studies in Part 1 also indicated, primary price data were published in only few papers, and they were usually focused on a low number of countries and medicines. Despite its limitation as data provider, scientific literature can prove to be useful in offering additional (background) data for the analysis and interpretation of prices (e.g., a global price survey on sofosbuvir and ledipasvir/sofosbuvir was based on the collection of medicine price data from national sources, but a discount mentioned in literature was considered for the calculation of discounted prices [2]). It is also possible to compare in a metaanalysis the results of different (national) price surveys (Cameron et al. [3] reviewed prices of 36 low- and middle-income countries (LMIC) that had been assessed and documented in 45 price studies using the World Health Organization (WHO)/Health Action International (HAI) methodology, for instance).

Ad c) Primary data collection is required in settings where no price data have yet been published. This is, for instance, the case in many LMIC, in particular in the private sector. If medicine prices are not regulated, they tend to vary between dispensaries and retailers of a country (cf. also Chapters 2.3–2.5). To survey medicine prices in these contexts, the WHO/HAI methodology was developed (cf. Chapter 6.2), and it was frequently used for conducting price studies, as shown in Part 1. Even in high-income countries with solidarity-based systems and price regulation for major parts of the pharmaceutical market, primary data collection might be needed to survey data from sectors with no price information. For instance, prices of nonprescription medicines are usually not regulated and often vary between pharmacies and nonpharmacy retailers [4]. Procurement prices can differ between hospitals [5]. List prices are known, but lower discounted prices, which were negotiated (e.g., for high-priced medicines), tend to be confidential [6,7]. For surveying such price data, information needs to be retrieved directly from involved parties (e.g., industry, supply chain actors, public authorities).

The three approaches described are resource- and time-intensive in different extent. Although retrieving data from national price databases is obviously less time-consuming than an on-site survey in several regions of a country, time and efforts for consulting price sources should not be underestimated. The selection of appropriate data sources and the collection of data should be considered appropriately in the planning of a study.

8.1.2 Assessment of Data Sources

The starting point for methodological decisions, including the choice of the data source, is the purpose of a price study. Are price data collected for research (that, eventually, may also provide evidence to policy-makers), or are they required for use in EPR? In case of the first-mentioned purpose, different aims can be pursued with the study. To mention a few:

- The study aims to compare the average medicine price level, or the prices of specific medicines, or of averages in selected therapeutic groups, of a country with other countries.
- The study aims to analyze the development in medicine prices (e.g., for all marketed medicines on average, for selected medicines, or for specific therapeutic groups) over time, and/or it aims to investigate the impact of a policy measure on medicine prices.
- The study aims to identify possible price differences in a country (between outpatient and inpatient sectors, between different dispensers, between regions).
- The study aims to explore savings' potentials attributable to generic and biosimilar medicines.
- The study aims to analyze the relevance of different price components (e.g., what is the contribution of distribution margins or taxes to final prices, in a country and in comparison with other countries).

The purpose of the use of medicine price data is key, and the methodological design of a price study (or of a price data collection for EPR purposes) needs to be developed, being aligned to the objective and perspective of the price study (cf. also Chapter 9). The purpose of the price survey shall also guide the choice of the medicine price data source.

In addition, data sources should meet some minimum criteria. According to the authors, a reliable and useful medicine price data source should

1. provide medicine price information at the date(s) required,
2. offer medicine price information for the whole defined area, or at least in a representative way,
3. cover the medicines (i.e., pharmaceutical presentations) required for the purpose of the data collection,
4. present data for the required price type (or a price type that allows determining the required price type),

5. be accessible (at a cost that the user can afford), and
6. be reliable and sustainable.

In addition to these mandatory prerequisites, the following further characteristics of data sources are considered to be supportive:

- an easy and time-saving procedure to retrieve the data, and
- the provision of additional information.

Table 8.1 provides guidance to researchers in the selection of data sources for price surveys, analyses, and comparisons. A checklist of questions to address is provided. The different criteria presented should be understood as being interlinked (e.g., does the data source provide price information for defined nonprescription medicines at pharmacy retail price level for a representative number of pharmacies in the country over the last 4 years, at monthly intervals?). Although the authors are aware that the criterion of accessibility frequently drives the choice of a data source, this should not be the sole aspect to be considered. For definitions of technical terms (e.g., price type, pharmaceutical presentation) kindly refer to previous Chapter 7.

In practice, the different aspects have to be well balanced and assessed with a view to the aim and planned methodology of the price study. In some cases, even indicative criteria may play a major role in the process. As suggested in Table 8.1, consultation of a demo version or results of a sample query can support the decision, and this likely avoids time and resources that would be needed at a later stage when unexpected data gaps are identified. In any case, identification and selection of the most appropriate data source(s) is a time-intensive and crucial process.

8.2 MEDICINE PRICE SERVICES AND DATABASES

To take an informed decision about the choice of the data sources, researchers and experts should be aware about different tools (databases, price lists) that offer medicine price information.

In the following, some illustrative examples of price data sources will be presented. This is not intended to be comprehensive. Selected examples comprise medicine price databases and services that were frequently mentioned in the medicine price studies discussed in Part 1 and some collaborative projects that international agencies and not-for-profit organizations developed. Because the authors do not have access to all existing medicine price data sources, the description of selected price data sources will be based on literature. We do not advise in favor of, nor against, any of the described data sources, but we recommend researchers to assess them in line with the criteria presented in Table 8.1.

Note: Guidance about conducting on-site price surveys in accordance with the WHO/HAI methodology is provided in Chapter 6.2.

8.2.1 Public Sector Data Sources

At national levels, common price data sources include

1. those that contain procurement price data, and
2. those managed by public authorities that are responsible for pricing and/or reimbursement decisions.

Ad 1) In several countries over the world, public services procure (essential) medicines for hospitals or outpatient use in the public sector. Procurement (tender) prices are frequently stored in databases that are freely accessible. Examples of such procurement databases are the Maltese Procurement Database www.etenders.gov.mt or the Philippines database www.philgeps.gov.ph. Chapter 2.4 provides examples of procurement databases in Latin America.

Tendering of goods above a defined threshold needs to be published (i.e., publication of the call and the outcomes). This is also applicable for medicines. In the European Union, the Tenders Electronic Daily (TED) platform (ted.europa.eu) provides information about such tenders. However, tender information may relate to the bulk of medicines purchased and does not always allow determining the price of the single medicine (presentation).

Ad 2) In countries with price regulation for the whole country, public authorities responsible for pricing and/or reimbursement tend to own and manage the medicine price data. Some of them publish them, either electronically in databases or through the provision of lists on their websites, or by the publication of hard copy books. The idea behind printed versions is to hand them over to doctors to encourage them to prescribe more rationally, especially when therapeutically equivalent medicines at lower prices are available. This price information can also be built into prescription software programs. In some other countries, authorities have these lists, catalogs, or registers in their internal information systems and do not disseminate them.

In the European Union (EU), the so-called Transparency Directive [8] stipulates that all Member States publish medicine price data for reimbursable medicines (i.e., those medicines that are, at least partially, funded by a public payer). As a result, price data in the reimbursement segment should be accessible for the 28 EU Member States.

The WHO provides a list of price data sources globally. This "medicine price information sources" website [9] offers links to several data sources run by national pricing and/or reimbursement authorities.

One of the price sources indicated on the WHO list is the Pharma Price Information (PPI) service offered by the Austrian Public Health Institute. PPI was also mentioned as a data source in several European price studies presented in Chapter 2.1. PPI offers price data (at exfactory, wholesale, and pharmacy retail price levels gross and net) of all 28 EU Member States, Norway, and Switzerland [10].

The PPI service was established to support, according to the Austrian General Social Insurance Law, the Austrian Pricing Committee, which calculates the EU average price as part of the EPR process in Austria [11]. At request, PPI also offers price data to researchers and any other interested people, against a charge to cover for the working time of the PPI experts to retrieve the data. As a medicine price service, PPI does not provide access to primary data sources but delivers a defined data set. Price data can be requested for trade names or active ingredients (e.g., all generic versions or selected ones, such as the highest-priced and the lowest-priced generics).

8.2.2 Collaborative Initiatives

In recent years, there have been some initiatives of researchers, public authorities, and nongovernmental institutions to compile national price data. Some of these collections are accessible only to those who contribute by providing data, whereas other data sources are publicly accessible.

8.2.2.1 Management Sciences for Health

The Management Sciences for Health (MSH) guide [12,13] has been a well-established initiative for several years: since 1986, the nonprofit health organization MSH has been publishing an annual guide of international reference prices for medicines. Price data are provided by buyers and, usually not-for-profit, suppliers such as international development agencies or government authorities.

The MSH International Medical Products Price Guide is available in print versions as well as electronically (with a search function). It is free of charge but requires registration for customized queries. Further information on this guide can be found in Chapter 6.2 (Box 6.2.2).

MSH reference prices serve to provide a benchmark to assess surveyed national prices [12,13]. They have been recommended as the most useful standard as a comparator, particularly in the context of LMIC and they are part of the WHO/HAI methodology [14,15]. Thus, it is a supplementary price data source that researchers may use in addition to national sources.

8.2.2.2 Early Advances in Europe: European Commission's Projects

In Europe, the work of building a medicine price database dates back to the late 1990s. The initial project, ECPHIN, with institutional support from the European Commission's (EC) Joint Research Centre, was set out to create a database on the basis of voluntary contributions from Member States and built the technical basis. Within the framework of the next project, EudraNet, it was then fed with price data from Member States; however, it was stopped after some time [16]. The EC explained that it was difficult to undertake comparisons due to the different times and means of data delivery [17].

The research project entitled "EURO-MED-STAT. Monitoring expenditure and utilisation of medicinal products in the European Union countries. A public health approach", cofunded by the EC, aimed to identify and evaluate data sources in European countries, to compare existing data and to make suggestions for a minimum data set for European registers of medicines [18,19]. Although the focus was on expenditure and utilization, price data were also included: the Library of EU Pharmaceutical Indicators [20] described sources that also contained medicine prices, and a sample database to test the feasibility of a common tool from a research perspective was established based on information provided by project partners in the involved countries (usually administrative data). The database contained some price data and allowed cross-country comparisons.

The EURO-MED-STAT project was designed as a 24-month activity, starting in 2002, and despite some follow-up initiatives the collaboration eventually came to an end. However, the research database containing price information with no indication of the date of the data, continued to be publicly accessible in the Internet. The authors of this chapter are aware that this created an incentive for some researchers to use out-dated data from this easy-to-handle source.

At the time of the production of this book (2018), the EURO-MED-STAT database is no longer accessible.

8.2.2.3 EURopean Integrated Price Information Database (Euripid)

A few years after the EURO-MED-STAT research project, the Hungarian National Health Insurance Fund Administration developed a medicine price database that was fed with data provided by competent authorities of some European countries. The Common European Drug Database (CEDD) was established as a pilot version and included price data of Austrian, Czech, Finnish, Hungarian, Irish, Lithuanian, Norwegian, Polish, Slovenian, and Slovakian medicines [21]. This database was, and still is, freely accessible, and it contains prices as of 2008/2009.

Based on the pilot database, the Hungarian National Health Insurance Fund Administration established the EURopean Integrated Price Information Database (Euripid) database with the support of an EC grant (2010—13) [22]. Euripid contains price data of reimbursable medicines. After the end of the EC grant, participating countries established the Euripid Collaboration which later received another EC grant in mid-2015 [23].

Public authorities for pricing and/or reimbursement of the participating countries provide price data of their country and, in return, they have access to the Euripid database. By the end of 2015, Euripid contained data from 27 European countries, of which 25 countries are EU Member States [24]. Only authorities that provide data to Euripid are granted access to the database. Supranational and international organizations (e.g., European Commission, WHO) may have access if the Board of Participants approves, and an agreement regarding a contribution is concluded. Scientists can also address the owners of the database (euripid.eu) to discuss with them a request for price data they need for research purposes.

8.2.2.4 Decisiones Informadas en Medicamentos Platform in Latin America

In Latin America, the regional platform Decisiones Informadas en Medicamentos (DIME) offers minimum public procurement prices for selected 38 medicines in eight countries of the region (Chile, Colombia, Costa Rica, Dominican Republic, Ecuador, El Salvador, Mexico, and Peru) [25]. The medicines were chosen because of their impact on the public budgets and cover, among others, the therapeutic areas of cancer, diabetes, hepatitis C, immune-suppressing agents, and HIV antivirals. For further information and price examples refer to Chapter 2.4.

The DIME platform that is sponsored by the Inter-American Development Bank is freely accessible. The authors of Chapter 2.4 highlighted that a major challenge and limitation of DIME is to have regular updates. Consulting DIME (http://www.proyectodime.info/) shows that the date of the prices is not indicated.

8.2.2.5 Western Pacific Platform for Procurement Prices

The Price Information Exchange for Essential Medicines (PIEMEDS) website contains procurement prices in the public sector for medicines. WHO collects and processes the data that participating countries in the Western Pacific region share voluntarily for this PIEMEDS system.

At the start of the pilot in 2009, 40 medicines were included. The list has been extended to cover the medicines of the 2017 WHO Essential Medicines List. PIEMEDS is password protected. On registration, price information is freely available for some medicines (essential medicines), whereas only country representatives/authorized users are granted access to the complete data set that also includes high-priced medicines [26].

8.2.2.6 WHO Global Price Reporting Mechanism for HIV, Tuberculosis, and Malaria

The WHO AIDS Medicines and Diagnostics Service (AMDS) established the Global Price Reporting Mechanism (GPRM) database to record international transactions of HIV, tuberculosis, and malaria commodities purchased by national programs in LMIC.

This web-based database allows users to search for the price and volumes sold of the included medicines in countries, regions, by income category, human development index category, manufacturer, and type of manufacturer (generic and on-patent medicines). Analyses of the antiretroviral (ARV) price evolution are published regularly in AMDS summary reports.

Access is free. Data up to the level of individual procurement operations can be made available to research groups on request and approval by the AMDS partners [27].

The database (http://apps.who.int/hiv/amds/price/hdd) is regularly updated [9]. It was noted that it is not always clear what is included in the price [28].

8.2.2.7 Vaccine Product, Price, and Procurement Platform

The Vaccine Product, Price, and Procurement (V3P) mechanism is a web platform that offers vaccine product, price, and procurement data with the goal of increasing price transparency and informing decisions around vaccine introduction and implementation [29]. It includes a database of vaccine prices that was launched in June 2014 [30].

The price database contains publicly accessible information from WHO, United Nations Children's Fund (UNICEF), and the Pan American Health Organization (PAHO) Revolving Fund as well as information from participating countries [29]. By 2015, 40 countries shared data with WHO for this project [31]. The database is freely accessible.

The V3P price database allows country analyses and evaluations over time, but it does not disclose the countries that delivered the data. The income groups (e.g., high-income countries) and the UN regions (e.g., African region) are indicated.

Although V3P has been praised as an important project to improve price transparency [31], it might not be applicable as a data source for price surveys in which access to primary data is required.

8.2.3 Other Providers

In the private sector, key providers of price data include

1. publishing houses and information systems companies,
2. pharmacy associations, and
3. consumer organizations.

Ad 1) The services offered by publishing houses usually comprise market research data of high-income countries and sometimes also of emerging markets. The publishing houses either offer direct access to a (web-based) source with individual price data that are password protected or they provide a defined data set in line with the specifications made by the user. Data provision of these sources is, in general, connected with costs that can be substantial from a researcher's perspective.

The best-known data sources in this area that have also been frequently quoted in price studies are VIDAL and IMS Health. The VIDAL group is a French health-care informatics and information systems company that reports to offer a range of products related to medicine information, including price data in some cases, for countries in Europe, the Middle East, and Latin America [32]. IMS Health, which is meanwhile renamed IQVIA, reports to provide a range of information, technology, and service solutions in health care [33]. The core business related to medicines is sales data, but IMS also offers price data. Although research projects normally do not have the budget to afford access to the IQVIA databases, researchers may address IMS to discuss the delivery of a defined data set. On its website, the IMS Institute for Health-care Informatics, at the time of writing called IQVIA Institute, has been inviting requests for academic research support [34].

A word of warning: Apart from these and further well-established publishing houses, new commercial providers have come on the market. Although some new providers may offer valuable data not covered by others, caution should still be exercised. Unknown providers should be carefully assessed in advance (the checklist as presented in Table 8.1 *aims to provide some support).*

Ad 2) Some pharmacy associations, or publishing houses commissioned by them, offer price information, usually at the pharmacy retail price level. Access to these data can be connected with costs.

Ad 3) Another option for accessing price data, again primarily pharmacy retail prices, is websites that are maintained by consumer organizations to provide guidance to the patients. These data sources tend to be provided in settings where medicine prices differ between pharmacies (and further dispensaries, including internet pharmacies). Data of such services can be adjusted on a regular (often daily) basis, usually with the storage of historic data.

REFERENCES

[1] World Health Organization. WHO guideline on country pharmaceutical pricing policies. Geneva. 2013.

[2] Iyengar S, Tay-Teo K, Vogler S, Beyer P, Wiktor S, de Joncheere K, et al. Prices, costs, and affordability of new medicines for Hepatitis C in 30 countries: an economic analysis. PLoS Medicine 2016;13(5):e1002032.

[3] Cameron A, Ewen M, Ross-Degnan D, Ball D, Laing R. Medicine prices, availability, and affordability in 36 developing and middle-income countries: a secondary analysis. The Lancet 2009;373(9659):240–9.

[4] Habl C, Antony K, Arts D, Entleitner M, Fröschl B, Leopold C, et al. Surveying, assessing and analysing the pharmaceutical sector in the 25 EU member states. Country profiles. Vienna: Österreichisches Bundesinstitut für Gesundheitswesen (ÖBIG); 2006.

[5] Vogler S, Habl C, Leopold C, Mazag J, Morak S, Zimmermann N. PHIS Hospital Pharma Report. Vienna: Pharmaceutical Health Information System (PHIS); commissioned by the European Commission and the Austrian Federal Ministry of Health; 2010. Available from: http://whocc.goeg.at/Literaturliste/Dokumente/BooksReports/PHIS_Hospital%20Pharma_Report.pdf.

[6] WHO Regional Office for Europe. Access to new medicines in Europe: technical review of policy initiatives and opportunities for collaboration and research. Copenhagen. 2015.

[7] Morgan S, Vogler S, Wagner AK. Payers' experiences with confidential pharmaceutical price discounts: a survey of public and statutory health systems in North America, Europe, and Australasia. Health Policy 2017;121(4):354–62.

[8] European Commission. Council directive 89/105/EEC of 21 December, 1988 relating to the transparency of measures regulating the prices of medicinal products for human use and their inclusion in the scope of national health insurance systems. 1988. Available from: https://eur-lex.europa.eu/legal-content/EN/TXT/HTML/?uri=CELEX:31989L0105&from=EN.
[9] World Health Organization. Medicine price information sources. Available from: http://www.who.int/medicines/areas/access/med_price_info_sources/en/.
[10] Gesundheit Österreich GmbH. Pharma price information (PPI) service. Vienna. 2017. Available from: https://goeg.at/Pharma_Price_Information.
[11] Vogler S, Kilpatrick K, Babar Z-U-D. Analysis of medicine prices in New Zealand and 16 European countries. Value in Health 2015;18(4):484–92.
[12] Management Sciences for Health (MSH). International drug price indicator guide. 2017. Available from: https://www.msh.org/resources/international-drug-price-indicator-guide.
[13] Management Sciences for Health (MSH), World Health Organisation (WHO). International medical products price indicator guide. 2015 edition. Arlington. 2016.
[14] WHO, HAI. Medicine Prices. A new approach to measurement. Working draft for field testing and revision. World Health Organization, Health Action International; 2003.
[15] WHO, HAI. Measuring medicine prices, availability, affordability and price components. 2nd ed. Geneva: World Health Organization, Health Action International; 2008 Available from: http://www.who.int/medicines/areas/access/OMS_Medicine_prices.pdf.
[16] Bouvy J, Vogler S. Background paper 8.3 pricing and reimbursement policies: impacts on innovation. In: World Health Organization, editor. Priority medicines for Europe and the world. 2013 Update. Geneva: World Health Organization; 2013.
[17] European Commission. Written question E-2545/97 by Mihail Papayannakis (GUE/NGL) to the commission. Official Journal of the European Communities 1997. https://de.scribd.com/document/43765638/Untitled.
[18] Rosian I, Vogler S, Vander Stichele R, Larsen L, Odegaard B, Brahm AK, et al. EURO-MED-STAT–Monitoring expenditure and utilization of medicinal products in the European Union countries: a Public Health approach. European Journal of Public Health 2003;13(Suppl. 3):95–100.
[19] Walley T, Folino-Gallo P, Barry M, Bruzzone M, De Joncheere K, Rosian I, et al. The EurMedStat proposals on indicators for price and utilisation. Italian Journal of Public Health 2006;3(1):15–21.
[20] EURO-MED-STAT Working Group. The liberary of European union pharmaceutical Indicators. 2004. http://ec.europa.eu/health/ph_projects/2001/monitoring/fp_monitoring_2001_frep_12_1_en.pdf.
[21] National Health Insurance Fund Administration of Hungary. Common European Drug database CEDD. 2008. Available from: http://cedd.oep.hu/].
[22] European Commission DG Entreprise. Call for proposals - development of a database on the pricing of medicinal products in the EU. Grant Programme. 2009. Available from: http://ec.europa.eu/DocsRoom/documents/2790/attachments/1/translations/en/renditions/pdf.
[23] EURIPID. In: Presentation of the proposal of EURIPID Collaboration for DG SANCO call on Statistical data for medicinal product pricing. Presentation for the Workshop with EFPIA; 2014. Brussels.
[24] Vogler S, Lepuschütz L, Schneider P, Stühlinger V. Study on enhanced cross-country coordination in the area of pharmaceutical product pricing. Luxembourg: Gesundheit Österreich Forschungs- und Planungs GmbH; Publications Office of the European Commission; 2016.

[25] Decisiones Informadas en Medicamentos (DIME). Available from: http://www.proyectodime.info.
[26] World Health Organization. PIEMEDS. Price information exchange for essential medicines. 2017. Available from: https://piemeds.com/.
[27] WHO AIDS Medicines and Diagnostics Service. Global price reporting mechanism for HIV, tuberculosis and malaria. Available from: http://www.who.int/hiv/amds/gprm/en/.
[28] WHO AIDS Medicines and Diagnostics Service. Procurement & supply management toolbox. 2012. Available from: http://psmtoolbox.org/en/tool-details%7CPricing%7CGlobal-Price-Reporting-Mechanism-GPRM-%7C35.
[29] World Health Organization. Vaccine product, price and procurement (V3P) web platform. July 2017. Available from: http://www.who.int/immunization/programmes_systems/procurement/v3p/platform/en.
[30] World Health Organization. Global vaccine action plan. Monitoring, evaluation & accountability. Secretariat annual report 2014. Geneva. 2015.
[31] Strategic Advisory Group of Experts on Immunization. 2015 assessment report of the global vaccine action plan. 2015. Published online: http://www.who.int/immunization/global_vaccine_action_plan/SAGE_GVAP_Assessment_Report_2015_EN.pdf?ua=1.
[32] VIDAL Group. VIDAL drug information systems. Available from: http://www.vidal-dis.com/.
[33] IMS Health. Quinteles IMS health. Available from: https://www.imshealth.com/.
[34] QuintilesIMS Institute. Research at the QuintilesIMS institute. Available from: http://www.imshealth.com/en/thought-leadership/quintilesims-institute/research-support.

CHAPTER 9

Preparing Price Studies – Key Methodological Decisions

Sabine Vogler, Peter Schneider, Nina Zimmermann
WHO Collaborating Centre for Pharmaceutical Pricing and Reimbursement Policies, Pharmacoeconomics Department, Gesundheit Österreich GmbH (GÖG/Austrian Public Health Institute), Vienna, Austria

LIST OF ABBREVIATIONS

ATC	Anatomical Therapeutic Chemical Classification
CIF	Cost, insurance, freight
DDD	Defined daily dose
EMA	European Medicines Agency
EPR	External price referencing
EU	European Union
EphMRA	European Pharmaceutical Market Research Association
GDP	Gross domestic product
GST	General sales tax
HAI	Health Action International
IMF	International Monetary Fund
IMS	Intercontinental Medical Statistics
LMIC	Low- and middle-income country/ies
MWPP	Manufacturer price/wholesale price/pharmacy retail price net/ pharmacy retail price gross; alternatively: manufacturer, wholesaler, pharmacy and patient
MSP	Manufacturer's selling price
NMRA	National Medicines Regulatory Authority
OECD	Organisation for Economic Co-operation and Development
OMP	Orphan medicinal product
PDD	Prescribed daily dose(s)
PPP	Purchasing power parities
SU	Standard unit(s)
UHC	Universal health coverage
US	United States
VAT	Value-added tax
WHO	World Health Organization

Medicine Price Surveys, Analyses, and Comparisons
ISBN 978-0-12-813166-4
https://doi.org/10.1016/B978-0-12-813166-4.00015-2

9.1 INTRODUCTION

Key methodological decisions have to be taken when a medicine price survey, analysis and/or comparison is planned. This chapter aims to provide guidance for researchers, students, policy-makers and further experts who intend to conduct a price study.

The chapter builds on previous ones. In Chapters 2 to 4, the overview of price studies globally, for certain medicine groups and over time highlighted different purposes and perspectives of research undertaken in the area of medicine price studies, and it presented differences in findings that depend on the selected methodological approach. Chapter 6 (that provided an overview of methodologies) confirmed the need for guidance on methodological choices in the preparation of a study plan: besides the WHO/HAI methodology for the specific case of on-site medicine price surveys and a few papers on methodological aspects of cross-country price comparisons, literature to guide those interested in conducting a medicine price survey is scarce. Since price comparisons are more complex, they will be discussed in further detail in this chapter. Chapter 7 (terminology) and Chapter 8 (data sources) are preparatory chapters and will be referred to, where appropriate.

The chapter will present different dimensions (parameters) that should be considered in the planning of a price study but it is not a manual. Different options of how to address each of the parameters will be discussed with a view to their implications. Eventually, investigators have to balance their research interests (that may require large data sets) against practical limitations in terms of staff capacity, budget and deadlines.

9.2 PURPOSE AND PERSPECTIVE

Before getting started, the major questions that have to be addressed are as follows:

Why is the price research conducted?

What is its purpose?

Which objectives does it aim to achieve?

The purpose of a medicine price survey can range from pure academic interest to an obligation for public authorities to use price data in the pricing decision process. The latter usually implies collection of medicine price data in other countries as part of the external price referencing (EPR) policy, in which the price of a medicine is based on the prices of that specific product in other countries (for details see Chapters 11 to 15 that are devoted to the EPR policy). Even if EPR is not applied, price data can still be relevant in the policy context. For instance, they can be used as an input factor to a pharmacoeconomic analysis — which is often required for pricing and reimbursement purposes — or to provide a starting point for price negotiations and further procurement purposes.

At the same time, academic research in the area of medicine prices will likely not remain in the 'ivory tower' but can be of interest for policy-makers. International price comparisons, for instance, will, most probably, raise the attention of policy-makers of the included countries (for further reflections on the political sensitiveness of the medicine price studies see Box 9.1).

BOX 9.1 Political Relevance of Medicine Price Research

Research of medicine prices can be highly politically sensitive since it addresses crucial policy issues such as patient access to needed medicines, including equity considerations (across and within countries, different population groups etc.), affordability for the patients and long-term sustainability of the healthcare system (see also Chapter 11). In addition, medicine prices are not only of relevance in the policy area of health but they also relate to industrial and trade policies. With the emergence of new, high-priced medicines in recent years (that challenge the financial sustainability of healthcare systems even in rich countries and remain unaffordable for patients in most countries globally) prices of medicines (and their affordability) got high on the political agenda in high-income countries [1,2]. Medicine price studies help generate data and evidence and thus contribute to improved transparency though, as illustrated in this book, large gaps in transparency continue to exist since medicine price information is lacking for several countries around the world, for specific settings such as the private or the hospital sectors and for specific price types, for example, discounted prices. Not all stakeholders appear to have an interest in transparency and publication of medicine price data.

As a result, studies of medicine prices — even if initiated solely out of research interest in an academic setting — may quickly end up in political debate. As for other areas of research, criticism frequently addresses the methodological choices taken. The WHO/HAI manual on 'Measuring Medicine Prices, Availability, Affordability and Price Components' stressed the relevance of a sound methodology that can be defended: 'People who may be exposed and criticized by the study's findings may prefer to attack the methods used in the study rather than address the results' [3].

Examples of research objectives with regard to medicine price studies include:

- How much do patients pay for (selected) medicines in the private sector? If the same medicines are procured for the public sector, which prices are paid by government?
- Do the prices in the hospital sector in a country (e.g., the country where the researchers, or their funding body, are based) differ from the prices in the outpatient sector? Is this the case for the same medicines, or for the top-selling medicines of each sector, for instance?
- How high is the difference between the prices of originator and generic medicines, and is the variation similar to the price differences between reference products and biosimilar medicines?
- Which components (e.g., add-ons such as mark-ups in the supply chain, duties and taxes) contribute to the final price of a medicine that the patient pays, and to which extent? Are there differences in the relevance of defined price components between settings (e.g., public/private or outpatient/hospital sectors), regions and countries?
- Can consumers purchase medicines over the Internet at lower prices? (Note: most probably, the research objective will be combined with further research questions such as legal requirements and quality issues.)
- Is there 'regional equity' within a country: do ex-factory and final retail prices of medicines (e.g., specific therapeutic groups, non-prescription medicines) differ within a country, and how much? Are there differences between urban and rural areas?
- Are prices of the same medicines lower at non-pharmacy retailers than at pharmacies? (The research question can be combined with further study objectives, such as exploring possible differences in the performance of the dispensers.)
- Are actual prices (e.g., due to discounts in the supply chain or granted by industry to public payers) lower than list prices indicated in price lists or price databases?
- Which medicines are priced above a certain amount?
- Can the assertion that all hospitals (or other procurers) are granted the same prices be confirmed?
- Do price data of the same medicines differ in different price sources? How much and why?
- How have medicine prices developed over time?
- Has a policy reform (e.g., implementation of price control, change in the methodology of a pricing policy, liberalisation of the prices of

non-prescription medicines, information campaigns to patients, higher co-payments, measures to promote generic uptake) impacted medicine prices (e.g., in general, in specific settings or therapeutic areas)?
- What is the average price level for all or defined medicines across a country and within a country (e.g., different settings, sectors)?

As suggested for some of the questions listed above, these study aims can (and should) be supplemented by investigating possible causes for the status quo and differences. These illustrative study objectives were phrased to address research on one country. In addition, most of the above-mentioned research questions can also be addressed in cross-country comparative studies.

Furthermore, medicine price data can be used for further research purposes, such as to conduct studies on availability and affordability of medicines, for instance:
- How high is the financial burden for patients to purchase a medicine (e.g., for a chronic condition)?
- Are there differences in the average medicine price levels in countries that apply different pricing policies (e.g., EPR, value-based pricing)?
- Is there a conversion of average medicine price levels in countries that apply EPR and cross-reference to each other?
- What would be the share of public pharmaceutical expenditure to fund defined high-priced medicines and to offer them to all patients that need them?
- Can the asserted 'strategic market launch' approach of pharmaceutical industry (i.e., staggered market entry of medicines, with an earlier introduction in higher-priced countries and delayed launch in lower-priced countries) be confirmed?
- Which is the expected impact of the implementation of a policy measure, and can it be quantified (e.g., in terms of savings for public payers, financial burden for patients)?
- Has the introduction of centralised procurement resulted in lower prices?
- How do results differ if nominal medicine price data are weighted by economic indicators (e.g., by PPP or by GDP)?
- Who (e.g., consumers, public payers, supply chain actors) benefits from discounted prices?

While these lists are not comprehensive, they illustrate the range of study objectives that researchers may like to work on. Research can be carried out based on own research interest, to support policy decisions and/or in response to research questions defined by a funding body, and this will likely also shape the study objectives.

Another key decision that has to be taken at the very start of each research project is the perspective from which the study will be conducted. It is closely linked to the study objective(s). Major perspectives for price studies include:

- patient (consumer) perspective,
- perspective of (public) payer(s) and/or procurer(s) (e.g., hospital),
- public health and/or overall healthcare system perspective (i.e., aiming to balance the individual public payers and patient perspective, considering aspects such as equity, affordability and long-term sustainability of the healthcare system),
- industry perspective,
- wholesale, distributor, pharmacy and other supply chain actor's/dispensary's perspective.

Another dimension is whether the study is conducted from a national (or regional) perspective, and from a supra-national (e.g., for the African region) or global perspective. A cross-country price comparison can be conducted from a national perspective, in order to investigate the ranking of prices in the own country compared to other countries. If performed from a global perspective, the study objective would be different such as to explore whether, or not, the medicine prices correspond to the economic situation of the surveyed countries, for instance.

9.3 KEY METHODOLOGICAL DECISIONS

Based on the key decisions of study purpose, objectives and perspective, researchers have to take a couple of methodological choices. Major dimensions of the methodological design include:

- the geographic area (country/countries, region(s) etc.),
- the sector/setting (public/private, outpatient/in-patient)
- the medicines included (e.g., therapeutic groups)
- the price type (e.g., ex-factory price/pharmacy retail price, list price/discounted price) and
- the timing of the price data.

These five dimensions are basic and are also relevant for price data collection in non-comparative environments. The range of methodological choices taken for these dimensions will be described in Sections 9.3.1–9.3.5. For cross-country comparisons, further specifications are necessary and will be described in Section 9.3.6. A summary is provided in Table 9.1. Experience from price studies has shown practical difficulties, in

Table 9.1 Methodological choices

Dimension (parameter)	Rationale	How to proceed	Preferred option(s)	Possible options (depending on research purpose)	Not advised/'Don'ts'
Selection of country/countries	To select the country or countries that are able to appropriately respond to the research purpose (e.g., data generation for areas/countries without data, understanding a given country's average price level in comparison to other countries)	Gain knowledge about the policy framework in countries considered for possible inclusion in the study (e.g., identify areas/settings of price regulation and publication of prices, intra-country variation of prices, data gaps) and analyse the feasibility of survey and analysis, assess in advance possible limitations and develop the methodology accordingly, including contingency strategies	Develop country selection criteria that are in line with the research objective. Balance higher comparability of candidate comparator countries (e.g., in terms of income, healthcare system, pharmaceutical policy, utilisation) against the added value of data generation for countries with limited price information. No 'one-size-fits-all' approach.	Use of comparator countries that have differences in country characteristics is possible for research purposes but weighting (e.g., for utilisation and income of countries) should be considered, in particular for studies to explore average price levels.	Choice of countries solely based on practical issues (e.g., availability of a set of price data) disconnected from the research question. Use of countries with very limited data points for the comparison of average price levels of countries (however, an alternative presentation of data, e.g., at the level of individual medicines may be meaningful and can be considered) Use of completely non-comparable countries for policy purposes (inclusion in EPR)

Continued

Table 9.1 Methodological choices—cont'd

Dimension (parameter)	Rationale	How to proceed	Preferred option(s)	Possible options (depending on research purpose)	Not advised/'Don'ts'
Selection of sector(s)	To identify areas not covered in previous price studies, to investigate intra-country differences in medicine prices and to be able to consider appropriately particularities of price regulation, access to price data and price variation in and among sectors	Gain knowledge about country-specific characteristics of the pharmaceutical system and its sectors and settings	Decide based on findings of preliminary research of the policy framework and data availability whether you aim to cover the whole pharmaceutical market or you prefer selecting one or further sectors Outline the limitations in case of comparison of two or more sectors that are different	Comparison of prices in different sectors (e.g., public and private sectors; outpatient and in-patient sectors) can be feasible but differences in the sectors should be considered (e.g., one national price for the whole country for outpatient medicines vs. different prices in hospital in a given country; different price types applicable for different sectors) Cross-country comparison of medicines of	Ignoring the relevance of different sectors and settings

				defined sectors (however, researchers should be aware of possible differences in the definition of sectors between countries)	
Product basket	To ensure the selection of relevant medicines whose price data analysis is meaningful for answering the research question, to identify the medicines according to the defined classification and to ensure comparability in cross-country analyses	Specify the classifications relevant for the research purpose in the cross-specific contexts and sort out how they have been implemented in national practice and data sources (e.g., how to identify orphan medicines, generics or cancer medicines).	Search for information at presentation level (defined pharmaceutical form, strength and pack size), and further (needed) specifications (e.g., patent, prescription or reimbursement status, availability in the market) Compare medicines of the same presentation Compare	In case of a comparison of per unit prices of identical presentations, deviation related to the pack size is acceptable: per unit prices of medicines of the same pharmaceutical form and strength can be compared if the pack sizes differ slightly (comparison to the closest pack size)	Non-available medicines (unless they are only temporarily unavailable) Non-comparable medicines Build average prices of active ingredient without considering the patent status of the product Lack of contingency plan on how to deal with data gaps

Continued

Table 9.1 Methodological choices—cont'd

Dimension (parameter)	Rationale	How to proceed	Preferred option(s)	Possible options (depending on research purpose)	Not advised/'Don'ts'
			originators to originators and generics to generics		
Price data	To ensure to conduct a price study (and not an analysis of costs or expenditure)	Check whether, or not, the data that are surveyed or received relate to medicine prices or to 'price proxies' (e.g., expenditure data)	Use of price data, with primary data at the level of 'presentations' (defined pharmaceutical form, strength and pack size) – further manipulations are possible	For certain research objectives and in case of complete unavailability of price data, 'price proxies' might be acceptable. However, these studies should not be labelled price studies.	Use of 'price proxies' and interpreting these data as price data.
Unit of measurement	To ensure an appropriate presentation of price data context and to make price data comparable	Work with primary data (i.e., those for which no measurement units have been applied) and do the measurement calculation yourself If not possible: Know which	Measure price data per unit basis (e.g., per tablet, per vial) to conduct price analyses and comparisons	• Price data per DDD (rather a unit for measurement of pharmaceutical utilisation) • Price data per course of treatment for studies that have	Price data per weight unit Use of aggregated price data that do not allow deducing primary medicine prices and units

		measurement units were applied to each of the price data points		a broader research scope (e.g., assessment of affordability)	
Price types	To interpret price data correctly (note: price types reflect perspective) and to ensure that prices of the same stages in the supply chain are compared	Understand different stages of a price along the supply chain and identify different factors (e.g., regulations such as statutory mark-up schemes, taxes and practice) that determine price components Investigate which price types are available in a country and which price types they correspond to in other countries Explore the possibility of	Compare prices of the same price type Missing data for price types can be calculated in case of statutory mark-up/margin systems	Missing price types can be calculated based on average wholesale (or pharmacy) margins Assumptions should be justified by further research (e.g., that the mark-up regulation valid for a regulated setting such as prescription-only medicine is also applied in a regulated setting, e.g., non-prescription medicines)	Comparison of prices of different price types Wrong interpretation of supply chain remuneration and taxes (e.g., mixing up of mark-ups and margins)

Continued

Table 9.1 Methodological choices—cont'd

Dimension (parameter)	Rationale	How to proceed	Preferred option(s)	Possible options (depending on research purpose)	Not advised/'Don'ts'
		determining data for missing price types			
Time period	To analyse medicine price data that are comparable in terms of the dates they refer to	Decide which date(s) of the data you require and then check access of these data	Have access to primary data for needed dates (that are clearly indicated) during the whole time of the study	Comparing data of different points in time adjusted for inflation and deflation is possible	Use of data from national databases without knowing to which date they refer to

The table summarises key methodology dimensions of a price study that should be considered in the development of the study protocol. The advice is based on experiences with price studies analysed and conducted by the authors, and it is open for challenge. While some approaches are recommended, the researchers' final decision will always depend on the study's purpose and objectives, and options listed here as less preferred could still be chosen in specific contexts.
Source: The Authors.

particular with regard to data availability and comparability. These dimensions discussed in the following sections were also mentioned in Chapter 6 (cf. in particular Table 6.1), though authors of presented methodology papers tended to focus on only a few elements.

In this chapter, several technical terms are used. While they will be defined and explained whenever necessary, readers may also like to consult Chapter 7 that provides a summary of major terms and their definitions.

9.3.1 Geographic Area

As for other methodological decisions in the design of a study, the overall purpose and research objective impact the decision of whether data of one or more countries will be surveyed and analysed (cf. Section 9.3.6.1 on the selection of countries for comparative cross-country studies).

A single-country study may aim to survey medicine prices of sectors for which no, or few, price data are available, in order to contribute to evidence generation. This is, for instance, a major purpose of price surveys conducted using the WHO/HAI methodology of measuring medicine prices, availability, affordability and price components [3]. Such surveys tend to be performed in countries with no, or limited, price regulation, and on-site data collection as recommended by the WHO/HAI manual will be needed. However, also in countries with regulated and published medicine prices, on-site data collection might be needed for so-called 'black box areas' that are not covered by price regulation and in which prices of the same medicines vary and are largely unknown (e.g., non-prescription medicines, hospital setting, cf. Section 9.3.2). Further purposes of single-country price studies include evaluation of policy measures (e.g., interrupted time-series analyses) and intra-country comparisons of sectors and settings.

The selected country is often the one where the researcher, or the funding body, is based, or has a special interest. Variation in countries represented in price studies is large, as the overview of medicine price surveys, analyses and comparisons in Chapters 2 to 4 illustrated. However, there seems to be a focus on high-income industrialised countries, in particular large countries with major pharmaceutical markets. These are usually countries in which medicines are marketed earlier and for which price data are more easily accessible. In addition, research groups tend to be based in high-income countries, interest of commissioning and funding bodies tends to concentrate on large and high-income countries and researchers working on low- and middle-income countries (LMIC) and/or small markets face more difficulties in getting their findings published (e.g., frequently not scope of scientific journals). In addition, conducting analyses in countries with lower levels of price regulation can be more challenging because primary data may have to be collected first before conducting an analysis. Despite these challenges, researchers are encouraged to do price surveys and analyses on countries with limited price information since they will thus provide an important contribution to data generation.

As price studies presented in Chapters 2 to 4 had highlighted, there are nearly always differences in prices of identical medicines between countries. This is a result of pricing being a competence of individual countries. In several countries, there is even variation in prices between regions of a country, between sectors (e.g., different prices for identical medicines in the public and private sectors) and between dispensers. Such intra-country differences are likely a result of lack of price regulation (for details see Box 9.2).

Already in the phase of developing the study protocol, knowledge about the policy framework of the country, and countries respectively, intended for inclusion is key. As explained in Box 9.2, there is high likelihood of intra-country differences in medicine prices if price regulation is lacking. In these cases, the methodology has to be designed appropriately, for example, by planning collection of price data of identical medicines from a representative sample of different dispensers. In contrast, if price regulation is in place and one price per medicine is valid throughout the whole country, retrieval of prices from a national data source is most likely sufficient.

Intra-country comparisons may explore possible variation between geographic regions (e.g., of different income, or different population groups) and also between urban and rural, more remote areas and between areas of different infrastructure and transport facilities, of different consumption patterns related to medicines and also other goods (e.g., healthy food) or services (e.g., private healthcare services), of different relevance and density of healthcare providers and medicine dispensers.

Key message: The economic situation and the policy framework (e.g., medicine price regulation) can impact the availability of medicine price data and, in response, the choice of methods for the data survey. Researchers should have sufficient knowledge about the investigated country (regulation, access to data, findings of previous price studies) already at the planning phase.

BOX 9.2 Price Regulation Impacting Cross-national, Cross-regional and Cross-sectional Variation in Medicine Prices

The government of a country may decide whether, or not, it regulates medicine prices since pharmaceutical pricing policies are, in general, a national competence. Even in the European Union (EU) that has a harmonised process for marketing authorisation, Member States set medicine prices solely for their own country, as part of national decision-making. As a consequence, medicine prices tend to vary between countries. There are only a few exemptions: Countries jointly procure medicines (e.g., in the Eastern Caribbean region, Gulf Cooperation Council [4]), and a country may use the prices that were set in other countries (e.g., Luxembourg uses prices from its neighbouring countries like Belgium, France or Germany, while adding a specific percentage rate [5]).[1]

In practice, price regulation does not cover all medicines, for all price types, in all sectors of a country. Price control can target one or more price types, for example, solely the manufacturer price or additional price types across the supply chain such as the wholesale price or pharmacy retail price by regulating the respective add-ons. Selected medicine groups may be covered by price regulation: Price-regulated medicine groups are usually subsidised medicines (thereafter called reimbursable medicines), that is, medicines whose expenses are, at least partially, covered by a third party payer (frequently a public payer) and/or prescription-only medicines, that is, medicines that require a medical prescription. It should be noted that an overlap between reimbursable medicines and prescription-only medicines is often observed. In some countries (e.g., Austria), price regulation targets only the outpatient sector, not the in-patient sector. Price regulation may address only on-patent medicines, while manufacturers are allowed to price at their discretion off-patent products such as generic and biosimilar medicines. In many LMIC, medicine prices are controlled in the public sector (usually a price is set through a public procurement process), while there is no price control for medicines in the private sector.

As a result, the dimensions of geographic area, sector, medicine group and price type are inter-linked.

As studies presented in Chapters 2 to 4 have shown, price regulation contributes to lower — and therefore more affordable — medicine prices. In addition, price control helps improve transparency since in non-regulated settings medicine prices are usually not published and thus not known. In such an environment, prices tend to vary within a country (regional differences including variation between urban and rural areas; and additionally among dispensers), and frequent changes may also occur.

Background information on countries and their pricing regulation: see studies presented in Chapters 2 to 4 and the overview of global pricing policies in 'Pharmaceutical Prices in the 21st Century' [6].

[1] In fact, this constitutes a variant of the external price referencing (EPR) policy (cf. Chapters 11 to 15).

9.3.2 Sectors and Settings

Researchers may decide to conduct a survey with the aim of collecting data in a sector for which no such information has yet been systemically gathered, or they aim to design the study as an intra-country comparative analysis between sectors.

Possible sectors (settings) include:

- Public versus private sectors: In many countries globally, the healthcare sector, including the pharmaceutical sector, is split into a public and a private sector. Medicines of the public sector are usually procured, and also dispensed, by government entities that tend to fund them completely or to a large extent. Thus, there is sort of price control through the public procurement process. In the private sector, medicine prices are usually freely set by the manufacturers and further market players along the supply chain (cf. Section 9.3.4). Researchers may aim to compare prices between the public and the private sector. It can be done for same medicines dispensed through both channels, or for all or defined groups of medicines in the sectors. In the latter case, interpretation is key because differences may be attributable to the characteristics of the medicines (e.g., more high-priced therapeutic groups such as oncology medicines, patent status) included.
- It should be noted that for most high-income countries with advanced universal health coverage (UHC), through a comprehensive social health insurance system, for instance, such as in the Member States of the EU, the distinction between public and private sectors is not relevant. For those countries, a common differentiation is between reimbursable and non-reimbursable medicines (some authors also talk of reimbursement and non-reimbursement sectors [or segments or markets, respectively]). A medicine is usually classified as either reimbursable or non-reimbursable.[2] Similar to what was said above about public and private sectors, a comparison of average medicine price levels in the reimbursement and non-reimbursement sectors is, in general, not meaningful because different types of medicines are attributed to the different sectors.

[2] However, a non-reimbursable medicine may also be reimbursed if defined criteria are met (e.g., reimbursement granted on a patient-named basis upon individual approval of a specialist doctor of a reimbursement agency).

- Outpatient versus hospital sectors: Studies may investigate prices of medicines that are solely dispensed in the outpatient sector or of those administered only in hospitals, or they compare the two sectors. For a price survey addressing these segments, the following aspects should be considered appropriately in the development of the study methodology. First, identifying 'hospital medicines' might be a challenge: Some countries have specific definitions of hospital medicines or hospital-exclusive medicines [7]. In practice, due to differences in the healthcare delivery systems, some medicines may be administered in an outpatient setting in some countries, while the respective 'point of care' is a hospital in other countries [8]. Furthermore, the setting 'hospital' can be defined differently across countries (for instance, a survey showed differences in national definitions compared to the OECD definition of the term 'hospital' [7]). Secondly, some medicines can be supplied in both outpatient and hospital sectors, while for other medicines use is limited to one sector (e.g., due to regulation, clinical guidelines or delivery practice of suppliers). Third, different price types are relevant for the two settings given their different supply chains (see Section 9.3.4). Fourth, even for countries with a national price regulation it might be difficult to survey a 'national hospital price'. In some countries, price regulation only targets the outpatient sector. Even in case of published hospital prices, they may relate to the maximum prices. In many countries with price regulation, medicines are procured individually by hospitals (or by groups of hospitals), and, as a result, there might be, or not, different prices of the same medicines between hospitals in the country. For the outpatient sector, this is rarely the case for regulated ex-factory (or wholesale) prices.

Further sectors include on-patent and off-patent markets (that comprise the segments of originator medicines whose patent expired, generic medicines and biosimilar medicines), medicines that are, or are not, subject to a medical prescription (prescription-only medicines and non-prescription medicines), medicines for specific indications or diseases (e.g., orphan medicines, medicines to treat non-communicable diseases such as cancer, chronic obstructive pulmonary or cardiovascular diseases) and medicines that account for high expenditure medicines (so-called 'high-cost' medicines). Some of the medicine groups listed will be discussed in the next section (cf. Section 9.3.3).

Key messages: Medicines may be attributable to different sectors (e.g., public/private sector, reimbursed/non-reimbursed medicines, outpatient/hospital sector, on-patent/off-patent medicines). Definitions of the sectors and settings may differ between countries, and it can be challenging, sometimes impossible, to determine the sector to which medicines have been classified. Consideration of sectors is key even for studies that are not comparable across countries, regions or sectors since the affiliation to a sector can have implications on the medicine price data to survey and analyse (e.g., different price types are applicable, data source only covers certain sectors).

9.3.3 Medicines

Price studies do usually not investigate the entire pharmaceutical market, but tend to focus on one or a few specific medicine groups (or segments or settings). A few examples for such groups were mentioned in Section 9.3.2. With regard to therapeutic groups, the review of price studies presented in Chapter 3 highlighted that price studies on cancer medicines and HIV/AIDS medication were conducted more frequently than for other indications. An increase in price studies on Hepatitis C medicines in the last years was observed: this illustrates how the topics selected for research are linked to the political agenda. Orphan medicines and medicines that have been accounting for high shares of public pharmaceutical expenditure (often called 'high-cost' medicines though neither research and development costs nor production costs are necessarily high) were also in the scope of recent price studies. Interest of payers and competent authorities in prices of these medicines is in line with prioritisation that decision-makers have to undertake in order to deal efficiently with scarce resources since a rather low number of medicines can account for a comparably high share of public pharmaceutical expenditure [9]. Similarly, in materials management, the technique of the so-called ABC analysis has been used for inventory categorisation and prioritisation. Products are classified into three categories: A, B and C. It is advised that A items are subject to tight controls and accurate records, whereas the controls can be less strict for B and, in particular, C items. A items tend to account for 70%—80% of total value of an inventory. In drug utilisation research, the 'DU90%' methodology is based on the same principle: It recommends assessing the quality of prescribing for those medicines that account for 90% of pharmaceutical consumption. Comparative analyses between the 90% and the 10% segments confirmed the robustness of the methodology [10]. These findings suggest that the inclusion of a rather low number of products in a comparison may be sufficient for specific research purposes under the condition that the medicines are selected appropriately.

Different approaches have to be applied to identify the defined groups, and required time and other resources will differ depending on the selected classification criterion. Therapeutic groups can be identified rather easily thanks to the Anatomical Therapeutic Chemical (ATC) classification system of the WHO (see also Box 9.3). In the European Union, medicines that received a designation of an orphan medicinal product (OMP) from the European Medicines Agency (EMA) are labelled as such in the EMA database. Information about the prescription status of medicines can be found in national databases that inform about the marketing authorisation status of medicines, usually maintained by the National Medicines Regulatory Authority (NMRA). Sometimes, price databases also indicate the prescription and/or reimbursement status of medicines. These examples illustrate that even if medicines are appropriately classified preparatory work is needed to draw up the list of selected medicines.

A few countries (e.g., Italy [11], Germany [9]) offer statistics of medicines that account for highest shares in pharmaceutical budgets, but in other countries these data need to be requested from authorities and payers. Published data are often available at the level of active ingredients (ATC 5 code). This is usually not sufficient for the sample selection since more details of the 'presentations' (pharmaceutical form, strength, pack size of the medicines) are needed and have to be sought. In some countries, data of top-selling medicines might be considered confidential and will not be shared, even not as supportive evidence to help optimising the selection of medicines included in the sample. Alternatively, sales data can be supportive in selecting top medicines but these data have usually been collected by market research institutions. Thus, they can be connected with costs that exceed the budget of researchers. In addition, these sales data have usually been collected for large pharmaceutical markets of high-income countries (HIC) and are rarely available for LMIC.

As explained in Section 9.3.2, some definitions to classify differ between countries. A medicine that received a designation as OMP valid for the whole EU is not necessarily labelled as orphan medicine in Canada, the United States or Australia. Even within the EU and its harmonised regulation of marketing authorisation and of the prescription status of medicines, differences between Member States exist related to which products are classified as medicines, and which not, and which medicines are subject to medical prescription status. The patents of a medicine can expire at different times across countries; as a result, generic and biosimilar versions may be available in some national markets whereas they have not yet been granted

BOX 9.3 ATC Classification and DDD Measurement Systems

The Anatomical Therapeutic Chemical (ATC) as the classification system and the Defined Daily Dose (DDD) as a unit of measure have been developed in the field of the drug utilisation research from the 1960s on. The WHO recommended the ATC/DDD system as the international standard for drug utilisation studies in 1981. The WHO Collaborating Centre for Drug Statistics Methodology located at the Norwegian Institute of Public Health is in charge of coordinating the development and use of the ATC/DDD system.

In the ATC classification system, the active substances are classified in a hierarchy with five different levels according to the organ or system on which they act and their therapeutic, pharmacological and chemical properties. The system has 14 main anatomical/pharmacological groups or first levels. Each ATC main group is then divided into second levels that could be either pharmacological or therapeutic groups. The third and fourth levels are chemical, pharmacological or therapeutic subgroups and the fifth level is the chemical substance.

The classification of metformin illustrates the structure of the code:

A	Alimentary tract and metabolism (1st level, anatomical main group)
A10	Medicines used in diabetes (2nd level, therapeutic subgroup)
A10B	Blood glucose lowering drugs, excl. insulins (3rd level, pharmacological subgroup)
A10BA	Biguanides (4th level, chemical subgroup)
A10BA02	Metformin (5th level, chemical substance)

The second, third and fourth levels are often used to identify pharmacological subgroups when it is considered more appropriate than therapeutic or chemical subgroups.

There is the issue that some active substances can have different ATC-5 code in case of use for different indications.

There are other classification systems; the best-known is the European Pharmaceutical Market Research Association (EphMRA) classification in which medicines are classified in a hierarchy of three and sometimes four levels mainly according to their indications and use. Despite a similar structure at the higher levels, the ATC classification and the EphMRA classification differ. The EphMRA classification serves a different purpose, namely to support marketing strategies of the pharmaceutical companies, and has been used by IQVIA (previously IMS [Intercontinental Medical Statistics]) in their marketing research statistics. Awareness of the differences between the two systems is important. A harmonisation between the ATC and EphMRA classifications has been discussed but is not considered to be the aim.

A DDD is defined as the assumed average maintenance dose per day for a medicine used for its main indication in adults. It is a technical unit created for

BOX 9.3 ATC Classification and DDD Measurement Systems—cont'd

the measurement of pharmaceutical consumption that could also be expressed in the number of units, number of prescriptions or by the physical quantity of medicines. As for the ATC classification, the DDD measurement unit facilitates international comparisons since other variables tend to differ between countries and over time. However, it should be noted that pharmaceutical utilisation data presented in DDD provide a rough estimate of consumption and not an exact picture of actual use. It is stated that 'the DDD is nearly always a compromise based on a review of available information including doses used in various countries when this information is available' [12]. The DDD is sometimes a 'dose' that is rarely if ever prescribed because it might be an average of two or more commonly used doses. As a result, the DDD does not necessarily correspond to the recommended or prescribed daily dose (PDD). Therapeutic doses for individual patients and patient groups will often differ from the DDD as they will be based on individual characteristics such as age, weight, ethnic differences, type and severity of disease, and pharmacokinetic considerations.

DDDs are only assigned for medicines that were given an ATC code. Only one DDD is assigned per ATC code and route of administration (e.g., major medicine groups without DDDs are topical products [most products in ATC group D], sera [ATC group J06], vaccines [ATC group J07], antineoplastic agents [ATC group L01], general and local anaesthetics [ATC group N01], ophthalmologicals and otologicals [most products in ATC group S], allergen extracts [ATC group V01] and contrast media [ATC group V08]).

The ATC/DDD system aims to serve as a tool for drug utilisation research and monitoring, with a view to improve the quality of use of medicines. The ATC/DDD system is intended for pharmaceutical consumption statistics, to facilitate comparability of these data between countries. It has not been developed for the purpose of medicine price comparisons or support in pricing support. The 2018 Guidelines for ATC classification and DDD assignment stated: 'There is a strong reluctance to make changes to classifications or DDDs where such changes are requested for reasons not directly related to drug consumption studies. For this reason the ATC/DDD system by itself is not suitable for guiding decisions about reimbursement, pricing and therapeutic substitution' [12].

Sources: WHO Collaborating Centre for Drug Statistics Methodology. Guidelines for ATC classification and DDD assignment 2018. Oslo; 2017.

market authorisation in other countries. Information about expected patent expiries in national markets is difficult to access.

Medicines may be available in different pharmaceutical forms (e.g., tablet, solution for injection), different strengths (5 and 10 mg), different pack sizes (e.g., 28 and 30 tablets) and different containers (e.g., blister, bottle, pre-filled syringe, vial). Further variations are possible in cases of additional equipment (e.g., supplementary needles, needle-guard). In the present book, a medicine in a defined pharmaceutical form, strength and pack size will be called 'presentation'. A survey that aims to cover the full market, or a defined medicine group, will likely collect price data of all presentations of the selected medicines. In other cases, findings will be more meaningful if one relevant presentation per medicine is selected. Usually, this will be the presentation that accounts for highest (public) pharmaceutical expenditure or sales (value component from the payer's or industry's perspective) and for highest number of prescriptions or packs sold (volume). Again, to identify the respective presentations, further data (e.g., reimbursement claim data provided by a third party payer that ideally cover the whole national market; sales data by market research institutions) are required. The provision of such data can be linked to additional costs, and will likely take some time. This will be complicated in international comparisons since in other countries different presentations of a medicine can be marketed, and their relevance in sales may differ. Different approaches of how to ensure the comparability of medicines selected will be discussed in Section 9.3.6.

A study protocol should also inform about the chosen methodological approach with regard to off-patent medicines (if applicable) unless it has been decided that the price research will be limited to the originator medicines. The WHO/HAI methodology recommends collecting price data of selected presentations of an originator medicine and the lowest-priced version of a generic [3]. This methodology allows the comparison of price variation between two identical medicines, based on the assumption that the originator medicine is the highest-priced version. Alternative approaches to investigate price data of medicines in the off-patent segment include collecting the price of the originator and the generic version that accounts for highest sales or expenditure (if such data are available) or of the originator, the highest-priced generic and the lowest-priced generic. The latter approach allows learning how much prices of originator medicines are higher than for generic medicines prices and if there is a difference in the price of the highest-priced and lowest-priced generic, and how much. In addition, the different generics of the same medicine can be weighted by volume which is an approach particularly used in cross-country comparisons (cf. Section 9.3.6.4).

Ideally, price studies should only consider medicines that are actually available because otherwise medicine price data would not be meaningful in terms of patient access to medicines. This aspect is also incorporated in the WHO/HAI methodology that aims to survey both availability and prices of medicines [3]. In principle, on-site surveys are required to assess actual availability of selected medicines at different points of dispensing (e.g., community pharmacies). Databases (e.g., of an NMRA) in some countries offer indications of market availability of medicines. This is usually not done at the level of individual points of dispensing, but at the national level: information is provided whether, or not, the medicine has been marketed, and whether it has been withdrawn from the market; some databases also report temporary non-availability (e.g., due to production or delivery shortages). Such information allows excluding medicines that are not available at the time of survey. It should be noted that this information about market availability is often provided in different sources than the medicine price data.

Major messages: A key element of the study protocol is the choice of medicines to be included. Specific therapeutic groups, medicines with defined prescription, reimbursement or patent status or those that account for comparably high shares of the public pharmaceutical expenditure can be selected, depending on the study objective. The identification of the selected medicines can be challenging in some countries and settings. Researchers should allow enough time for the selection of the medicines for inclusion; they may need to wait for data requested from authorities or other data providers.

9.3.4 Price Data

In the design of a price research three aspects, that are somewhat interrelated, should be considered:

- Should the study be based on medicine price data? How is the term 'price' defined, and how does it differentiate from other monetary values?
- Which unit of measurement (e.g., per pack size, per weight, per DDD) should be chosen?
- Which price type(s) (e.g., alongside the distribution chain) should be surveyed and analysed?

9.3.4.1 Definitions of Medicine Price and 'Price Proxies'

In some studies that claim to be medicine price analyses, notions such as 'cost' or 'expenditure' are analysed and are interpreted as measurement of price. However, this is not correct. 'Price' defines the value component whereas pharmaceutical expenditure is price multiplied by volume. Box 9.4 provides an overview of definitions related to medicine prices and price proxies.

As for any research, clarity in terms and entities analysed is key in medicine price surveys, analyses and comparisons. There are several important research questions that require other data than medicine prices. Expenditure data help determine government spend on specific medicines, or are indications for the share of public budget, for instance.

As reiterated throughout this chapter, it depends on the research objective, purpose and perspective of the study whether, or not, if price or other monetary data, or a combination (e.g., to analyse the impact of price, volume and structural effects in pharmaceutical expenditure) are required.

Some 'price studies' are based on other monetary proxies given the lack of (access to) price data (and missing resources or other barriers such as confidentiality to collect primary data of medicine prices). In certain cases, working with 'price proxies' might be acceptable since it is one approach to generate evidence but the limitations should be clearly mentioned. However, such studies should not be called price studies.

Major message: Researchers who aim to retrieve and analyse secondary 'price data' are strongly advised to explore in advance whether, or not, the information labelled as price data in a data source actually relates to prices.

9.3.4.2 Units of Measurement

Usually, medicine prices are indicated per pack. For the purpose of the study, the data need to be indicated in a measurement unit that allows further analyses and particularly comparisons. There might be few scenarios in which the indication of price data per pack, without further transformation in another unit of measurement, can be acceptable. For instance, this approach can be chosen in order to showcase that prices in the own, lower-resourced country are higher than other, higher-income countries. But doing so, it is essential that medicines of the same pharmaceutical form, strength and pack size are compared.

A frequently used unit of measurement is the number of 'units' in a pack. These units are easy to determine if they are countable, such as per the number of tablets or capsules. They are more challenging to determine

BOX 9.4 Definitions of Price and Further Monetary Terms

The definition of **medicine price** that is applied on this book (cf. Chapter 7 on terminology) is as follows: 'Value component of pharmaceutical expenditure. Typically, it is indicated per pack, but it can also refer to items in a pack or to standard units. It can be indicated for different price types'. This definition has been provided by the Organisation for Economic Co-operation and Development (OECD) that relates, more generally, to the **price of a good or service**: The latter is defined by OECD as 'the value of one unit of that good or service' (definition according to the System of National Accounts) or as 'the value of one unit of a product, for which the quantities are perfectly homogeneous not only in a physical sense but also in respect of a number of other characteristics' (definition according to the European System of National and Regional Accounts) [14].

The OECD Glossary of Statistical Terms defines **expenditures** as 'the values of the amounts that buyers pay, or agree to pay, to sellers in exchange for goods or services that sellers provide to them or to other institutional units designated by the buyers' [14]. In simpler words, expenditure is price multiplied by volume. **Pharmaceutical expenditure** may include further goods than medicines. OECD, for instance, has been surveying expenditure on 'medical goods' that are split in medicines (called 'pharmaceuticals' in the OECD terminology) and other medical non-durables. Pharmaceuticals are then sub-divided into prescribed and non-prescribed medicines (called in 'over-the-counter (OTC)' in OECD context), with a separate subclass for other non-durable goods. Examples of pharmaceuticals include medicinal preparations, branded and generic medicines, patent medicines, serums and vaccines, vitamins and minerals and oral contraceptives [14,15].

The terms 'expenditure' and 'expenses' are sometimes used interchangeably. Overall, '**expenses'** rather relate to individual parties, such as market actors (e.g., 'funding spent on operating a business, either by paying salaries for employees, purchasing new equipment or supplies or spending money on marketing the business with the goal of increasing profits' [16]).

Some authors used the term '**cost(s)**' as a synonym for 'expenditure(s)'. In economic context, however, there is a difference between these two notions since the term 'costs' refers to input factors (for production or delivery of service). The OECD defines costs as 'the value in alternative uses of the factors of production used by a firm (labour costs, materials costs, capital costs). Costs may be fixed or variable. Total costs refer to the sum of fixed and variable costs' [14].

Sales is another monetary term applied in this context. Like expenditure, expenses and costs, the term 'sales' includes both value and volume components. It is a term of business and trade, and it 'measures gross operating revenues less rebates, discounts, and returns' [14]. The perspective of the business operator (e.g., pharmaceutical company) is applied.

Continued

BOX 9.4 Definitions of Price and Further Monetary Terms—cont'd

Glossaries and classification systems of relevance: OECD Glossary of Statistical Terms [14], System of Health Accounts of Eurostat, OECD and WHO [15], Glossary of pharmaceutical terms of the WHO Collaborating Centre for Pharmaceutical Pricing and Reimbursement Policies [17].

in cases of liquids such as oral solution or suspension for injection. For a price survey, appropriate units of measurement can be the vial, ampoule and further containers.

Several price studies (see Chapters 2 to 4) analysed price data per standard units (SU). This is the case for data that researchers received from IMS (today known under the name IQVIA) which developed this definition. An SU is defined as 'the smallest dose of a product, equivalent to one tablet or capsule for an oral dosage form, one teaspoon (i.e. 5 mL) for a syrup and one ampoule or vial for an injectable product' [18]. It is thus similar to 'units' as presented above. This methodology has been applied by IQVIA to all medicines on the market in all countries of which the institute has data. It should be noted that IQVIA has a focus on sales data, and the primary purpose of the SU methodology development was apparently to make sales data comparable (for market research analysis).

Studies also used price data indicated per DDD. As explained in Box 9.3, a defined daily dose is the assumed average maintenance dose per day for a medicine used for its main indication in adults. It is a major unit of measurement to ensure comparability in drugs utilisation research. The WHO Collaborating Centre for Drug Statistics Methodology that is responsible for the coordination of the use of the ATC/DDD system has been advising against the use of DDD in pricing and reimbursement decisions since the DDD methodology has been developed for the measurement and comparison of pharmaceutical consumption.

Some research papers, including those that aimed to assess the affordability of medicine prices for patients or public payers, expressed the price per a course of treatment or within a defined period of time such as a month (for medicines to treat chronic diseases such as asthma, diabetes or cardiovascular diseases). While these units are strictly speaking not purely price data anymore since they contain an element of utilisation, this approach can be very useful for some research questions. It is important, however, that in comparative studies the same 'course of treatment' for the same medicines in different countries, regions, setting and over times.

A few studies presented price data per weight units such as kilogram or gram. Such methodology apparently assumes that prices of medicines would be linked to weight though, in practice, prices of medicines depend on several other factors, including its assumed 'value', the willingness-to-pay of purchaser and financial constraints of patients and payers that limit the ability to pay (see also Chapter 13.5). Unless justified by particular research objectives (e.g., cross-country comparison of prices of an active ingredient per gram paid and of actual production costs of this active ingredient per gram), using weight units to measure prices is not advised.

If data are provided from different sources (e.g., prices of different countries) and presented per units, there is the risk that different units might be applied in some cases.

Major message: In general, it is recommended to retrieve or receive primary data and to work further on them by rescaling per selected unit of measurement. Alternatively, getting a set of price data with and without the rescaling to unit measurement is also acceptable and can help reduce the workload. Whatever unit of measurement will be eventually chosen, researchers should know the unit's size of each presentation studied and should have the possibility to adapt them if needed (e.g., define a different course of a treatment if the study refers to children, for instance).

9.3.4.3 Price Types

Medicine price surveys, analyses and comparisons can be conducted for different price types (price components) that reflect different perspectives.

9.3.4.3.1 Price Components along the Supply Chain

Different price types are, among others, attributable to an increase of prices along the supply chain. This is due to remuneration for the intermediaries involved and customs, duties, taxes and further add-ons.

The WHO/HAI methodology to measure medicine prices, availability, affordability and price components [3] defined five stages (cf. also Chapter 6.2):

- The first stage is the manufacturer's selling price (MSP), which is the price the manufacturer charges for the medicine, and/or the cost, insurance, freight (CIF) price for imported medicines. The latter reflects the costs of insuring and shipping the medicines to the countries of destination; there are different shipping terms (such as Ex-Works, Free on Board and Delivered Duty Unpaid) that vary with regard to the split of costs between seller and buyer.

- The second stage is the so-called landed price that describes the cost of a medicine after it has arrived in a country, has cleared all customs and import requirement and is then supplied to the main distributor (e.g., the importer, the wholesaler or a Central Medical Store). The landed price contains the import tariffs, inspection and port charges (including costs for quality control testing), importer's mark-up, local transport costs and any national taxes that are levied on the medicines purchased by the importer or supplier as add-ons to the MSP or CIF.
- The third stage refers to the wholesale selling price or central medical stores prices. This price component contains any wholesale mark-ups added by the wholesaler (or Central Medical Stores) as well as regional or state taxes levied at this stage and transport costs to move goods from the wholesaler to the retailer.
- The fourth stage is called retail price in the private sector or dispensary price in the public sector. A major component adding to the previous stage is the retail mark-up that retailers add to cover their costs, including their profit. Additionally, local or town taxes may be levied at this stage.
- The fifth and final stage is called 'dispensed price' in the WHO/HAI methodology. It contains the sales taxes such as a value-added tax (VAT) or a general sales tax (GST) and fees (e.g., a dispensing fee) that are collected when the medicine is dispensed.

Apart from national (or regional and local) taxes and duties, the extent of the add-ons can differ between different supply chain actors involved at the different stages (e.g., importers, wholesalers, pharmacies, drugstores and other retailers) which will result in different final 'dispensed prices' for the customers.

Regulation of wholesale and pharmacy mark-ups, in addition to regulation of ex-factory prices, can contribute to uniform prices across a country. The rationale of regulating wholesale and pharmacy remuneration is to remunerate the supply chain actors appropriately for the services while ensuring the final consumer prices are not increasing through mark-ups and add-ons along the supply chain.

The WHO/HAI methodology that was designed to cover countries without price regulation is supplemented by another taxonomy of price components that is particularly applicable for countries with regulation for more than one price type (e.g., European countries). Though this taxonomy (including variants) is widely applied (see also price studies presented in

Chapters 2 to 4), it has no specific name. For the purpose of this book, it will be called MWPP price taxonomy[3]. It defines four major price types:

- Ex-factory price (also called manufacturer price or ex-manufacturer price): the price at the level of industry, charged by a pharmaceutical manufacturer
- Wholesale price (also called pharmacy purchase price or pharmacy purchasing price): the price charged by wholesalers to the retailers (usually community pharmacies); it is based on the ex-factory price and additionally includes any remuneration for pharmaceutical wholesale (e.g., in the form of a wholesale mark-up or a wholesale margin).
- Pharmacy retail price (also called consumer price or sometimes public price[4]) net: the price charged by community pharmacies to the general public; it is based on the pharmacy purchasing price and additionally includes any pharmacy remuneration (such as a pharmacy mark-up, a pharmacy margin or dispensing fee). If net, it does not include VAT or other taxes.
- Pharmacy retail price (and synonyms) gross: The pharmacy retail price including VAT or other taxes.

These price types (or some of them) are found in many price databases and price lists. Some countries also use CIF prices instead of the ex-factory prices.

The MWPP taxonomy based on three stages does not differ much from the classification of the WHO/HAI methodology: The key difference is that the WHO/HAI methodology specifies the landed price as a separate price component to consider the different intermediaries that may levy duties and charges. Also, the WHO/HAI methodology reminds that taxes might be levied at any stage, not only at the dispensing level. In the MWPP classification the dispensing fee is considered as one form of pharmacy remuneration and thus integrated in the pharmacy retail price net.[5]

For medicines that are procured by public entities (e.g., hospitals), these add-ons are not applicable. As a result, no further price components of the

[3] MWPP stands for manufacturer (price), wholesale (price), pharmacy (retail price net) and pharmacy (retail price gross). It can also be read as referring to the actors involved: manufacturer, wholesaler, pharmacy and patient.

[4] The use of the term 'public price' is not recommended since it might lead to confusion with the notion of a 'public funded price' (reimbursement price).

[5] Some price databases indicate pharmacy retail prices that include the pharmacy mark-ups but not the dispensing fee.

supply chain are considered; only the procurement price or hospital price are relevant for the price study.

9.3.4.3.2 Reimbursement Prices

Another price type is the so-called reimbursement price. It relates to the amount covered by a third party payer such as a reimbursement authority and, as such, reflects the perspective of the (public) payer. It confirms the strong linkage between prices/pricing and reimbursement. It could be argued that this is not a price per se but a share of the price but such argument also applies for other price components that form the final consumer price. An example of a reimbursement price is the so-called reference price in an internal price referencing system. This is a reimbursement policy in which identical medicines or similar medicines are clustered into so-called reference groups. The reference price refers to the maximum amount that the third party payer funds. A reference price system requires the availability of equivalent or comparable medicines (e.g., generics) to build the clusters.

While reference prices are usually published (also to signal patients the willingness-to-pay of the public payer), other reimbursement prices (e.g., for on-patent medicines) are to be found in only a few price databases. Frequently, they are not exactly called 'reimbursement price'; they have to be identified due to the description of their role (in local language). In Austria, there is the explicit price type of a reimbursement price that is called 'sickness fund price', and it is published. The Austrian 'sickness fund price', that covers the compensation for the manufacturer, the wholesaler and the pharmacy, lies above the wholesale price and below the pharmacy retail price. In other price databases, there are sometimes indications (e.g., a percentage reimbursement rate) that assist with calculating of the reimbursement price. In this context, it is important to understand the respective national pricing and reimbursement system and to know to which price type the reimbursement rate should be applied (usually to the pharmacy retail price net).

As stated above, the reimbursement price is a maximum amount. What is indicated as reimbursement price in price databases may exceed the actually paid amount of the social health insurance or any other third party payer. This is predominantly attributable to two reasons:

- Further co-payments (e.g., a prescription fee) might be charged to patients (e.g., Austria, Estonia, Poland), or a percentage co-payment of the reference price (in a reference price system) might additionally be applicable (e.g., Portugal). Though this is not confidential, it might be challenging to survey the data correctly.

- In addition to what is officially published, confidential discounts and price-reducing arrangements might be applicable.

9.3.4.3.3 List Prices and Confidentiality

Price data that can be retrieved from price lists and databases will always be the officially published list prices. However, for all price types presented above, lower, discounted prices can exist due to price-reducing arrangements agreed between supply chain actors and between industry or supply actor chain and the public payer. To name a few:

- Discounted ex-factory prices, due to
  - Statutory discounts charged by the third party payer to pharmaceutical industry,
  - Negotiated discounts and similar arrangements between the third party payer to pharmaceutical industry,
- Discounted wholesale prices, due to
  - Negotiated discounts granted by a manufacturer to a wholesale pharmacy
- Discounted pharmacy retail prices, due to
  - Statutory and negotiated discounts (e.g., in a framework agreement) charged by the third party payer to pharmacies,
  - Negotiated discounts granted by wholesale to pharmacies.

The examples listed above describe cases that have been observed in reality.

It has sometimes been argued that discounts and similar price-reducing arrangements cannot be assessed in price surveys due to confidentiality. This is true in many cases but not always:

- Discounts and similar arrangements are not always confidential. Some countries ask pharmaceutical industry, wholesale or the community pharmacy sector to contribute to the pharmaceutical bill by granting statutorily regulated discount on the manufacturer price, wholesale price or pharmacy retail price, respectively. Usually, these discounted prices are not listed in price databases but the extent of discounts has been published in legislation (e.g., Germany, Greece, Spain) or a framework agreement (Ireland) and is known. Thus, this kind of information can be used in price studies if the discount is applicable to the individual medicines (e.g., a fixed deduction, or a percentage rate). If the discount is more complex and not linked to the price of the individual product (e.g., payback if a defined sales amount will be exceeded), these arrangements cannot be considered.

- In many cases, discounts and further price-reducing arrangements have been agreed on a conditional basis between the parties. The parties either involve the market player (industry and wholesale, wholesale and pharmacy), or a (public) payer and a market player. In these cases, it is almost impossible to include 'actual' price data in a study. A few studies (cf. Chapter 2.1) surveyed such discounted prices; this was usually done through on-site surveys (with researchers ensuring confidentiality and anonymity to the data providers). It should be noted that even if the challenge of assessing confidential data set were solved, many of these agreements (so-called managed-entry agreements, cf. also Chapter 13.5.3) might be arranged in a complex way as discussed above (e.g., depending on sales volume, discounts being determined ex-post) that a consideration in terms of individual price data is actually impossible.

The non-availability of actual (discounted) price data is a limitation of most price studies that should be acknowledged. It is particularly an issue with high-priced medicines that are known to be frequently subject to these managed-entry agreements. A few countries (e.g., Austria, Australia) indicate in their price database the existence of such agreements per product [2], and for a few further markets information might be available in literature about the existence (rarely about the extent) of these discount arrangements.

Major messages: Price data can be indicated at different price types (price components in the supply chain, reimbursement-related price data). Further price components that impact the final price should be considered if this is in line with study objective. Non-availability of data for certain price type is a limitation to be acknowledged but shall not discourage researchers to publish findings of a price study.

9.3.5 Time Period

Another dimension of the methodology of medicine price studies concerns the time aspect: the survey and analysis of data can relate to one specific point in time (cross-sectional study) or can extend over a time period (longitudinal study, time-series analysis).

9.3.5.1 Cross-sectional Studies

Surveys and analyses of price data at specific points in time are easier to conduct than time-series analyses; still a few issues need to be considered.

As reiterated throughout this chapter, the purpose and objective of the study determines methodological choices. At the same time, data availability can, in practice, impact the design, and price data might only be available at specific points in time — different from those originally intended to be included in the study. Some databases provide, for instance, daily updates, while others offer monthly, quarterly or bi-annually updated price information. This can be a particular issue in case of a cross-country analysis, with price data available in different data sources that relate to different points in time. Though not the preferred approach, an analysis of price data that refer to different points in time can be conducted if it complies with the purpose of the study, covers up for missing price information and ensures quality of the data. In case of large variations in timing of the data analysed and compared (e.g., different years), it is recommended adjusting the prices for inflation and deflation, respectively. For instance, Cameron et al. corrected for inflation and deflation secondary price data retrieved from WHO/HAI price surveys conducted in several countries in different years that were then used in a cross-country comparison [19].

Several of the recommendations given in Chapter 8 about careful selection of the data source related to the timing of the data: Is it known which date the data in the source refer to? How do I recognise that data were updated? If I want to collect data at certain points in time, (how) is it possible in a data source that changes frequently (e.g., daily) and only displays most updated data?

9.3.5.2 Time-Series Analyses

Interrupted time-series analyses are considered to be the strongest, quasi-experimental approach for evaluating longitudinal effects of interventions [20] and are thus appropriate tools to evaluate the impact of a policy measure on medicine prices. This method involves constructing a time series of data (e.g., price data) and testing statistically for a change in the time periods before and time periods after implementation of an intervention (e.g., a pricing policy measure).

It has been recommended to collect at least 12 data points before and 12 data points after the intervention [20]. This can be a challenge in settings with limited data availability and will require additional efforts in data collection. Even if no primary data survey from dispensers is needed, retrieving such data from data sources that do not allow for easy handling of historical data can be cumbersome.

Major messages: The date to which the medicine price data relate to must be known. Cross-sectional comparison of data of different periods in time should be avoided and, if done, adjustments for inflation and deflation should be undertaken. Time-series analyses of medicine price allow evaluation of policy interventions.

9.3.6 Specific Decisions Related to Cross-Country Comparisons

Cross-country comparisons require additional decisions. Comparability needs to be ensured, and covering up for data gaps has to be balanced against a strict definition of comparability. Researchers also need to decide whether, or not, price data will be weighted, for example, to account for different (sales) volumes and/or different income levels of the countries investigated.

9.3.6.1 Comparator Countries

A few papers [21–24] discussed criteria for the selection of comparator countries included in a price study (cf. Chapter 6.1). They tended to stress that the selection of comparable countries is a challenge given existing variation in healthcare settings, regulation, policies and practice that impact prices and utilisation of medicines. Pharmaceutical utilisation is influenced by several factors, including clinical guidelines, culture and religion, for instance [25,26]. Some authors argued that solely countries of similar pharmaceutical pricing policy environment, similar pharmaceutical market, similar country size, similar income and similar pattern of medicine consumption should be included in cross-country price comparisons [21,22]. The importance of comparability in terms of the two latter aspects (income, utilisation) was particularly stressed.

The authors of this chapter support a more flexible approach with regard to comparator countries and reiterate that the purpose of a study determines methodological choices, including the selection of comparator countries. For policy decisions (i.e., price data collection for use in EPR), comparability in several dimensions, as listed above (e.g., similar income and utilisation patterns), is important. This has also been stressed by the WHO Guideline on Country Pharmaceutical Pricing Policies [27]; for further information see Chapter 14 on guidance documents for EPR. Nonetheless, a price comparison between countries that differ, somewhat considerably, in some of the presented parameters is still possible and can be justified if it contributes to the research question (e.g., if the study aims to gather information on countries of different income levels or aims to assess affordability [24]). The WHO/HAI manual argued that a comparison of countries of different economic situations can help conveying a message to policy-makers such as that the given country pays higher prices than other countries of considerably higher income [3]. Morel et al. showed for instance that some middle-income countries paid higher medicine prices than some high-income countries, while other middle-income countries paid lower prices than some low-income countries [28].

If the research aims to explore differences between *average* price levels of countries (instead of comparing single prices of individual medicines), then weighting of price data should be considered. This has been, in particular, proposed for the two above-mentioned dimensions of pharmaceutical consumption and income of countries and will be discussed in separate sections (cf. Sections 9.3.6.4 and 9.3.6.5).

A focus on a specific sector (setting) can also be made in a cross-country comparison: for instance, prices of medicines used in hospitals or of those procured through public tendering can be compared between countries. Clear definitions of the settings across the countries are required to ensure including same or similar medicines in the selected settings. Researchers may be confronted with the challenge of having a sufficient number of medicines in the intersecting set of the different countries (see also Section 9.3.6.2). The study protocol could include reflections about the minimum number of needed data points since in some cases, despite preparatory checks of data availability, the data collection may show a low number of medicines with robust medicine price data in some countries that an exclusion of countries from the price analysis might be required.

Major message: In principle, comparability of the included countries should be sought in terms of their income, medicine utilisation pattern and policy framework. But the choice of countries that are not similar may be justified and even reasonable for certain research objectives.

9.3.6.2 Comparable Medicines

In order to deal in international comparisons with cross-country differences of medicine particularities, researchers may select medicines that comply with the defined classification criteria in the 'base country' and use these selected medicines in comparator countries. They should acknowledge the possible risk that the selected medicines may not correspond to the defined criteria in foreign contexts (e.g., there may not be prescription-only or hospital-exclusive medicines in other countries). Depending on the research objective, in some cases, however, it might be necessary to first identify the defined medicines in all comparator countries, and then either include all medicines that comply with the selection criteria in any of the countries or consider the lowest common subset.

Lack of data for (comparable) medicines that are scope of the investigation is one major limitation of price comparisons. This might be attributable to the fact that medicines considered for possible inclusion in the study are not marketed in comparator countries. This results from a variety of reasons: Given widespread use of EPR, marketing authorisation holders may bring new high-priced medicines in the market in lower-income countries at a later stage (months and even years after marketing in the first-launch country). The staggered market launch aims to not reduce the benchmark price that is based on EPR in several countries (cf. chapter 13.2.1). Furthermore, medicines may not be launched in markets that are considered unattractive for business. This is the case for several LMIC with limited ability-to-pay: neither public payers nor patients have sufficient funds to pay the prices charged for some essential medicines [29]. Small countries (i.e., low population number), even in high-income settings, may suffer from limited availability because pharmaceutical companies may not consider low-volume markets of commercial interest, also in the light of costs incurred due to regulatory requirements (e.g., translations in country language) [30]. An argument brought forward by industry is that for some medicines prices are too low to ensure business viability. In recent years, governments and the public health community have observed with concern the market withdrawal of well-established and widely used 'old' medicines with low prices [31]. Differences in availability between countries can also be attributed to cross-country variation in epidemiology and 'treatment culture', including prescription patterns. This comes back to the argument discussed above of choosing reference countries of similar morbidity pattern and medicine utilisation that likely increases the number of similar medicines. However, even in comparable countries the same active ingredients might be marketed in different pharmaceutical forms, strength and pack sizes. It has been argued that differences take into account country-specific prescribing, dispensing and use patterns [22]. Differences could also be the result due to pharmaceutical industry's marketing strategies ('product differentiation') [32]. In any case, these differences complicate cross-country comparisons. Finally, temporary shortages that are an increasing problem globally [33] may also be responsible for non-availability of medicines on the market.

9.3.6.2.1 Strategies to Optimise Medicine Selection for Cross-Country Comparison

Ideally, if resources allow, researchers are advised to check the availability of the medicines planned for inclusion (in selected presentations, i.e., in defined pharmaceutical form, strength and pack size) in the comparator countries. This could save unpleasant surprises at a later stage when price data are collected. Ex-ante verification is, in particular, recommended if the sample of medicines is intended to be small. Some national databases inform whether, or not, the medicine has been marketed. However, researchers should be aware of the fact that the information about the marketing authorisation status of medicines in national databases does not automatically imply that the medicine has been brought into the market. In the European Union, defined medicines (e.g., biotechnological medicines) have been granted a centralised marketing authorisation. Nonetheless, not all of these centrally authorised medicines have been marketed. From a high-income country, Austria, it was reported that 50%—60% of the medicines authorised were actually on the market [34].

The authors acknowledge that an ex-ante assessment of market availability of selected medicines is often not possible (no such data freely accessible), or would incur disproportional costs or efforts. In such cases, researchers might also like to define a larger sample of medicines that would allow for the exclusion of a few products at a later stage when the collected (price) data reveal data gaps.

Some data sources contain price data even if the medicines were not actually marketed. In some price databases the availability status is indicated, and a few databases even inform about 'temporary non-availability'. In some countries, information about the marketing status and availability of medicines can be derived from additional sources (cf. also Chapter 8). Researchers are invited to balance the need for further information about medicines' availability against the efforts of additional research.

The study protocol should also specify whether, or not, price data of medicines that are not marketed would be included in the research. While acknowledging that eventually the study objective is decisive, the authors tend to prefer not including price data of medicines that have not been marketed. These are kind of 'fake prices' not linked to reality and actual delivery to patients. The inclusion of these medicines into price databases appears to be rather linked to pharmaceutical policy and companies' responses to it (e.g., an MAH may have an interest to have price data published in a high-priced country that is frequently referenced to by other countries that apply EPR). However, there might be good reasons to still include medicines that are only temporarily not available in the products' basket of the study.

9.3.6.2.2 Like-for-Like Comparison

Researchers are encouraged to critically assess if it can be justified to move away from a strict definition of comparable units for the benefit of inclusion of further data points to cover up for gaps.

The authors of this chapter are in favour of a rather narrow approach. We recommend a like-for-like comparison that allows only a few exceptions. A like-for-like medicine price comparison means that medicine prices analysed on a per unit basis (cf. Section 9.3.4.2) should have

- the same pharmaceutical form (e.g., film-coated tablet),
- the same strength (e.g., 5 mg), and
- the same pack size (e.g., 30 tablets).

In a narrow range, exceptions to the pack size are considered acceptable. The authors are supportive to take alternatively the closest pack size (e.g., 28 tablets) if the same is not available. This is also in line with the recommendation of the WHO/HAI methodology [3]. It should be noted that the comparison is done at the unit basis (e.g., $^{\text{pack price}}/_{30}$ and $^{\text{pack price}}/_{28}$ are compared and not the pack prices of a 30-tab pack and a 28-tab pack). A comparison to medicines of more distant pack size (e.g., 500 or 100 tablets) might be, however, problematic since different marketing considerations and procurement strategies can be reflected in the price of large packs. Upon critical assessment, consideration of same medicines that only differ in pharmaceutical form (e.g., similar oral forms such as tablets, film-coated tablets, capsules, hard capsules) might be also acceptable if no data are available for the presentation in the identical pharmaceutical form in the comparator countries. In this respect, variation has been observed in terms of how pharmaceutical forms are indicated in national databases between countries (e.g., sometimes only 'tablet' or 'oral form' is indicated, whereas other data sources are more explicit in specifying). Similarly, the way of how strength and dosage of same medicines are indicated in national databases can differ.

Do not search for trade names. Medicines are marketed under different trade names. Thus, the identification of identical medicines should not be done by trade names. Searches should be based on the name of the active ingredient or by ATC-5 (however, one active ingredient may have different ATC-5 codes). Researchers should be aware that active ingredients are spelled differently in national languages. As explained in Chapter 8, some price databases allow for the search at ATC-5 or of active ingredients, whereas others do not. In such cases, researchers have to consult further sources (e.g., a register of authorised medicines) or do additional research.

A specific aspect in terms of ensuring comparability is that the reimbursement, prescription and patent status of the investigated medicines or its affiliation to a specific setting (e.g., considered as hospital medicine) may differ between countries. In some cases, this can have implications on data availability or on prices (e.g., the price of an originator medicine that went off-patent and now faces competitors in the market is lower compared to countries where that product is still on-patent). Researchers are advised to consider such particularities in the interpretation of price data.

Major messages: It is recommended to define in advance comparator criteria of the medicines (e.g., comparison of only medicines that are for hospital use or defined as prescription-only in other countries, consideration of solely medicines in the market) in line with the research objective and check the feasibility of assessing this information. Ideally, medicines of the same pharmaceutical form, strength and pack size should be compared; slight deviations in pack size are acceptable.

9.3.6.3 Comparable Price Types

Medicine prices can be surveyed, analysed and compared at different price types. As explained in Section 9.2, the perspective of the investigation determines the choice of price type studied: for example, ex-factory prices (manufacturer prices) from industry's or Ministry's of Trade perspective, (pharmacy) retail prices (consumer prices) from patients' perspective and reimbursement prices from public payers' perspective.

It is key to compare medicine prices of the same price type in cross-country comparisons. Comparison of different price types will lead to wrong conclusions.

In Section 9.3.4.3, it was shown that several stages along the supply chain result in different price types. Different kinds of add-ons (e.g., taxes, duties, tariffs, mark-ups) can be added at the various stages, which limits comparability. It can be challenging to determine the price type of published price data in national databases, which apply their country's perspective and terminology. For example, in England, the so-called 'trade price' is published. It is the first price in the supply chain. Is it the ex-factory price, as some have been arguing? To answer this question, the policy framework in England has to be studied: The ex-factory price is not price-regulated, and there is no control of the wholesale margin. This margin is negotiated on a confidential basis between industry and wholesalers and is not published [35]. The price type ('trade price') that is published corresponds to the wholesale price in other countries and should be considered as such in international price comparisons.

Working with secondary data, researchers might be tempted to choose price types for the analysis based on the existing data in the national databases. However, in regulated settings, data for further price types can be calculated. Taxes at different stages, wholesale and pharmacy mark-ups and margins can be used to calculate from pharmacy retail prices gross down to ex-factory prices, and to determine consumers prices by adding the relevant mark-ups. In most European countries, wholesale and pharmacy mark-ups and margins are statutorily regulated as maximum mark-ups and margins but in practice the maximum amounts are always fully exploited. Cautions should be given to details of the design of the remuneration schemes for supply chain actors. **It should be carefully checked whether a mark-up** (i.e., add-on to the lower price stage) **or a margin** (i.e., share of the next highest price type, thus representing the percentage of the selling price that is profit) **is applied**, and the two concepts should not be mixed up (cf. also Chapter 7 on the terminology). Attention should be paid to the scope of the regulation that may only relate to reimbursable or prescription-only medicines or different groups of medicines.

While prices at different price types can be calculated if statutory wholesale and pharmacy remuneration is based on flat and regressive mark-up or margin schemes, this is not always possible if pharmacy remuneration is not linked to medicine prices, but based on a tariff to remunerate services. If researchers aim to include such countries for a comparison of pharmacy retail prices, they could calculate data of this price type based on assumptions, while acknowledging the limitations. For instance, if a dispensing fee is applied, it can be included in the pharmacy retail price. Increasingly, a mix of price-related pharmacy remuneration (e.g., flat mark-up or margin, regressive scheme) and price-independent, performance-based funding of pharmacy services (e.g., dispensing fee) has been introduced. In these cases, the performance-based remuneration should also be considered in the final pharmacy retail price, if possible; otherwise, it should be acknowledged that pharmacy retail prices are likely under-estimated. Performance-based remuneration of pharmacy services that are not included in national price databases can explain possible lower pharmacy retail prices of some countries in international comparison.

The authors of this chapter consider it appropriate to take assumptions in certain cases. For instance, the regulation of supply chain actors (wholesale/pharmacy) that only addresses a specific segment (e.g., reimbursable medicines) might be used to calculate missing price types of non-reimbursable medicines if research had confirmed that in practice same margins are applied for reimbursable and non-reimbursable medicines. Similarly, application of average margins is an option. Apart from the above-mentioned example of England, some further European countries regulate prices at wholesale price level while ex-factory prices are the result of commercial negotiations between the manufacturer and wholesalers [35]. To allow for a comparison of ex-factory prices in Europe, wholesale prices of these countries could be discounted by an average wholesale margin. Since the individual deals between industry and wholesale are confidential in these countries, there are few publications on average wholesale margin [36,37]. An updated version of average wholesale margins can be found in the Regulation on Procedural Rules for Calculation of the EU average price [38] in Austria that published average wholesale margins of other European countries used in their EPR regulation.

It is fair to say that assumptions limit the validity of a price study. Thus, researchers have to balance robustness of data against availability issues, and this decision shall again be guided by the study objective. Since it is key to understand the policy framework in the comparator countries, researchers are encouraged to extend their preliminary research beyond literature review and contact country experts at a very early stage, or even invite them to collaborate on the study.

A cross-country price study may also aim to identify differences in the price components between countries [3]. For instance, as shown in European price comparisons some countries (e.g., Italy, Austria) have comparably high pharmacy retail prices though their ex-factory prices do not rank that, whereas ex-factory prices of other countries (e.g., Denmark, Sweden) rank high in comparison but pharmacy retail prices do not [39]. This points to comparably high, or low, wholesale or pharmacy mark-ups and signals to policy-makers a possible need for action on the design of regulation of specific price types.

Major messages: Medicine prices must be compared for the same price type in cross-country comparisons. Researchers have to understand the price type of data included in national price databases. In case of statutory mark-up (or margin) schemes, price data can be calculated for price types for which no data are available;

information about average mark-ups and margins can also be used to determine price types.

9.3.6.4 Weighting for Volume (Price Indices)

A key decision is whether, or not, to compare prices of individual medicines (so-called single price comparisons) or to draw conclusions on average price levels of countries, or sub-markets. In the latter case, it has been suggested weighting data for volume components, that is, to calculate price indices.

Many price studies did not account for volume. Such single price comparisons can be done for a comparably low number of medicines (though comparability has to be ensured), and it does, in principle,[6] not require further data than prices.

Statements about average price levels across countries might be of interest for the whole market or defined submarkets (e.g., off-patent market). They are connected to some challenges:

- A high number of data is required which may involve extensive data collection and/or access to data from a provider (possibly linked to costs).
- In the countries of the comparison, there may be different utilisation patterns with regard to included medicines. Thus, price indices have been proposed as they adjust the price data for volume.

Price indices are measures of relative price changes to allow for showing average differences between countries (or time periods). Different types of price indices have been developed. The widely applied Laspeyres index uses volume weights of the base country, whereas the Paasche index uses the volume weights of comparator countries (for definitions refer to Box 9.5). Each of the indicators has its strengths and limitations. By weighting for volume in the other countries of the comparison, the Paasche index requires several data. As a result, the Laspeyres price index is more frequently computed for practical reasons. In theory, the Fischer index that combines mechanisms of Laspeyres and Paasche price indices is considered as the 'ideal' index, but it requires more data than the other two indices and is thus often not feasible [40].

[6] Supplementary data might still be required to define price data (e.g., information of units per pack, price types, related to the prescription, patent or reimbursement status) or exchange rate information.

BOX 9.5 Price Indices

A price index compares the prices of a set of products at different points in time, or at different locations (countries). It is an economic measure of relative price changes, consisting of a series of numbers arranged so that a comparison between the values for any two or more periods or countries will show the average change in prices between periods or the average difference in prices between countries, respectively.

Commonly used price indices are the Laspeyres index and the Paasche index.

The Laspeyres price index is used for measuring the price development of the basket of goods and services consumed in the base period. It answers the question of how much a basket that consumers bought in the base period would cost in the current period. It is defined as a fixed-weight, or fixed-basket, index that uses the basket of goods and services and their weights from the base period. It is also known as a 'base-weighted index'.

The Paasche price index is an index formula used for measuring the price development of the basket of goods and services that is consumed in the current period. The question it answers is how much a basket that consumers buy in the current period would have cost in the base period. So it is also defined as a fixed-weight, or fixed-basket, index, because it uses the basket of goods and services and their weights from the current period. It is therefore also known as a 'current weighted index'.

There are further indices such as the Fischer price index. This is an index formula used in price statistics for measuring the price development of goods and services, on the basis of the baskets from both the base and the current period. It is defined as the geometric average of the Laspeyres price index (which only uses the base period basket) and the Paasche price index (which only uses the current period basket).

In medicine price comparisons the parameter 'period' is substituted by 'country' (base country instead of the base period, comparator countries instead of the current period).

Sources: Eurostat. Statistics explained, Luxembourg; 2018. Available from: http://ec.europa.eu/eurostat/statistics-explained/index.php/Main_Page [40]; Eurostat. European price statistics. An overview, Luxembourg; 2008. Available from: http://ec.europa.eu/eurostat/documents/3217494/5700847/KS-70-07-038-EN.PDF/6b78bcc3-b219-4038-80d2-4180a9410678?version=1.0 [41].

Results of price comparisons based on indices are sensitive to the choice of the index formula. This was also documented in research that applied different indices for a medicine price comparison. Results derived by applying the Paasche index were found to be usually lower than Laspeyres results [21,42,43]. This may result from a possibly higher consumption of medicines with lower prices in their countries.

Possible volume data to consider for weighting are sales data, prescription, dispensing data or claims data expressed in volume. Each of these data sets represents a different perspective, and it should be checked whether, or not, the volume data set refers to the same sub-market as the price data. Building price indices requires double efforts with regard to data availability: access to price as well as volume data is needed (at least for one country in case of the Laspeyres price index).

Analysing medicine prices based on price indices is definitively an interesting approach if conclusions about average price levels between countries shall be drawn. Weighting by volume allows taking the national prescribing culture, epidemiology and marketing strategies into consideration. However, two challenges need to be addressed: to ensure data availability and sufficient skills and knowledge to build and analyse price indices.

Still, there is no need to base every cross-country comparison on price indices. Unweighted single price comparisons for a low number of medicines — even for one single medicine — can be of interest to researchers, policy-makers and media because they showcase price variation between countries. Most cross-country price studies presented in Chapters 2 to 4 were conducted on basis of unweighted comparisons for individual products of interest, for example, in the areas of the HIV/AIDS, cancer or hepatitis C medication.

If data availability, resources and capacity allow, researchers might be interested in applying different methodologies (unweighted and different price indices) and compare differences in findings.

Major messages: Possible use of price indices should be considered during the planning phase of a price study. Indices are particularly relevant for the determination of average price levels in cross-country comparisons. Different price index methods require different amounts of additional data (e.g., volume data) and will lead to different results.

9.3.6.5 Choice of Conversion Rate and Weighting for Income

Since price data of other countries are usually available in other currencies (unless for countries with a common currency), decisions have to be taken related to the exchange rate. The two major options are either conversion of data using exchange rates or weighting for purchasing power parity (PPP). For definitions see Box 9.6.

BOX 9.6 Exchange Rates

Exchange rates are defined as the price of one country's currency in relation to another. They may be expressed as the average rate for a period of time or as the rate at the end of the period. Exchange rates are classified by the International Monetary Fund (IMF) in three broad categories, reflecting the role of the authorities in the determination of the exchange rates and/or the multiplicity of exchange rates in a country: (1) the market rate which is used to describe exchange rates determined largely by market forces (in which the rate 'floats'); (2) the official rate which is used to describe the exchange rate determined ('fixed') by authorities; and (3) arrangements falling between the two, in which the rate holds a stable value against another currency or a composite of currencies. This indicator is measured in terms of national currency per US dollar.

Purchasing power parities (PPP) are the rates of currency conversion that equalise the purchasing power of different currencies by eliminating the differences in price levels between countries. In their simplest form, PPP are price relatives that show the ratio of the prices in national currencies of the same good or service in different countries. PPP are also calculated for groups of products and for each of the various levels of aggregation up to and including GDP. The basket of goods and services priced is a sample of all those that are a part of final expenditure: household consumption, government services, capital formation and net exports, covered by GDP.

PPP are generally used for research and analysis, for statistics and administrative purposes. The Organisation for Economic Co-operation and Development (OECD), together with the Statistical Office of the European Commission (Eurostat), developed this concept. Further users besides OECD and the European Commission include the IMF, the United Nations, the World Bank, government agencies, universities and research institutes, public and private enterprises, the media and individuals.

Sources: OECD. OECD glossary of statistical terms. Paris: OECD Publishing; 2008. Availablie from: https://read.oecd-ilibrary.org/economics/oecd-glossary-of-statistical-terms_9789264055087-en - page2 [14]; Eurostat, Organisation for Economic and Co-operation Development. Eurostat-OECD methodological manual on purchasing power parities. Luxembourg: OECD Publishing; 2012; OECD. OECD health data Paris: OECD; 2018. Available from: https://data.oecd.org/ [44].

One limitation of exchange rates is their volatility. If conversion by exchange rates is applied, researchers should carefully decide which kind of exchange rate is more appropriate for their research (average vs. a rate at a specific point in time). Average rates relating to longer periods of time (e.g., average exchange rate of the month or quarter before the date of price collection) can reduce the exchange rate volatility but are less specific in relation to the timing of the data collection.

Exchange rates are determined by the supply and demand for different currencies. However, different factors including currency speculation, interest rates, government intervention and capital flows between countries influence supply and demand for currencies. As a result, exchange rates suffer from the limitation that they do not reflect the relative purchasing powers of currencies in their national markets [44].

In response, the concept of PPP has been developed, and its use is recommended, particularly in the context of GDP and pharmaceutical expenditure data [44]. However, PPP do not come without limitations, either. As statistical constructs, they provide best available estimates of country's economies and their general price level in relation to other countries in comparison. Furthermore, since they were constructed to address the general economy, the underlying basket of goods and services to calculate the PPP is not pharmaceuticals-related. The main use of PPP is to convert GDP and expenditures of different countries into real GDP and real expenditures [46]. Eurostat and OECD developed a method to calculate PPP for household purchases of medical goods and services [44] but PPP published by OECD and Eurostat for further use do not consider medicines. This is a limitation in the use of PPP and should be considered in the interpretation of the results.

If not contradictory to the study objective, researchers are encouraged to apply both approaches (exchange rates and PPP conversion) to demonstrate the differences. As a trend, price data converted in PPP tend to be lower for higher-income countries and higher for lower-income economies compared to price data converted by exchange rates.

As an alternative to price data by PPP, prices could also be adjusted by per capita GDP expressed in PPP [47]. This would also equalise differences in the economic situation and income of the comparator countries.

Major message: Conversion of national price data by purchasing power parities can be considered.

9.4 LIMITATIONS AND CONCLUSIONS

Conducting a medicine study can be challenging. In the planning of the research, several methodological choices have to be taken.

This chapter aims to convey two major messages:

- Invest sufficient time and resources in the study protocol.
- The study objective and purpose should be the guiding principle for the development of the methodology.

While this chapter aims to provide practical advice (see also the checklist in Table 9.1), it is not intended to be a 'cook book' that makes strong recommendations (such as: 'researchers have to survey price data of outpatient medicines of at least three countries of similar income, convert the price data by using PPP and then calculate a Laspeyres index'). Though some options are preferred, there might be good reasons for choosing other approaches. A price study will always have limitations, but researchers should be aware of these limitations and clearly spell them out.

We acknowledge that we could not always provide references (given lack of literature) and that some of recommendations, or preferred options, are based on our practical long-term experience with medicine price surveys, analyses and comparisons. We also acknowledge that the chapter had a stronger focus on countries with price regulation because the authors' experience mainly relates to these countries.

This chapter did not aim to focus solely on price comparisons, as other literature tends to do, as surveys and intra-country analyses also require sufficient methodological reflection. On-site surveys, however, were not described in this chapter since they have already been covered by the WHO/HAI methodology that was presented in depth in Chapter 6.2.

A discussion of different formats to present analysed data (e.g., different types of tables and graphs such as bar charts or box plots) was not scope of this chapter. The choice of the format for data representation will depend on the methodology that was used to analyse the price data. A few, rather simple approaches of presenting data of a price comparison of single medicines are offered as part of the exercises in Chapter 10.

As a concluding remark, it should be reminded that in addition to the development of the methodology, further preparatory work is required. A sufficient budget needs to be ensured to cover possible cost of access to databases, purchase of data or travels in case of on-site surveys. Availability and quality of data sources should be checked (cf. Chapter 8). A team of data collectors and investigators has to be built and trained. Procedures and rules for surveying data and documenting results as well as decisions (e.g., justified protocol deviations) need to be established and communicated. Mechanisms for quality assurance (e.g., validation of surveyed data by senior researchers, invitation of reviewers to comment on the study protocol and preliminary results) should be established. Last, but not least, given the high political relevance of medicine price research and analysis (see Box 9.1), approaches to manage expectations and reactions of stakeholders should be considered (e.g., involvement of policy-makers and further stakeholders in an advisory board, production of a layperson summary of the study and cooperation with the university communication department).

REFERENCES

[1] WHO Regional Office for Europe. Copenhagen; Access to new medicines in Europe: technical review of policy initiatives and opportunities for collaboration and research. 2015.

[2] Vogler S, Paris V, Ferrario A, Wirtz VJ, de Joncheere K, Schneider P, et al. How can pricing and reimbursement policies improve affordable access to medicines? lessons learned from European countries. Applied Health Economics and Health Policy 2017:1–15.

[3] WHO, HAI. Measuring medicine prices, availability, affordability and price components. 2nd ed. Geneva: World Health Organization, Health Action International; 2008 Available from: http://www.who.int/medicines/areas/access/OMS_Medicine_prices.pdf.

[4] Espín J, Rovira J, Calleja A, Azzopardi-Muscat N, Richardson E, Palm W, et al. How can voluntary cross-border collaboration in public procurement improve access to health technologies in Europe? Policy Brief 2016;21.

[5] Vogler S, Lepuschütz L, Schneider P, Stühlinger V. Study on enhanced cross-country coordination in the area of pharmaceutical product pricing. Luxembourg: Gesundheit Österreich Forschungs- und Planungs GmbH; Publications Office of the European Commission; 2016. Available from: http://ec.europa.eu/health/systems_performance_assessment/docs/pharmaproductpricing_frep_en.pdf.

[6] Babar Z-U-D. Pharmaceutical prices in the 21st Century. Springer; 2015.

[7] Vogler S, Habl C, Leopold C, Mazag J, Morak S, Zimmermann N. PHIS hospital pharma report. Vienna: Pharmaceutical Health Information System (PHIS); commissioned by the European Commission and the Austrian Federal Ministry of Health; 2010. http://whocc.goeg.at/Literaturliste/Dokumente/BooksReports/PHIS_Hospital Pharma_Report.pdf.

[8] Leopold C, Vogler S, Habl C, Mantel-Teeuwisse AK, Espin J. Personalised medicine as a challenge for public pricing and reimbursement authorities—A survey among 27 European countries on the example of trastuzumab. Health Policy 2013;113(3):313–22.

[9] Schwabe U, Paffrath D, Ludwig W-D, Klauber J. Arzneiverordnungsreport 2017. Berlin: Springer; 2017.

[10] Bergman U, Popa C, Tomson Y, Wettermark B, Einarson T, Åberg H, et al. Drug utilization 90%—a simple method for assessing the quality of drug prescribing. European Journal of Clinical Pharmacology 1998;54(2):113–8.

[11] Osservatorio Nazionale sull'Impegno dei Medicinali. L'Uso dei Farmaci in Italia. Rapporto Nazionale. Anno 2016. Rom: Agenzia Italiana del Farmaco (AIFA); 2017.

[12] WHO Collaborating Centre for Drug Statistics Methodology. Guidelines for ATC classification and DDD assignment 2018. 2017. Oslo.

[13] Wolrd Health Organization. ATC/DDD toolkit. Geneva. 2018. Available from: http://www.who.int/medicines/regulation/medicines-safety/toolkit/en/.

[14] OECD. OECD glossary of statistical terms. Paris: OECD Publishing; 2008. Available from: https://read.oecd-ilibrary.org/economics/oecd-glossary-of-statistical-terms_9789264055087-en - page2.

[15] OECD, Eurostat, World Health Organization. A system of health accounts 2011. Paris: OECD Publishing; 2017. Revised edition.
[16] Jane M. Difference between Disbursements & expenses. 26, September 2017. Available from: https://bizfluent.com/info-8568724-difference-between-disbursements-expenses.html.
[17] WHO Collaborating Centre for Pharmaceutical Pricing and Reimbursement Policies. Glossary of pharmaceutical terms. Update 2016. Vienna. 2016. Available from: http://whocc.goeg.at/Literaturliste/Dokumente/MethodologyTemplate/Glossary_Update2016_final.pdf.
[18] Leopold C, Zhang F, Mantel-Teeuwisse AK, Vogler S, Valkova S, Ross-Degnan D, et al. Impact of pharmaceutical policy interventions on utilization of antipsychotic medicines in Finland and Portugal in times of economic recession: interrupted time series analyses. International Journal for Equity in Health 2014;13(1):53.
[19] Cameron A, Ewen M, Ross-Degnan D, Ball D, Laing R. Medicine prices, availability, and affordability in 36 developing and middle-income countries: a secondary analysis. The Lancet 2009;373(9659):240–9.
[20] Wagner AK, Soumerai SB, Zhang F, Ross-Degnan D. Segmented regression analysis of interrupted time series studies in medication use research. Journal of Clinical Pharmacy and Therapeutics 2002;27.
[21] Danzon PM, Kim JD. International price comparisons for pharmaceuticals. PharmacoEconomics 1998;14(1):115–28.
[22] Andersson F. Methodological aspects of international drug price comparisons. PharmacoEconomics 1993;4(4):247–56.
[23] Walley T, Folino-Gallo P, Barry M, Bruzzone M, DeJoncheere K, Rosian I, et al. The EurMedStat proposals on indicators for price and utilisation. Italian Journal of Public Health 2006;3:15–21.
[24] Machado M, O'Brodovich R, Krahn M, Einarson TR. International drug price comparisons: quality assessment. Revista Panamericana de Salud Publica 2011;29(1):46–51.
[25] Morgan SG, Leopold C, Wagner AK. Drivers of expenditure on primary care prescription drugs in 10 high-income countries with universal health coverage. Canadian Medical Association Journal 2017;189(23):E794–9.
[26] Frost DW, Cook DJ, Heyland DK, Fowler RA. Patient and healthcare professional factors influencing end-of-life decision-making during critical illness: a systematic review. Critical Care Medicine 2011;39(5):1174–89.
[27] World Health Organization. WHO guideline on country pharmaceutical pricing policies. Geneva. 2013. Available from: http://apps.who.int/medicinedocs/documents/s21016en/s21016en.pdf.
[28] Morel CM, McGuire A, Mossialos E. The level of income appears to have no consistent bearing on pharmaceutical prices across countries. Health Affairs 2011;30(8):1545–52.
[29] Cameron A, Ewen M, Auton M, Abegunde D. The world medicines situation 2011. Medicines prices, availability and affordability. Geneva: World Health Organization; 2011.
[30] de Labry Lima AO, Espín Balbino J, Rovira Forns J. Literature review on entry of medicines in European small markets. Pharmaceuticals Policy and Law 2012;14(2):187–93.
[31] Vogler S, Zimmermann N, Ferrario A, Wirtz VJ, de Joncheere K, Pedersen HB, et al. Pharmaceutical policies in a crisis? Challenges and solutions identified at the PPRI Conference. Journal of Pharmaceutical Policy and Practice 2016;9(1):1.
[32] Health Action International. Fact or fiction? What healthcare professionals need to know about pharmaceutical marketing in the European Union. 2016.

[33] Gray A, Manasse Jr HR. Shortages of medicines: a complex global challenge. Bulletin of the World Health Organization 2012;90(3):158.
[34] Zimmermann N, Vogler S. PPRI/PHIS pharma profile Austria. Vienna: Pharmaceutical Pricing and Reimbursement Information (PPRI)/Pharmaceutical Health Information System (PHIS); 2012.
[35] Vogler S, Martikainen JE. Pharmaceutical pricing in Europe. In: Babar Z-U-D, editor. Pharmaceutical prices in the 21st Century. Springer; 2015. p. 343–70.
[36] Kanavos P, Schurer W, Vogler S. Pharmaceutical distribution chain in the European union: structure and impact on pharmaceutical prices. London/Vienna: EMINet/LSE/GÖG; 2011.
[37] Indecon. Section 4: wholesale pharmacy data in selected countries. 2007.
[38] Bundesministerium für Gesundheit und Frauen. Regelung für die Vorgehensweise der Preiskommission bei der Ermittlung des EU-Durchschnittspreises gemäß § 351c Abs. 6 und Abs. 9a ASVG [Regulation on Procedural Rules for Calculation of the EU average price according to § 351c 6 and 9a General Social Insurance Law]. 2017.
[39] Vogler S, Schneider P, Zimmermann N. Preisvergleich kostenintensiver Arzneimittel 2015 [Price comparison of high-cost medicines 2015]. Vienna: Gesundheit Österreich GmbH; 2016.
[40] Eurostat. Statistics explained. Luxembourg. 2018. Available from: http://ec.europa.eu/eurostat/statistics-explained/index.php/Main_Page.
[41] Eurostat. European price statistics. An overview. Luxembourg. 2008. Available from:, http://ec.europa.eu/eurostat/documents/3217494/5700847/KS-70-07-038-EN.PDF/6b78bcc3-b219-4038-80d2-4180a9410678?version=1.0.
[42] Danzon PM, Chao L-W. Cross-national price differences for pharmaceuticals: how large, and why? Journal of Health Economics 2000;19(2):159–95.
[43] Wouters OJ, Kanavos PG. A comparison of generic drug prices in seven European countries: a methodological analysis. BMC Health Services Research 2017;17(1):242.
[44] Eurostat. Organisation for Economic Co-operation and Development. Eurostat-OECD methodological manual on purchasing power parities. Luxembourg: OECD Publishing; 2012.
[45] OECD. OECD health data. Paris: OECD; 2018. Available from: https://data.oecd.org/.
[46] Konijn P. Pharmaceutical products—comparative price levels in 33 European countries in 2005. Statistics in Focus, Economy and Finance. Eurostat 2007;45:1–3.
[47] Busse R, Panteli D, Schaufler J, Schröder H. Europäischer Preisvergleich für patentgeschützte Arzneimittel [European Price Comparision for On-Patent Medicines]. Springer; 2016.

CHAPTER 10

Training Exercises for Medicine Price Surveys, Analyses and Comparisons

Nina Zimmermann, Peter Schneider, Sabine Vogler
WHO Collaborating Centre for Pharmaceutical Pricing and Reimbursement Policies, Pharmacoeconomics Department, Gesundheit Österreich GmbH (GÖG/Austrian Public Health Institute), Vienna, Austria

LIST OF ABBREVIATIONS

FC	Fantasian Crowns
GDP	Gross domestic product
PPP	Purchasing power parities

10.1 PURPOSE

The exercises in this chapter offer training opportunities. They should support to practically apply the principles and content discussed in this book.

10.2 TRAINING MATERIAL: EXERCISES

You are one of the advisers to the Minister of Health in your country, and you are responsible for pharmaceutical policy. The Minister of Health gives you a phone call: At a recent public event he was addressed by a journalist who claims that prices of medicines in your country are among the highest of the geographic region and that patients face high co-payments and issues with access to medicines. The journalist asked the Minister about plans for reducing medicine prices. The Minister of Health wants to know whether, or not, the journalist was right. Thus, he commissions you to conduct a price study in order to survey, analyse and compare prices in your country with those of the four neighbouring countries (Fantasia, Belladonna, Heavensgate, Redland).

Medicine Price Surveys, Analyses, and Comparisons
ISBN 978-0-12-813166-4
https://doi.org/10.1016/B978-0-12-813166-4.00016-4

10.2.1 Exercise 1 – Preparation of the Study (Methodology)

Q1: Which five dimensions do you have to consider when designing a medicine price study?

1.
2.
3.
4.
5.

Q2: Which medicines would you select for your study?

____

____

____

Q3: Where do you get the price data of the neighbouring countries? Which price sources do you select?

____

____

____

Q4: Which price type would you compare in your price study (e.g., manufacturer prices, wholesale prices) and why? Do you consider discounted prices?

____

____

____

Q5: You are interested in the comparison of the reimbursed prices between countries: What do you have to consider in this case?

____

____

____

Q6: Exchange rates – which ones would you select and why? (monthly, average of 6 months or a yearly average?)

____

____

____

Q7: Will you present the medicine prices adjusted by volume or other weights (e.g., PPP or GDP per capita)? If yes, why and if no, why not?

____

10.2.2 Exercise 2 – Price Data Calculation

You decided to focus on the comparison of the ex-factory prices (which are statutorily regulated using external price referencing) of the top-selling products in your country and to compare them to the four neighboring countries (Fantasia, Belladonna, Heavensgate, Redland).

10.2.2.1 Q1: One of the Top-Selling Products Is Glupic

You would like to compare its prices as of 1 May 2018:

- Name: Glupic
- Active ingredient: Sobratinib
- ATC code: L77AB54
- Company: Pharmasuper Sale
- Pharmaceutical form: Film-coated tablet
- Strength: 100 mg
- Pack size: 60
- Ex-factory price in your home country: Euro 1126.41

Please calculate the correct ex-factory prices of this medicine in the four neighboring countries and complete the table below (advice: please calculate all prices before you check the solutions section in the Annex).

	Ex-factory prices in Euro				
Product	**Home country**	**Fantasia**	**Belladonna**	**Heavensgate**	**Redland**
Glupic, 100 mg, 60 film-coated tablets	1126.41				

- Fantasia:
  - wholesale mark-ups are not regulated in Fantasia; an average margin of 10% is assumed
  - in the national price database you will find the following **wholesale price** for this product: 7769.60 Fantasian Crowns
  - Exchange rate to Euro: 1 Euro = 7.437 Fantasian Crowns (FC)
  - Q: What is the price of this product in Fantasia expressed in FC and in Euro?
- Belladonna:
  - VAT rate on medicines in Belladonna = 5%
  - Please find below an excerpt of the national price list:
  - Which product do you select for the price comparison and what is the ex-factory price to be included in the comparison?

Name of medicinal product	Package	Active substance	Marketing authorisation holder	Maximum ex-factory price in Euro (incl. VAT)
Blackebap tablet, film coated 100 mg	Pack with 60 tabs in blister(s)	Sobratinib	Remidica Ltd	878.72
Blackebap tablet, film coated 400 mg	Pack with 30 tabs in blister(s)	Sobratinib	Remidica Ltd	1788.94
Sobratinib occard tablet, film coated 100 mg	Pack with 60 tabs in blister(s)	Sobratinib	Occard Healthcare	194.17
Sobratinib occard tablet, film coated 400 mg	Pack with 30 tabs in blister(s)	Sobratinib	Occard Healthcare Limited	364.97
Glupic caps 100 mg	Pack with 60 caps in blister(s)	Sobratinib	Pharmasuper Sale	1430.39
Glupic tablet film coated 100 mg	Pack with 120 tabs in blister(s)	Sobratinib	Pharmasuper Sale	2495.12
Glupic tablet film coated 400 mg	Pack with 30 tabs in blister(s)	Sobratinib	Pharmasuper Sale	2846.45
Sobratinib capsule, hard 100 mg	Pack with 96 caps in blister(s)	Sobratinib	Better Life Ltd.	1696.98
Sobratinib capsule, hard 100 mg	Pack with 48 caps in blister(s)	Sobratinib	Better Life Ltd.	972.67
Sobratinib capsule, hard 100 mg	Pack with 120 caps in blister(s)	Sobratinib	Better Life Ltd.	1996.09
Sobratinib capsule, hard 100 mg	Pack with 60 caps in blister(s)	Sobratinib	Better Life Ltd.	1144.32
Sobratinib turbo tablet, film coated 100 mg	Pack with 60 tabs in blister(s)	Sobratinib	Turbo Pharma BV	1144.32
Sobratinib turbo tablet, film coated 400 mg	Pack with 30 tabs in blister(s)	Sobratinib	Turbo Pharma BV	2277.17

- Heavensgate:
- Please find below an excerpt of the national positive list (the prices indicated are pharmacy retail prices in Euro).
- Heavensgate has a statutorily regulated linear wholesale mark-up of 3% for all medicines and a statutorily regulated linear pharmacy mark-up of 18% for reimbursable medicines and 20% for non-reimbursable medicines. Reimbursable medicines are exempt from VAT; for other medicines a VAT rate of 5% applies.
- Which product do you select for the price comparison, and what is the ex-factory price to be included in the comparison?

01.05.2018

Pos	ATC	Kódigo	Nominido	Ditoploplnok	Priso
1259	L77AB54	74895	GLUPIC 100 mg filmumm tabletky	tbl flm 120 × 100 mg (blis.PVC/AI)	209570
1257	L77AB54	74866	GLUPIC 400 mg filmumm tabletky	tbl flm 30 × 400 mg (blis.PVDC/AI)	876.62

- Redland
  - Please find below an excerpt of the national price list.
  - Which price do you select for the price comparison? What is the ex-factory price?

CIP	36578941
Nuturalisa de medacamentuliu	AA
Numero AMMM	45786
Nomina	GLUPICI 100MG, Flaksa 60 tablutki
grander pekning	njet

beguna data	**fini data**
07.03.2008	16.10.2019

Fabrikatus nomus
HellsBells Pharma

pixorate fabrikatus	**pixorate patientus**	**pagachi ministerium**	**datare validi**
814,47	917,47	100%	01.07.2018
838,46	945,43	100%	01.01.2018
1048,07	1172,28	100%	01.01.2016
1151,73	1272,16	100%	07.03.2008

10.2.3 Exercise 3 – Price Data Presentation and Data Analysis

Findings can be presented in different formats. Apply some for the example of Glupic.

10.2.3.1 Q1: Price Differences to the Neighbouring Countries

Please complete the following table and interpret the results:

The price of Heavensgate is not taken into account.

	In %
Price difference in home country/min.	
Price difference in home country/∅	
Price difference in home country/max.	

∅.... average of the prices in the comparator countries, min. = lowest price in the comparator countries, max. = highest price in the comparator countries.

Interpretation of the results:

____

____

____

10.2.3.2 Q2: Index Calculation

Price indices are measures of relative price changes to allow for showing average differences between countries (or time periods). Different types of price indices have been developed. Simple index calculations use the values of the home country as basis. Widely applied Laspeyres index uses volume weights of the base country, whereas the Paasche index uses the volume weights of comparator countries.

For the example of Glupic, please calculate a simple index (home country = 100%) and draw possible conclusions for your home country:

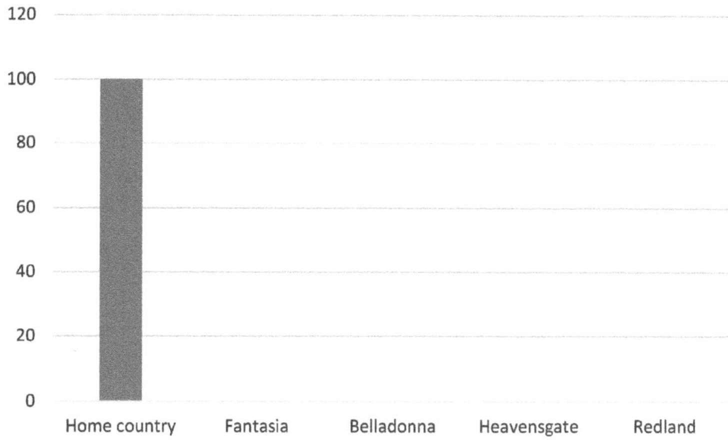

Interpretation:

____

____

____

10.2.3.3 Q3: Box Plot Data Presentation

Another way to present the data is drawing a box plot. A box plot is a visual method to show the distribution and centres of a data set. Measures of distribution include the interquartile range and the mean of the data set. Measures of centre include the mean (average) and the median.

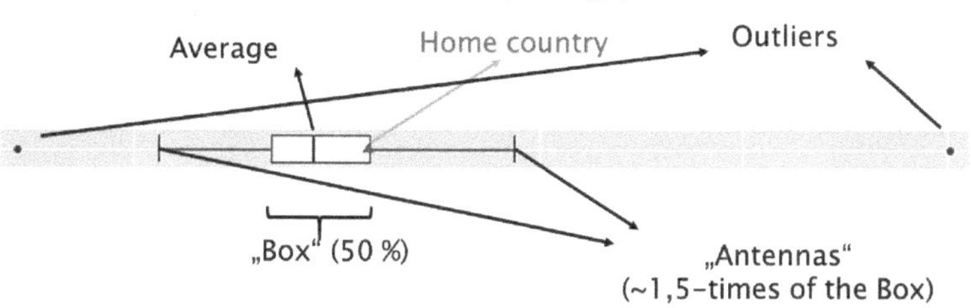

A box plot is a way to show a five number summary in a chart. The main part of the chart (the 'box') shows where the middle portion of the data is: the interquartile range. At the ends of the box, you find the first quartile (the 25% mark) and the third quartile (the 75% mark). The far left of the chart (at the end of the left "antenna" or 'whiskers') is the minimum (the smallest number in the set) and the far right is the maximum (the largest number in the set). The median is represented by a vertical bar in the centre of the box. The value of the home country is presented in a triangle. The advantage of box plots is that they require a sample size of only five (in this case, five countries; however, samples of less than five should be avoided since box plots reflect sample variability) [1].

Drawing a box plot for solely one product is not very meaningful. In addition to Glupic, you also surveyed the price data for following products:

	Ex-factory prices in Euro (per pack)				
Product	**Home country**	**Fantasia**	**Belladonna**	**Heavensgate**	**Redland**
Heart Core, 150 mg, 28 capsules	406	352.8	721	323.12	351.4
SomePills, 100 mg, 14 film-coated tablets	2.38	3.08	3.22	1.54	1.68
Respira, 25 mg, 1 vial containing powder and solvent for prolonged-release suspension for injection	13.77	15.12	14.21	9	8.5
Supermill, 300 mg, 30 modified release tablets	546.6	593.4	713.1	529.2	530.4
Injectao, 50 mg, 1 vial, solution for injection	3500	3555	4500	3500	3500

	Ex-factory prices in Euro (per pack)				
Product	**Home country**	**Fantasia**	**Belladonna**	**Heavensgate**	**Redland**
Braintrain, 500 mg, 21 capsules	411.39	479.22	511.98	452.13	437.64
Sanita, 300 mg, 1 pre-filled syringe	24.59	28.54	26.7	22.67	19.32

Please present the data of Glupic and further medicines in a box plot and kindly mark the value in the home country. You find in the Internet tutorials how to do it (e.g., by using Excel or R).

Box plot:

10.2.3.4 Q4: Prices in Purchasing Power Parities (PPP)

Purchasing power parities can be used as currency conversion rates to convert expenditures expressed in national currencies into an artificial common currency (the Purchasing Power Standard, PPS), thus eliminating the effect of price level differences across countries [2].

Purchasing power parities refer to a reference value (e.g., 'average values in the Eurozone' = 100).

Why would you present price data in purchasing power parities (PPP)?

____

____

____

Please calculate the prices of Glupic in EUR purchasing power parity (PPP).

	Home country	Fantasia	Belladonna	Heavensgate	Redland
Exchange rate in EUR PPP	1056	0.84	0.98	–	1.06
Glupic, 100 mg, 60 film-coated tablets – ex-factory prices in Euro					
Glupic, 100 mg, 60 film-coated tablets – ex-factory prices in EURO PPP					

Interpretation?

____

____

____

REFERENCES

[1] Krzywinski M, Altman N. Points of significance: visualizing samples with box plots. Nature Publishing Group; 2014.

[2] Eurostat. Purchasing Power Parities. http://ec.europa.eu/eurostat/web/purchasing-power-parities accessed on 20 May 2018.

PART 3

Using Medicine Price Comparisons for Policy-Making

CHAPTER 11

Price Comparison as a Pricing Policy Option—Introduction into Pharmaceutical Policies

Sabine Vogler
WHO Collaborating Centre for Pharmaceutical Pricing and Reimbursement Policies, Pharmacoeconomics Department, Gesundheit Österreich GmbH (GÖG/Austrian Public Health Institute), Vienna, Austria

LIST OF ABBREVIATIONS

AIDS	Acquired immune deficiency syndrome
EML	Essential medicines list
EPR	External price referencing
HIV	Human immunodeficiency virus
HTA	Health technology assessment
LMIC	Low- and middle-income countries
MEA	Managed-entry agreement(s)
SDG	Sustainable development goals
UHC	Universal health coverage
UN	United Nations
US	United States
WHO	World Health Organization

11.1 NEED FOR PHARMACEUTICAL REGULATION AND POLICIES

Medicines are no normal goods, and pharmaceutical markets are no normal competitive consumer markets in which suppliers and purchasers meet.

In case of a normal good, a person knows his/her own needs and purchases this good if its marginal benefit exceeds the price paid. For medicines (as well as any other "health goods"), "price elasticity" is low because people need the treatment. This is aggravated by the fact that patients in solidarity-based health-care systems often do not know the price.

Health-care markets in countries with social protection for citizens are usually characterized by the involvement of three parties:

- the patient: who benefits from the medicine, but usually does not pay its price (or not fully),

Medicine Price Surveys, Analyses, and Comparisons
ISBN 978-0-12-813166-4
https://doi.org/10.1016/B978-0-12-813166-4.00017-6

- the doctor: who prescribes the medicine (thus, as an "agent," taking the "consumption decision" on behalf of the patient), and
- the third-party payer: who covers (parts of) the expenses of the medicine.

The health-care, including pharmaceutical, system is characterized by information asymmetry because the prescribing doctor likely has higher knowledge than the patient. Therefore, patients are often not able to make an informed decision over choosing and paying medicines for their own benefit. At the same time, prescribing doctors tend not to know all relevant therapeutic alternatives [1]. While prescribing, doctors should act as "perfect agents" for their patients; (small) transaction costs can be involved (e.g., searching for lowest-priced medicines). In addition, "moral hazard" can occur in solidarity-based systems. Moral hazard refers to the fact that patients demand (and receive) too much care relative to the social optimum solely because of the existence of a health insurance system; in case of pharmaceuticals, patients get too many and/or too expensive medicines prescribed. Studies indicated moral hazard in physicians' prescribing (e.g., prescribing of originator medicines despite the existence of generics) [2,3].

As a consequence, there is a need for regulation and policy in the field of medicines.

11.1.1 Regulation—to Ensure Safety of Medicines and Pharmaceutical Provision

Medicines can result in major harm and may even lead to severe cases of diseases and death if produced, stored, supplied, dispensed, and used in a nonappropriate way. Thus, for the sake of safety, governments need to regulate clinical trials, production, distribution, prescription, dispensing, and use of medicines.

Unfortunate events have catalyzed the development of pharmaceutical regulation. In 1937, over 100 people in the United States died of diethylene glycol poisoning after taking a sulfanilamide elixir, which used the chemical as a solvent without any safety testing. This facilitated the introduction of the US Federal Food, Drug, and Cosmetic Act that asked for premarket notification of new medicines in 1938 [4]. The second catastrophe that influenced the development of pharmaceutical regulation far more than any event in history was the "Contergan scandal." In the early 1960s, it was revealed that the stillbirths and deformities of thousands of children were due to ingestion of thalidomide that had been sold under the trade name "Contergan" as a nonprescription sleeping and tranquillizing agent in 47 countries since 1957. The German company Grünenthal had advertised the medicine as entirely harmless, and many pregnant women used thalidomide because it also helped alleviate morning sickness occurring in the early months of pregnancy [5]. In Europe, the thalidomide disaster was a major starting point to establish and strengthen pharmaceutical regulation.

Today, key regulatory functions for medicines include

- Licensing of the manufacture, import, export, distribution, promotion, and advertising of medicines,
- Assessing the safety, efficacy, and quality of medicines and issuing a marketing authorization for individual products,
- Inspecting and surveillance of manufacturers, importers, wholesalers, and dispensers of medicines,
- Controlling and monitoring the quality of medicines on the market,
- Controlling promotion and advertising of medicines,
- Monitoring safety of marketed medicines, including collecting and analyzing adverse reaction reports,
- Providing independent information on medicines to professionals and the public [6].

11.1.2 Pharmaceutical Policies—to Contribute to Affordable Access to Medicines

Although pharmaceutical regulation addresses issues of patient safety, quality, and effectiveness of medicines (before, during, and after market launch), the objective of improved patient access to essential medicines (cf. Box 11.1 on essential medicines) is addressed through pharmaceutical policies [7].

Access to essential medicines is part of the fundamental human right to health as enshrined by the Universal Declaration of Human Rights of 1948 (Article 25, [9]) and the International Covenant on Economic, Social, and Cultural Rights of 1966 (Article 12, [10]). Access to essential medicines is also recognized in the Sustainable Development Goals (SDG). As part of a new sustainable development agenda (following up on the eight Millennium Development Goals that were scheduled to end in 2015 [11]), countries adopted the set of SDG to end poverty, protect the planet, and ensure prosperity for all. The SDG were adopted in September 2015, and

BOX 11.1 Essential Medicines

Essential medicines are those that satisfy the priority health-care needs of the population. They are selected with due regard to public health relevance, evidence on efficacy and safety, and comparative cost-effectiveness.

Essential medicines are intended to be available within the context of functioning health systems at all times in adequate amounts, in the appropriate dosage forms, with assured quality and adequate information, and at a price the individual and the community can afford.

In 1977, the World Health Organization (WHO) published the first Model List of Essential Medicines that served as a guide for the development of national and institutional essential medicine lists. Since then, the WHO Model List of Essential Medicines has been updated every 2 years.

Based on World Health Organization. Essential medicines. 2017. Available from: http://www.who.int/medicines/services/essmedicines_def/en/.

each goal has specific targets to be achieved over the next 15 years. SDG 3.8 particularly mentions the importance of "access to safe, effective, quality, and affordable essential medicines and vaccines for all" as a central component of Universal Health Coverage (UHC) [12].

As part of the SDG, all UN Member States have agreed to aim to achieve UHC by 2030. UHC is understood that all individuals and communities receive the health services they need without suffering financial hardship (Box 11.2).

The World Health Organization (WHO) proposed a "framework for collective action" to equitable access to essential medicines that should consider the following elements:

- rational selection and use of medicines (e.g., reimbursement lists based on treatment guidelines, regularly updated guidelines based on best evidence, trainings);
- affordable prices (e.g., price information, generic policies);
- sustainable financing (e.g., increase in public funding, increase in health insurance coverage, better use of out-of-pocket payments); and
- reliable health and supply systems (e.g., integrate medicines in health sector development, assure medicines' quality, promote rational use).

WHO's concept of "essential medicines" and its Model List of Essential Medicines (Box 11.1) are key tools to support access to essential medicines.

BOX 11.2 Universal Health Coverage

Universal health coverage (UHC) means that all people and communities can use the promotive, preventive, curative, rehabilitative, and palliative health services they need, of sufficient quality to be effective, while also ensuring that the use of these services does not expose the user to financial hardship.

This definition of UHC embodies three related objectives:

1. Equity in access to health services—everyone who needs services should get them, not only those who can pay for them.
2. The quality of health services should be good enough to improve the health of those receiving services.
3. People should be protected against financial risk, ensuring that the cost of using services does not put them at risk of financial harm.

UHC is an integrated approach to improve health outcomes, and it does not mean free coverage for all possible health interventions, regardless of the cost because no country can provide all services free of charge on a sustainable basis. It is not only about ensuring a minimum package of health services but also about ensuring a progressive expansion of coverage of health services and financial protection as more resources become available. UHC is not only about individual treatment services but also includes population-based services such as public health campaigns, adding fluoride to water, and controlling mosquito breeding grounds.

UHC emphasizes not only what services are covered but also how they are funded, managed, and delivered. The three dimensions to consider are who? what? and to what extent? Working toward UHC means taking steps toward equity, development priorities, social inclusion, and cohesion.

Moving toward UHC requires strengthening health systems in all countries, and this is something that every country can do.

Based on World Health Organization. Universal health coverage (UHC). 2016. Available from: http://www.who.int/medicines/services/essmedicines_def/en/.

Even if the term "Essential Medicines List" (EML) is rather used in the context of low- and middle-income countries (LMIC), the principle of careful selection of essential medicines for public supply and reimbursement is of relevance for high-income countries as well [14] (these lists are usually called "reimbursement lists" or "positive lists" in high-income countries [15]). Based on these principles, high-priced medicines are not per se excluded from being classified as essential medicines. To reflect treatment advances of public health relevance, the WHO also included new, typically expensive medicines in its revised essential medicines model lists (e.g., inclusion of 12 antiretroviral medicines for HIV/AIDS in 2002 and medicines in the indications of tuberculosis, cancer, and hepatitis C in 2015) [16]. Although the WHO decided that these products should be available to all people who need them in all countries, appropriate pricing policies and sustainable funding are required at country level to ensure actual access to these medicines.

11.2 TAXONOMIES OF PHARMACEUTICAL POLICIES

The previous section has shown the interconnectivity of different elements that can contribute to more affordable patient access to medicines. As a result, it is needed a mix of policies that balances partially conflicting policy objectives (e.g., equity, cost-containment, affordability) and expectations of different stakeholders.

Policies (policy options, policy measures) are defined as "instruments, tools, and approaches that allow policy-makers to achieve defined objectives" [15]. As such, only governments (represented by public authorities and/or public payers) can design policies. Stakeholders (e.g., pharmaceutical industry, doctors) can develop strategies to achieve their objectives, possibly in reaction to government policies. For instance, a pharmaceutical company can design a pricing strategy that aims to maximize profits (e.g., price discrimination by charging different prices on different countries). However, the approaches of private stakeholders are not (public) policies but strategies and plans. In this book, the terms "policy" and "policies" relate solely to actions and measures taken by governments.

A common categorization of pharmaceutical policies is the classification into supply-side and demand-side measures. Supply-side policies are applied by governments (e.g., public authorities and public payers in the health-care system) to control prices and/or profits, to manage access, and/or to determine coverage, whereas demand-side policies are directed at stakeholders who prescribe medicines (usually physicians), who dispense medicines (pharmacies), and who ask for medicines (patients) [17,18]. The distinction between supply-side or demand-side measures is not always completely clear (e.g., copayments can be both understood as part of the payers' supply-side policy relating to the design of the reimbursement system or as a demand-side measure that addresses patients; elements in the supply chain remuneration to promote generics' uptake—e.g., lower margins for these medicines—can be interpreted as an incentive for patients to ask for a generic, thus a demand-side policy).

Another frequently applied distinction is the one into "pricing" and "reimbursement": Pricing policies are defined as "regulations and processes used by government authorities to set the price of medicines as part of exercising price control" [15], and reimbursement policies relate to the "coverage of the cost by a third party payer (e.g., Social Health Insurance/ National Health Service)" [15]. In practice, pricing and reimbursement practices are sometimes closely connected, which makes the classification of policies a challenge. For instance, some pricing policies are only applicable for reimbursable medicines, i.e., medicines that are funded, at least partially, by public payers. Also, the processes of public authorities to set a medicine price and determine its reimbursement are interlinked in some countries (e.g., Sweden [19]).

There are further, however, less commonly used methods to categorize policies, such as

- related to their level in the health-care system (e.g., national, regional, municipal, or cross-national and international measures; policies targeted at the outpatient vs. the hospital sectors);
- per stakeholder addressed by the measure (e.g., industry, wholesale, patients);
- measures that solely target the price of medicines or that impact volume, or both;
- a categorization per objective that the policy primarily aims to achieve (e.g., cost-containment, efficiency gains, affordability).

Combinations of the approaches are possible, and this makes the distinction between categories even more strenuous. Table 11.1 provides an overview of selected policies with the attempt to classify them in terms of pricing and reimbursement, as well as of supply-side and demand-side measures.

11.3 INTRODUCTION INTO PRICING POLICIES

Governments can choose among different policy options to set medicine prices. In principle, there is the key distinction between a nonpolicy (so-called free pricing) and price control (price regulation). Under free pricing, private actors (e.g., manufacturers, importers, wholesalers, pharmacists) set the medicine prices, with or without notifying authority of their decision. In these cases, governments are purely "price takers."

Table 11.1 Major pricing and reimbursement policies for medicines classified in terms of supply-side and demand-side measures

Category	Supply-side measures	Demand-side measures
Pricing	• **External price referencing** Practice of using the price(s) of a medicine in one or several countries to derive a benchmark or reference price for the purposes of setting or negotiating the price of the product in a given country. • **Value-based pricing** No clear definition. Through this policy, authorities set prices for new medicines and/or decide on reimbursement based on the therapeutic value that a medicine offers, usually assessed through health technology assessment (HTA) or economic evaluation. • **Cost-plus pricing** Pricing policy that determines a medicine price by taking into account production costs, promotional expenses, research and development, administration costs, overheads, and a profit that is considered "reasonable." • **Conditional pricing** A pricing policy that links the price of a medicine to specific outcomes or criteria (managed-entry agreements are one variant of this pricing, and reimbursement, policy).	—

	• **Tendering** Any formal and competitive procurement procedure through which tenders (offers) are requested, received, and evaluated for the procurement of goods, works or services, and as a consequence of which an award is made to the tenderer whose tender/offer is the most advantageous. • **Differential pricing**[1] Cross-country approach of setting the price of a medicine in accordance with the ability to pay, and/or the economic situation of the involved countries. The pricing decision would be taken in a collaborative approach by the governments of the involved countries or an international organization. • **Generic pricing policies** Specific pricing policies for generic medicines, such as a price link, in which the price of generics is set into relationship to the originator price. • **Profit control** Cap on manufacturer's profit; below this threshold, the manufacturer is free to price its medicines (indirect price regulation).	

Continued

Table 11.1 Major pricing and reimbursement policies for medicines classified in terms of supply-side and demand-side measures—cont'd

Category	Supply-side measures	Demand-side measures
	• **Statutory remuneration for wholesale and pharmacies** Remuneration awarded by governments to supply chain actors for handling their services, in form of price-dependent markups or margins, or (dispensing) fees. • **Regulation of taxes, duties, and further price components** Statutory limits on further price components as the medicine moves from manufacturer to the patients.	
Reimbursement	• **Essential medicines list/reimbursement list/ positive list** A formulary that contains medicines eligible for reimbursement. • **Managed-entry agreement (MEA)** An arrangement between a manufacturer and payer/ provider that enables access to (coverage/ reimbursement of) a health technology subject to specified conditions.	• **Prescribing by international nonproprietary name** Requirement for physicians to prescribe medicines by its active ingredient name instead of the brand name. • **Pharmaceutical budgets for prescribers** Ex-ante determination of a value threshold that doctors may prescribe during a period.

	• **Health Technology Assessment (HTA)** A multidisciplinary process that summarizes information about the medical, social, economic, and ethical issues related to the use of a health technology in a systematic, transparent, unbiased, robust manner; not a policy itself but evidence to inform policy-making. • **Reference price systems/internal reference pricing** A reimbursement policy in which public payers fund a defined amount for identical or similar medicines grouped within a cluster.	• **Generic substitution** Practice of substituting a medicine with a less expensive medicine at pharmacy level. • **Copayment** Patient's contribution toward the expenses of a medicine covered by the public payer.

[1]See Chapter 7 on terminology for the distinction to price discrimination ("Ramsey pricing"), which is a pricing strategy of manufacturers.

The authors based on King DR, Kanavos P. Encouraging the use of generic medicines: implications for transition economies. Croatian Medical Journal 2002;43(4):462–9; Vogler S, Zimmermann N, Habimana K. Study of the policy mix for the reimbursement of medicinal products. Proposal for a best practice-based approach based on stakeholder assessment. Vienna: Commissioned by the European Commission; 2014, definitions taken or adapted from WHO Collaborating Centre for Pharmaceutical Pricing and Reimbursement Policies. Glossary of pharmaceutical terms. Update 2018. Vienna; 2018. Available from: http://whocc.goeg.at/Glossary/Search.

Applying price control, governments can set medicine prices based on a legal provision (e.g., law, decree; so-called statutory pricing). Government officials (e.g., public payers) can also negotiate with suppliers or distributors or they use competitive mechanisms such as tendering.

Different pricing policies can be used (and are appropriate)

- for different groups of medicines,
- for different sectors, and
- for different price types.

11.3.1 Medicines Groups

For instance, different pricing policies might be applied for prescription-only medicines and nonprescription medicines, for reimbursable and nonreimbursable medicines, and for on-patent and off-patent medicines. In the off-patent market, specific pricing policies can be chosen for generics and for biosimilar medicines. Governments can decide to use particular pricing policies for medicines that claim to provide added therapeutic benefits, or for orphan medicines (e.g., a pricing policy that considers the value of these medicines).

11.3.2 Sectors

Because of variation in organization and funding frameworks between the outpatient (i.e., ambulatory) and the hospital sectors in many countries, pricing policies differ between these sectors [20].

Another major distinction for health and pharmaceutical systems concerns the split into a public and a private sector. The latter refers to the totality of privately owned institutions and individuals providing health care, including private insurers [21]. Although public health care is usually provided by the government through national health-care systems, it can be provided in the private sector through "for profit" hospitals and self-employed practitioners, and "not for profit" nongovernment providers, including faith-based organizations [22]. The key procurement policy in the public pharmaceutical sector of many LMIC is tendering, whereas free pricing is applied in the private sector. In terms of reimbursement, medicines in the public sector tend to be provided either for free or they are partially funded by the state, whereas patients have to fully pay for medicines supplied in the private sector. In countries with an advanced UHC (e.g., European countries), the terms "public" and "private" pharmaceutical sectors are not used, but a distinction is made between the "reimbursement sector" ("reimbursement market") and the "non-reimbursement sector". Medicines in the nonreimbursement sector are not funded by the state (full out-of pocket payments), and there is often (but not always) free pricing. In the reimbursement sector, authorities of many high-income countries have moved beyond tendering and have been applying further pricing policies.

11.3.3 Price Types

Pricing policies do not only concern the ex-factory price, i.e., the price at the level of industry, charged by a pharmaceutical manufacturer. There are specific policies targeted at the market actors in the supply chain (e.g., distributors, wholesalers, community pharmacies). Furthermore, as taxes, duties and further tariffs can impact final medicine prices, policies can be applied to cap them.

The following chapters of Part 3 present and discuss in-depth the policy of external price referencing (EPR) which is a pricing policy at the manufacturer price level (and wholesale price level in some countries) that considers medicine prices in other countries. Thus, knowledge about conducting price surveys, analyses, and comparison is required for this pricing policy. Other pricing policies do either not consider medicine prices or relate to medicine prices in the same country. Further pricing policies at the manufacturer price level will be presented in Chapter 13, in which alternative pricing policies to EPR are discussed.

REFERENCES

[1] Puig-Junoy J. Price regulation systems in the pharmaceutical market. The Public Financing of Pharmaceuticals an economic approach. Cornwall: Edward Elgar Publishing Limited; 2005. p. 35–58.
[2] Lundin D. Moral hazard in physician prescription behavior. Journal of Health Economics 2000;19(5):639–62.
[3] Hellerstein JK. The importance of the physician in the generic versus trade-name prescription decision. The RAND Journal of Economics 1998:108–36.
[4] Rägo L, Santoso B. Drug regulation: history, present and future. In: Drug benefits and risks: international textbook of clinical pharmacology. revised 2nd ed. 2008. p. 65–77.
[5] Dally A. Thalidomide: was the tragedy preventable? The Lancet 1998;351(9110):1197–9.
[6] World Health Organization. WHO policy perspectives on medicines. Geneva: No. 7. In: Effective medicines regulation: ensuring safety, efficacy and quality; 2003.
[7] World Health Organization (WHO). How to develop and implement a national drug policy. Geneva. 2nd ed. 2001.
[8] World Health Organization. Essential medicines. 2017. Available from: http://www.who.int/medicines/services/essmedicines_def/en/.

[9] United Nations. Universal declaration of human rights. 1948. Available from: http://www.un.org/en/universal-declaration-human-rights/.
[10] United Nations. International covenant on economic, social and cultural rights. 1966. Available from: http://www.ohchr.org/EN/ProfessionalInterest/Pages/CESCR.aspx.
[11] United Nations. Millenium development goals and beyond 2015. 1966. Available from: http://www.un.org/millenniumgoals/.
[12] United Nations. Sustainable development knowledge platform. 2017. Available from: http://www.un.org/millenniumgoals/.
[13] World Health Organization. Universal health coverage (UHC). 2016. Available from: http://www.who.int/medicines/services/essmedicines_def/en/.
[14] Hogerzeil HV. The concept of essential medicines: lessons for rich countries. British Medical Journal 2004;329(7475):1169.
[15] WHO Collaborating Centre for Pharmaceutical Pricing and Reimbursement Policies. Glossary of pharmaceutical terms. Update 2018. Vienna. 2018. Available from: http://whocc.goeg.at/Glossary/Search.
[16] Gray AL, Wirtz VJ, t Hoen EF, Reich MR, Hogerzeil HV. Essential medicines are still essential. The Lancet 2015;386(10004):1601–3.
[17] King DR, Kanavos P. Encouraging the use of generic medicines: implications for transition economies. Croatian Medical Journal 2002;43(4):462–9.
[18] Vogler S, Zimmermann N, Habimana K. Study of the policy mix for the reimbursement of medicinal products. Proposal for a best practice-based approach based on stakeholder assessment. Vienna: Commissioned by the European Commission; 2014.
[19] Moïse P, Docteur É. Pharmaceutical pricing and reimbursement policies in Sweden. Paris: OECD; 2007.
[20] Vogler S, Habl C, Leopold C, Mazag J, Morak S, Zimmermann N. PHIS hospital pharma report. Vienna: Pharmaceutical Health Information System (PHIS); Commissioned by the European Commission and the Austrian Federal Ministry of Health; 2010. http://whocc.goeg.at/Literaturliste/Dokumente/BooksReports/PHIS_Hospital Pharma_Report.pdf.
[21] Mackintosh M, Channon A, Karan A, Selvaraj S, Cavagnero E, Zhao H. What is the private sector? Understanding private provision in the health systems of low-income and middle-income countries. The Lancet 2016;388(10044):596–605.
[22] Basu S, Andrews J, Kishore S, Panjabi R, Stuckler D. Comparative performance of private and public healthcare systems in low- and middle-income countries: a systematic review. PLoS Medicine 2012;9(6):e1001244.

CHAPTER 12

Practice of External Price Referencing

Peter Schneider, Sabine Vogler
WHO Collaborating Centre for Pharmaceutical Pricing and Reimbursement Policies, Pharmacoeconomics Department, Gesundheit Österreich GmbH (GÖG/Austrian Public Health Institute), Vienna, Austria

LIST OF ABBREVIATIONS

ASVG	Allgemeines Sozialversicherungsgesetz (General Social Insurance Law, Austria)
CAPA	Central Administration for Pharmaceutical Affairs (Egypt)
CIF	Cost, insurance and freight
DDD	Daily defined dose
EC	European Commission
ECB	European Central Bank
EPR	External price referencing
EU	European Union
EURIPID	EURopean Integrated Price Information Database
G-BA	Gemeinsamer Bundesausschuss (Joint Federal Committee, Germany)
GCC	Gulf Central Committee
GCC-DR	Gulf Central Committee for Drug Registration
GDP	Gross domestic product
GMP	Good manufacturing practice
HiT	Health Systems in Transition
IPR	Internal price referencing
MAH	Marketing authorisation holder
MoH	Ministry of Health
NMA	National Medicines Agency
NPM	Non-prescription medicine(s)
PIR	Precio internacional de referencia (international reference price, term used in Mexico)
POM	Prescription-only-medicine(s)
PPI	Pharmaceutical Price Information
PPP	Purchasing power parity
PPRI	Pharmaceutical Pricing and Reimbursement Information (a network of competent authorities for pharmaceutical pricing and reimbursement)

Medicine Price Surveys, Analyses, and Comparisons
ISBN 978-0-12-813166-4
https://doi.org/10.1016/B978-0-12-813166-4.00018-8

Pharmaceutical policy aims to achieve three – to a certain degree opposing – objectives: (1) to improve access to medicines for patients, (2) to ensure the sustainability of public pharmaceutical budgets and (3) to reward pharmaceutical manufacturers for innovative medicines. Policy-makers are responsible for choosing the most appropriated policy options and implementing them in a design that best achieves their health priorities while striking the balance between the three objectives.

As described in the previous chapter (Chapter 11), policy-makers may opt for different policies to regulate prices of medicines. Pricing refers to the policy of setting the price of a medicine at certain points in the pharmaceutical distribution chain which includes wholesale and pharmacy remuneration margins and product taxation [1]. Regulation of pharmaceutical prices – if in place at all – is a national competence. Even in the European Union (EU) where the marketing authorisation of pharmaceuticals has been harmonised for more than a decade, the government of every single country sets medicine prices. In doing so, policy-makers of EU member states have to respect common provisions such as the Transparency Directive issued by the European Commission (EC) [2].

At country level, pricing is typically the competence of the Ministry of Health (MoH) or National Medicines Agency (NMA).[1] The most common pricing policy in European countries and increasingly worldwide is external price referencing (EPR). EPR – which is also known under different names such as external referencing pricing (ERP), cross-reference pricing [3], geographic price referencing [4], international reference pricing [5] or price cap regulation [6] – is defined as '*the practice of using the price(s) of a medicine in one or several countries in order to derive a benchmark or reference price for the purpose of setting or negotiating the price of the product in a given country*' [7]. There is no '*the*' EPR-policy but the practice of EPR can vary among countries with respect to its particular design [8].

This chapter aims to provide an overview of how EPR mechanisms have been designed. In the first part this will be presented at a global scale and in the second part a focus will be laid on European countries.

[1] However in some countries, decisions on pricing are combined with decisions on reimbursement, that is, the policy of covering the cost of a medicine by a public payer, having a committee which takes the decisions on both.

12.1 OVERVIEW OF USE OF EPR WORLDWIDE

EPR is one of the most commonly used strategies to control prices of on-patent pharmaceuticals. The reason of its increasing popularity has been described as 'a relatively simple and easy-to-apply system compared to economic evaluation, for example' [8]. While in Europe the practice of EPR has been extensively surveyed and information about different designs can be found in several publications and reports [8–13], the literature on EPR in other parts of the world – with the exemption of high-income countries like Canada – is sparse. Ibrahim MM, Rida NA, Babar Z and Owusu Y [14] provided a systematic review of pharmaceutical pricing policies in developing countries, including EPR as one dimension. Kaló Z, Alabbadi I, Al Ahdab OG et al. [15] focussed on Middle East countries (i.e., Egypt, Jordan, Kuwait, Lebanon, Qatar, Saudi Arabia and United Arab Emirates) and conducted a survey with local experts on EPR regulations. Babar Z-U-D [16] provided a detailed report of international medicine pricing issues through country level case studies from around the globe and presented pricing policies of several low- and middle-income countries (e.g., Ethiopia, Qatar, Vietnam) and regions (e.g., European countries). Babar Z-U-D [17] focussed on pharmaceutical policy in countries with developing healthcare systems and included descriptions of pharmaceutical pricing in the examined countries.

EPR is applied in one form or another in Brazil [18], Canada [19], Colombia [20,21], Ecuador [22], Egypt [15,23], Iran [8], Japan [9], Jordan [8], Kuwait [15], Lebanon [8], Malaysia [24], Mexico [25], Pakistan [27], Qatar [15,30], Saudi Arabia [15,28], South Africa [8,31], South Korea [32], Sultanate of Oman [8], Taiwan [29], Tuvalu [26], United Arab Emirates (UAE) [8,15] and Vietnam [33]. This section looks at the practice of EPR in the mentioned 23 countries and aims to describe similarities and differences of chosen approaches when regulating pharmaceutical prices.

12.1.1 Relevance of EPR

In Malaysia, there is no formal price regulation of pharmaceuticals. However, the Ministry of Health (MoH) – as the largest healthcare service provider – procures medicines for the public sector. One type of procurement is national tenders which are evaluated by different criteria depending on the type of medicine. For single source products, the main criterion for evaluation is EPR, and reference countries are selected based on economic status, population size and other factors [24].

In Iran, the role of EPR seems twofold: With respect to determining prices for pharmaceuticals EPR is the main criterion for all medicines. However, for reimbursement decisions, competent authorities use EPR as a supportive criterion together with five further criteria: (1) comparative effectiveness, (2) budget impact analysis, (3) cost modelling for one therapeutic course in outpatient care, (4) average monthly increases in sales in the half-year prior the reimbursement application and (5) opinions and comments of certain departments of major medical universities [34].

Saudi Arabia has also defined several criteria, and seven of the nine criteria are related to pharmaceutical price comparison, suggesting a higher relevance of the EPR component [28]. In Egypt, the role of EPR varies depending on the availability of information. EPR is the main criterion to determine the maximum retail price of a branded medicine. In case, the product is marketed in fewer than five countries, EPR is a supportive criterion together with a study on the therapeutic effectiveness of the product in question in comparison to its therapeutic alternatives [23].

12.1.2 Reference Countries

The number of reference countries in the examined countries ranges between 1 and 36.

The Mexican basket is defined to contain a total of six reference countries, but for each pricing decision the countries will be selected individually based on sales data. The six countries in which the medicine had the highest sales in the previous quarter will be chosen. The international reference price (Precio internacional de referencia, PIR) is calculated as the average of the ex-factory prices in the defined six countries, and price data are weighted by sales data. The PIR is adjusted each year and the marketing authorisation holder (MAH) is required to provide the necessary information, which can be subject to an annual verification by an external auditor [25].

Among the group of the studied countries (globally except European countries), the country with the largest number of officially defined reference countries is Saudi Arabia. The Gulf country considers cost, insurance and freight (CIF) prices from 30 countries in which the product is marketed [15].

Some countries also defined second-line (or backup) reference countries that are taken into account under certain circumstances (e.g., if no price data are found in first-line (or priority) countries). In South Korea prices of seven industrialised countries (France, Germany, Italy, Japan, Switzerland, the UK and the US) are considered for the pricing of new medicines. In addition, the national price agreement guidelines suggest also including Taiwan and Singapore — both countries with similar economic conditions to Korea — into the group of reference countries in cases when decisions on reimbursement are taken [32].

Until 2011, Kuwait only had one country in the reference basket: the Pharmacy and Medical Control Department within the Ministry of Health based the maximum retail price on the price in the country of origin. In 2011, the government abolished any price controls of medicines, with the expectation that this would result in lower prices. However, medicine prices increased, and in response, the government joined the 'price harmonisation' process for medicine prices enacted in the countries of the Gulf Central Committee for Drug Registration (GCC-DR), i.e., Bahrain, Kuwait, Oman, Qatar, Saudi Arabia and UAE (for further information on the GCC-DR see Box 12.1) [30]. The price harmonisation process that started in 2012 aimed to align the CIF price of all presentations marketed in GCC countries in a common currency and to restrict price rises due to

BOX 12.1 Gulf Central Committee for Drug Registration (GCC-DR)

Bahrain, Kuwait, Oman, Qatar, Saudi Arabia, the United Arab Emirates (UAE) and Yemen established the Gulf Central Committee for Drug Registration in 1999, with the executive office being located in Riyadh (Saudi Arabia). The main objective of the GCC-DR is to coordinate health policies and programmes among the participating countries via exchange of information, knowledge, techniques and expertise. The responsibilities of GCC-DR include

- the centralised procedure for marketing authorisation of pharmaceuticals;
- registration of pharmaceutical companies;
- inspection of pharmaceutical companies for good manufacturing practice (GMP) compliance;
- review of technical and post-marketing surveillance reports.

Source: [36]

foreign currency fluctuation. The lowest CIF price found in the GCC countries is taken as the reference price, and all other countries lower their prices to this reference price. Medicine prices in the Kingdom of Saudi Arabia — which traditionally has the lowest price in the region — usually serve as reference prices for the GCC member states [35].

When deciding on reference countries, there seems to be a tendency to include neighbouring countries or countries of comparable economic conditions. Countries from Southeast Asia benchmark to Southeast Asian countries, and the countries from the Gulf region brought forward the above-mentioned price harmonisation.

Among the examined countries, Vietnam was the only country in which specific criteria for selecting reference countries were defined by a government decree. In order to qualify as reference country, the following statistical indices or organisation structures have to be similar to those of Vietnam: (1) the per capita gross domestic product (GDP) per year; (2) the per capita GDP at purchasing power parities (PPP) per year and (3) networks of providing services for preventive medicines, medical examination and treatment, functional rehabilitation, and health improvement and medicine supply [37].

12.1.3 Scope of Medicines

Four of the examined countries regulate prices of all medicines with EPR: Egypt, Iran, Saudi Arabia and South Korea [23,28,32,38]. In Saudi Arabia, the prices determined through EPR serve as ceilings and are relevant primarily in the case of private purchases by individuals in pharmacies. Saudi authorities are required to price each medicine before marketing authorisation because the determined price has to be printed on the package of each product in a clear way [28]. South Korea determines the so-called 'maximum allowable price' which, as a form of price cap, sets an upper limit of remuneration based on prices in other countries [32]. Egypt and Iran differentiate the EPR methodology for different types of medicines. EPR is used for originator medicines while for locally produced and imported generic medicines both countries use EPR in combination with a price link [23,38,39]. The latter is a practice of setting a medicine price in relationship to the price of a reference medicine. Usually, the generic price is set at a certain percentage lower than the one of the originator reference medicine [7].

The other countries apply EPR only to a subgroup of medicines. In Brazil, the medicines agency attributes the medicines during the marketing authorisation process to one of the following six categories: (1) New patent-protected medicines that present better efficacy or a better safety profile compared to established treatments; (2) 'me-too' medicines, which are similar, identical or 'closely related' to a medicine already approved by the National Medicines Agency; (3) new presentations of a medicine already marketed in the same strength; (4) new presentations of medicines already marketed, but in a different strength; (5) medicines that offer a new strength form or a new combination of active ingredients already available in Brazil and (6) generic medicines. While medicines of categories 2, 3 and 4 are priced according to some (weighted) internal price referencing (IPR, i.e., consideration of prices of the same or similar medicine in the country), EPR is applied to medicines of categories 1, 5 and 6 [18]. Similarly, Canada applies EPR mainly for patented medicines for the duration of their patent life [19].

In several countries the pharmaceutical sector is divided into a private and public sector. Frequently, there is no price regulation in the private sector, but medicine prices in the public sector are controlled. This is, for instance, the case in Tuvalu. The pharmacy department of Princess Margaret Hospital procures medicines to be dispensed in the public sector through tendering. Tendering procedures in Tuvalu are specified in the public procurement regulations that are regularly updated. One evaluation criterion is that '*the procuring entity shall determine the prevailing market rate for the goods [...] based on evidence of the price it previously paid, the price it paid for similar goods [...] and the price paid by other purchasers for the same goods [...]*' [26]. Thus, some form of price comparison or benchmarking could take place during the evaluation process of public procurement.

12.1.4 Price Types

While European countries mainly consider ex-factory prices when applying EPR (cf. Section 12.2.4), this is not always the case in other regions. Since in several of the countries the world over, ex-factory price data are usually not available, price comparisons for EPR are frequently made at CIF or wholesale prices instead (seven investigated countries). Still, among the investigated countries, Brazil, Canada, Jordan, Iran and Saudi Arabia compare ex-factory prices when using EPR [18,19,28,38,40].

Egypt was the only country that reported applying EPR at the pharmacy retail price level. In accordance with the pricing decree 499/2012, the MAH is obliged to submit to the Central Administration for Pharmaceutical Affairs (CAPA) the prices in the reference countries where the medicine is marketed. This list should indicate the pharmacy retail prices including all discounts [23].

12.1.5 Calculation Method

Globally, the most commonly used method to derive an EPR-based price appears to be the consideration of 'lowest price' in the reference countries or a slightly modified approach. The National Commission on Pricing of Medications in Colombia calculated the maximum pharmacy retail price as the average of the three lowest prices in the reference countries [41]. In Jordan, the Jordan Food and Drug Administration regulated the maximum pharmacy retail prices in the private sector and determined the price through one of four options: (1) the price requested by the supplier based on CIF export price, (2) the price in the country of origin, (3) the export price to Saudi Arabia or (4) the median price in a basket of at least three out of seven European countries (i.e., UK, France, Spain, Italy, Belgium, Greece and the Netherlands). The option that achieved the lowest price was taken [40,42,43].

The Iranian Pharmaceutical Pricing Act as of 2011 provided different formulae for different types of medicines: The price of an on-patent medicine was calculated by considering price(s) in either the country of origin or the reference countries (Greece, Turkey, Spain, Saudi Arabia and Algeria), and it had to be set below the prices in these countries. The price of domestically produced or imported generics was set at least 60% lower than the lowest price of the originator in the reference countries (40% for orphan medicines) or at the level of the lowest price of that generic medicine (of the same manufacturer in reference countries) [38,39]. In 2012, Egypt introduced a similar pricing policy: Originator medicines were priced according to the lowest retail price in the reference countries. If the originator medicine was marketed in fewer than five countries, it would be priced based on (1) comparative study of the product and its alternatives, or (2) the lowest pharmacy retail price in the countries where it is marketed. As already mentioned above, in the case of generic medicines a combination of EPR and generic price link was used [23].

A unique formula was reported to be used in Colombia's EPR policy: the benchmark price was based on the price in the 'third quartile'. Prices were collected from 17 reference countries, then sorted (highest ranking first), and the competent authority for pricing set a price close to the price of countries number 12 and 13 [44].

For South Africa, it was suggested to introduce EPR in the private sector and to apply a phased approach. In phase 1, the price of a medicine was proposed to be set on the basis of the average of prices in the country basket including South Africa. This phase was supposed to be an interim period lasting for 2 years, and afterwards medicine prices would be set according to the lowest price in the basket. This proposal provided also for exemptions in certain circumstances and the opportunity to use weighted prices for those manufacturers who supplied both the public and private sectors [31,45].

12.2 OVERVIEW OF USE OF EPR IN WHO EURO REGION

The European region of the World Health Organization (WHO EURO) comprises 53 countries in a geographical area that spans from the Atlantic to the Pacific oceans.

Information for this section was obtained from different sources: literature published on EU Member States [1,13,46], European Economic Area (EEA) countries Switzerland, Norway and Iceland [9,11,12] and countries of the Balkan and Eastern European countries [47,48] provided some information about EPR. In addition, a survey of details of existing EPR policies was conducted. Members of the Pharmaceutical Pricing and Reimbursement Information (PPRI) network[2] [49] were asked to participate in this survey in Q2/2017; responses from 25 countries were received.

Through this two-tiered data collection approaches, data were collected on 41 countries of the European region. Information refers to the year 2017.

36 of 41 surveyed countries (for an overview of the included countries see Fig. 12.1) in the WHO EURO region apply EPR, or EPR elements, for some of the medicines. Belarus, Kazakhstan, Sweden, Ukraine and the UK do not apply the pricing policy of EPR. Sweden has implemented value-based pricing (VBP) as the pricing and reimbursement policy for new medicines, whereas the Pharmaceutical Price Regulation Scheme (PPRS) in the UK regulates the profit that companies can achieve on sales to the national health system, rather than regulating prices directly. Belarus, Kazakhstan and Ukraine have no price control for the private sector;

[2] The PPRI network consists of more than 90 institutions, mainly public authorities for pharmaceutical pricing and reimbursement information from 46 countries, mostly in the WHO European region.

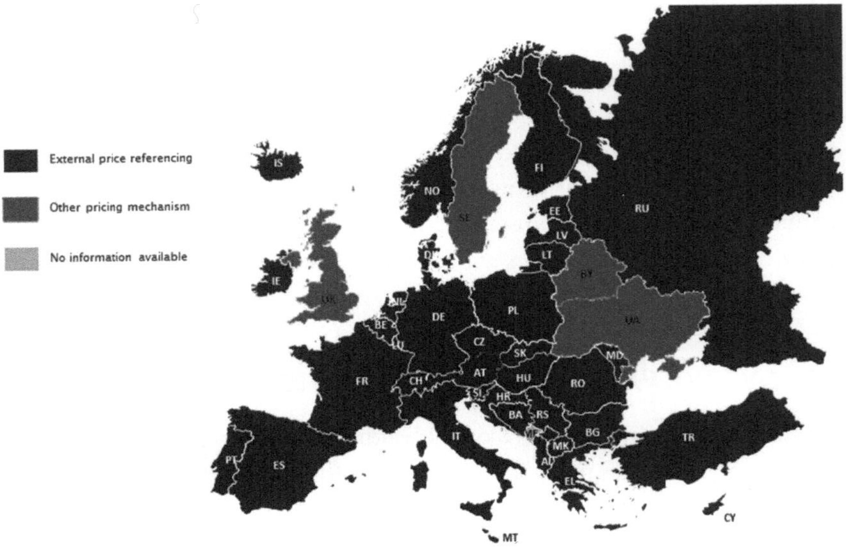

Figure 12.1 Use of EPR in European countries.

medicines in the public sector are tendered through public procurement. It should be noted that Ukraine has run a pilot project on EPR.

12.2.1 Relevance of EPR

EPR can be either used as the sole or main policy to determine medicine prices or as an additional element to provide information in the pricing process. 26 out of the 36 WHO EURO countries that apply EPR use it as the sole or main pricing policy (Fig. 12.2). In some countries, however, the implementation of EPR in a specific form is limited to specific sectors (e.g., outpatient sector) and/or medicines (cf. Section 12.2.4). In Slovenia, for instance, EPR is, in principle, the main policy for setting the maximum allowed price, but in case of medicines with 'extraordinary prices' other pricing policies are applied, and price data of other countries are solely used as additional source of information. In Ireland, EPR is used as a supportive policy to set prices for new on-patent medicines, whereas it is strictly applied for re-alignments of existing prices (cf. Section 12.2.7 on price monitoring and revisions). EPR was reported to be used as main policy for setting the price of new medicines in Turkey, though the price evaluation commission has still the right to change them.

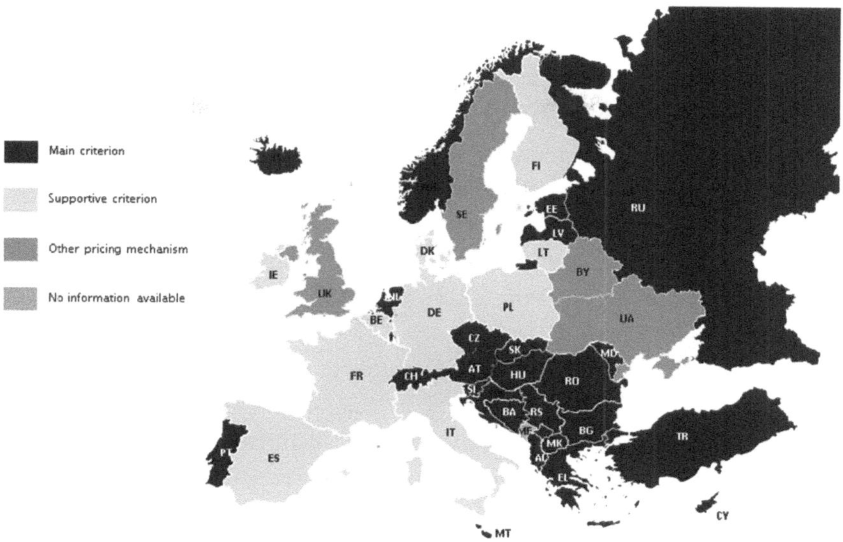

Figure 12.2 Role of EPR in the price setting process in European countries.

In 10 countries EPR is used as a supportive criterion in the decision process: this means that prices in other countries are considered together with a broad range of other factors when determining a 'reasonable' price. Those factors include, but are not limited to:

- the cost of the therapy cycle;
- benefits to be gained from the medicine use from the patient's perspective;
- relative benefits compared to treatment alternatives;
- effects on the healthcare system ('budget impact');
- funds available for reimbursement;
- reward for innovation.

In the German system, EPR is a supportive policy and is combined with elements of free pricing and value-based pricing (VBP). Since a reform act in 2011 medicines with a new active ingredient are subject to an early benefit assessment (VBP element) which is conducted in the first year after market launch. At launch, the MAH has the right to set prices (free pricing element), and after 1 year medicine prices are revisited. Whether price re-negotiations are opened or not depends on the decision of the Joint Federal Committee (Gemeinsamer Bundesausschuss, G-BA) and is based on the results of the early benefit assessment and the expert hearings [50]. During these price negotiations prices of selected countries can also be taken into consideration (EPR element).

12.2.2 Reference Countries

Table 12.1 provides an overview of the reference countries (indicated in rows) of the European countries as of 2017.

The number of reference countries ranged between 1 (Luxembourg) and 31 (Poland). The countries that were most frequently mentioned as reference countries were France (23), Italy (22), Spain (20), Belgium and Slovakia (19).

The choice of reference countries seems to point to the importance of two selection criteria:

1. **Comparable economic conditions**: Countries tended to include countries with an overall comparable economic situation in the basket: For instance, comparing a country's gross domestic product (GDP) per capita with the average per capita GDP of its reference countries, high interrelation was found in Denmark, Estonia, Finland, Germany, Italy, Lithuania and Malta. However, Bulgaria, Romania and Turkey included rather higher-income countries in their baskets, whereas high-income countries Switzerland and Norway rather reference to countries with lower income than their own.
2. **Geographic proximity**: Countries tended to include their respective neighbouring countries. For instance, the three Baltic countries, Estonia, Latvia and Lithuania, had each other in their reference baskets. A similar pattern was also observed for Northern, Southern and South-eastern European countries.

In some countries the reference countries were not explicitly defined. As such, they were selected on a case-by-case basis, for example, from a pool of countries – 'Eurozone countries' (i.e., those EU Member States who share the euro as common currency) or countries included in the EURopean Integrated Price Information Database EURIPID (i.e., an EU Member States driven initiative of a medicine price database fed by data supplied by pricing and reimbursement authorities, cf. Chapter 8.2 for further details). In addition, a few countries (Bosnia and Herzegovina, Bulgaria, Cyprus, Italy) defined 'first-line' (i.e., highly prioritised) countries and additional 'backup', and alternative, countries. In these cases, price information was first searched from first-line countries; if, however, price data were not available, prices from defined 'backup' countries, if available, were used.

Table 12.1 Reference countries used in ERP in European countries

C	AT	BE	BG	CY	CZ	DE	DK	EE	EL	ES	FI	FR	HR	HU	IE	IT	LT	LU	LV	MT	NL	PL	PT	RO	SE	SI	SK	UK	CH	IS	NO	BA	BY	MD	MK	RS	RU	TR	Other
AT																																							
BE																																							
BG																																							
CY																																							
CZ																																							
DE																																							
DK																																							
EE																																							
EL																																							
ES																																							
FI																																							
FR																																							
HR																																							
HU																																							LI
IE																																							
IT																																							
LT																																							
LU																																							Country of origin
LV																																							
MT																																							
NL																																							
PL																																							LI
PT																																							
RO																																							
SE																																							
SI																																							
SK																																							
UK																																							
CH																																							
IS																																							
NO																																							
AL																																							
BA																																							
BY																																							
MD																																							
MK																																							
RS																																							
RU																																							KZ, UA
TR																																							
	16	19	13	10	17	19	17	13	17	20	16	23	10	15	14	22	14	8	14	8	17	15	15	12	15	15	19	18	4	4	6	0	1	0	1	3	1	2	

Country abbreviations: *AL*, Albania; *AT*, Austria; *BA*, Bosnia and Herzegovina; *BE*, Belgium; *BG*, Bulgaria; *BY*, Belarus; *CH*, Switzerland; *CY*, Cyprus; *CZ*, Czech Republic; *DE*, Germany; *DK*, Denmark; *EE*, Estonia; *EL*, Greece; *ES*, Spain; *FI*, Finland; *FR*, France; *HR*, Croatia; *HU*, Hungary; *IE*, Ireland; *IS*, Iceland; *IT*, Italy; *KZ*, Kazakhstan; *LI*, Liechtenstein; *LT*, Lithuania; *LU*, Luxembourg; *LV*, Latvia; *MD*, Moldova; *MK*, Macedonia; *MT*, Malta; *NL*, Netherlands; *NO*, Norway; *PL*, Poland; *PT*, Portugal; *RS*, Serbia; *RU*, Russia; *SE*, Sweden; *SI*, Slovenia; *SK*, Slovakia; *TR*, Turkey; *UA*, Ukraine; *UK*, United Kingdom.

12.2.3 Scope of Medicines

The survey showed variation in the scope of medicines subject to EPR. In principle, EPR can be applied to all kind of medicines, but there are administrative and technical limitations: a broader scope will likely increase administrative burden, and it may be doubted if EPR coverage for all medicine groups is the most appropriate policy. In the surveyed European countries, medicines that were subject to EPR included prescription-only medicines (POM), reimbursable medicines, generics with no corresponding originator in the reimbursement list, parallel imported products, hospital products or reimbursed non-prescription medicines (NPM). Albania, Luxembourg, Macedonia, Moldova and Serbia applied EPR to NPM, for instance.

There is a tendency to apply EPR predominantly to medicines in the outpatient sector. Notable exemptions are Denmark, Iceland and Slovenia. Denmark reported to use EPR solely in the hospital sector, and in Iceland and Slovenia maximum prices in both outpatient and hospitals sectors were set based on price comparison. Most commonly, EPR is focused on reimbursable medicines (i.e., medicines that are, at least partially, funded by the state); 15 countries reported to have this scope. But additional provisions can exist. In Finland, EPR is not applied for medicines that have been immediately included in the reference price system, that is, internal reference pricing. Nine surveyed European countries reported to regulate prices of POM based on EPR. In Turkey, both POM and NPM are subject to EPR though different formulae apply for the two groups.

Other surveyed countries defined certain medicine types for which EPR applies; this makes it difficult to assign them into one of the abovementioned groups. In addition to pharmaceutical products (chemical and biological) and pharmaceutical products approved as hybrid, Greek legislation also provides for applying EPR to pharmaceutical products that do not have data exclusivity when there is a lack of competition on the market. Further countries to be mentioned in the context are Belgium (originator medicines), Spain (new reimbursed medicines), Germany and France (innovative medicines in both countries). Hungary specified six types of medicines to be subject to EPR.

12.2.4 Price Types

As medicines move along the supply chain, further price components are added on at each stage. This results in different price types, which could be

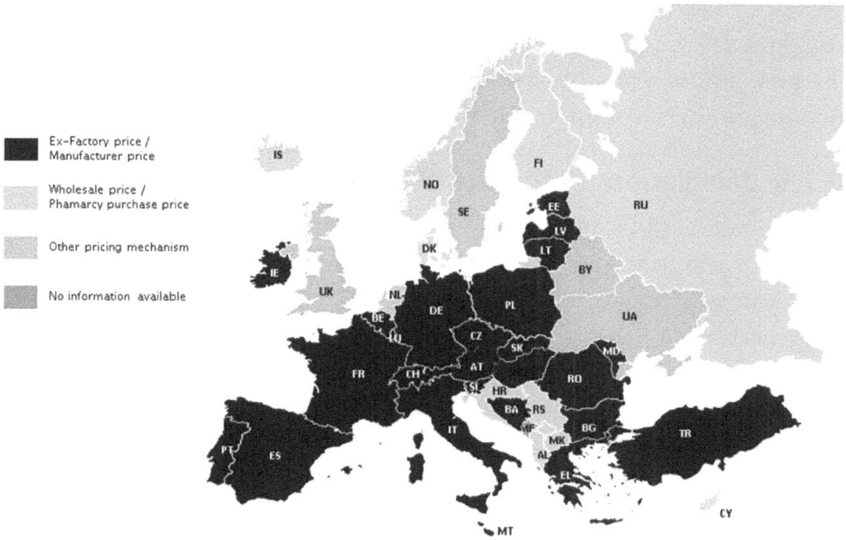

Figure 12.3 Selection of price types used in EPR in the European countries.

considered in EPR. Fig. 12.3 shows that nine countries decided to set prices at pharmacy purchasing price (wholesale price) level; in these countries, the extent of wholesale margin is the result of negotiations between pharmaceutical manufacturer and wholesaler, and it is confidential [51].

The majority of European countries (25 countries) referred to the ex-factory price (manufacturer price) when doing EPR, but exemptions are possible. For instance, in Latvia wholesale prices can be considered in cases when (1) the price in Denmark is one of the three lowest prices in the basket, (2) the ex-factory price is not available or (3) the MAH indicates a reduced (or no) wholesale margin in the application process. In Germany, MAH is obliged by law to report 'real' list prices, that is, prices reduced by any discounts that the manufacturer has granted. The Swiss handbook for the inclusion of medicines in the national reimbursement list stipulates consideration of the German statutory manufacturer discount[3] [52]. In 2017, the Austrian Parliament passed an amendment to the General Social

[3] Discounts are reductions of (published) list prices; manufacturer discounts relate to reductions granted by pharmaceutical companies to third party payers. Usually, discounts are negotiated between the two parties and remain confidential. In addition, a few countries apply statutory manufacturer discounts that are based on laws and are published.

Insurance Law (Allgemeines Sozialversicherungsgesetz, ASVG) that brought a few procedural changes for setting medicine prices in Austria. The new procedures provide for a consideration of statutory manufacturer discounts in three countries (Germany, Greece and Spain) [53].

12.2.5 Calculation Method of the Reference Price

The methodological approach for the calculation of the reference price includes at least three aspects:

- exchanges rates
- application of weights
- formula used for calculating the reference price

Reference baskets are usually composed of countries that do not have the same currency and require conversion of collected price information into the domestic currency. The majority of surveyed European countries — for which information on this topic was available — source the exchange rates from their national central banks or the European Central Bank (ECB). However, there is a widespread variation between the choices of exchange rate type: daily, 3-month average, 6-month average and 12-month average are applied in European countries.

Among the surveyed countries, Germany was the only one with legal provision that allows weighting of prices by estimated annual turnover of the respective medicine and purchasing power parities (PPP) of other countries. In all other countries prices are not adjusted by weights, but authorities reported that through reference countries of comparable per capita GDP (cf. Section 12.2.2) a kind of weighting could implicitly be achieved.

Different formulas to calculate the reference price can be applied, which are presented in Fig. 12.4. The most frequently used formula was to calculate the average price or a slightly modified method such as the average of the three lowest prices of reference prices (18 countries). In eight countries, the reference price was calculated based on the lowest price in the reference countries. Some countries applied a mix of calculation methods: In Iceland and Portugal the average price was determined for outpatient medicines, whereas hospital medicine prices are set using the lowest-price method. In Slovenia elements of both approaches were combined: for newly launched medicines prices were set according to the lowest price obtained in the reference countries whereas a maximum of 72% of the average of highest- and lowest-priced generic was allowed for

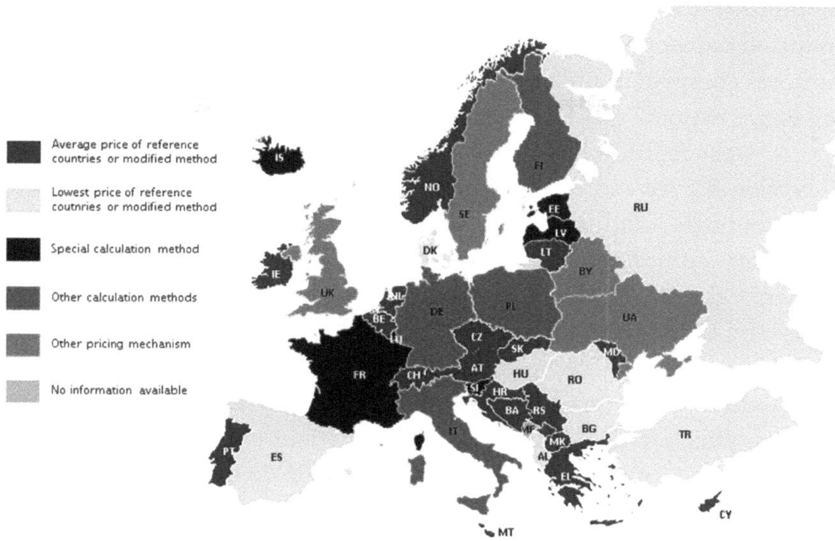

Figure 12.4 Formulas applied for calculating the reference price used in EPR in the European countries.

generics. Four countries had no specific formula in place, since prices of other European countries were only used as supportive information in price negotiations with the MAH. For instance, the German high court ruled that price calculations were not allowed to follow a fixed algorithm but had to take into account the specifications of the individual case. Three countries indicated a formula distinctive from other European countries: The prices determined in Estonia cannot exceed the highest price in the reference countries. In Latvia, the reference price was the third lowest price in the country basket but should not be higher than the price in Lithuania or Estonia. French prices should be similar to those in the reference countries and should not be below the lowest price in the four reference countries.

12.2.6 Data Provision and Validation

This and the following chapter refer to the Member States of the EU plus Norway, Switzerland and Iceland, as the required information has not yet been surveyed in a structured way in the countries of the WHO EURO region. In this group, 29 countries apply EPR.

In 23 of the countries that apply EPR, the pricing authority asked the MAH to supply the price information of the reference countries.

Additionally, the Cypriot and Czech competent authorities for pricing conducted independent price searches to validate the information. In seven countries, competent authorities searched prices independently. Frequent sources are national official websites and databases that are publicly accessible as well as EURIPID that is operated by competent authorities (cf. Section 8.2 for more information on EURIPID).

26 countries validated price information in one or the other form. Competent authorities that conducted an independent price search considered the prices found to be correct unless the MAH proved the contrary by submitting sufficient evidence (e.g., invoices). In countries, in which pharmaceutical companies provided the price information, prices were validated either through national databases, official sites or EURIPID, and it was done either on a regular basis or randomly. In Austria, according to the Austrian General Social Insurance Law, the competent authority for pricing, the Austrian Federal Ministry of Labour, Social Affairs, Health and Consumer protection, could ask the Austrian Public Health Institute to check the price data submitted by the MAH. The Austrian Public Health Institute does so by using their price information service (Pharma Price Information/PPI) established for this purpose.

12.2.7 Price Monitoring and Price Revisions

In 23 countries, the legal framework provided for revision of the EPR-based prices. In Denmark and Ireland revisions also took place in regular intervals, but they are based on a voluntary agreement between public payers and the pharmaceutical industry instead of legislation. Countries with legislation on revision or monitoring had either fixed dates or fixed intervals, ranging from 1 month to 5 years. Out of the 26 countries with price monitoring and price revisions, 18 did this exercise on a regular basis and the remainder at certain occasions. The duration of the intervals ranged from 3 months to even 5 years. In some cases regular price monitoring or revisions are linked to certain medicines: in Norway the prices of 250 substances which represented around three quarter of the reimbursement market in value were annually revised, and in Spain and Ireland prices of off-patent medicines were regularly updated once a year. Five countries (Belgium, Croatia, Denmark, Germany and Hungary) reported that they had no regular intervals for price revision. Competent authorities from two countries (Germany and Hungary) did neither revise nor monitor the prices of medicines at all. Despite existence of the respective law in Hungary, the regulation to specify details has not yet been implemented at the time of the survey.

12.3 OVERVIEW OF APPROACHES TO DEAL WITH CHALLENGES IN EPR

EPR may appear to be a relatively easy method for determining prices for medicines, but the comparison of prices is not as straightforward as it seems. This chapter presents identified approaches of how pricing authorities have been dealing with some of the methodological challenges linked to EPR.

12.3.1 Non-availability of Price Information

Non-availability of price information in the reference countries is particularly an issue for countries that base their price setting solely or predominantly on EPR. Countries' strategies to deal with the challenge of non-availability can be classified into four broad categories[4]:

1. **Define alternative criteria**: The first approach is to define alternative criteria and procedures that will be used when price data are available from an insufficient number of reference countries. Usually fewer than half of the countries in the reference basket are considered as insufficient. Several countries defined one or several backup countries: In Estonia, prices from all other EU Member States can be referred to when price information from all first-line reference countries is missing. However, authorities reported that this was only done in very rare cases. Some countries (e.g., Portugal and Lithuania) accept official documentation of the medicine price in the country of origin that the MAH provides as alternative to missing price data in the reference countries. Italy and Spain, both of which reported large country baskets (24 and 22 respectively), defined priority countries due to geographic neighbourhood (Spain) or comparable economic conditions (Italy).
2. **Require data availability in a minimum number of reference countries**: The second approach identified is that countries define a minimum number of countries whose price information is available as a prerequisite to set the price. If this requirement is not met, a temporary

[4] Countries may be attributed to more than one category since, in practice, a clear distinction is not always possible.

price can be determined or the price setting procedure is interrupted ('clock-stop'). Until April 2017, a price of a new medicine in Austria was set if the product has already been marketed in at least half of the EU Member States (for a change in legislation see below).

3. **Regular price revisions**: Ireland sets prices based on available information but provides for a review at any point in time as soon as price information from reference countries will be available. In April 2017, Austria introduced similar provisions: The 'EU average price' is calculated on the basis of available price information but re-evaluated in regular intervals, that is, 6, 24, 48 and 60 months after the price application has first been submitted.
4. **Proceed with available information**: Some countries (e.g., Finland and Spain) simply proceed with price data of those countries where available. This approach can go along with regular price adjustments.

12.3.2 Non-availability of Price Data at Required Types

When medicines move along the supply chain, their price increases due to add-ons at each stage, resulting in different price types. Price data from the reference countries might not be available for the price type (e.g., ex-factory price) used in EPR (cf. Section 12.2.4) due to different reasons. One reason could be differences in the reporting standard of the reference countries (different price types are published). Another reason is lack of regulation for distribution remuneration and, as a result, no known data for some price types.

In case of non-availability of price data at required types, some governments tend to calculate them based on known or assumed distribution remuneration. The size of the margins or mark-up (schemes) is usually published if the distribution remuneration has been regulated. If there is lack of regulation and adds-on in the reference countries are not known, some countries calculate respective price types based on average margins that were identified through research. In Switzerland and Austria the procedural rules of the pricing committees publish the average wholesale margins applicable to derive ex-factory prices in the reference countries.

12.3.3 Non-availability of the Defined Presentation (Differences in Pack Size, Pharmaceutical Form or Strength)

In response to non-availability of the defined presentation, several countries introduced rules as follows (one or several rules may apply): (1) If in the reference countries medicines are available in other pack sizes (with different prices) than the one defined for comparison, the closest pack size of the assessed medicine is used as reference. The maximum allowed range between pack sizes can be defined as a percentage band as done in the Czech Republic or as absolute limit as this is the case in Norway or Bulgaria. (2) If the pharmaceutical form in the reference countries is different from the one of the assessed medicine, some countries use a comparable pharmaceutical form as reference whereas others do not allow referencing to other pharmaceutical forms. (3) However, if the defined medicine is only available in different strength, most of the countries do not consider different strength. Exceptions are France, where authorities consider prices per course of treatment, and Hungary, where the closest strength of the assessed medicine is used as reference.

REFERENCES

[1] Panteli D, Arickx F, Cleemput I, Dedet G, Eckhardt H, Fogarty E, et al. In: Busse R, Figueras J, McKee M, Mossialos E, Nolte E, van Ginneken E, editors. Pharmaceutical regulation in 15 European countries. Copenhagen: The European Observatory on Health Systems and Policies; 2016.

[2] Council Directive 89/105/EEC of 21 December 1988 relating to the transparency of measures regulating the pricing of medicinal products for human use and their inclusion in the scope of national health insurance systems.

[3] Stargardt T, Schreyogg J. Impact of cross-reference pricing on pharmaceutical prices: manufacturers' pricing strategies and price regulation. Applied Health Economics and Health Policy 2006;5(4):235–47.

[4] Gregson N, Sparrowhawk K, Mauskopf J, Paul J. Pricing medicines: theory and practice, challenges and opportunities. Nature Reviews Drug Discovery 2005;4(2):121–30.

[5] Håkonsen H, Horn AM, Toverud E-L. Price control as a strategy for pharmaceutical cost containment—what has been achieved in Norway in the period 1994–2004? Health Policy 2009;90(2):277–85.

[6] Brekke KR, Holmås TH, Straume OR. Are pharmaceuticals still inexpensive in Norway? A comparison of prescription drug prices in ten European countries. SNF Report No. 08/10. 2010.

[7] WHO Collaborating Centre for Pharmaceutical Pricing and Reimbursement Policies. Glossary of pharmaceutical terms. Update 2016. Vienna: Gesundheit Österreich GmbH (GÖG); 2016.

[8] Espin J, Rovira J, de Labry AO. Working paper 1: external price referencing – review series on pharmaceutical pricing policies and interventions. Geneva: World Health Organization and Health Action International; 2011.

[9] Rémuzat C, Urbinati D, Mzoughi O, El Hammi E, Belgaied W, Toumi M. Overview of external reference pricing systems in Europe. Journal of Market Access and Health Policy 2015;3.

[10] Ruggeri K, Nolte E. Pharmaceutical pricing: the use of external reference pricing. 2013.

[11] Toumi M, Rémuzat C, Vataire A-L, Urbinati D. External reference pricing of medicinal products: simulation-based considerations for cross-country coordination. Final Report. European Commission; 2014.
[12] Vogler S, Lepuschütz L, Schneider P, Stühlinger V. Study on enhanced cross-country coordination in the area of pharmaceutical product pricing. Commissioned by the European Commission, Directorate-General for Health and Food Safety. Brussels: Publications Office of the European Union; 2016.
[13] Europe Economics. External reference pricing London. 2013.
[14] Ibrahim MM, Rida NA, Babar Z, Owusu Y. Pharmaceutical pricing strategies in Developing countries: a systematic review. Value in Health 2016;19(7):A455.
[15] Kaló Z, Alabbadi I, Al Ahdab OG, Alowayesh M, Elmahdawy M, Al-Saggabi AH, et al. Implications of external price referencing of pharmaceuticals in Middle East countries. Expert Review of Pharmacoeconomics and Outcomes Research 2015;15(6):993–8.
[16] Babar Z-U-D. Pharmaceutical prices in the 21st century. Switzerland: Springer: Cham; 2015.
[17] Babar Z-U-D. Pharmaceutical policy in countries with developing healthcare systems. Springer; 2017.
[18] Drug market regulation chamber - Council of Minister. Resolution CMED No. 2, dated 5 March 2004. In: Published on the Federal Official Gazette of 07 October 2005 and by resolution CMED no. 4 dD, published on the Federal Official Gazette of 12 March 2007; 2004.
[19] Paris V, Docteur É. Pharmaceutical pricing and reimbursement policies in Canada. 2007.
[20] Romero M. Financial incentives and pharmaceutical prices: the Colombian case.
[21] Vacca C, Acosta A, Rodriguez I. Precios de Referencia Internacional y Análisis de Costo Minimización para la Regulación de Precios de Medicamentos en Colombia. Value in Health 2011;14(5, Suppl.):S16–9.
[22] Durán CE, Lucio R, Rovira J. Pharmaceutical policy in Ecuador. Pharmaceutical policy in countries with developing healthcare systems. Springer; 2017. p. 221–36.
[23] Wanis H. Pharmaceutical pricing in Egypt. In: Z.-U.-D. Babar, Pharmaceutical prices in the 21st century. Springer; 2015. p. 59–78.
[24] Hassali MA, Tan CS, Wong ZY, Saleem F, Alrasheedy AA. Pharmaceutical pricing in Malaysia. In: Z.-U.-D. Babar, Pharmaceutical Prices in the 21st Century. Springer; 2015. p. 171–88.
[25] Moïse P, Docteur E. Pharmaceutical pricing and reimbursement policies in Mexico. 2007.
[26] Government of Tuvalu. Public procurement regulations 2014 made under section 2 of public procurement act. 2013. p. 2014.
[27] Nguyen TA, Knight R, Roughead EE, Brooks G, Mant A. Policy options for pharmaceutical pricing and purchasing: issues for low- and middle-income countries. Health Policy and Planning 2015;30(2):267–80.
[28] Alrasheedy AA, Hassali MA, Wong ZY, Aljadhey H, AL-Tamimi SK, Saleem F. Pharmaceutical policy in Saudi Arabia. Pharmaceutical policy in countries with developing healthcare systems. Springer; 2017. p. 329–47.
[29] Lee Y-C, Yang M-C, Huang Y-T, Liu C-H, Chen S-B. Impacts of cost containment strategies on pharmaceutical expenditures of the National Health Insurance in Taiwan, 1996–2003. Pharmacoeconomics 2006;24(9):891–902.
[30] Nada A, Manal Z, Mohamed Izham M. An exploratory insight on pharmaceutical sector and pricing policies in Qatar. Global Journal of Pharmacy and Pharmaceutical Science 2017;1(4).

[31] Suleman F, Gray A. Pharmaceutical policy in South Africa. Pharmaceutical policy in countries with developing healthcare systems. Springer; 2017. p. 285–302.
[32] Lee I-H, Bloor K. Pharmaceutical pricing policies in South Korea. In: Z.-U.-D. Babar, Pharmaceutical prices in the 21st Century. Springer; 2015. p. 151–69.
[33] Nguyen AT, Knight R, Mant A, Cao QM, Brooks G. Medicine pricing policies: lessons from Vietnam. Southern Med Review 2010;3(2).
[34] Ansaripour A, Uyl-de Groot CA, Steenhoek A, Redekop WK. The drug reimbursement decision-making system in Iran. Value in Health Regional Issues 2014;3:174–81.
[35] Hasan RSI, Lessing C. Pharmaceutical pricing policies in the Gulf countries' Council (GCC) and the United Arab Emirates (UAE). In: Z.-U.-D. Babar, Pharmaceutical prices in the 21st century. Springer; 2015. p. 297–307.
[36] Lakkis MM. Global and regional drug regulatory harmonization initiatives. Drug Information Journal 2010;44(3):289–97.
[37] Nguyen TA, Roughead EE. Pharmaceutical pricing policies in Vietnam. In: Z.-U.-D. Babar, Pharmaceutical prices in the 21st century. Springer; 2015. p. 321–42.
[38] Zaboli P, Hashemi-Meshkini A, Varmaghani M, Gholami H, Vazirian I, Zekri H-S, et al. Pharmaceutical laws and regulations in Iran: an overview. Journal of Research in Pharmacy Practice 2016;5(3):155.
[39] Hashemi-Meshkini A, Keshavarz K, Nikfar S, Vazirian I, Kebriaeezadeh A. Pharmacists remuneration models in Iran and selected countries: a comparative study. Iranian Journal of Pharmaceutical Research 2013;12(4):995.
[40] El-Dahiyat F, Curley LE. Pharmaceutical policy in Jordan. Pharmaceutical policy in countries with developing healthcare systems. Springer; 2017. p. 237–60.
[41] Knowledge Ecology International. PhRMA's asks regarding special 301, drug pricing and reimbursement. 2010.
[42] Abbott RB, Bader R, Bajjali L, ElSamen TA, Obeidat T, Sboul H, et al. The price of medicines in Jordan: the cost of trade-based intellectual property. Journal of Generic Medicines 2012;9(2):75–85.
[43] Ghazi Jarrar L. Pharmaceuticals pricing policy in Jordan (presentation held on 20/21 May, 2008 in Riyad. available under. In: Riyad, editor. Administration JFaD; 2008. https://www.sfda.gov.sa/ar/news/Documents/PharmaceuticalPricingPolicyinJordan.pdf.
[44] Rodrigues C. Latin America's pharmaceutical prices: the perfect storm is here. 2015. Eye for Pharma, http://social.eyeforpharma.com/market-access/latin-americas-pharmaceutical-prices-perfect-storm-here.
[45] Gray A, Suleman F. Pharmaceutical pricing in South Africa. In: Z.-U.-D. Babar, Pharmaceutical prices in the 21st century. Springer; 2015. p. 251–65.
[46] Barros PP. Pharmaceutical policies in European countries. Advances in Health Economics and Health Services Research 2010;22:3–27. Epub 2010/06/26.
[47] Dauti M, Alili-Idrizi E, Ahmeti-Lika S, Malaj L. Overview on Generics policies and pharmaceutical pricing in the European countries and the Republic of Macedonia. European Scientific Journal 2015;11(3).
[48] Marcheva M, LublianaTosheva-Konteva GP. Pricing and reimbursement of medicines in central and East European countries. World Journal of Pharmacy and Pharmaceutical Sciences 2013;2(6):4311–28.
[49] Vogler S, Zimmermann N, De Joncheere K. The Pharmaceutical Pricing and Reimbursement Information (PPRI) network—a decade of exchange of information and policy research? Journal of Pharmaceutical Policy and Practice 2015;8(Suppl. 1):E4.
[50] Ognyanova D, Zentner A, Busse R. Pharmaceutical reform 2010 in Germany. Eurohealth 2011;17(1):11–3.

[51] Vogler S, Schneider P. Vergütung der Arzneimitteldistribution in den europäischen Ländern. Gesetzliche Regelungen und Durchschnittsspannen. Wien: Gesundheit Österreich Forschungs- und Planungs-GmbH; 2015.
[52] Eidgenössisches Departement des Innern (EDI). Handbuch betreffend der Spezialitätenliste. In: Bern, editor. (BAG) BfG; 2017.
[53] Änderung des Allgemeinen Sozialversicherungsgesetzes. 2017.

CHAPTER 13

Assessment of External Price Referencing and Alternative Policies

Sabine Vogler
WHO Collaborating Centre for Pharmaceutical Pricing and Reimbursement Policies, Pharmacoeconomics Department, Gesundheit Österreich GmbH (GÖG/Austrian Public Health Institute), Vienna, Austria

LIST OF ABBREVIATIONS

AMR	Antimicrobial resistance
ATC	Anatomical Therapeutic Chemical Classification
CADTH	Canadian Agency for Drugs and Technologies in Health
CAPR	Competent Authorities Responsible for Pricing and Reimbursement (a network in the European Union)
CEA	Cost-effectiveness analysis
DNDi	Drugs for Neglected Diseases Initiative
EPR	External price referencing
EU	European Union
EUnetHTA	European Network for Health Technology Assessment
EURIPID	EURopean Integrated Price Information Database
GBP	Great Britain Pound
GCC	Gulf Cooperation Council
GDP	Gross domestic product
HAI	Health Action International
HIC	High-income country/countries
HTA	Health technology assessment
ICER	Incremental cost-effectiveness ratio
JPA	Joint Procurement Agreement
LMIC	Low- and middle-income country/countries
MEA	Managed-entry agreement(s)
MMV	Medicines for Malaria Venture
MSH	Management Sciences for Health
NHS	National Health Service
OECS	Organization of Eastern Caribbean States
PAHO	Pan American Health Organization
PBS	Pharmaceutical Benefits Scheme (Australia)
PDP	Product development partnership(s)
PHARMAC	Pharmaceutical Management Agency
PPP	Purchasing power parity/parities

Medicine Price Surveys, Analyses, and Comparisons
ISBN 978-0-12-813166-4
https://doi.org/10.1016/B978-0-12-813166-4.00019-X

PPRI	Pharmaceutical Pricing and Reimbursement Information (a network of competent authorities of pharmaceutical pricing and reimbursement)
PPS	Purchasing power standard(s)
QALY	Quality-adjusted life year
R&D	Research and development
RPS	Reference price system(s)
SADC	Southern African Development Community
UHC	Universal health coverage
UN	United Nations
US	United States
USD	United States of America Dollars
VBP	Value-based pricing
WHO	World Health Organization
WTP	Willingness-to-pay

External price referencing (EPR) has been increasingly used all over the world, and expectations about its benefits are high. At the same time, concerns about limitations of this pricing policy have been expressed, and there have been calls for exploring alternative approaches to deal with high-priced medicines [1,2]. This chapter starts by critically reviewing the benefits and limitations of EPR that have been documented and discussed in literature and policy debate (Sections 13.1 and 13.2). Based on some simulation scenarios of the EPR methodology (Section 13.3), Section 13.4 proposes options for change in the design of the pricing policy. Section 13.5 concludes by presenting alternative policies to set medicine prices that consider other criteria for decision-making.

13.1 BENEFITS OF EPR

Possible benefits of EPR include:

1. It is a policy to set and control medicine prices (price regulation).
2. It may contribute to long-term financial sustainability by containing pharmaceutical expenditure and possibly generate savings for public payers.
3. It is considered to be technically simple. Administrative efforts are expected to be low.
4. Extensive experience with EPR implementation has been made globally.
5. In case of non-achievement of objectives, changes in the methodology can have some impact.

6. Cross-country collaboration that is currently on the rise can improve intended results and/or facilitate implementation.
7. EPR is not a stand-alone policy. EPR, or some of its elements, can be used in combination with other pricing and/or reimbursement measures.

13.1.1 Price Regulation

First of all, by its nature, EPR is a pricing policy, that is, a government action to determine and control medicine prices.

In countries without price regulation (such as many low- and middle-income countries (LMIC) and the United States) medicine prices were usually higher than in regulated settings. Thus, they are not affordable for patients who have to pay fully out-of-pocket for medicines or are charged with high co-payments [3,4]. Similarly, in several countries without price regulation prices in the private sector were higher than in the public sector (see also the findings of the price studies in Chapter 2). For instance, according to a study of 36 LMIC, prices of originator medicines were more than over 20 times the international MSH reference prices as defined in the WHO/HAI methodology (for details on the WHO/HAI methodology [5] see Chapter 6.2).

The World Health Organization (WHO) recommends implementation of price regulation because there are strong indications for its ability to contribute to more affordable access to medicines (see also the WHO Guideline on Country Pharmaceutical Pricing Policies [6] in Chapter 14). Despite its presumed and observed limitations, EPR is one policy for governments to statutorily set medicine prices. Even if only parts of the medicines on the market are price regulated, this can already be a major step forward. Essential medicines (cf. Box 11.1 in Chapter 11.1 for the concept of essential medicines) constitute typical candidates for price control.

13.1.2 Cost-Containment, Savings and Financial Sustainability

Several studies investigated the impact of EPR to contribute to financial sustainability, by either containing costs (expenditure) or even providing savings. A common outcome measure studied in this context is public pharmaceutical expenditure because in countries with advanced universal health coverage (UHC) medicines subject to EPR regulation are usually funded or co-funded by third party payers. Some studies analysed the development of prices after the implementation of EPR, or in comparison to non-EPR applying countries, whereas others did simulations.

Table 13.1 provides a selection of studies that investigated cost-containing effects of EPR. As also noted in Chapters 2 to 4, evidence is

Table 13.1 Evidence about EPR's ability to contribute to cost-containment

Author(s)	Title	Country/ countries studied	Period	Key results	References
Windmeijer et al., 2006	Pharmaceutical promotion and GP prescription behaviour	Netherlands	1994–99	The study measured the effects of implementation of EPR. Medicine prices were reduced by about 15% on average. Prices of medicines without a reimbursement price were affected the most. In addition, several medicines clustered in a group (i.e., medicines of identical and/or similar therapeutic benefit, including generics) were forced to lower their prices.	[7]
Håkonsen et al., 2009	Price control as a strategy for pharmaceutical cost containment – what has been achieved in Norway in the period 1994–2004?	Norway	1994–2004	The study looked at medicine prices' development before and after the introduction of EPR in 2000. It concluded that consistent use of EPR and subsequent price revisions led to substantial price reductions of many medicines. In the year of its introduction, EPR resulted in medicine price reduction by 2.0% (the consumer price index	[8]

				increased to 3.1% in that respective year).	
Merkur/ Mossialos 2007	A pricing policy towards the sourcing of cheaper drugs in Cyprus	Cyprus	2003	The effect of EPR on medicine prices was simulated. Overall, Cyprus was identified as a high-priced country. Based on the simulations the study concluded that EPR would lower prices and contain costs: The pharmacy retail prices would be lowered by 33% to 39% in cases of high-priced medicines, and by 26% to 33% for the medicines with highest sales.	[9]
Leopold et al., 2012	Impact of External Price Referencing on Medicine Prices – A Price Comparison Among 14 European Countries	14 European countries	2007/2008	Prices of a sample of 14 on-patent medicines were studied in cross-country analysis of European countries, several of which with EPR, and a few not. Medicine prices were in general	[10]

Continued

Table 13.1 Evidence about EPR's ability to contribute to cost-containment—cont'd

Author(s)	Title	Country/ countries studied	Period	Key results	References
				lower in cases where the country applied EPR compared to countries that did not.	
Filko/ Szilagyiova, 2009	The Slovak experience in the international price benchmarking for prescription drugs	Slovakia	2008	Following a change of the EPR methodology the proportion of pharmaceutical expenditure as share of total health care spending declined to approximately 25%.	[11]
Toumi et al., 2014	External reference pricing of medicinal products: simulation-based considerations for cross-country coordination	26 European countries	Not known	The study simulated the effects of EPR on medicine prices in 26 European countries. It concluded that when EPR were applied as the sole criterion for pricing, it would decrease medicine prices by about 15% after 10 years. For countries applying EPR, periodic price revisions were identified as the main requirement for price reductions.	[12]

The references are listed in the table.
Overview provided by the authors.

mainly focussed on high-income countries. Overall, research documented that EPR is able to contribute to savings for public payers or at least contain growing expenditure.

Studies to assess the effect of EPR do not come without limitations. It can be difficult to analyse policy interventions because they are not randomized clinical trials but are conducted in real-life settings, where further influencing factors and policy interventions may influence their outcomes. It is thus not always clear whether, or not, reductions in medicine prices or in public expenditure can solely be attributed to the introduction of EPR. According to information provided by policy-makers, high savings were reported shortly after the introduction of EPR but they were reduced over time [13]. As such, EPR proved to be effective in terms of cost-containment, even very successful in the beginning, but apparently it lost its impact after some time. Such 'fade-out effects' have also been observed with other policies, and they confirm that for any policy, including EPR, adjustments are necessary in the course of time. As it will be shown later, the effectiveness of EPR in terms of cost-containment is dependent on its design, and methodological choices can have an impact.

13.1.3 Simplicity

Espin et al. (2011) described EPR as 'a relatively simple and easy-to-apply system compared, for example, to economic evaluation' and considered its easy-to-handle use as a main advantage of this pricing policy [14].

EPR does not require large investments into health technology assessment (HTA) such as the establishment of an HTA structure (agency) and capacity-building of staff, which would be a prerequisite for value-based pricing (VBP). In contrast to VBP, EPR does not require the development of (complex) methodologies to assess the value of a medicine. Still, doing high quality EPR is not easy and may require non-negligible resource investment (see Section 13.2 for further discussion).

13.1.4 Experience

Several countries worldwide apply EPR, and some of them introduced it years ago. As a result, policy-makers and technical people have gained experience with EPR implementation.

Unfortunately, practical experience of EPR implementation is not well documented, as studies tend to focus on mapping exercises and analyses of certain aspects. Additionally, there are few guidance documents of how to conduct EPR (for few examples see Chapter 14). But in recent years collaborations of public authorities through informal networks (e.g., the

Pharmaceutical Pricing and Reimbursement Information [PPRI] network [15]) and more formalised collaborations (e.g., the Competent Authorities Responsible for Pricing and Reimbursement/CAPR network [16], the so-called BeNeLuxA collaboration [17]) that aim to share information and experience of policy practice have increasingly been established.

13.1.5 Methodological Optimisation

Any (pharmaceutical) policy can yield different results depending on its methodological set-up, and this is also and in particular the case for EPR. Studies [12,13] based on simulations provided evidence of how methodological choices can impact outcomes and thus contribute to the achievement of the intended policy objectives. Details will be presented in Section 13.3.

In case of non-achievement of objectives, policy-makers do not necessarily need to change to another pricing policy, but can undertake smaller changes in the methodological design. A stepwise adaption and optimisation of EPR over time is possible.

13.1.6 Collaboration

EPR is a pricing policy that is based on information from other countries. Apart from cross-learning of countries about experiences, as mentioned above, contacts to experts (in pricing authorities, for instance) can help technical people in identifying price data sources, assessing their benefits and limitations and receiving advice on the interpretation of price data in national data sources.

In this context, a common price database of public authorities that allows easy access is an asset. In the European region, an advanced collaborative approach for sharing medicine price data is the so-called EURIPID price database of competent authorities (cf. Chapter 8.2.2). Given increased collaborations between countries, it can be expected that this may lead to the establishment of further price databases of public authorities, also in other regions, and this will facilitate the application of EPR. The importance of sharing price information has been recognised by the report of the United National Secretary-General's High-Level Panel on access to medicines, which recommended the establishment of an international database of prices of medicines [1].

13.1.7 Combination With Other Policies

While medicine prices of other countries are not considered to be the most appropriate indicator to reflect the (added) therapeutic value of a medicine (see below the limitations in Section 13.2), policy-makers stressed that price data provide, at least, some benchmarks (personal communication). A weak benchmark is considered superior to a situation without any information, and it offers a starting point for further analyses and collection of further data.

In practice, EPR is frequently used as a supplementary policy that is accompanied by other policies, tools and criteria for setting the price or determining the reimbursement amount (cf. Chapter 12). Even countries that do not apply EPR (e.g., Sweden, UK) review the prices of medicines in other countries and use them as additional background information in their pricing and reimbursement process.

The non-exclusivity of EPR is one of its benefits: EPR, or elements of EPR (e.g., consideration of price data in other countries), can be combined with other pricing and/or reimbursement measures.

13.2 LIMITATIONS OF EPR

Possible limitations of EPR include:

1. It incentivizes launch delays and non-availability of medicines.
2. Its savings potential is not fully utilised due to incomplete, non-transparent and incorrect price information.
3. It requires capacity-building, and it can be cost- and resource-intensive.
4. It does not reflect value and is not considered as a mechanism to reward innovation.
5. EPR is considered to be not 'fair'.
6. EPR is exposed to exchange rate volatility.
7. EPR is expected to lead to spillover effects including price convergence.

13.2.1 Availability Issues

A frequently mentioned limitation of EPR concerns its potential to contribute to accessibility issues. EPR incentivizes marketing authorisation holders to launch medicines first in countries with high prices of medicines, and delay market entry, or not market at all, in lower-priced countries [12–14,18–25].

As the practice from Europe shows, high-priced countries such as Germany, Austria, Denmark and Sweden (cf. Chapter 2.1) are among the first launch countries [13]. There are indications of delayed availability for lower-priced European countries (e.g., Central and Eastern European countries) where medicines are being brought into the market 2 to 3 years after its marketing in early launch countries [26].

While there are strong indications that EPR contributes to launch delays in lower-priced countries, attention should be taken to not attributing every availability issue to the EPR policy. Several new medicines (e.g., cancer medicines, orphan medicines) are not marketed in lower-resourced countries [27,28] because these health systems do not have the ability to pay high prices. In the European Union (EU), parallel trade is allowed, and shortages of medicines in EU Member States with lower prices have been observed due to parallel exports to higher-priced countries [29,30]. However, according to an analysis of medicine shortage reporting systems in European countries, 'economic reasons' (i.e., widespread use of EPR) accounted for only 1% of shortages (3% in case of oncology medicines), compared to 16% (and 27% respectively) of shortages being caused by production problems [31].

13.2.2 Incomplete, Non-transparent and Incorrect Price Information

While EPR savings potential is, in principle, acknowledged and documented (cf. Section 13.1.2), it is not always fully exploited due to limited access to (correct) price information.

As highlighted in different chapters of this book, there is no price information available for numerous countries over the world, particularly those without price regulation. They are thus not appropriate candidates as reference countries. Even for countries with existing price databases, availability of medicine price data might not be complete. In accordance with the European Union (EU) Transparency Directive [32], Member States have to publish prices of reimbursable medicines; as a result, prices of non-reimbursable medicines are often not available. This concerns particularly non-prescription medicines that are usually not reimbursed, and in some countries price data for the hospital sector are also not published (e.g., Portugal [33]).

A major source of limited price transparency is discounts and other price-reducing agreements. These arrangements, which are summarised in the European setting under the umbrella term of managed-entry agreements (MEA), are commonly used for new, premium-priced medicines and are, in general, confidential [34–36]. As shown in Chapter 2 (particularly Chapter 2.1), there are few studies that aimed to bring light into this 'black box', and not all of them were able to report exact amounts of discounts for the investigated medicines. For the time being, access to confidential price information appears to be not possible for policy-makers.[1] It would require joint forces of governments across countries to move forward with initiatives of price transparency [37].

[1] In this context, it should be reminded that the German EPR legislation aims to refer to actual (discounted) medicine prices in the reference countries (cf. Chapter 12).

Even if these discounts arrangements were disclosed, there might be some technical issues to solve. Some MEA do not solely target the price of a medicine but are designed in a more complex way (such as price—volume agreements or bundling), so the exact extent of discounts per medicine will be difficult to determine. In some cases it can only be assessed ex-post.

A few countries have mandatory manufacturer discounts (either statutorily regulated such as in Germany or Spain or based on framework agreements, e.g., Ireland) [13]. These discounts have officially been published but they are rarely taken into consideration by EPR-applying countries.

Price information might also be incorrect if public authorities rely on a sole source and do not have the resources to validate price data to be used in EPR.

13.2.3 Capacity-Building and Investments

While it has been acknowledged that other policies such as VBP can require very large investments in terms of time and other resources (Section 13.1), it is fair to note that EPR is not a simple task either. Capacity has to be built with staff who will conduct the data collection and the comparison with prices of other countries [18,38]. Furthermore, policy-makers and experts that develop (and further adapt) an EPR methodology should have a good understanding of the principles and impact of this policy.

To address the limitation of incomplete information that was highlighted in the previous section, additional efforts are required to identify missing data in commonly used sources for EPR (e.g., time to search in supplementary databases maintained by competent authorities in different countries). It can also be time-intensive to search for supplementary information such as the prescription or reimbursement status or hospital use of the respective medicines that might be required in the EPR process, depending on its methodology design[2].

Appropriate data sources for price information have to be identified: some databases require a payment to gain access, and others might not be designed in a way that they allow for quick and easy handling (see also Chapter 8). Certain methodological choices such as large country baskets or regular price reviews can add substantially to the workload of implementing EPR.

[2] For instance, an EPR system could be designed in a way that it only considers prices in other countries if the respective medicine is reimbursed or it is not exclusively used in hospitals in the reference countries.

Finally, as stated above, validation of data would be needed to ensure a quality-based EPR process. This does not come without further costs either (working time of staff or consultants, cost of additional data sources).

13.2.4 Non-consideration of Value

In contrast to other pricing and reimbursement policies, particularly VBP (cf. Section 13.5.1), the value concept has not been built into EPR. In fact, EPR neither reflects the willingness-to-pay nor the ability-to-pay of a country [39]. Value considerations may come into play indirectly, by importing the value attributed to the medicine in the reference countries that apply these concepts [38].

EPR has been described as 'path-dependent' [18,24], meaning that input information required for decision-making can impact the final outcome. It has been argued that prices, and price decreases, obtained through EPR appear to be mainly influenced by the applied methodology, without necessarily paying attention to factors intrinsic to the healthcare system in which it operates.

Industry has been arguing that innovation is not sufficiently rewarded if value is not considered. This would reduce industry's incentive to invest into research and development (R&D) [40] (cf. also Section 13.5.7 about 'delinkage').

13.2.5 Fairness

Different stakeholders have criticized EPR for not being a 'fair policy'. It has been argued that lower-income countries would pay the same price as higher-income countries (which is rarely the case, but there is price variation, cf. the price studies presented in Chapters 2-4), and this would not be fair from a public health perspective.[3] Industry has been arguing that prices based on EPR may not provide a 'fair' reward for R&D and that EPR 'is fundamentally flawed from an economical point of view and will ultimately lead to greater inequalities in patient access across Europe' [40].

Achieving a common understanding about a 'fair price' is a challenge. There are different perspectives on what constitutes a 'fair' reward for industry that still preserves access to patients. In this context, the WHO

[3] It should be noted that in the WHO/HAI review to inform the WHO Guideline on Country Pharmaceutical Pricing Policies it was stated that the underlying assumption justifying the use of EPR that the prices in the reference countries are somehow right, appropriate or fair.

launched a global dialogue, the 'Fair Pricing Forum' to discuss options to develop a fairer pricing system that ensures the sustainability of health systems and promotes innovation [41].

13.2.6 Exchange Rate Volatility

A technical limitation linked to the design of EPR is designed concerns exchange rate volatility. Apart from common currency areas (e.g., the euro zone), medicine prices in the reference prices are denominated in local currencies [12,18,24,42].

13.2.7 Price Convergence and Other Spillover Effects

The scientific literature and policy papers mentioned negative spillover effects of EPR, relating to consequences for other countries [14,24,40]. Different impacts were referred to under the umbrella term of 'spillover effects'.

Convergence of medicine prices is considered to be one spillover effect [24]. EPR is expected to lead to uniform or, at least, converging prices. This is based on the rationale that in some regions of the world (e.g., EU) there is extensive cross-referencing between countries that tend to have other EU Member States in their baskets and, in return, are also referenced by them (cf. Chapter 12.2). A few studies that investigated price data of over 1 a decade ago suggested convergence of (list) prices of new medicines within the EU [43,44]. However, more recent studies did not confirm such convergence across EU Member States [45–47]. One study [45] even showed an increase in dispersion for two countries (Germany – upward trend and Greece – downward trend). This development might be attributable to the global financial crisis that hit some European countries during the study period (2007–15). See also Chapter 4 for details of studies that analysed the existence of price conversion and price dispersion.

Another frequently mentioned spillover effect relates to the fact that the price levels of other countries and their price developments can be exported through EPR. While pricing authorities and public payers of EPR-applying countries benefit from low price levels in reference countries and from price revisions that reduce prices, industry has a different viewpoint. Commonly reported practices of industry to avoid these spillover effects are the reduction of transparency and a strategic sequencing of the launch of medicines [14,18]. As described above, this will impact on lower-priced reference countries that will suffer from lower availability. Industry might not provide medicines or might offer them at high (list) prices only, to some lower-priced countries that could be candidates for being reference countries to others.

13.3 IMPACT OF SIMULATIONS OF EPR MODELS

This section presents simulation scenarios that investigated impacts of changes in the EPR methodology on medicine prices.

Unless stated differently, the simulations are based on data published in the frame of the 'Study on enhanced cross-country coordination in the area of pharmaceutical product pricing' [13] that compared different methodological choices. The 'base case' scenario was defined as follows:

- A 'real-life' setting was used by taking into account the parameters of the pricing policies in the 28 EU Member States, Iceland, Norway and Switzerland (EPR implemented in 28 countries and non-use of EPR in the outpatient sector in Denmark, Sweden and UK; EPR dimensions relating to the basket of reference countries, the calculation method to derive the benchmark rate, the frequency of price revisions, the methodology for the conversion of the exchange rate as in place in the first quarter of 2015).
- In the simulations, Germany was considered as first launch country, and its launch price was set at 100 euros. The prices of non-EPR countries were fixed at 100 as well.
- Prices based on EPR would only be determined after the prices in the defined (minimum) number of reference countries were available.
- Prices were held constant until a re-evaluation was due according to legislation. No price deflation or inflation was considered.
- Exchange rates were assumed constant across time.
- For simplicity, EPR was assumed to be the sole pricing policy in the EPR-applying countries.

To kick-off, a launch price of 100 euro was assumed for Germany and of 70 euro for Italy. The simulations referred to ex-factory prices and were always run for a period of 10 years (120 months).

Due to changes over the years that implied an increasing number of countries with price data available in their basket and price revisions, price erosion will occur. After 10 years, the simulations showed an average price of 78.1 euro in the EPR-applying countries, varying between 94.0 euro (Austria) and 67.8 euro (Hungary). Country-specific details on the base case and some simulated scenarios are presented in Table 13.2.

Table 13.2 Results of simulation scenarios of different EPR methodologies in 28 EPR-applying countries – prices after 10 years

Countries	Base case	Discounts	Revisions	Income adjustment	Basket change (4/30 countries)	Minimum price	Exchange rate (yearly/monthly)
AT (Austria)	*94.0*	82.0	76.5	88.2	94.0/85.0	70.0	94.0/94.6
BE (Belgium)	*94.0*	82.0	76.5	88.9	94.0/85.0	70.0	94.0/94.6
BG (Bulgaria)	*70.0*	19.0	69.5	32.9	67.5/83.9	54.7	62.5/58.1
CH (Switzerland)	*93.0*	66.0	86.5	129.5	77.1/84.2	62.3	95.8/98.2
CY (Cyprus)	*74.0*	47.0	70.0	57.6	66.2/72.4	48.0	75.6/76.3
CZ (Czech Republic)	*70.0*	35.0	69.5	45.5	67.8/83.9	56.2	62.7/58.1
DE (Germany)	*89.0*	72.0	79.9	80.0	87.7/85.0	77.9	88.9/90.4
EE (Estonia)	*70.0*	32.0	69.5	50.6	67.8/83.9	56.0	62.8/59.2
EL (Greece)	*70.0*	22.0	69.5	58.0	67.5/83.9	54.7	62.6/59.0
ES (Spain)	*70.0*	29.0	69.5	62.5	67.5/83.9	55.8	62.7/59.3
FI (Finland)	*78.6*	37.2	74.7	87.0	74.6/81.5	52.7	91.2/91.8
FR (France)	*82.2*	34.5	79.7	82.8	76.9/84.2	54.7	90.0/90.3
HR (Croatia)	*67.8*	11.4	65.7	41.1	70.5/77.0	50.1	66.4/63.1
HU (Hungary)	*70.0*	56.0	69.5	35.6	70.0/70.0	70.0	62.5/61.1
IE (Ireland)	*89.1*	59.2	82.5	82.9	77.1/84.2	57.3	91.3/92.0
IS (Iceland)	*88.8*	72.8	84.8	91.9	73.6/80.6	54.7	99.4/99.3
IT (Italy)	*70.0*	23.2	69.5	70.0	67.5/83.9	54.7	65.0/59.7
LT (Lithuania)	*70.1*	13.7	69.5	42.2	77.0/84.2	55.8	64.4/61.6

Continued

Table 13.2 Results of simulation scenarios of different EPR methodologies in 28 EPR-applying countries – prices after 10 years—cont'd

Countries	Base case	Discounts	Revisions	Income adjustment	Basket change (4/30 countries)	Minimum price	Exchange rate (yearly/monthly)
LU (Luxembourg)	*94.0*	82.1	76.5	95.7	67.5/83.9	70.0	94.0/94.6
LV (Latvia)	*70.0*	34.5	69.5	47.1	67.5/83.9	54.7	65.2/62.4
MT (Malta)	*75.5*	25.2	74.0	55.4	77.1/84.2	56.2	74.0/72.0
NL (Netherlands)	*81.6*	55.4	75.1	75.1	68.8/75.3	56.3	84.8/86.5
NO (Norway)	*84.0*	50.5	73.1	99.4	63.7/78.9	53.9	87.4/80.2
PL (Poland)	*70.6*	16.4	69.8	40.6	76.9/84.2	54.7	67.2/64.7
PT (Portugal)	*78.2*	22.2	75.2	56.1	77.0/84.0	55.8	81.9/79.9
RO (Romania)	*70.0*	18.5	69.5	34.4	67.5/83.9	54.7	66.4/64.7
SI (Slovenia)	*82.2*	32.1	76.5	58.9	67.5/83.9	63.0	90.0/90.3
SK (Slovakia)	*70.0*	24.3	69.5	47.1	67.5/83.9	54.3	62.6/59.2
Average price (against base case)	*78.1*	*41.2* *−47.2%*	*73.6* *−5.8%*	*65.6* *−16.0%*	*73.0/82.2* *−6.5%/ +5.3%*	*58.2* *−34.2%*	*77.3/75.8* *−1.0%/−3.0%*

Base case: based on EPR methodology as in place in the countries in Q1/2015.
Discounts: assumption of the consideration of statutory discounts in Germany, Greece and Ireland and an additional 20% (confidential) discount in Germany, France, Italy, the Netherlands, Spain and UK.
Revisions: assumption of price reviews and subsequent price adjustments every 6 months during the period of the 10 years investigated.
Income adjustment: assumption of adjustment of price data by purchasing power parities (PPP) in all 28 countries of the sample.
Basket change: assumption of a basket of four reference countries: Germany – high-priced country (alternatively Sweden for Germany to refer to), Finland and Portugal – middle-priced countries (alternatively the Netherlands), Italy – low-priced country (alternatively Spain); selection of countries based on ranking derived from base case scenario. Another assumption of referencing to 30 countries (all other EPR-applying and non–EPR-applying countries of the sample); results of further scenarios presented in the text and in Fig. 13.1.
Minimum price: assumption to derive the benchmark price based on the minimum price in the reference countries.
Exchange rate: conversion of price data in foreign currency based on average yearly exchange rate, and on average monthly exchange rate.
Author's own presentation and illustration based on data published in [13]

13.3.1 Consideration of Discounts

One scenario was based on the assumption that EPR-applying countries considered a discount of 20% of the referenced prices in large economies (i.e., Germany, France, Italy, the Netherlands, Spain and UK) plus the statutory manufacturer discounts in Germany, Greece and Ireland. Simulations suggested a substantial impact of the consideration of discounts: The average official list price in the 28 EPR-applying countries after 10 years dropped to 41.2 euro, corresponding to a 47.2% decrease compared to the base case scenario.

While the 20% discount was a simple assumption of a price reduction whose extent is not known in reality, the statutory discounts in Germany, Greece and Ireland are based on legislation (Germany and Greece) and a framework agreement (Ireland). The statutory manufacturer discounts relate to obligatory payments of industry to the public payers, and its amount has been published. Even if solely the statutory discounts of the three countries were taken into account, the impact was already considerable. The average official list prices in the EPR-applying countries fell to 57.15 euro (a drop of 26.8% compared to base case scenario). This was particularly attributable to the reduction of the Greek prices as several European countries had Greece in their basket and determined their EPR benchmark based on the lowest price in the basket (cf. Chapter 12.2). It can be concluded that a consideration of discounts in other lower-priced countries could have an important effect on the benchmark price.

13.3.2 Regular Price Revisions

Another scenario was based on the assumption that all EPR-applying countries reviewed the prices in the reference countries every 6 months and subsequently adjusted their prices. Compared to the base case that also included countries which did not regularly adjust prices, the average price fell down by 5.8% to 73.6 euro. Major reductions were observed in countries that did not revaluate at all during the period of the 10 years.

13.3.3 Consideration of Economic Parameters

It has been suggested considering the economic situation of the reference countries. One possibility to do so is by adjusting price data for purchasing power parities (PPP) instead of using nominal exchange rates.

This would have a major impact for individual countries. Simulations showed that medicine price data of lower-income countries were reduced, while the adjustments led to higher prices in high-income countries. In particular, prices in Switzerland and Norway increased by 40% and 18% respectively, whereas Bulgarian, Romanian and Hungarian prices decreased by 53, 51 and 49% respectively. Overall, the average price after 10 years dropped by 16% to 65.6 euro.

13.3.4 Changes in the Basket of Reference Countries

Several experts stressed the importance of a strategic choice of the reference countries (see also the guidance documents in Chapter 14). The results of the simulations (Fig. 13.1) tend to confirm this recommendation.

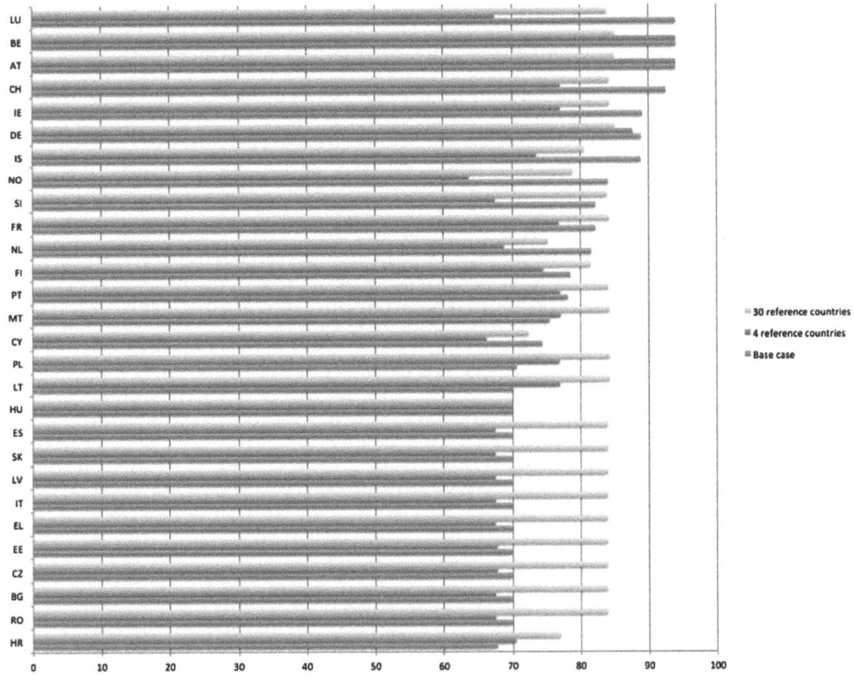

Figure 13.1 Results of simulation scenarios of changes in the basket of reference countries in 28 EPR-applying countries – prices after 10 years. Panel 1: Change in the size of the basket. Assumption of a basket of four reference countries: Germany – high-priced country (alternatively Sweden instead of Germany), Finland and Portugal – middle-priced countries (alternatively the Netherlands), Italy – low-priced country (alternatively Spain); selection of countries based on ranking derived from base case scenario and of 30 countries (all other EPR-applying and non–EPR-applying countries of the sample). Panel 2: Change in the reference countries included. Assumption of a basket of reference countries that does not include countries in the quintile of the lowest per capita GDP and of a basket of reference countries that does not include countries in the quintile of the highest per capita GDP.

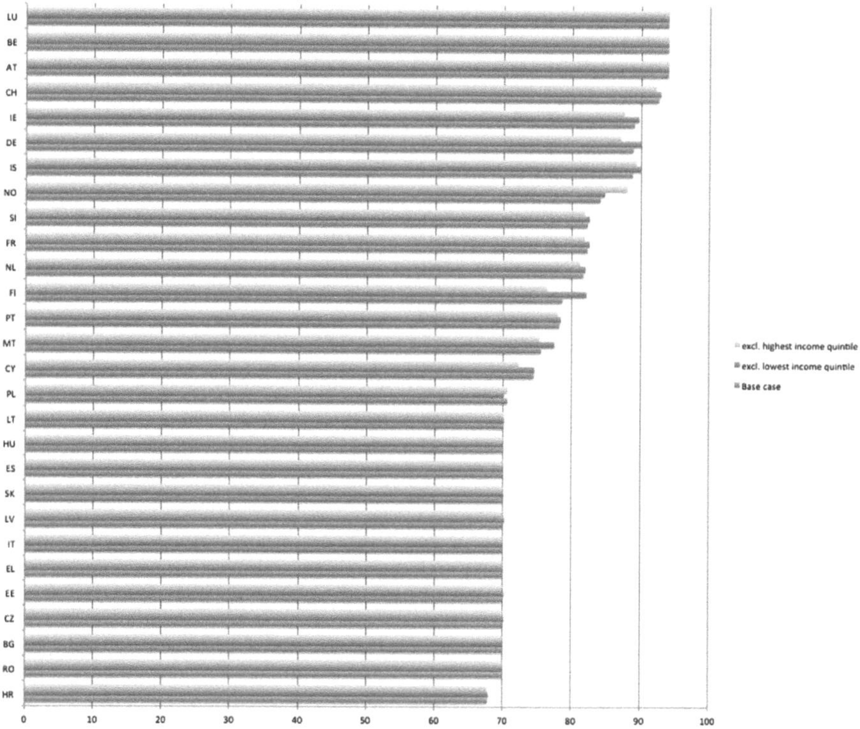

Figure 13.1 Cont'd

One simulation was run for a scenario that assumed the application of a strategically chosen basket of solely four reference countries that represented different price levels (one high-priced, two middle-priced and one low-priced country). A small basket also offers the advantage of lower administrative efforts. The simulation showed a decrease in the average price by 6.5% down to 73 euro. The impact differed between countries, thus reflecting the differences in existing EPR methodologies: while some had major price drops (e.g., Luxembourg −28%, Norway −24% and Slovenia −18%), prices increased in other countries (Croatia, Lithuania, Malta, Poland) compared to the base case. If the EPR-applying countries referred to all 30 other (EPR-applying and non-applying) countries of the sample, the average price of the EPR-applying countries would increase by 5.3% to 82.2 euro. It was sometimes argued that Greece should not be referenced to since the prices of the European low-priced country declined during the global financial crisis. However, not referencing to Greece would not change much: while the average price increased by 0.5% (up to

78.5 euro) compared to the base case, only a few countries were targeted. A considerable price increase was seen in only one country, Cyprus, that determined the EPR benchmark on an average of the prices of four reference countries, including Greece. A simulation of a scenario that did not include countries with per capita gross domestic product (GDP) in the lowest quintile showed similar results: an average increase to 78.5 euro (0.5%) in comparison to the base case that addressed some high-priced and high-income countries. There was no impact on lower-priced countries that tend not to include these high-priced countries in their baskets. Baskets that did not include medicines of the highest quintile in terms of per capita GDP as reference countries only had a slightly lower drop compared to the base case (an average price of 77.9 euro, i.e., a decrease of 0.3%).

13.3.5 Changes in the Calculation Method

There are different calculation approaches to derive the EPR price, such as taking the average of available price data in the reference countries, the minimum or some weighted average. Referencing to the minimum will likely drive prices down, and this was also confirmed by the simulation results. The base case scenario included some European countries that calculated the reference price based on the average (see also Chapter 12.2.5). As a result, the average price in the EPR-applying countries amounted to 58.2 euro and was thus 34.2% lower than in the base case scenario.

13.3.6 Choice of the Exchange Rate

In Section 13.2.6, exchange rate volatility was mentioned as one of the limitations of the EPR policy. Given the eurozone within the EU, this is maybe less an issue in Europe than in other regions of the world. But even in the EU some EPR-applying countries and some reference countries do not have the euro.

While in the simulations of changes in the exchange rate methodology the differences in price changes were lower than in the other scenarios, the choice of the exchange rate still matters. Exchange rates based on shorter intervals will likely increase prices, as this is also illustrated by the example of monthly and yearly exchange rates in Table 13.2, but there is the trade-off of higher volatility.

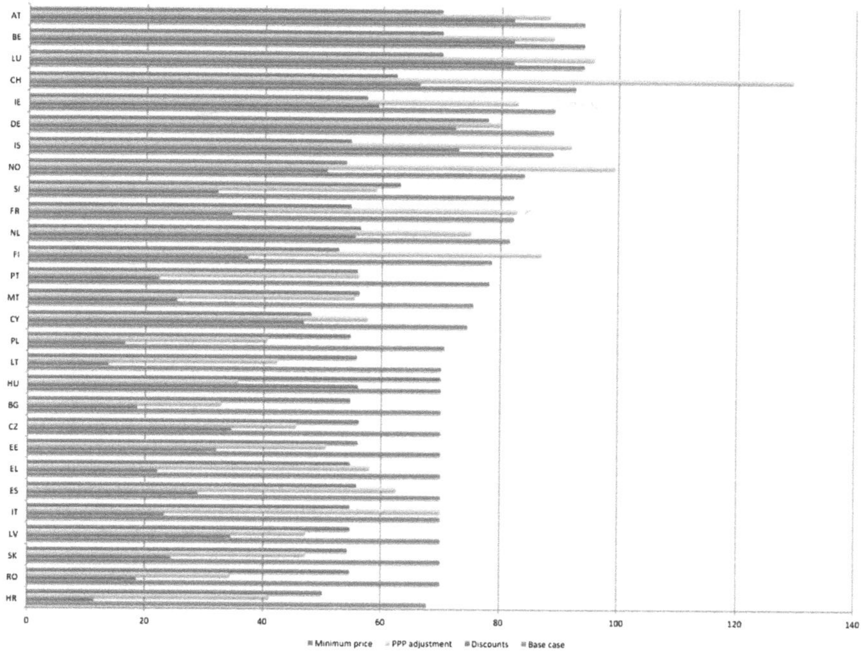

Figure 13.2 Results of simulation scenarios with highest impacts in the 28 EPR-applying countries — prices after 10 years.

13.3.7 Key Impacts

To conclude, the scenarios of consideration (or assumption) of discounts, determining the EPR price based on the minimum price in the reference countries and of adjustment of price data by PPP had the highest impact in the simulations. Fig. 13.2 presents the scenarios that showed the highest impacts.

For a description of the base case and the simulated scenarios see notes of Table 13.1.

13.4 IMPROVEMENTS IN EPR

In the light of identified benefits and limitations of EPR, options for improvement will be discussed in the next two sections. This section is devoted to technical changes related to EPR and its methodology, while the next section looks at further policy options for pricing medicines.

Based on experience with EPR and simulations presented in the previous sections, Table 13.3 provides some suggestions of how to improve the

Table 13.3 Options for improving the EPR policy

Dimensions	Recommendations
Overarching principles	
Procedures	Rules and procedures of EPR should be clear and transparent. This contributes to smooth and effective implementation of EPR by technical staff, and it signals to stakeholders what they can expect, which improves planning security.
Capacity	Since EPR is not a simple tool, sufficient capacity has to be built.
Focus	It is recommended to define strategically the scope of medicines subject to EPR. Governments should consider not applying EPR to the whole market. For some medicines and market segments other policies might be more appropriate (e.g., governments could benefit from generic competition in the off-patent sector).
Access to data	Access to reliable medicine price data should be available continuously, if possible at no or moderate costs and with easy use. Governments should have explored data sources of candidate reference countries before drafting the EPR methodology.
Validation	Validation is key and should be incorporated in the EPR processes. Ideally, price data should be available from more than one source per country to allow for checking. Governments should consider ensuring validation of price data used for EPR as an integral part of the EPR process. For instance, price data provided by the marketing authorisation holder in the pricing application could be systematically reviewed by a specified validation service (e.g., a defined unit of technical staff in the pricing authority or a trusted third party).
Monitoring and evaluation	EPR should be regularly monitored as to whether it is (still) able to achieve the defined results. The evaluation should include an analysis of success factors and limitations to allow adaption of the policy. Governments are recommended to stipulate the scope and frequency of evaluations in the EPR legislation.

Methodological design	
Consideration of discounts	EPR is flawed by non-transparent price information. To obtain lower prices and thus ensure long-term sustainability of healthcare systems, governments would require information of discounted prices. EPR would lead to lower prices if discounted prices in the reference countries were considered. Since this information is usually not available due to confidentiality agreements between industry and payers, governments could consider referring to prices that were reduced due to published statutory manufacturer discounts where applicable. Governments could also assume the extent of discounts on prices in the reference countries (based on publications, if applicable, or their own experience with offered discounts) and thus to determine the reference price based on assumed reduced prices.
Careful selection of reference countries	Governments are urged to carefully select their reference countries. This regards the number and choice of countries (balancing additional workload due to large baskets against possible benefits of the inclusion of certain countries). The medicine price levels on average and for specific medicines (in particular those planned to be subject to EPR) in candidate reference countries should be explored in advance, and based on this knowledge, reference countries should be defined in line with intended policy objectives (e.g., having a mix of high- and lower-priced countries to allow for higher prices and provide incentives for industry, or focussing on low-priced countries for cost-containment purposes). Further criteria that governments may like to consider in the selection are accessibility of price data (including national language issues, costs of databases), pharmaceutical consumption patterns and similarities in the healthcare and pharmaceutical sector of the reference countries.

Continued

Table 13.3 Options for improving the EPR policy—cont'd

Dimensions	Recommendations
Regular price revisions	Government should consider designing the EPR methodology to provide for price revisions, e.g., by defining price revision intervals in legislation. The frequency of price revisions should be balanced: while no or rare price revisions are a missed opportunity in terms of cost-containment, the workload of price revisions should not be underestimated, and sufficient trained staff should be available. To ease the burden, price revisions could be planned for parts of the medicines under EPR (e.g., for those medicines that account for highest public pharmaceutical expenditure).
Selection of calculation methodology	Governments should also consider the impact of the calculation methodology on medicine prices. Depending on the intended objectives, other calculations methods than average, median or lowest price in the reference countries are possible (e.g., average of the three or five lowest countries in a large country basket).
Backup strategies for non-availability of price data	Non-availability of price data is a reality that governments should take into consideration when they develop their EPR methodology. In particular, they will be confronted with data gaps if they include reference countries with lower medicine price levels, and/or with limitations in published price information. The EPR methodology should define possible contingency strategies (e.g., alternative countries, repetition of the price collection at certain intervals with subsequent price revision).
Income levels	In designing their EPR methodology, governments should consider whether, or not, they aim to adjust medicine prices by indicators reflecting the income levels of the reference countries. In doing so, they are recommended to check the appropriateness of different indicators (e.g., a common measurement in the field is purchasing power parities which is, however, based on a general basket of goods).
Exchange rate stability	An EPR methodology should also include directions on the exchange rates applied. Exchange rate volatility that will occur unless the EPR-applying countries and reference countries are members of a currency union. Average exchange rates for lower periods of time (e.g., average annual exchange rate) tend to even out short-term outliers but their advantage of higher stability has to be balanced against more precise shorter-term (e.g., monthly) exchange rate averages.

Note: The recommendations represent the author's views based on evidence in literature and experience in EPR.

EPR methodology. As a practical advice, it is recommended that governments run simulations and test different baskets of countries and data sources before the EPR methodology is finalised. Piloting of EPR is a good way to learn about possible pitfalls and make adjustments to the methods before they are implemented and used to inform pricing decisions.

In general, improvements in transparency (i.e., moving away from confidential discounts) would allow public purchasers and payers to take more informed decisions. With reductions in information asymmetry, they could assess the complete market situation, also taking into consideration future developments of new medicines that can bring therapeutic advance but might also considerably impact public budgets. By being better informed, pricing authorities could develop long-term investment and disinvestment strategies. It has been argued that despite some expected short-term 'pain' in terms of industry's reduced willingness to offer discounts, the improvement of price transparency is expected to contribute to a more affordable access to medicines in the long run [37].

One of the advantages of EPR is that it is not a stand-alone policy but can be combined with other policies and tools. Some of the pricing policies that will be described in the next section are not necessarily mutually exclusive to EPR but can be used in a supplementary way in order to develop the more appropriate policy mix in line with defined objectives.

13.5 ALTERNATIVES TO EPR

While EPR is a commonly used pricing policy, it is not the sole policy option in this field. This section presents further policies to price medicines that include pricing policies (commonly) applied in several countries and more 'innovative' models in early stages or under discussion. The latter are being developed to address identified limitations of current pricing policies in terms of ensuring affordable access to medicines. Table 13.4 provides a summary of the described pricing policies currently in place. Some of these policies are no 'pure' pricing policies, but also contain reimbursement elements.

As explained in Chapter 11, pricing *policies* are understood as regulations and processes used by government authorities. Actions taken by stakeholders (e.g., industry, wholesalers) to influence or change medicine prices are referred to as pricing *strategies*. This section concerns pricing policies of public authorities, while pricing strategies of private sector actors are not in the scope. Particular attention will be given to ensure clarity for cases

Table 13.4 Overview of further pricing policies

		Practice		Criteria			Assessment	
Policy	**Definition**	**Geographic scope**	**Scope of medicines**	**Prices in other countries**	**Other criteria**	**Relation to EPR**	**Benefits**	**Limitations**
Value-based pricing (VBP)	No clear definition. Through this policy authorities set prices for new medicines and/or decide on reimbursement based on the therapeutic value that a medicine offers, usually assessed through HTA or economic evaluation.	In HIC supportive instruments such as HTA or economic evaluations are commonly used in pricing and/or reimbursement of new medicines. However, an integrative approach of pricing and reimbursement based on value has been implemented in only a few countries (e.g., Sweden, Australia).	Typically applied for new medicines (without competitors)	No	Cost-effectiveness is a key criterion but other factors (e.g., comfort of use, cost savings in other parts of the health system, gains in labour productivity) may also play a role.	Mutually exclusive. However, in practice, some countries use VBP elements in pricing, while EPR offers a starting point.	Use of HTA and CEA allows generation of evidence and more informed decisions; policy-makers can signal their priorities to industry.	Difficult to implement; need for capacity-building, no incentives for a MAH to stay below the WTP threshold; ability-to-pay (affordability) is not considered
Cost-plus pricing	Pricing policy that takes into account production costs, promotional expenses, research and development (R&D), administration costs, overheads and profits to determine a medicine price.	Some LMIC; however a declining number of countries.	No information in literature.	No	Production costs in the broader sense (including material cost, R&D costs)	Mutually exclusive. However, costs and prices in other countries can be used as background information in price negotiations.	No evidence to support the use of cost-plus pricing as an overall pricing policy.	Difficult to assess production costs; authorities depend on information provided by manufacturers

Conditional pricing	Pricing policy that links the price of a medicine to specific outcomes or criteria. It comprises a range of agreements under different names (e.g., managed-entry agreements, risk-sharing, pay-for-performance).	Many HIC; also in some middle-income countries and emerging markets	New, typically high-priced medicines; medicines with limited evidence about their therapeutic benefit	No	Defined health outcomes (performance-based); aspects of the purchasing arrangement (e.g., minimum number of purchases).	Frequently used to negotiate the reimbursement price after preliminary determination of a price based on EPR.	Allows (early) access to medicines that would be unaffordable otherwise. Allows payers to manage uncertainty. Collection of real-world data.	Confidentiality connected to most conditional pricing arrangements. Increases information asymmetry and weakens the bargaining power of authorities. Difficult to implement, to monitor and to stop. No established methodology. Capacity-building is required.
Internal price referencing	Practice of using prices of identical or similar medicines in a country to set the price of a medicine	Applied in many countries with reimbursement systems (mainly HIC)	Medicines for which therapeutic alternatives are available (particularly generics, less frequently used for biosimilar medicines)	No	Prices of same and similar medicines in the same country	Complementary and supplementary (some countries use both external and internal price referencing)	Simple to handle, ensures lower prices of alternative medicines	Does not fully exploit the efficiency potential of lower-priced medicines, static method
Competitive pricing	Procedure that benefits from competition between suppliers, such as tenders	Globally, in many countries over the world (particularly for the public	Medicines procured by public authorities, or by	No	Key criterion: price offered in the bid; additional criteria (e.g.,	Usually exclusive. Possibility to tender for medicines with	Savings for procurers due to price competition	Risk of non-availability and shortages

Continued

Table 13.4 Overview of further pricing policies—cont'd

		Practice		Criteria			Assessment	
Policy	**Definition**	**Geographic scope**	**Scope of medicines**	**Prices in other countries**	**Other criteria**	**Relation to EPR**	**Benefits**	**Limitations**
	with a call for bids that are assessed, and the most advantageous one being selected	sector, including the hospital sector)	healthcare providers (e.g., hospitals). Possibility to have tenders in the off-patent market		supply conditions) can apply	regulated prices based on EPR		
Collaborative pricing	Joint initiatives of pricing authorities and/or procurers to achieve coordinated (not necessarily uniform) prices (examples: governments-lead differential pricing (DP) policy, joint procurement [JP])	DP: mainly LMIC (and least-developed countries), frequently under the lead of an international organisation JP: experience from few countries (e.g., in the Americas), planned by European countries	DP: few therapeutic groups (e.g., HIV/AIDS, malaria) JP: essential medicines; possible scope could be high-priced medicines	No	Ability-to-pay	Usually exclusive	Improved transparency, better purchasing and bargaining power due to reduction in information asymmetry, eventually 'fairer' and lower prices and improved patient access	Commitment of all authorities and agencies involved is required to comply with agreed procedures, risk of failure of collaboration if only one partner steps out. Possibly higher prices in the short run.

CEA, cost-effectiveness analysis; *DP*, differential pricing; *EPR*, external price referencing; *HIC*, high-income countries; *HTA*, Health Technology Assessment; *JP*, joint procurement; *LMIC*, low- and middle-income countries; *MAH*, marketing authorisation holder; *R&D*, research and development; *VBP*, value-based pricing; *WTP*, willingness-to-pay.

Compilation by the author; references are provided in the text.

(e.g., in literature) in which the same terminology (e.g., VBP, cost-plus pricing, differential pricing) is used to describe policies (government) and strategies (private sector).

13.5.1 Value-Based Pricing

Under the value-based pricing (VBP) policy, the 'value' that a medicine offers determines the price.

However, there is no clear or agreed definition of VBP. In a narrow approach, VBP (in the context of the English National Health Service/ NHS) is defined as '(the price) that ensures that the expected health benefits [of a new technology] exceed the health predicted to be displaced elsewhere in the NHS, due to their additional cost' [48]. This is aimed at achieving optimal resource allocation by ensuring that resources would not have been better spent in another way. Applying a broader approach, any policy linking the price of a medicine to its added therapeutic benefit could be considered within the category of VBP [39].

Leading VBP countries are Australia, New Zealand and also Canada (the latter also applies EPR). Australia was the first country to require pharmaceutical companies to produce economic data in support of their application for inclusion of a new medicine on the Pharmaceutical Benefits Scheme (PBS); the first set of formal pharmacoeconomic guidelines was published in 1992 [49,50]. In 1993, the Canadian Agency for Drugs and Technologies in Health (CADTH) and the Pharmaceutical Management Agency (PHARMAC) in New Zealand published pharmacoeconomic guidelines for their processes [51,52]. In Europe, Sweden introduced a 'real' VBP system in 2002: with pricing and reimbursement processes being completely integrated, eligibility for reimbursement is assessed against three criteria – the human value principle to guard against discrimination of individuals, the need and solidarity principle that gives priority to those in greatest need and the cost-effectiveness principle [53]. England that has been applying pharmacoeconomic principles for years intended to move to a 'full' VBP scheme in 2014 [54]. Eventually, this plan was not implemented ('Value based pricing is dead.' [55]). In terms of applying a broader definition of VBP, England continues to use a value-considering approach in pricing and reimbursement, and this is also the case for many European countries [39,56].

One reason for limited clarity related to the VBP policy might be that the terminology was adopted from a concept applied by the pharmaceutical industry. In optimizing their pricing strategies, pharmaceutical companies aim to understand how the purchasers (e.g., public payers) value the differentiated worth of a medicine (compared to alternatives) or how much they are willing to pay for it (willingness-to-pay/WTP concept).

The assessment of the value of new medicines can consider different dimensions: in addition to improvements in length and quality of life, criteria such as comfort of use, cost savings in other parts of the health system and gains in labour productivity for patients and carers can also be taken into account. It can be focussed on the healthcare system or apply a broader society approach.

VBP usually relies on the cost-effectiveness analysis (CEA) in which an incremental cost-effectiveness ratio (ICER) is determined. Usually, the quality-adjusted life years (QALY) approach is applied to assess the benefits of a healthcare intervention (including medicines). In general, an intervention is considered cost-effective if the ICER (e.g., price per QALY) is below a predetermined threshold. While above the ICER threshold a new medicine would, in theory, not be reimbursed, in practice policy-makers may deviate from the ICER threshold, and have done so in the past, in case of unmet medical need, rarity and severity of the disease treated and public pressure [39,57]. Few countries communicate their WTP threshold. For instance, a threshold of 20,000–30,000 GBP for England has been published [58], which has been supplemented by further thresholds for end-of-life medication and ultra-rare diseases in recent years [59]. Implicit thresholds exist in several countries [60].

In order to support pricing and reimbursement decisions, HTAs are performed. HTA is defined as 'a multidisciplinary process that summarises information about the medical, social, economic and ethical issues related to the use of a health technology in a systematic, transparent, unbiased, robust manner. Its aim is to inform the formulation of safe, effective, health policies that are patient focused and seek to achieve best value' [61]. HTA is a tool to support prioritization, with the aim to obtain better value for money. It is not a policy of its own. The findings of HTA still need to be appraised by policy-makers [62]. In European countries, the use of HTA is advanced: in some countries it is applied for all new medicines and in others for medicines with uncertain clinical benefits or expected high budget impacts. Frequently at least one HTA institution is in place in the European countries [56], and cross-country collaboration exists, particularly through the EUnetHTA project (see Box 13.1). In the other regions of the world, especially in LMIC, HTA is more broadly understood, as 'a systematic

BOX 13.1 European Experience in Health Technology Assessment (HTA)

To foster collaboration on HTA across European countries, the European Network for Health Technology Assessment (EUnetHTA) project was initiated. Strategic objectives of the EUnetHTA collaboration were defined to include a reduction of overlaps and duplications of efforts, an increase of HTA input into decision-making – and hence of the impact of HTA – and an improved link between HTA and healthcare policy-making [64].

The EUnetHTA collaboration started in 2007, with the financial support of the European Commission, and has grown to a network of 78 organizations (HTA agencies, research institutions and ministries of health) from 29 countries in the form of a joint action (i.e., a cooperation between government authorities and researchers, co-funded by the European Commission). EUnetHTA has contributed to establish a common methodology to evaluate clinical aspects (effectiveness or comparative effectiveness) of new technologies by developing the so-called 'core model' that provides practical guidance for the performance of core and rapid HTA reports [65]. In practice, the results of the HTA reports still continue to vary between countries, and a large majority of institutions and countries apply a wider scope than what is covered in the clinical domains of the HTA Core Model.

With EUnetHTA Joint Action 3 ending in 2020, the future of the HTA collaboration among European Union Member States is yet to be decided. Following up on an inception impact assessment in 2016 that presented policy options of different degrees of cooperation in HTA across European countries [66], the European Commission published a proposal in February 2018: this draft legislation proposes the establishment of a Member State Coordination Group on HTA that will act as the responsible authority to oversee joint work in the areas of joint clinical assessments, joint scientific consultations, the identification of emerging health technologies and voluntary cooperation [67].

approach to evaluate the properties, effects, and impacts of health technologies or intervention' [63].

VBP addresses one of the main drawbacks of EPR, namely the fact that it does not take into account value. With VBP, the value of new medicines is put into the centre, and tools such as CEA and HTA aim to result in more sound assessments. However, in order to perform HTA and pharmacoeconomic evaluations, extensive capacity-building is required. It has been discussed whether, or not, small countries require large HTA agencies, or if they could use evidence from other countries and translate it into their settings.

A major element of VBP is the WTP of public payers. If payers disclose their WTP, this could create an incentive for the development of products that generate increased added value [38,68]. It has been argued that by signalling their public health priorities (e.g., related to R&D), policy-makers and payers could become more active whereas the current pharmaceutical policy framework appeared to be supply-driven [69,70]. At the same time, VBP offers opportunities to industry for 'gaming', in particular in the choice of the comparators and the threshold [18]. In a VBP system with published cost-effectiveness thresholds, marketing authorisation holders are incentivized to price up to the threshold [71]. Furthermore, it might be sometimes difficult to identify what payers define as 'value'. In response, new approaches to assessing the value of medicines and other health technologies have been proposed and trialled, such as multi-criteria decision analysis [72].

In the 'Fair Pricing Forum' organised by the WHO, it was argued that 'a 'value-based' pricing model is not viable in many countries because it does not take into account affordability and total cost' [41].

13.5.2 Cost-Plus Pricing

Cost-plus pricing describes a policy that determines a medicine price by taking into account production costs, promotional expenses, investments into R&D, administration costs, overheads and profits. The manufacturer (or a supply chain actor) informs the pricing authority about the costs incurred and is granted a profit margin considered 'reasonable' that is determined based on these pieces of information provided. Cost-plus pricing may be applied at ex-factory, wholesale and retail price levels.

There is limited evidence about the implementation and outcomes of cost-plus pricing. Use of this pricing policy was reported from in several countries of the world, particularly in LMIC. Countries identified to use cost-plus pricing were Vietnam, China, Sri Lanka, Bangladesh, Iran and Pakistan but some countries (e.g., India, Colombia) have discontinued applying this pricing method [6,73]. In the European region, some countries (e.g., Cyprus – for locally produced generics, France, Greece, Spain, Slovakia, Turkey) used cost-plus in their pricing decisions 2 decades ago [74–76], but as of today (2018) no EU Member State uses a cost-plus pricing policy any longer.

The WHO Guideline on Country Pharmaceutical Pricing Policies recommends countries not to use cost-plus as an overall pharmaceutical pricing policy [6]. While there is a lack of analytic studies on the impacts of this pricing policy, no evidence has been identified to support the use of cost-plus pricing [6]. Apart from the critical decision about the extent of profit margin that policy-makers would consider 'reasonable', a major limitation of this policy is that pricing authorities depend on the manufacturer's information about their production and further costs. This could incentivize manufacturers to 'manipulation of costing data' [6] which may result in higher prices. Obtaining independent information is very difficult and practically impossible for most policy-makers.

While several countries discontinued using cost-plus as an overall pricing policy, authorities have been considering data on production cost and other costs as additional price information for the price negotiations (e.g., in Spain [77]).

In recent times, discussion has centred around implementing a 'new cost-plus pricing' policy, as a possible response to high prices of new medicines. It is not intended to re-install a cost-plus pricing policy that solely relies on costing data, but it has been proposed to use production costs as a threshold. This argument is brought forward in the light of some premium-priced medicines whose production costs only account for a tiny fraction of the prices charged. One aspect of this 'new cost-plus pricing' debate is the call for transparency of costing data. Research was conducted to assess production costs: for instance, manufacturing costs for 12-week courses of direct-acting antivirals to cure hepatitis C virus were estimated to be US$ 21–63 for ribavirin, US$ 10–30 for daclatasvir, US$ 68–136 for sofosbuvir, US$ 100–210 for faldaprevir and US$ 130–270 for simeprevir [78]. In some US states 'pharmaceutical cost transparency acts' were passed in 2016. Under these acts, it is mandatory for manufacturers to disclose their production costs of some high-priced medicines [79]. Despite these efforts to enhance transparency, there is still little knowledge about production costs and marketing costs, as well as about R&D costs (cf. also Section 13.5.7). Publications about assessments of R&D costs show large variation [1].

13.5.3 Conditional Pricing

Authorities may decide to link the price of a medicine to specific criteria such as health outcomes (i.e., 'success' of a medicine in the treatment of a disease). Industry may also propose conditions (e.g., procurement-relevant aspects such as a minimum number of units purchased or confidentiality in return for a discount). Conditional pricing is particularly applied to new medicines with uncertainty around their value, and in these cases real-world data about the effectiveness in clinical practice need to be collected. Conditional pricing falls under a variety of terms and taxonomies. 'Risk-sharing' and 'pay-for-performance' are commonly used terms to describe such pricing and reimbursement policies [80,81]. In the European Union, the notion 'managed-entry agreement(s)' (MEA) has been established as umbrella term for these conditional policies [35]. An MEA is defined as 'an arrangement between a [pharmaceutical] manufacturer and payer/provider that enables access to (coverage or reimbursement of) a health technology subject to specific conditions' [82].

Typically, MEA are distinguished into two categories: either financial-based (or non-health outcome-based) schemes or performance-based (or health outcome-based) schemes. Financial-based MEA may include (price or dose dependent) discounts, price or utilisation capping or price—volume agreements. Performance-based MEA are more complex in design and comprise, among others, variants such as outcome guarantees (i.e., an agreement where the manufacturer provides rebates, refunds or price adjustments if the product fails to meet the agreed outcome target), coverage with evidence development (i.e., reimbursement where additional data gathered in the context of clinical care would further clarify the impact of the medicine) and patient eligibility linked to patient registries to measure post-marketing clinical outcomes [35].

MEA are typically used for new medicines with high prices that are not affordable for public payers. Financial-based MEA are more common than performance-based MEA that are more difficult to handle. Nearly all high-income countries have implemented MEA, and there are indications about use of conditional pricing and reimbursement arrangements in upper-middle income countries and emerging markets [28,34—36,56,80,81,83,84].

Frequently, MEA are add-on arrangements taken after an initial price has been determined based on other pricing methods, usually EPR. In order to agree on a price that payers can afford, a lower (reimbursement) price is negotiated, taking the EPR benchmark as a starting point. The arrangements about conditions, including the discounted price, are usually kept confidential. There is interest on behalf of the industry to keep the officially communicated list prices high as other countries will refer to them through EPR. Thus, conditional pricing arrangements with confidential price information exercise negative spillover effects on other EPR-applying countries that risk overpaying [38] (cf. Section 13.2.7).

A conditional pricing arrangement likely offers the advantage to the procurer of getting (earlier) access to a medicine that would otherwise not be affordable. This is also beneficial for patients. Confidentiality, however, weakens the purchasing power of payers since they have no alternative but to trust the industry's promise that they 'got the best deal' [37]. Manufacturers may systematically ask for higher departing prices in expectation of an MEA [85]. It has been argued that by agreeing to MEA public payers implicitly accept to high (list) prices [86].

Apart from the prospect of getting lower prices, payers may also opt for conditional pricing because it allows them to manage uncertainty, particularly if evidence about the medicine's value is limited [35]. This is particularly the case for performance-based MEA that, in combination with patient registries, help collect real-life clinical data. It is advised to use conditional pricing with a disinvestment strategy as it might be difficult to stop funding at a later stage after patient expectations have been created [17].

While confidential discounts have been in place for a long time, the more formalised use of MEA and the increased use of performance-based agreements have been implemented more recently through experimenting and learning-by-doing. There is no standard methodology for MEA. Particularly performance-based MEA are challenging to implement, and data collection and monitoring of the progress can be time-intensive. Payers can encounter high administrative and transaction costs [80,85,87]. In addition to sufficient time resources, education and training of involved staff are required [88].

13.5.4 Internal Price Referencing

While external price referencing concerns a pricing policy in which 'external' prices, that is, prices from other countries, are considered, medicine prices in the same country are used for internal price referencing. Internal price referencing is defined as the 'practice of using the price(s) of identical medicines (ATC 5 level) or similar products (ATC 4 level) or even with therapeutic equivalent treatment (not necessarily a medicine) in a country in order to derive a benchmark or reference price for the purposes of setting or negotiating the price or reimbursement of the product in a given country' [89]. Thus, a prerequisite for this pricing policy is the availability of comparable medicines. Typically internal price referencing is done after patent expiry of a molecule and the launch of generic or biosimilar medicines.

A specific type of internal price referencing is the so-called generic price link. This policy refers to the practice of setting the price of a generic in relationship to the originator medicine, usually at a certain percentage lower than the originator price. The design of the generic price link policy may vary, with different percentage rates for first, second and subsequent generics coming into the market, and in some cases originator medicine prices might also be required to decrease after the market entry of generics. Internal price referencing can also be applied for parallel imported medicines and for biosimilar medicines.

As of 2016, 30 out of 42 surveyed countries (40 countries of the WHO European region, Canada and South Africa) reported to have a generic price link in place. 15 of these 30 countries with a 'generic price link' applied such a link policy also for biosimilar medicines (Austria, the Baltic States, Croatia, the Czech Republic, France, Iceland, Italy, Kazakhstan, Norway, Portugal, Romania, Slovakia and South Africa). A few countries with a 'generic price link' explicitly indicated not to use price linkages for biosimilar medicines (Belgium, Bulgaria, Finland and Turkey) while other countries applying a generic price link failed to report if they also used this policy to price biosimilar medicines [90].

If a linkage policy is applied for generics as well as for biosimilar medicines, the required difference between originator price and biosimilar price tends to be lower than the price difference between originator and generic. Thus, biosimilar medicines are granted higher prices. For instance, in the Czech Republic the first generic medicine had to be priced 32% below the originator, whereas the price of the first biosimilar had to be only 15% lower than the reference product. Few countries (Iceland, Italy, Kazakhstan, Latvia and South Africa) have same price differences for generic and biosimilar medicines, in comparison to originator and reference medicines, respectively [90].

Austria used to apply the same price difference for generic and biosimilar medicines but changed its legislation in April 2017. Since then, the first generic is priced at least 50% (48% prior to April 2017) below the price of the originator medicine that went off-patent. The second and each subsequent 'follower' is required to have a price difference related to the previously included generic: the price of the second generic has to be 18% (formerly 15%) lower than the one of the first generic, and the price of the third generic has to be 15% (formerly 10%) lower than the price of the second generic. The price of the originator product has to be reduced by at least 30% within 3 months after inclusion of the first generic into the reimbursement list, and with inclusion of the third generic into the reimbursement list the prices of the originator and the first and second generic must be reduced to the price of the third generic. Further generics have to offer price deductions of at least € 0.10 to be included in the reimbursement list. Price differences between biosimilars and the reference medicine have been stipulated as follows since April 2017: the first biosimilar medicine has to be priced at least 38% below the reference medicine. The price of the second biosimilar has to be at least 15% lower than the first biosimilar and the third biosimilar has to be priced at least 10% below the second biosimilar. For the remaining rules the same procedure as for generics applies (the reference medicine has to reduce its price by 30% within 3 months, for instance) [91].

A variant of internal price referencing is a so-called reference price system (RPS). Despite the term 'price' in its name it is rather a reimbursement policy. An RPS is defined as 'a reimbursement policy in which identical medicines (ATC 5 level) or similar medicines (ATC 4 level) are clustered (reference group). The third party payer funds a maximum amount (= reference price), while the patient must pay the difference between the reference price and the actual pharmacy retail price of the medicine, in addition to any co-payments (e.g. prescription fees, or percentage co-payment rates)'. An RPS encourages patients to ask for lower-priced generics (or biosimilar medicines) because they would otherwise be charged higher co-payments. RPS are in place in many high-income countries. As of 2017, 22 of the 28 EU Member States had an RPS (all but Austria, Cyprus, Luxembourg, Malta, Sweden and UK) [92].

Internal price referencing requires the availability of identical or similar medicines on the market. An RPS can complement a price link policy, and demand-side measures such as prescribing by International Non-Proprietary Name and generic substitution can support the effectiveness of the price link policy. However, a price link is rather static, and it has been argued that there are lost opportunities, since more competitive methods would likely achieve higher savings (see next section). An exploratory study on a few medicines in European countries showed that differences between originator and generic prices were higher in countries that had implemented competitive pricing policies in combination with demand-side measures to enhance generic uptake [93].

13.5.5 Competitive Pricing

Competitive pricing can be applied in settings where competition is possible, with multiple suppliers for same or similar medicines (e.g., therapeutic equivalents). Tendering and tendering-like procedures are mechanisms of competitive pricing and/or competitive procurement.

While the term 'procurement' refers more generally to the process of purchasing goods and services, tendering is a specific formal and competitive procurement procedure. In a tendering procedure, 'tenders (offers) are requested, received and evaluated for the procurement of goods, works or services, and as a consequence of which an award is made to the tenderer whose tender/offer is the most advantageous' [89]. In many cases, it is the (lowest) price that makes a bid most advantageous, but other criteria such as supply conditions, payment terms, frequency of delivery or packaging can also play a role [94].

Tendering is the key procurement method in the public sector in many countries over the world [95]. In high-income countries tendering mainly occurs in the hospital sector; it is done by individual hospitals and hospital groups or through pooling of regional hospital procurement at national level by procurement agencies [94]. Use of tendering, or tendering-like systems, in the outpatient sector is less frequent. It is in place in the outpatient off-patent sector in some European countries (e.g., Denmark, Germany, the Netherlands, Romania Slovenia) [96]. One example in this respect is the Dutch 'preferential pricing policy' that was introduced more than a decade ago. In 2005, all health insurers launched joint tenders for off-patent medicines in the outpatient sector. In 2008, they were no longer permitted to collectively run tenders (since Dutch health insurers should compete) and have been launching individual tenders since then. The range of medicines subject to the preferential pricing policy and the frequency of tenders vary between health insurers. Over time, tender terms tend to be extended, reaching durations of up to 1 or 2 years [97,98].

Strategic procurement considers the lifecycle of a medicine. Tendering, or other procurement methods, can achieve lower prices as soon as competition comes into play (usually starting with full or partial analogue competition between therapeutic alternatives, followed by generic, or biosimilar, competition). The price-reducing effect of competition has been shown, for instance for HIV/AIDS medicines. In Brazil, the price of HIV/AIDS medicines was reduced by 82% over 5 years due to generic competition whereas prices of medicines without generic competitor remained rather stable, falling 9% over the same period of time. For LMIC, a strong impact of the generic competition was observed in the price of AIDS triple-therapy that dropped from USD 10,000 per patient and year to USD 350 within 1 year [99]. However, competitive procurement practices bear the risk of shortages and non-availability of medicines, with suppliers being driven from the market. It was advised maintaining a naturally balanced competitive situation [100].

A study [98] that investigated the impacts of tendering for outpatient off-patent medicines in three European countries (Belgium, Denmark and the Netherlands) confirmed that competitive pricing was able to achieve high savings for public payers. In the Netherlands, savings due to tendering were estimated to amount to 352 million euro in 2009, 654 million euro in 2012 and 679 million euro in 2014 [101]. The study also pointed out the risk of non-availability of medicines if the policy has not been appropriately implemented. In none of the three investigated countries a withdrawal of companies from the market as a result of tendering could be confirmed. The study identified a robust legal and organisational framework, a strategy to avoid or, at least, deal with, shortages, an appropriate stakeholder management and demand-side policies to promote generic uptake as key prerequisites for a successful introduction of tendering [98]. While the 'winner-takes-it-all' principle is able to drive prices down to low levels, a 'divide-the-pie' strategy may be more appropriate to ensure a 'healthy market'.

13.5.6 Collaborative Pricing

Collaborative pricing is applied by a group of procurers (e.g., public payers, agencies) that jointly set the price of a medicine, or jointly purchase it. Collaborative pricing and procurement can be based on intra-country or cross-country cooperation. Two major policies that can be subsumed under collaborative pricing are differential pricing and joint procurement.

13.5.6.1 Differential Pricing

Differential pricing, also called tiered pricing, is based on the idea of having different prices for different purchasers. 'Price discrimination' and 'Ramsey pricing' are sometimes used as synonyms. These terms refer to business strategies of market players in the private sector: under price discrimination (Ramsey pricing) suppliers segment the market by differentiating consumer groups and charging different prices in accordance with perceived or assumed consumers' price elasticity and willingness-to-pay. In the field of medicines, this would translate into a company's strategy to charge higher prices to higher-income countries and lower prices to poorer economies. Interpreting differential pricing as government action, it describes a cross-country policy of setting the price of a medicine in accordance with the ability-to-pay and/or economic situation of the countries forming a collaboration, based on coordinated decisions taken by the public authorities of the involved countries or by an international organisation. Alternative names for these collaborative pricing approaches are equity pricing [102] and minimum-level pricing [103]. This section refers to differential pricing as a policy of governments and not as a business strategy.

Differential pricing has mainly been used in LMIC. Traditionally, it tended to be limited to few therapeutic areas (e.g., HIV/AIDS, malaria) or specific products (vaccines). Purchasers were frequently international organisations such as United Nations (UN) agencies [104]. Although differential pricing has not always been successful in improving patients' access to essential medicines, there were indications that for some least-developed countries access improved in situations in which medicines would otherwise have been unaffordable [104—106]. More recently, differential pricing has been implemented to increase access to medicines for non-communicable diseases, particularly as part of public—private partnerships to improve access [107,108]. Differential pricing is, in general, considered as a tool to contribute to improved access to medicines and not as a cost-containment measure. Generic competition has shown to reduce prices more effectively than differential pricing [106,109].

Given the launch of high-priced medicines in recent years, it has been discussed if high-income countries could use differential pricing, or similar collaborative pricing approaches, as an option to achieve fairer and more equitable medicine prices. For European countries, a commonly mentioned barrier for a successful implementation of differential pricing is parallel trade that is allowed in the EU. It would undermine the effectiveness of differential pricing if medicines with lower prices from lower-income countries would be exported to higher-income countries. It was argued that this challenge could be addressed through legal solutions: export bans and notifications could be imposed on medicines whose prices were set based on differential pricing. Some EU Member States that had faced large waves of parallel exports already applied such measures. A second frequently mentioned barrier to differential pricing is the widespread implementation of EPR since differential pricing and EPR are considered as mutually exclusive [110]. To respond to this limitation, cooperating countries could agree on not applying EPR for differentially priced medicines [13].

If differential pricing were applied as a collaborative approach of governments, the involved countries would need to agree on principles, mechanisms and rules. It would be key to reach a common understanding about the procedure (e.g., the extent of mark-downs or mark-ups to reflect the different ability-to-pay levels of countries). Having agreed on the differentiation of prices between the involved countries, the issue of how to set the starting price still needs to be settled, and an appropriate methodology has yet to be developed. While the Ramsey pricing *strategy* of pharmaceutical companies tends to be based on confidential discounts (in order not to reduce the EPR-based prices in other referring countries), a governments-run differential pricing *policy* must be transparent in terms of procedures as well as outcomes such as prices [99,103].

A study [13] exploring the feasibility of introducing differential pricing as a collaborative policy of EU Member States concluded that, though commonly mentioned limitations (existence of EPR and parallel trade) could be addressed, differential pricing did not seem to be a realistic policy option in the EU for the time being: it would require strong political commitment from ideally all EU Member States to agree on a collaborative framework. Against the backdrop of its limited feasibility in the EU, it has been suggested including traits of differential pricing, such as adjustments of prices for PPP, in the EPR methodology.

13.5.6.2 Joint Procurement

Another collaborative approach is joint procurement of medicines which aims to achieve efficiency gains through reduced information asymmetry and improved purchasing power. For instance, public purchasers may jointly negotiate. This may, or may not, lead to the same price for all parties involved.

In European countries, the topic of joint procurement is high on the political agenda. The 'sofosbuvir case' appears to have been a turning point in the debate on pharmaceutical policies. A French initiative in 2014 sought a collaborative approach with other European countries to get a lower price for sofosbuvir but it was not successful. In 2014, the 'Joint Procurement Agreement (JPA) of medical countermeasures' [111] (i.e., procurement of vaccines, for instance, to be prepared for an outbreak of a serious cross-border threat to health such as a pandemic) entered into force, and some EU Member States expressed hope that its scope could be extended to high-priced medicines against cancer and multiple sclerosis and orphan medicines. But for the time being, this is not intended [17].

As EU-wide joint procurement did not seem feasible in the short run, EU Member States started to seek cooperation between smaller groups of countries. In Europe, cross-country collaborations that also aim to jointly procure include the collaboration of Belgium, the Netherlands,

Luxembourg and Austria (called BeNeLuxA) [112], the Baltic Partnership Agreement of the three Baltic countries, the Romanian and Bulgarian Initiative and the Central Eastern European and South Eastern European Countries Initiative [113]. Cross-country cooperations for joint procurement also exist in other regions of the world: pooled procurement initiatives comprise the Southern African Development Community (SADC), of the East African Community, of the Organization of Eastern Caribbean States (OECS) Pharmaceutical Procurement Service and of the Gulf Cooperation Council (GCC) [114]. 27 Latin American and Caribbean countries signed agreements with the Pan American Health Organization (PAHO) to use the PAHO Strategic Fund which is a mechanism for pooled procurement of essential medicines and strategic health supplies that save lives [115].

Besides joint procurement, some cross-country collaborations (e.g., BeNeLuxA, the Nordic cooperation) also collaborate in other areas to improve their knowledge base and to be better prepared (e.g., sharing of information, horizon scanning) [17,113].

13.5.7 New Business Models ('Delinkage')

In the previous sections, approaches of how pricing authorities and procurers can set and determine medicine prices based on defined criteria and mechanisms were presented. The chapter would not be complete without, at least briefly, addressing the discussion about 'delinkage'.

The concept of 'delinkage' relates to a set of options that aim to change the way in which innovation is financed, by separating the costs of R&D and the price of the medicines (and other health products). More generally, it is used to refer to a call to fundamentally reform the R&D system [110] that is considered to be 'broken' [116,117].

The pharmaceutical industry has been justifying premium prices for new medicines (not all of them with added therapeutic benefit [118,119]) with its investments into R&D, and 'society tolerates — and even encourages — high prices for new medicines [...] to stimulate research and development (R&D) for new products' [110].

For years, experts engaged in the 'delinkage' debate have been stressing the lack of transparency with regard to actual R&D costs. The 2016 UN High Level Panel on Access to Medicines report [1] that also called for 'delinkage' showed the variation in costs to develop a new medicine that had been published, which presented data ranged from 4.2 billion USD (data published by a consulting company, PWC, in 2012) to the frequently quoted 2.6 billion USD of the Tufts Institute [120] and to considerably lower numbers published by Light and Warburton (180–231 million USD) [121] and by the Drugs for Neglected Diseases initiative (DNDi) (100–150 million euro). The DNDi figures took into account the attrition in the field of R&D for infectious diseases and the inherent risk of failure; otherwise DNDi reported costs of 30–40 million euro for the development of a new chemical entity [122].

Some experts have been arguing that the term 'delinkage' does not appropriately describe the intended policy options since, in practice, no link between prices and (unknown) R&D costs appears to exist. In addition, it has been recommended to take the share of public funding in the development of medicines into consideration since several new medicines marketed by pharmaceutical companies were initially developed by researchers that had received government funding for their research and whose start-up businesses were bought by 'big pharma' [123].

It has thus been proposed by some experts to talk of new (business) models instead of 'delinkage'. However, the discussion of these models is not new; it has been on-going for several years [124–126]. Proposed alternatives include expanding direct government funding of R&D, R&D subsidies and innovation inducement prizes (i.e., rewarding for the successful development of a new medicine by a cash prize) [127–130].

Experiences with, for example, the DNDi and the Medicines for Malaria Venture (MMV) highlight the potential of product development partnerships (PDP). These PDP have been dedicated to the R&D of medicines of neglected diseases using public and philanthropic funds, and have been able to develop medicines at relatively low costs [116,122].

Proponents of 'delinkage' have been urging to draw on the lessons learnt from PDP and to implement the piloted models at larger scales.

As for other policies (e.g., differential pricing, cf. Section 13.5.6.1), the debate has reached high-income countries. One reason is the high prices of new medicines that challenge the long-term sustainability of healthcare systems, and another one is the spread of antimicrobial resistance (AMR). New mechanisms for funding R&D have been proposed and trialled to incentivize the development of new effective antibiotics [117,131,132].

Information on 'delinkage' and new business models is not included in Table 13.4 because it is not considered to be a pricing policy. The debate, however, confirms that pricing policies are inter-connected with other pharmaceutical policy options.

13.5.8 Future Directions

Despite its limitations, EPR as a pricing policy is unlikely to disappear in the near future. While EPR methods can be improved by doing simulations and scenario analyses to inform changes, other limitations such as contributing to availability issues and non-transparency remain. This is why policy-makers should consider implementing it in conjunction with other policy instruments instead of using it as a stand-alone pricing policy.

REFERENCES

[1] United Nations Secretary General's High-Level Panel on Access to Medicines. Report of the United Nations secretary general's high-level panel on access to medicines. Promoting innovation and access to health technologies; September 2016.

[2] Council of the European Union. Council conclusions on strengthening the balance in the pharmaceutical systems in the EU and its Member States. June 17, 2016. Available from: http://www.consilium.europa.eu/press-releases-pdf/2016/6/47244642812_en.pdf.

[3] Xu K, Evans DB, Kawabata K, Zeramdini R, Klavus J, Murray CJ. Household catastrophic health expenditure: a multicountry analysis. The Lancet 2003;362(9378):111−7.

[4] Wagner AK, Graves AJ, Reiss SK, LeCates R, Zhang F, Ross-Degnan D. Access to care and medicines, burden of health care expenditures, and risk protection: results from the World Health Survey. Health Policy 2011;100(2):151−8.

[5] Cameron A, Ewen M, Ross-Degnan D, Ball D, Laing R. Medicine prices, availability, and affordability in 36 developing and middle-income countries: a secondary analysis. The Lancet 2009;373(9659):240−9.

[6] World Health Organization. WHO guideline on country pharmaceutical pricing policies. Geneva. 2013. Available from: http://apps.who.int/medicinedocs/documents/s21016en/s21016en.pdf.

[7] Windmeijer F, De Laat E, Douven R, Mot E. Pharmaceutical promotion and GP prescription behaviour. Health Economics 2006;15(1):5−18.

[8] Håkonsen H, Horn AM, Toverud E-L. Price control as a strategy for pharmaceutical cost containment—what has been achieved in Norway in the period 1994−2004? Health Policy 2009;90(2):277−85.

[9] Merkur S, Mossialos E. A pricing policy towards the sourcing of cheaper drugs in Cyprus. Health Policy 2007;81(2):368−75.

[10] Leopold C, Mantel-Teeuwisse AK, Seyfang L, Vogler S, de Joncheere K, Laing RO, et al. Impact of external price referencing on medicine prices−a price comparison among 14 European countries. Southern Med Review 2012;5(1):34−41.

[11] Filko M, Szilagyiova P. Case 3: the Slovak experience in the international price benchmarking for prescription drugs. Value in Health 2009;12(7):A229.

[12] Toumi M, Rémuzat C, Vataire A-L, Urbinati D. External reference pricing of medicinal products: simulation-based considerations for cross-country coordination. Final Report. European Commission; 2014. Available from: https://www.redaccionmedica.com/contenido/images/erp_reimbursement_medicinal_products_en-1.pdf.

[13] Vogler S, Lepuschütz L, Schneider P, Stühlinger V. Study on enhanced cross-country coordination in the area of pharmaceutical product pricing. Luxembourg: Gesundheit Österreich Forschungs- und Planungs GmbH; Publications Office of the European Commission; 2016. Available from: http://ec.europa.eu/health/systems_performance_assessment/docs/pharmaproductpricing_frep_en.pdf.
[14] Espin J, Rovira J, de Labry AO. Working paper 1: external price referencing – review series on pharmaceutical pricing policies and interventions. Geneva: World Health Organization and Health Action International; 2011. Available from: http://www.haiweb.org/medicineprices/24072012/ERPfinalMay2011.pdf.
[15] Vogler S, Leopold C, Zimmermann N, Habl C, de Joncheere K. The Pharmaceutical Pricing and Reimbursement Information (PPRI) initiative–experiences from engaging with pharmaceutical policy makers. Health Policy and Technology 2014;3(2):139–48.
[16] Pani L, Montilla S, Németh G, Russo P, Viceconte G, Vogler S. Balancing access to medicines and sustainability in Europe: an analysis from the network of competent authorities on pricing and reimbursement (CAPR). Pharmacological Research 2016;111:247–50.
[17] Vogler S, Paris V, Ferrario A, Wirtz VJ, de Joncheere K, Schneider P, et al. How can pricing and reimbursement policies improve affordable access to Medicines? Lessons learned from European countries. Applied Health Economics and Health Policy 2017:1–15.
[18] Kanavos P, Nicod E, Espin J. Short-and long-term effects of value-based pricing vs. External price referencing. London. 2010. Available from: http://whocc.goeg.at/Literaturliste/Dokumente/FurtherReading/Short-%20and%20long-term%20effect%20of%20value-based%20pricing.pdf.
[19] Rémuzat C, Urbinati D, Mzoughi O, El Hammi E, Belgaied W, Toumi M. Overview of external reference pricing systems in Europe. Journal of Market Access & Health Policy 2015;3.
[20] Danzon PM, Epstein AJ. Effects of regulation on drug launch and pricing in interdependent markets. Emerald Group Publishing Limited; 2008.
[21] Danzon PM, Towse A. Differential pricing for pharmaceuticals: reconciling access, R&D and patents. International Journal of Health Care Finance and Economics 2003;3(3):183–205.
[22] Danzon PM, Wang YR, Wang L. The impact of price regulation on the launch delay of new drugs—evidence from twenty-five major markets in the 1990s. Health Economics 2005;14(3):269–92.
[23] Kyle MK. Pharmaceutical price controls and entry strategies. The Review of Economics and Statistics 2007;89(1):88–99.
[24] Kanavos P, Fontrier A-M, Gill J, Efthymiadou O, Boekstein N. The impact of external reference pricing within and across countries. London: London School of Economics; 2017.
[25] Stargardt D-VT, Schreyögg J. Impact of cross-reference pricing on pharmaceutical prices. Applied Health Economics and Health Policy 2006;5(4):235–47.
[26] Vogler S, Schneider P, Zimmermann N. Development of average European medicine prices: implications for the methodology of external price referencing policy [submitted].
[27] Hofmarcher T, Jönsson B, Wilking N. Access to high-quality oncology care across Europe. 2014.
[28] Ferrario A. Access to cancer medicines in Europe: an analysis of existing challenges and countries' responses [thesis]. London: The London School of Economics and Political Science (LSE); 2016.

[29] De Weerdt E, Simoens S, Hombroeckx L, Casteels M, Huys I. Causes of drug shortages in the legal pharmaceutical framework. Regulatory Toxicology and Pharmacology 2015;71(2):251−8.
[30] PGEU. PGEU statement on medicine shortages in European community pharmacies. 2013.
[31] Pauwels K, Huys I, Casteels M, Simoens S. Drug shortages in European countries: a trade-off between market attractiveness and cost containment? BMC Health Services Research 2014;14(1):1−9.
[32] European Commission. Council Directive 89/105/EEC of 21 December 1988 relating to the transparency of measures regulating the prices of medicinal products for human use and their inclusion in the scope of national health insurance systems. 1988. Available from: http://eur-lex.europa.eu/LexUriServ/LexUriServ.do?uri=CELEX:31989L0105:en:HTML.
[33] Vogler S, Vitry A, Babar Z-U-D. Cancer drugs in 16 European countries, Australia, and New Zealand: a cross-country price comparison study. The Lancet Oncology 2016;17(1):39−47.
[34] Pauwels K, Huys I, Vogler S, Casteels M, Simoens S. Managed entry agreements for oncology drugs: lessons from the European experience to inform the future. Frontiers in Pharmacology 2017;8:171.
[35] Ferrario A, Kanavos P. Managed entry agreements for pharmaceuticals: the European experience. EMINet 2013.
[36] Morel T, Arickx F, Befrits G, Siviero P, van der Meijden C, Xoxi E, et al. Reconciling uncertainty of costs and outcomes with the need for access to orphan medicinal products: a comparative study of managed entry agreements across seven European countries. Orphanet Journal of Rare Diseases 2013;8:198.
[37] Vogler S, Paterson KR. Can price transparency contribute to more affordable patient access to medicines? PharmacoEconomics − Open 2017;1(3):145−7.
[38] Bouvy J, Vogler S. Background paper 8.3 pricing and reimbursement policies: impacts on innovation. In: World Health Organization, editor. Priority medicines for Europe and the world 2013 Update. Geneva: World Health Organization,; 2013. 8.3-1−8.3-74.
[39] Paris V, Belloni A. Value in pharmaceutical pricing. OECD Health Working Papers, No. 63. Paris: OECD Publishing; 2013.
[40] EFPIA. EFPIA position paper: principles for application of international reference pricing systems. July 16, 2014.
[41] World Health Organization (WHO). Fair pricing forum. 2017 Meeting Report. Geneva. 2017. Available from: http://www.who.int/medicines/access/fair_pricing/FairPricingForum2017MeetingReport.pdf?ua=1.
[42] Kanavos P, Vandoros S, Irwin R, Nicod E, Casson M. Differences in costs of and access to pharmaceutical products in the EU. Brussels: European Parliament; 2011.
[43] OECD. Pharmaceutical pricing policies in a global market. Paris: OECD; 2008.
[44] Pammolli F, Riccaboni M, Bonassi C. Health services in an open transatlantic market: a European perspective. Sleeping Giant: Awakening the Transatlantic Services Economy; 2007. p. 77.
[45] Leopold C, Mantel-Teeuwisse AK, Vogler S, de Joncheere K, Laing RO, Leufkens HGM. Is Europe still heading to a common price level for on-patent medicines? An exploratory study among 15 Western European countries. Health Policy 2013;112(3):209−16.
[46] Kyle MK, Allsbrook JS, Schulman KA. Does reimportation reduce price differences for prescription drugs? Lessons from the European union. Health Services Research 2008;43(4):1308−24.
[47] Europe Economics. External price referencing. London. 2013.

[48] Claxton K. Oft, Vbp: Qed? Health Economics 2007;16(6):545–58.
[49] Henry D. Economic analysis as an aid to subsidisation decisions. PharmacoEconomics 1992;1(1):54–67.
[50] Langley P. The role of pharmacoeconomic guidelines for formulary approval: the Australian experience. Clinical Therapeutics 1993;15(6):1154–76.
[51] Detsky AS. Guidelines for economic analysis of pharmaceutical products. PharmacoEconomics 1993;3(5):354–61.
[52] Davis P. Pharmaceuticals and public policy: learning from the New Zealand experience. Health Policy 1993;24(3):259–72.
[53] Johan P, Gunilla R, Peter S. PPRI pharma profile Sweden. Stockholm: Dental and Pharmaceutical Benefits Agency; 2017. Available from: http://whocc.goeg.at/Literaturliste/Dokumente/CountryInformationReports/PPRI_Pharma_Profile_Sweden_2017.pdf.
[54] Claxton K, Sculpher M, Carroll S. Value-based pricing for pharmaceuticals: its role, specification and prospects in a newly devolved NHS. CHE Research Paper 60 2011.
[55] Rafferty J. NICE and value based pricing—is this the end. BMJ; 2014.
[56] WHO Regional Office for Europe. Access to new medicines in Europe: technical review of policy initiatives and opportunities for collaboration and research. Copenhagen. 2015.
[57] Simoens S, Picavet E, Dooms M, Cassiman D, Morel T. Cost-effectiveness assessment of orphan drugs: a scientific and political conundrum. Applied Health Economics and Health Policy 2013;11(1):1.
[58] McCabe C, Claxton K, Culyer AJ. The NICE cost-effectiveness threshold. PharmacoEconomics 2008;26(9):733–44.
[59] Barham L. Three NICE thresholds for cost-effectiveness: does that make sense?. November 25, 2016. Available from: https://pharmaphorum.com/views-and-analysis/three-nice-thresholds-for-cost-effectiveness-does-that-make-sense/.
[60] Shiroiwa T, Sung Y-K, Fukuda T, Lang H-C, Bae S-C, Tsutani K. International survey on willingness-to-pay (WTP) for one additional QALY gained: what is the threshold of cost effectiveness? Health Economics 2010;19(4):422–37.
[61] EunetHTA. What is Health Technology Assessment? Available from: http://www.eunethta.eu/about-us/faq#t287n73.
[62] Patera N-G, Wild C. Assessment – APPRAISAL – decision: (good) practice examples and recommendations. Decision Support Document Nr. 72 2014. Available from: http://eprints.hta.lbg.ac.at/1036.
[63] World Health Organization. 2015 global survey on health technology assessment by national authorities. 2015. Geneva.
[64] European Commission. European network for health technology assessment [EUnetHTA] [2005110]. Available from: https://webgate.ec.europa.eu/chafea_pdb/health/projects/2005110/summary (accessed 6 February 2018).
[65] EunetHTA. HTA core model online. October 2017. Available from: https://meka.thl.fi/htacore/.
[66] European Commission. Inception impact assessment – strengthening of the EU cooperation on health technology assessment (HTA). 2016. Available from: http://ec.europa.eu/smart-regulation/roadmaps/docs/2016_sante_144_health_technology_assessments_en.pdf.
[67] European Commission. Proposal for a regulation of the European Parliament and of the Council on health technology assessment and amending directive 2011/24/EU. Brussels, 2018. Available from: https://ec.europa.eu/health/sites/health/files/technology_assessment/docs/com2018_51final_en.pdf.

[68] Godman B, Gustafsson LL. A new reimbursement system for innovative pharmaceuticals combining value-based and free market pricing. Applied Health Economics and Health Policy 2013;11(1):79.
[69] Consultative Expert Working Group on Research and Development. Follow-up of the report of the consultative expert working group on research and development. Financing and Coordination (CEWG); 2016. Available from: http://www.who.int/phi/cewg/en/.
[70] Franken M, le Polain M, Cleemput I, Koopmanschap M. Similarities and differences between five European drug reimbursement systems. International Journal of Technology Assessment in Health Care 2012;28(4):349.
[71] Hughes DA. Value-based pricing. Incentive for innovation or zero net benefit? PharmacoEconomics 2011;29(9):731–5.
[72] Angelis A, Kanavos P. Value-based assessment of new medical technologies: towards a robust methodological framework for the application of multiple criteria decision analysis in the context of health technology assessment. PharmacoEconomics 2016;34(5):435–46.
[73] Nguyen TA, Knight R, Roughead EE, Brooks G, Mant A. Policy options for pharmaceutical pricing and purchasing: issues for low-and middle-income countries. Health Policy and Planning 2014:czt105.
[74] Kanavos P. Financing pharmaceuticals in transition economies. Croatian Medical Journal 1999;40:244–59.
[75] Vogler S, Habl C, Leopold C, Rosian-Schikuta I, de Joncheere K, Lyager Thomsen T. PPRI report. Vienna: Pharmaceutical Pricing and Reimbursement Information; 2008.
[76] Vural IE. Politics, reforms, and regulation of pharma prices and expenditures in Turkey over the 2000s. Pharmaceutical prices in the 21st century. Springer; 2015. p. 267–95.
[77] Martinez V, Ferré de la Peña P, Izquierdo G, Lens Cabrera C. PHIS pharma profile Spain. Vienna: Pharmaceutical Health Information System (PHIS); 2010.
[78] Hill A, Khoo S, Fortunak J, Simmons B, Ford N. Minimum costs for producing hepatitis C direct-acting antivirals for use in large-scale treatment access programs in developing countries. Clinical Infectious Diseases 2014;58(7):928–36.
[79] Sullivan T. New York introduces pharmaceutical cost transparency bill: policy and medicines. May 18, 2016. Available from: http://www.policymed.com/2015/05/new-york-introduces-pharmaceutical-cost-transparency-bill.html.
[80] Carlson JJ, Sullivan SD, Garrison LP, Neumann PJ, Veenstra DL. Linking payment to health outcomes: a taxonomy and examination of performance-based reimbursement schemes between healthcare payers and manufacturers. Health Policy 2010;96(3):179–90.
[81] Garrison LP, Towse A, Briggs A, de Pouvourville G, Grueger J, Mohr PE, et al. Performance-based risk-sharing arrangements—good practices for design, implementation, and evaluation: report of the ISPOR good practices for performance-based risk-sharing arrangements task force. Value in Health 2013;16(5):703–19.
[82] Klemp M, Frønsdal KB, Facey K. What principles should govern the use of managed entry agreements? International Journal of Technology Assessment in Health Care 2011;27(01):77–83.
[83] Neumann PJ, Chambers JD, Simon F, Meckley LM. Risk-sharing arrangements that link payment for drugs to health outcomes are proving hard to implement. Health Affairs 2011;30(12):2329–37.
[84] Babar Z-U-D. Pharmaceutical prices in the 21st century. Springer; 2015.

[85] Sophie G, Mattias N, Lorena SM, Irm V, Nancy T, Irina C. How to improve the Belgian process for managed entry agreements? An analysis of the Belgian and international experience. Brussels: Belgian Health Care Knowledge Centre (KCE); 2017.
[86] Vogler S, Zimmermann N, Ferrario A, Wirtz VJ, de Joncheere K, Pedersen HB, et al. Pharmaceutical policies in a crisis? Challenges and solutions identified at the PPRI Conference. Journal of Pharmaceutical Policy and Practice 2016;9(1):1.
[87] Adamski J, Godman B, Ofierska-Sujkowska G, Osinska B, Herholz H, Wendykowska K, et al. Risk sharing arrangements for pharmaceuticals: potential considerations and recommendations for European payers. BMC Health Services Research 2010;10:153.
[88] Lieven A, Luca P. Dynamic outcomes based approaches to pricing and reimbursement of innovative medicines. 2017.
[89] WHO Collaborating Centre for Pharmaceutical Pricing, Reimbursement Policies. Glossary of pharmaceutical terms. Update 2016. Vienna. 2016. Available from: http://whocc.goeg.at/Literaturliste/Dokumente/MethodologyTemplate/Glossary_Update2016_final.pdf.
[90] Vogler S, Schneider P. Do pricing and usage-enhancing policies differ between biosimilars and generics? Findings from an international survey. Generics and Biosimilars Initiative (GaBI) Journal 2017;6(2):79–88.
[91] Zimmermann N, Rainer L. Short PPRIPharma profile Austria 2017. Vienna: Gesundheit Österreich GmbH (GÖG); 2018.
[92] Gombocz M, Zimmermann N. Maßnahmen zur Einbindung von Patientinnen und Patienten in die ökonomische Verschreibung von Medikamenten [Interventions for patient involvement to enhance a more rational prescribing of medicines]. Vienna: Gesundheit Österreich Forschungs- und Planungs GmbH; 2017.
[93] Vogler S. How large are the differences between originator and generic prices? Analysis of five molecules in 16 European countries. Farmeconomia Health Economics and Therapeutic Pathways 2012;13(Suppl. 3):29–41.
[94] Vogler S, Habl C, Leopold C, Mazag J, Morak S, Zimmermann N. PHIS hospital pharma report. Vienna: Pharmaceutical Health Information System (PHIS); Commissioned by the European Commission and the Austrian Federal Ministry of Health; 2010. Available from: http://whocc.goeg.at/Literaturliste/Dokumente/BooksReports/PHIS_Hospital%20Pharma_Report.pdf.
[95] Seiter A. A practical approach to pharmaceutical policy. Washington DC: World Bank Publications; 2010.
[96] Dylst P, Vulto A, Simoens S. Tendering for outpatient prescription pharmaceuticals: what can be learned from current practices in Europe? Health Policy 2011;101(2):146–52.
[97] Kanavos P. Tender systems for outpatient pharmaceuticals in the European Union: evidence from The Netherlands and Germany. London: EMINET; January. 2012. Available from: http://www.progenerika.de/wp-content/uploads/2013/02/Anlage-2_Tendering-Report-EMINET-13OCT2012-FINAL.pdf.
[98] Vogler S, Gombocz M, Zimmermann N. Tendering for off-patent outpatient medicines: lessons learned from experiences in Belgium, Denmark and The Netherlands. Journal of Pharmaceutical Health Services Research 2017;8(3):147–58.
[99] T'Hoen E, Moon S, Pecoul B. Pills and pocketbooks. 2001.
[100] Ferrario A, Kanavos P, Humbert T, Iwamoto K, Bak Pedersen H. Challenges and opportunities in improving access to medicines through efficient public procurement in WHO European Region. Copenhagen. 2016.

[101] Zorginstituut Nederland. GIPeilingen 2014. Ontwikkelingen genees- en hulpmiddelengebruik [GIPeilingen 2014. Developments in pharmaceutical and medical products' use]. Diehmen: Genees- en hulpmiddelen Informatie Project; 2015. Available from: https://www.zorginstituutnederland.nl/binaries/zinl/documenten/publicatie/2015/10/27/gipeilingen-2014/gipeilingen-2014.pdf.
[102] Rovira J. Can EU citizens afford their medicines? The financial crisis and access to medicines in Europe. Presentation. Brussels: High Level Meeting. The European Parliament; 2013.
[103] Mossialos E, Dukes G. Affordably priced new drugs for poor populations: approaches for a global solution. The International Journal of Risk & Safety in Medicine 2000;14(1):1–29.
[104] Babar ZUD, Atif M. Differential pricing of pharmaceuticals: a bibliometric review of the literature. Journal of Pharmaceutical Health Services Research 2014;5(3):149–56.
[105] Yadav P. Differential pricing of pharmaceuticals: review of current knowledge, new findings and ideas for action. Zaragoza: MIT Zaragoza International Logistics Program; 2010.
[106] Moon S, Jambert E, Childs M, von Schoen-Angerer T. A 'win-win solution?': A critical analysis of tiered pricing to improve access to medicines in developing countries. Globalization and Health 2011;7:39.
[107] Access and affordability initiative. Access accelerated. 2018. Available from: https://accessaccelerated.org/initiative/access-and-affordability-initiative/.
[108] The New York Times. As cancer tears through Africa, drug makers draw up a battle plan. October 7, 2017. Available from: https://www.nytimes.com/2017/10/07/health/africa-cancer-drugs.html.
[109] Waning B, Kaplan W, King AC, Lawrence DA, Leufkens HG, Fox MP. Global strategies to reduce the price of antiretroviral medicines: evidence from transactional databases. Bulletin of the World Health Organization 2009;87(7):520–8.
[110] UNITAID. An economic perspective on delinking the cost of R+D from the price of medicines. Discussion paper. Geneva: World Health Organization; 2016.
[111] European Commission. Medical Countermeasures that could be procured in common under the joint procurement agreement. 2014. Available from: http://ec.europa.eu/health/preparedness_response/docs/jpa_note_scope_en.pdf. Luxembourg.
[112] BeNeLuxA Initiative. BeNeLuxA. Available from: http://www.beneluxa.org.
[113] Espín J, Rovira J, Calleja A, Azzopardi-Muscat N, Richardson E, Palm W, et al. How can voluntary cross-border collaboration in public procurement improve access to health technologies in Europe? Policy Brief 2016:21.
[114] TForG. GCC pooled procurement approach – focus on the Kingdom of Saudi Arabia. 2017. Available from: https://www.tforg.com/how-we-think/sweetspot-blog/2015/06/08/a-gcc-pooled-procurement-approach-focus-on-the-kingdom-of-saudi-arabia/.
[115] Pan American Health Organization. PAHO strategic fund. 2017. Available from: http://www.paho.org/hq/index.php?option=com_content&view=article&id=12163&Itemid=42005&lang=en.
[116] Moon S, Bermudez J, t Hoen E. Innovation and access to medicines for neglected populations: could a treaty address a broken pharmaceutical R& system? PLoS Medicine 2012;9(5):e1001218.
[117] Outterson K, Powers JH, Daniel GW, McClellan MB. Repairing the broken market for antibiotic innovation. Health Affairs 2015;34(2):277–85.
[118] OECD. New Health Technologies: Managing access, value and sustainability. Paris: OECD Publishing; 2017.
[119] Schwabe U, Paffrath D, Ludwig W-D, Klauber J. Arzneiverordnungs-report 2017. Berlin: Springer; 2017.

[120] DiMasi JA, Hansen RW, Grabowski HG. The price of innovation: new estimates of drug development costs. Journal of Health Economics 2003;22(2):151–85.
[121] Light DW, Warburton R. Demythologizing the high costs of pharmaceutical research. BioSocieties 2011;6(1):34–50.
[122] DNDi. An innovative approach to R&D for neglected patients: ten years of experience and lessons learned by DNDi. Drugs for Neglected Diseases (DNDi); 2014.
[123] Ministry of Health Welfare, Sport. Summary of medicines plan. The Hague. 2016. Available from: http://english.eu2016.nl/binaries/eu2016-en/documents/publications/2016/03/1/summary-of-medicins/summary-of-medicines-plan.pdf.
[124] World Health Organization. Global strategy and plan of action on public health, innovation and intellectual property. Geneva. 2011.
[125] Velásquez G, Seuba X. Rethinking global health: a binding convention for R&D for pharmaceutical products. South Center Research Papers 2011;42:29.
[126] Røttingen J-A, Chamas C. A new deal for global health R&D? The recommendations of the consultative expert working group on research and development (CEWG). PLoS Medicine 2012;9(5):e1001219.
[127] Knowledge Ecology International (KEI). Delinkage.org. Available from: http://delinkage.org/.
[128] Jayadev A, Stiglitz J. Two ideas to increase innovation and reduce pharmaceutical costs and prices. Health Affairs 2009;28(1):w165–8.
[129] Love J, Hubbard T. Bid idea: prizes to stimulate R& (and) D for new medicines, the. Chi-Kent L Rev 2007;82:1519.
[130] Agitha T. Alternative incentive models delinking R&D costs from pharmaceutical product price. Journal of Intellectual Property Rights 2013;18(5):491–8.
[131] The Review on Antimicrobial Resistance. Tackling drug-resistent infections globally. London: Final Report and Recommendations; 2016.
[132] So AD, Shah TA. New business models for antibiotic innovation. Uppsala Journal of Medical Sciences 2014;119(2):176–80.

CHAPTER 14

Policy Guidance

Sabine Vogler
WHO Collaborating Centre for Pharmaceutical Pricing and Reimbursement Policies, Pharmacoeconomics Department, Gesundheit Österreich GmbH (GÖG/Austrian Public Health Institute), Vienna, Austria

LIST OF ABBREVIATIONS

EC	European Commission
EMINet	European Medicines Information Network
EPR	External price referencing
EU	European Union
Euripid	EURopean Integrated Price Information Database
GDP	Gross domestic product
HAI	Health Action International
LMIC	Low- and middle-income countries
P	Principle
PPP	Purchasing power parities
PPRI	Pharmaceutical pricing and reimbursement information
WHO	World Health Organization

The previous chapters in Part 3 highlighted the relevance of medicine price comparisons for policy-making. Although there is a toolbox of different pricing policies, some of which are only relevant for selected medicine groups (e.g., off-patent medicines), the policy of external price referencing (EPR) has increasingly gained importance and is meanwhile applied in several countries over the world. As any policy, EPR has benefits and limitations, and as outlined in Chapter 13, its capacity as an effective policy in terms of defined objectives also depends on methodological choices.

In several countries, particular low- and middle-income countries (LMIC), medicine prices are not regulated. This can be attributable for intracountry price variation, high prices, and excessive out-of-pocket payments for patients because in countries without price regulation medicines are usually not funded, or cofunded, by public payers. To address these challenges and to offer protection from catastrophic payments on medicines, an increasing number of LMIC has been introducing price

Medicine Price Surveys, Analyses, and Comparisons
ISBN 978-0-12-813166-4
https://doi.org/10.1016/B978-0-12-813166-4.00020-6

regulation for parts of the medicines. In doing so, policy-makers have been asking for advice, in particular on the two following dimensions:

- *Which* pricing policy should be introduced? Is the EPR policy, commonly used by peer countries, considered as an appropriate option?
- *How* should EPR be implemented? Which methodological choices should be taken?

Policy-makers expect answers from international and supranational organizations and donor institutions. Some of these institutions produced, or commissioned, guidance documents (or studies whose findings allowed conclusions) that addressed the abovementioned questions, or one of them. The Guideline on Country Pharmaceutical Pricing Policies of the World Health Organization (WHO) is of key importance in this context. Therefore, a subchapter is devoted to this Guideline (Chapter 14.1), and Chapter 14.2 presents a few further guidance documents that relate to EPR. Only publications that address this policy at a global metalevel are presented; documents that relate to a specific country situation were excluded. The focus is on publication of supranational and international organizations (as authors, editors, or commissioners). Overall, there is paucity of guidance documents of EPR.

14.1 WORLD HEALTH ORGANIZATION GUIDELINE ON COUNTRY PHARMACEUTICAL PRICING POLICIES

The WHO Guideline on Country Pharmaceutical Pricing Policies was developed in 2011, and the final document [1] was published in 2013.

The guideline followed up on previous efforts and initiatives of WHO to improve medicines availability and affordability worldwide, in particular in LMIC. Such activities included, for instance, development of a standard survey methodology for measuring medicines prices and availability (the so-called WHO/Health Action International (HAI) methodology [2,3] that was described in Chapter 6.2) and its implementation for price surveys in several countries (see Chapter 2 for studies using the WHO/HAI methodology). In particular, the Guideline was built on a series of six reviews about different policies and aspects of medicine price management that were performed as part of the WHO/HAI project and were completed before the drafting of the Guideline (for information and recommendations made in the WHO/HAI policy review on EPR [4] see Chapter 14.2).

The scope of the Guideline was determined by three overarching policy questions:

1. Should countries use price control measures to manage medicine prices?
2. Should countries adopt measures to control add-on costs in the supply chain?
3. Should countries promote the use of quality-assured generic medicines as a strategy to manage medicine prices?

In case of a positive answer of these overarching questions, more specific questions were explored. With regard to the first question on price control, a subquestion was whether, or not, EPR could be effective in LMIC. Two other questions concerned the possible effectiveness of health technology assessments and cost plus price setting in LMIC.

The Guideline advocated the use of a combination of different pricing policies for medicines that should be carefully selected based on the objective, context, and health system. Transparency related to the policies, processes, and decisions was recommended, and the Guideline called for effective implementation and monitoring.

With regard to EPR, the WHO Guideline on Country Pharmaceutical Pricing Policies recommends considering its use, ideally as part of an overall strategy, and in combination with other pricing policies and methods. The Guideline also provides some advice with regard to the methodological choices for EPR. One recommendation asks for transparency of methods and processes, thus supplementing the general recommendation under "key principles", and another recommendation provides guidance with regard to selection criteria for reference countries: the choice of these countries is recommended to be "based on economic status, pharmaceutical pricing systems in place, the publication of actual versus negotiated or concealed prices, exact comparator products supplied, and similar burden of disease" [1]. The full wording of the recommendation on EPR and key principles of the Guideline is presented in Box 14.1.

In addition to the recommendations, the Guideline document provides background information based on collected evidence and expertise of panel members. It was stressed that the incorrect choice of reference countries is a major risk, that published prices do not necessarily reflect actual discounted and typically confidential prices, that verification of data sources of reference countries may be difficult, and that EPR may be deceptively perceived as a simple policy [1]. Although not part of the recommendations, the Guideline document also lists some requirements for the implementation of the EPR policy (Table 14.1).

Box 14.1 Recommendation on external price referencing (EPR) and key principles of the WHO Guideline on Country Pharmaceutical Pricing Policies

Use of EPR—Recommendation

Countries should consider using external reference pricing as a method for negotiating or benchmarking the price of a medicine.

Countries should consider using external reference pricing as part of an overall strategy, in combination with other methods, for setting the price of a medicine.

In developing an external reference pricing system, countries should define transparent methods and processes to be used.

Countries/payers should select comparator countries to use for EPR based on economic status, pharmaceutical pricing systems in place, the publication of actual versus negotiated or concealed prices, exact comparator products supplied, and similar burden of disease.

Key Principles

Countries should use a combination of different pharmaceutical pricing policies that should be selected based on the objective, context, and health system.

Countries should make their pricing policies, processes, and decisions transparent.

Pricing policies should have an appropriate legislative framework and governance and administrative structures, supported by technical capacity, and should be regularly reviewed, monitored (including actual prices), and evaluated and amended as necessary.

In promoting the use of affordable medicines, countries should employ a combination of pharmaceutical policies that address both supply and demand issues.

If regulation of pharmaceutical prices is introduced, effective implementation will be required to ensure compliance (e.g., incentives, enforcement, price monitoring system, fines).

Countries should adopt policies to promote the use of quality-assured generic medicines to increase access and affordability.

Countries should collaborate to promote exchange of information about policies, their impacts, and pharmaceutical prices.

Note: In the Guideline, the abbreviation "EPR" is used for external price referencing/external reference pricing. For consistency, it was changed to EPR.

From World Health Organization. WHO guideline on country pharmaceutical pricing policies. Geneva; 2013. Available from: http://apps.who.int/medicinedocs/documents/s21016en/s21016en.pdf.

Table 14.1 Implementation issues for external price referencing (EPR) addressed in the WHO Guideline on Country Pharmaceutical Pricing Policies

Dimension	Issues to be considered for the implementation of EPR
Technical capacity	Database management, data analysis
Data required	True negotiated prices rather than shadow prices
Infrastructure	Legislative framework for use of EPR
	Procedures on how to apply EPR, including criteria for choice of reference countries
	Procedures on how EPR feeds into the decision-making process
	A mechanism for monitoring the magnitude of applied mark-ups and medicine prices
Methodological considerations	Selection or calculation of the reference price (e.g., lowest price in the set, simple average of all products, weighted average)
	Date of the price in the reference countries (e.g., current price vs. price at launch)
	Adjustments required to account for confidential discounts or rebates in list prices and for level of economic development

From World Health Organization. WHO guideline on country pharmaceutical pricing policies. Geneva; 2013. Available from: http://apps.who.int/medicinedocs/documents/s21016en/s21016en.pdf.

14.2 FURTHER GUIDANCE DOCUMENTS OF EXTERNAL PRICE REFERENCING

Although limitations and benefits of EPR have been addressed in several research and policy papers (cf. Chapters 13.1 and 13.2), only few publications can be considered as guidance documents. Table 14.2 provides an overview of identified publications that either advice policy-makers about the use or nonuse of EPR under specific conditions or provide guidance on methodology and implementation issues.

As mentioned in Chapter 14.1, the WHO Guideline on Country Pharmaceutical Pricing Policies was based on the evidence collected, one of which was the WHO/HAI policy review on EPR [4]. This review discussed the feasibility of EPR and was also rather specific on implementation aspects by offering a checklist of issues and options to be considered when designing an EPR policy. The review proposed considering 11 elements as follows:

1. Single or multiple approaches for pricing (e.g., is EPR the sole approach, or is it applied together with other approaches?)
2. Scope of medicines regulated by EPR (e.g., all medicines, on-patent medicines, off-patent medicines, reimbursable medicines)

Table 14.2 Summary of recommendations on external price referencing (EPR) and its implementation in a selection of policy guidance documents

Title (short)	Type of publication and institution[1]	Recommendations on use of EPR	Recommendations on methodological choices	Ref.
Espin et al. (2011)	Review, part of the WHO/HAI review series on pricing policies	Recommendation to countries to consider the appropriateness of EPR by taking into account all alternative pricing policy options. It was argued that the use of EPR appears to be more justified for small, low-income countries, which might not have the technical capacity or the resources required for more complex price regulation mechanisms. Recommendation to implement EPR as objective and transparent as possible.	Checklist of issues to be considered: Single or multiple approaches for pricing; scope of medicines regulated by EPR, number of reference countries and criteria for their selection; sources of price information; type of price used for setting the price; formula or procedure to derive the price from the prices in the reference countries; exchange rate; procedure if price data from reference countries are not available; updates and revision; enforcement; monitoring and evaluation.	[4]
WHO 2013	WHO Guideline	Recommendation to consider the use of EPR as part of an overall strategy and in combination with other pricing policies	Recommendation addresses the choice of the reference countries, and in the background document of the Guideline considerations about the technical implementation are made.	[1]
Toumi et al. (2014)	Research study, commissioned by EC[2]	No explicit recommendation on the use or nonuse of EPR; however, EPR is considered as "an appropriate way forward for some countries" that "represents a flexible and efficient tool for decision makers"	Impact of frequent price revisions, iterative price cuts, large country baskets, price calculation methods, genericization impact and prices' sources were indicated as influent parameters.	[5]

Vogler et al. (2016)	Research study, commissioned by EC[2]	No recommendation on the use or nonuse of EPR	Four options for improvement are proposed: **1.** European price data base **2.** Reference to discounted prices **3.** Regular price reviews and revisions **4.** Consideration of economic indicators to weight price data	[6]
Schneider/ Habl (2017)	Best practice report as basis for development of a guidance document, commissioned by EC[2]	No recommendation on the use or nonuse of EPR	Seventeen principles for best practice in the use of EPR grouped around three overarching key principles: **1.** Clear objectives of pharmaceutical pricing that are harmonized with health system objectives and reviewed periodically **2.** Establishment of EPR in a simple and manageable way **3.** Well-defined methodology of price survey, with clear rules	[7]

EC, European Commission; *EPR*, external price referencing; *PPP*, Purchasing Power Parity/ies; *Ref.*, reference; *WHO*, World Health Organization.
[1]International or supranational institution that edited or commissioned the study and/or guidance document. No further publications (e.g., commissioned by other stakeholders such as pharmaceutical industry) were included.
[2]Disclaimer to be noted: The European Commission stressed that the content of the study represents the views of the contractor and is its sole responsibility, and it can in no way be taken to reflect the views of the EC.
Source: From the author

3. Number of reference countries and criteria for selecting them (e.g., low-priced countries, accessible price data, early entry of new medicines, socioeconomic similarities, similar policy objectives, neighboring countries)
4. Sources of price information (e.g., asking applicants, public official databases, ad hoc requesting of specific price information to authorities in other countries)
5. Type of price used for setting the price (e.g., transaction price vs. list price, exfactory price vs. importation price or retail price)
6. Formula or procedure to derive the price from the prices in the reference countries (e.g., average price, average price adjusted by gross domestic product (GDP) per capita, median price, lowest price)
7. Exchange rate (e.g., source, updates)
8. Procedure if price data from reference countries are not available when needed (e.g., use of available prices, inclusion of additional reference countries, provisional use of available price data, and revision as soon as further prices become available)
9. Updating and revision of the price based on EPR (e.g., use of EPR only for setting the initial launch price, periodic updates, and revisions)
10. Enforcement (e.g., rigid enforcement vs. use as a benchmark for negotiation)
11. Monitoring and evaluation (no monitoring and evaluation vs. comprehensive and rigorous monitoring and evaluation)

In the course of the last decade, the European Commission (EC) commissioned a few studies that aimed to investigate the practice and impacts of EPR with regard to defined policy objectives. Under the auspices of the EMINet (European Medicines Information Network) project (i.e. a consortium of three research institutions—Gesundheit Österreich GmbH, London School of Economics, and Andalusian School of Public Health— that collected evidence about pricing and reimbursement policies to support EU Member States), a comparative assessment of EPR and value-based pricing was conducted, and benefits and limitations of both policies were identified [8]. However, no recommendation on the use of EPR or methodological choices was made. This was also the case for another EC-commissioned study on EPR published in 2014 that ran different simulation scenarios on EPR with the aim to identify and assess EPR cross-country coordination issues [5]. Only one of the recently EC-commissioned studies provided guidance about EPR to policymakers: Although a recommendation about the use or nonuse of EPR was not its scope, the "study on enhanced cross-country coordination in the area of pharmaceutical product pricing" [6] aimed to explore improvements in the current EPR practice in European countries in terms of increased patients' access to medicines and savings for public payers. The study proposed four methodological and procedural options for improving EPR:

- European medicine price database:
  A European medicine price database, such as the existing Euripid database (cf. Chapter 8.2.2 and below), is considered to be extremely supportive for national public authorities that perform EPR and require easy access to reliable price data of their reference countries.
- Reference to discounted prices:
  With regard to cost-containment, the study suggested referencing to the "real prices" that are actually paid by the authorities in the reference countries because, as shown in simulations, this could decrease the prices. However, these discounted prices are typically agreed in confidential negotiations and are thus not known. As a back-up strategy, the study recommended considering at least price reductions resulting from statutory discounts (i.e., publicly available discounts based on legal provisions).
- Regular price reviews and revisions:
  Because periodic monitoring and subsequent price revisions are not systemically done in several countries, regular revisions were recommended. Given the strategic launch sequencing related to EPR (i.e., medicines are marketed with delay in lower-priced countries, see also Chapter 13.2), the implementation of this recommendation likely contributes to the cost-containment objective. Industry could also benefit from revisions in case of price increases.
- Adaptation of the EPR formulae by consideration of economic indicators to weight prices:
  As a proposal for improved access to medicines, it was suggested adjusting the price data of the reference countries by purchasing power parities (PPP) instead of applying nominal exchange rates, or by taking into account economic indicators such as GDP per capita. It was argued that this would introduce an element of fairness in the EPR policy. Furthermore, the lower prices (that are referred to) in lower-income countries are expected to contribute to better patient access to medicines, or at least fewer delays in accessibility in these countries.

A guidance document of major importance in this context is expected from the Euripid Collaboration. As described in Chapter 8.2.2 in Part 2, Euripid is the acronym for the EURopean Integrated Price Information Database that was established by the Hungarian National Health Insurance Fund Administration with the support of an EC grant (2010–13) [9]. Under the EC grant "Statistical data for medicinal product pricing" under the call HP-PJ-2014 [10] awarded in mid-2015, the Euripid Collaboration has been commissioned to develop a guidance document on a coordinated approach of national authorities regarding the use of EPR to avoid or at least mitigate negative impacts for patient access to medicines. At the editorial deadline of this book, the guidance document was not yet published. However, a "Euripid Best Practice Report on External Reference Pricing" [7], which the guidance document is intended to be based on, is publicly accessible. While the Best Practice report does neither debate the appropriateness of EPR nor discuss alternative policy options, it developed principles for best practice in the use of EPR based on an analysis done about current practices in European countries.

The Euripid Best Practice report identified 17 principles that were grouped around three overarching key principles [7]:

- Overarching principle A: The objective of the pharmaceutical pricing system should be clear and harmonized with health system objectives and reviewed periodically
  - Principle (P) 1: Define the objectives of pharmaceutical pricing policy
  - P 2: EPR is an important policy tool but it should be used in a mix with other tools and not as a stand-alone policy
  - P 3: EPR is a mechanism that determines the maximum price of a medicine
  - P 4: Build up capacity in the field of price comparison
  - P 5: Implement price monitoring to improve quality and comparability of price information of medicines
- Overarching principle B: An EPR system shall be set up in a simple and manageable way to keep the administrative burden at a reasonable level.
  - P 6: Marketing authorization holders should be required to provide prices in reference countries but they should be confirmed through independent price search
  - P 7: EPR should be preferably applied to on-patent medicines or medicines without generic alternatives at the market

  - P 8: EPR should be preferably applied at the level of the manufacturer or producer of the medicine
  - P 9: The size of the reference country basket should be in line with the objectives of EPR
  - P 10: The formula applied should reflect the objective of EPR
  - P 11: EPR should be seen in a broader, international context to avoid logic inconsistencies and to account for different abilities to pay
  - P 12: Prices determined through EPR should be regularly revised
- Overarching principle C: A well-defined methodology of price survey, with clear rules, is supportive for staff doing the price surveys and comparisons, and guarantees other stakeholders (e.g., pharmaceutical industry) a higher predictability of the results.
  - P 13: Differences in the reimbursement status of medicines in the reference country should be taken into account
  - P 14: When the pack size is different, define a band within which different packages are considered as equal or use unit prices
  - P 15: When the packaging/container is different, countries should agree on a "comparability catalogue"
  - P 16: When the pharmaceutical form is different, countries should follow clinical practice
  - P 17: The choice of exchange rate when applying EPR should reflect the objective of the pharmaceutical pricing policy

To conclude, research showed a scarcity of guidance documents of the use and implementation of EPR. The lack of guidance of how to design EPR coincides with a lack of guidance of how to conduct price surveys, analyses, and comparisons in general, as shown in Chapter 6.1. Limited availability of guidance can particularly be a challenge for policy-makers in LMIC without price regulation who aim to introduce medicine price control. Given the widespread use of EPR globally, policy-makers might be inclined to opt for this pricing policy, hoping to build on the experiences in the other countries. Existing evidence and guidance documents of EPR confirmed that there is no "one-size-fits-all" approach, but the implementation of EPR, like any policy, should be in line with the overall policy objective of the health-care, pharmaceutical, and pricing system. Because the design of EPR can impact the outcomes, it was recommended to take methodological choices with caution and a clear vision of their intended impacts. The selection of the reference countries, the scope of medicines covered under the EPR policy, issues of comparability and regular revisions were frequently mentioned among key methodological decisions.

REFERENCES

[1] World Health Organization. WHO guideline on country pharmaceutical pricing policies. Geneva. 2013. Available from: http://apps.who.int/medicinedocs/documents/s21016en/s21016en.pdf.

[2] WHO, HAI. Medicine Prices. A new approach to measurement. Working draft for field testing and revision. World Health Organization, Health Action International; 2003. Available from: http://www.haiweb.org/medicineprices/manual/manuals/MedicinePrices.pdf.

[3] WHO, HAI. Measuring medicine prices, availability, affordability and price components. 2nd ed. Geneva: World Health Organization, Health Action International; 2008 Available from: http://www.who.int/medicines/areas/access/OMS_Medicine_prices.pdf.

[4] Espin J, Rovira J, de Labry AO. Working paper 1: external price referencing – review series on pharmaceutical pricing policies and interventions. Geneva: World Health Organization, Health Action International; 2011. Available from: http://www.haiweb.org/medicineprices/24072012/ERPfinalMay2011.pdf.

[5] Toumi M, Rémuzat C, Vataire A-L, Urbinati D. External reference pricing of medicinal products: simulation-based considerations for cross-country coordination. Final report. European Commission; 2014. Available from: https://www.redaccionmedica.com/contenido/images/erp_reimbursement_medicinal_products_en-1.pdf.

[6] Vogler S, Lepuschütz L, Schneider P, Stühlinger V. Study on enhanced cross-country coordination in the area of pharmaceutical product pricing. Luxembourg: Gesundheit Österreich Forschungs- und Planungs GmbH; Publications Office of the European Commission; 2016. Available from: http://ec.europa.eu/health/systems_performance_assessment/docs/pharmaproductpricing_frep_en.pdf.

[7] Schneider P, Habl C. Euripid best practice report on external reference pricing (ERP). "Statistical data for medicinal product pricing" under the call HP-PJ-2014 (No. 664317). Funded by the Health Programme of the European Union. Vienna: European Commission Grant; 2017. Available from: http://metaweb.hu/wp-content/uploads/Euripid_BestPracticeReport_final_Feb2017.pdf.

[8] Kanavos P, Nicod E, Espin J. Short-and long-term effects of value-based pricing vs. external price referencing. London. 2010. Available from: http://whocc.goeg.at/Literaturliste/Dokumente/FurtherReading/Short-and long-term effect of value-based pricing.pdf.

[9] European Commission DG Entreprise. Call for Proposals - development of a database on the pricing of medicinal products in the EU. Grant Programme 2009. 2009. Available from: http://ec.europa.eu/DocsRoom/documents/2790/attachments/1/translations/en/renditions/pdf.

[10] European Commission. EC grant 'Statistical data and guidance document for medicinal product pricing and for the use of ERP [EURIPID]' [No. 664317]. 2014. Available from: https://webgate.acceptance.ec.europa.eu/chafea_pdb/health/projects/664317/summary.

CHAPTER 15

External Price Referencing Policy Brief

Sabine Vogler
WHO Collaborating Centre for Pharmaceutical Pricing and Reimbursement Policies, Pharmacoeconomics Department, Gesundheit Österreich GmbH (GÖG/Austrian Public Health Institute), Vienna, Austria

LIST OF ABBREVIATIONS

EPR	External price referencing
ERP	External reference pricing
LMIC	Low- and middle-income countries
UHC	Universal health coverage

15.1 WHAT IS EXTERNAL PRICE REFERENCING?

External price referencing (EPR) is defined as 'the practice of using the price(s) of a medicine in one or several countries in order to derive a benchmark or reference price for the purposes of setting or negotiating the price of the product in a given country' [1]. It is thus government action that pricing authorities can apply to set and determine medicine prices.

External price referencing is known under different names such as external reference pricing (ERP), international price comparison, international price benchmark and international referencing pricing. It differs from the pricing policy of internal price referencing (also known as internal reference pricing) that compares identical or similar medicines of the same country and that is typically used in the off-patent sector.

In this policy brief, the term 'external price referencing' (abbreviated EPR) is used.

15.2 WHERE IS EPR APPLIED?

EPR is applied in several countries all over the world. EPR is not a pricing policy solely for high-income countries, and its use has also been observed in low- and middle-income countries (LMIC) [2,3].

Medicine Price Surveys, Analyses, and Comparisons
ISBN 978-0-12-813166-4
https://doi.org/10.1016/B978-0-12-813166-4.00021-8

In Europe, EPR has been implemented in 26 of the 28 Member States of the European Union (all but Sweden and the United Kingdom) as well as in some countries outside the European Union (e.g., Norway, Switzerland, Turkey) [4]. EPR is also used in Canada, in some Latin American countries (e.g., Brazil, Colombia, Mexico), African countries (e.g., Egypt, South Africa) and countries in the Asia-Pacific region (e.g., Malaysia, Japan, South Korea). Increasing implementation of EPR has been observed during the last decade as more and more countries have made progress towards universal health coverage (UHC). When countries introduce price regulation, they frequently chose EPR as one of the policies.

Implementation of EPR does not necessarily imply its use for all medicines and in all settings. As a pricing policy, the scope of EPR tends to focus on medicines subsidised by the state [3,5,6]. In European countries, EPR tends to be predominantly used in the out-patient sector and is less frequently applied to medicines in the hospital setting [4]. EPR is predominantly used for new medicines but several countries also apply it for off-patent medicines [4].

15.3 WHY HAS EPR BEEN IMPLEMENTED?

EPR is a pricing policy, and as such, it aims to achieve lower medicine prices and thus help make medicines affordable to public payers and patients. A rationale that drives countries to use EPR may be that, broadly speaking, policy-makers aim to obtain prices that are not higher than in comparable countries [2]. Knowledge of published prices in other countries offers first indications to pricing authorities about the willingness-to-pay and ability-to-pay in other countries.

One reason why countries chose EPR out of the 'tool box' of pricing policies is that it can be implemented with fewer investments compared to other policies. For instance, value-based pricing considers health technology assessments and requires capacity development of specialised skills.

Furthermore, use of EPR in many countries all over the world likely contributed to its introduction in other countries since policy-makers may consider EPR's popularity as a proxy for its effectiveness.

15.4 HOW HAS EPR BEEN IMPLEMENTED?

The EPR methodology comprises several elements that policy-makers can use in different designs to achieve intended policy objectives.

There is large variation in the number of reference countries, ranging from 1 to up to 30 and more countries. Many countries (e.g., Croatia, France, the Netherlands, Turkey) use a smaller basket that includes around three to seven countries. Pricing authorities tend to refer to countries in the same region, frequently neighbouring countries or countries in the proximity [3]. Overall, governments tend to include countries of similar economic situation and similar medicine price level in their reference country basket [2]. Economic pressures (e.g., countries that were hit hard by the financial crisis such as Ireland and Portugal) have led to the inclusion of reference countries with lower price levels [7]. A few countries (e.g., Cyprus) defined alternative countries that are referenced in case that price data should not be available in first-line countries [4].

Methods of how to calculate the benchmark price differ between EPR-applying countries. Many countries set their price based on an average of prices in the reference countries while others relate to the lowest prices in the other countries. Several countries also apply more sophisticated formulae (e.g., Norway determines the average of the three lowest prices out of a basket of nine countries) [4,5].

Many countries (e.g., Jordan, Lebanon, Switzerland) determine the EPR-based benchmark at the ex-factory price level, while a few further countries set wholesale prices (e.g., Colombia, Finland) or pharmacy retail prices (e.g., Egypt) based on EPR [3,4]. Pricing authorities nearly always refer to the published list prices in the reference countries. In very few European countries (e.g., Austria, Germany) legislation requires consideration of discounted prices, usually mandatory manufacturer discounts to public payers. Price data of reference countries are converted into exchange rates, using daily rates or average rates covering longer periods of time, for example, quarterly exchange rates. German EPR legislation asks for weighting prices by economic parameters (purchasing power parities) but this appears to be the sole country worldwide to do so.

The marketing authorisation holder usually provides the required price information of the reference countries. In a small but increasing number of countries technical staff of the pricing authorities validate this information, usually by consulting price databases.

The level of detail in legislation varies between EPR-applying countries. A few of them have particular regulations that specify, for instance, approaches of how to deal with missing data (e.g., alternative reference countries, a broad definition of comparable medicines, price reviews at set intervals). Some regulations include definitions of the comparability of medicines subject to EPR.

15.5 DOES EPR IMPROVE PATIENT ACCESS TO MEDICINES? DOES IT CONTAIN COSTS?

Overall, EPR is not considered a policy that aims to improve patient access to medicines, that is, to bring medicines to countries and markets that have not had access before [4]. It is a pricing policy, and its major aim is to set and control medicine prices. EPR may contribute to contain the public pharmaceutical bill in a given country, and savings can be used to fund new medicines and help ensure long-term sustainability of a publicly funded healthcare system.

Several studies documented the ability of the EPR policy to lead to lower medicine prices [4,8–10]. EPR's effectiveness appears to be strongest immediately after its implementation but it tends to 'fade out' after some time. In practice, particularly for high-priced medicines, industry and payers have been concluding confidential discount agreements, and negotiated net prices are kept confidential. Since authorities reference to published list prices instead of real (discounted) prices, the savings' potential of EPR has not fully been exploited.

From a global public health perspective, EPR has negative spillover effects on countries with lower medicine price levels that may face availability issues following use of EPR in other countries. Limited access results from staggered market launch of medicines because marketing authorisation holders, who do not want to reduce the EPR-based benchmark price, launch medicines first in higher-priced countries and only later, or not all, in lower-priced countries.

15.6 WHAT SHALL POLICY-MAKERS CONSIDER WHEN THEY DECIDE TO IMPLEMENT EPR?

EPR is a pricing policy that may offer benefits, particularly in terms of cost-containment, for a given country. It is a relevant policy option in the area of pharmaceutical pricing that policy-makers may consider implementing to regulate prices of defined medicines in their country.

Policy-makers are advised to challenge the frequently mentioned argument that EPR would be an easy-to-implement policy. While it is true that EPR requires fewer investments than other pricing policies, still capacity has to be built and access to reliable price data be ensured. Use of EPR is linked to administrative burden whose extent depends on the design of the policy and practical implementation issues. The pricing policy benefits, however, from its widespread use: Governments that recently introduced EPR can draw from experiences gained by other countries that have applied this policy for years.

EPR is highly sensitive to its methodological choices. As for any other policy, there is no 'one-size-fits-all' approach since country-specific policy objectives and particularities have to be considered in the design of EPR and in pharmaceutical pricing policy in general. But consideration of the following principles and approaches can be beneficial:

- Defining and limiting the scope is suggested since for some medicines other policies may be more appropriate to achieve the intended policy aims. For off-patent medicines, for instance, competitive policies have proven to be able to bring prices down [11,12].
- EPR is not mutually exclusive and should be combined with other pricing policies (e.g., competitive pricing policies such as tendering for the off-patent market) and reimbursement tools (e.g., careful selection of medicines for inclusion in national essential medicine lists). Policy-makers should identify the most appropriate mix of policies that may include EPR for specific medicines and settings.
- EPR relates to setting medicine prices at defined price types (frequently ex-factory prices). Further price components (e.g., in the supply chain) should be addressed with appropriate policies (e.g., regulation of the remuneration for pharmacies such as statutory pharmacy mark-ups or a dispensing fee).
- Attention should be paid to carefully define the methodological design. Important parameters include the reference countries (which and how many), the calculation method (e.g., average or lowest of prices in the reference countries) and approaches to deal with non-availability of data (e.g., when a medicine is not available in the reference country). Backup strategies should be developed and, ideally, stipulated in legal provisions.
- Solutions should be sought to deal with the limitation that EPR-applying countries tend to overpay since they refer to published list prices instead of 'real' discounted prices that are usually confidential.

Policy-makers may like to adjust calculation methods (e.g., discounting for an assumed amount), or to consider, at least, published statutory discounts.

- Since the strategic launch of medicines by pharmaceutical companies tends to lead to higher prices in the beginning, regular price reviews should constitute an integral part of the EPR policy. The workload can be reduced if the reviews are limited to defined medicines (e.g., those priced above a specific threshold).
- Policy-makers are encouraged to define clear and transparent rules and procedures to ensure common understanding of technical experts involved in EPR and of stakeholders impacted by the policy. Price data should be published in an easily accessible manner to support other countries that also apply EPR. Transparency of price data (e.g., communication of discounted prices) or at least flagging any price-reducing arrangements in national data sources would strengthen the EPR policy.
- When newly introducing EPR, policy-makers are advised to run a pilot to test effectiveness and practicability of the developed methodology. During the development of the design and the pilot phase, input and support of other EPR-applying countries with experience can prove beneficial.
- Regular monitoring and evaluations of the policy are recommended to investigate whether, or not, EPR in its present design is able to achieve the defined policy aims and to identify possible unintended effects. Adjustments might be necessary after some time.

EPR is part of the current system that some experts consider 'broken' [13,14]. While for the time being policy-makers continue, for practical reasons, using the EPR policy to set prices of some medicines, they may also like to join forces with other countries to explore new approaches in pharmaceutical policy (beyond pricing). Such new models for developing, producing and supplying medicines should ensure patient access to needed medicines at 'fair' prices globally.

REFERENCES

The list contains several key references; more detailed evidence is referenced in Chapters 12–14.

[1] WHO. Collaborating Centre for pharmaceutical pricing and reimbursement policies. Vienna: Glossary of pharmaceutical terms. Update 2016; 2016. Accessible at: http://whocc.goeg.at/Literaturliste/Dokumente/MethodologyTemplate/Glossary_Update2016_final.pdf.

[2] Espin J, Rovira J, de Labry AO. Working paper 1: external price referencing — review series on pharmaceutical pricing policies and interventions. Geneva: World Health Organization and Health Action International; 2011. Available from: http://www.haiweb.org/medicineprices/24072012/ERPfinalMay2011.pdf.

[3] Espin J, Rovira J, Ewen M, Laing R. Mapping external reference pricing practices for medicines. Health Action International and the Andalusian School of Public Health; 2014.

[4] Vogler S, Lepuschütz L, Schneider P, Stühlinger V. Study on enhanced cross-country coordination in the area of pharmaceutical product pricing. Luxembourg: Gesundheit Österreich Forschungs- und Planungs GmbH; Publications Office of the European Commission; 2016. Available from: http://ec.europa.eu/health/systems_performance_assessment/docs/pharmaproductpricing_frep_en.pdf.

[5] Leopold C, Vogler S, Mantel-Teeuwisse AK, de Joncheere K, Leufkens HG, Laing R. Differences in external price referencing in Europe-A descriptive overview. Health Policy 2012;104(1):50—60.

[6] Toumi M, Rémuzat C, Vataire A-L, Urbinati D. External reference pricing of medicinal products: simulation-based considerations for cross-country coordination. Final Report. European Commission; 2014. Available from: https://www.redaccionmedica.com/contenido/images/erp_reimbursement_medicinal_products_en-1.pdf.

[7] Vogler S, Zimmermann N, de Joncheere K. Policy interventions related to medicines: survey of measures taken in European countries during 2010—2015. Health Policy 2016;120(12):1363—77.

[8] World Health Organization. WHO guideline on country pharmaceutical pricing policies. Geneva. 2013. Available from: http://apps.who.int/medicinedocs/documents/s21016en/s21016en.pdf.

[9] Håkonsen H, Horn AM, Toverud E-L. Price control as a strategy for pharmaceutical cost containment—what has been achieved in Norway in the period 1994—2004? Health Policy 2009;90(2):277—85.

[10] Leopold C, Mantel-Teeuwisse AK, Seyfang L, Vogler S, de Joncheere K, Laing RO, et al. Impact of external price referencing on medicine prices—a price comparison among 14 European countries. Southern Med Review 2012;5(1):34—41.

[11] Kaplan WA, Wirtz V, Nguyen A, Ewen M, Vogler S, Laing R. Policy options for promoting the use of generic medicines in low- and middle-income countries. Health Action International (HAI) 2016. Available from: http://haiweb.org/wp-content/uploads/2017/02/HAI_Review_generics_policies_final.pdf.

[12] Dylst P, Vulto A, Godman B, Simoens S. Generic medicines: Solutions for a sustainable drug market? Applied Health Economics and Health Policy 2013;11(5):1—7.

[13] Moon S, Bermudez J, t Hoen E. Innovation and access to medicines for neglected populations: could a treaty address a broken pharmaceutical R& system? PLoS Medicine 2012;9(5):e1001218.

[14] Outterson K, Powers JH, Daniel GW, McClellan MB. Repairing the broken market for antibiotic innovation. Health Affairs 2015;34(2):277—85.

CHAPTER 16

Conclusions

Sabine Vogler
WHO Collaborating Centre for Pharmaceutical Pricing and Reimbursement Policies, Pharmacoeconomics Department, Gesundheit Österreich GmbH (GÖG/Austrian Public Health Institute), Vienna, Austria

LIST OF ABBREVIATIONS

EPR	External price referencing
HAI	Health Action International
WHO	World Health Organization

This book dealt with the issue of medicine price surveys, analyses and comparisons from a public health perspective and was focussed on responding to the following questions:

- What is the evidence of medicine price information?
- What is the state-of-the-art methodology for conducting medicine price surveys, analyses and comparisons?
- What have been the experiences with the use of international medicine price comparisons for policy-making purposes?

Key findings of this book are:

- **There is still lack of medicine price information globally.** Medicine price studies tend to focus on high-income countries with large pharmaceutical markets and are mostly conducted as comparative analyses of few countries (determining average price levels based on price indices) and as time-series analyses (e.g., to assess the effects of policy interventions). Even in high-income countries there is lack of medicine price information for certain areas (usually those not covered by price regulation and/or with intra-country price variations), such as hospital medicines, non-prescription medicines and 'real' prices following discounts received in price negotiations. However, it is fair to say that an increase in medicine price information and analyses has been observed during the last 2 decades. This is, among others, attributable to the World Health Organization (WHO)/Health Action International

Medicine Price Surveys, Analyses, and Comparisons
ISBN 978-0-12-813166-4
https://doi.org/10.1016/B978-0-12-813166-4.00022-X

(HAI) project to measure availability and prices of medicines. In the course of this project, WHO and HAI developed a methodology to survey and analyse medicine prices and have been encouraging countries, particularly low- and middle-income countries, to conduct price surveys using this methodology. Globally, price studies have been focussed on medicine groups that are of concern from a public health perspective, such as those to treat HIV/AIDS and cancer. Increasingly high-priced medicines, including orphan medicinal products, were surveyed during the last years.

- **There is limited methodology guidance of how to conduct medicine price surveys, analyses and comparisons.** The sole generally accepted methodology standard is the above-mentioned WHO/HAI methodology to measure medicine prices, availability, affordability and price components that provides detailed guidance to survey on-site retail prices of defined medicines at different points of dispensing and procurement prices. It is a valuable method particularly for countries and settings where no price information has yet been recorded and published. For price studies in high-income countries (e.g., to determine average price levels of countries) that are predominantly based on secondary price data, often for large data sets received from (commercial) data providers or retrieved from national price lists, additional methodological guidance is required. A few scientific articles provided recommendations on the methodological set-up of cross-country medicine price comparisons. Comparability of the countries and choice of the price index method were key aspects covered. But no comprehensive manual to provide practical advice of how to identify sources of secondary price data and to assess their quality, for instance, was found.
- **There is widespread use of international medicine price comparisons for policy-making but evaluations of its impact are few.** An increasing number of countries introduced the policy of external price referencing (EPR) for at least parts of the medicines in their markets. Using EPR, governments set medicine prices in their country based on the prices of the same medicines in other countries. EPR is a common pricing policy, typically used for new medicines, and it has been implemented in many countries globally. It is linked to the expectation that it helps contain public pharmaceutical expenditure and eventually improve patient access to medicines. Despite EPR's popularity, only a small number of evaluations are available. They

usually focussed on investigating cost-containment effects and tended to show that EPR has led to lower medicine prices. Assessments of the EPR policy also suggested that methodological choices matter and can, even substantially, impact on medicine prices. Guidance on how to design EPR is provided in a few policy documents.

The purpose of this book was to bring together existing evidence of medicine price information and to offer advice on how to conduct price surveys, analyses and comparisons, including guidance of how to optimise the EPR design for better achieving intended policy objectives. Major messages include:

- **The purpose of a medicine price survey, analysis or comparison determines the methodology.** The starting point of each survey and analysis of medicine price data is the objective and purpose of the exercise: Are data collection and analysis done for research or for policy-making? Is there interest to obtain price data of a country or a geographic area, a sector or setting, of certain medicines at a defined price type for which no information has yet been available? Shall average price levels of countries be compared, and/or shall various methodological designs (e.g., unweighted price data, price indices such as Laspeyres or Paasche indices) be tested? Does the study aim to observe medicine price developments over time, and, if applicable, before and after the implementation of a policy measure? Are price data of other countries required to set prices based on the external price referencing policy? Shall the relevance of some price components (e.g., remuneration for pharmacies, local taxes) be explored?
- **There is no 'one-size-fits-all' solution but usually more approaches, with different implications, are possible.** The methodological design has to be developed to comply with the study objective. Guidance on how to conduct medicine price surveys, analyses and comparisons provided in this book aimed to raise awareness about the different parameters of the study design that should be considered but it is not aimed to be prescriptive on specific choices. Researchers have to assess the implications of different methodological approaches, and their decisions should be primarily guided by the study objective. In several cases, however, they need to balance choices against practical limitations such as gaps in data availability, budget limitations and deadlines.
- **Medicine price surveys, analyses and comparisons require careful preparation.** Even a 'simple' price survey in one country,

conducted for a handful of medicines, has to be thoroughly planned. Key decisions regard methodological choices on the country/countries, the region or other geographic areas, the sectors and settings (e.g., public vs. private sectors, outpatient vs. hospital sectors, on-patent vs. off-patent markets), the product sample, the price type (e.g., ex-factory price, retail price) and the unit of measurement. Based on these parameters of the study design, decisions have to be taken about the sources (primary data collection or use of secondary data?) and the processes to survey, validate, analyse, interpret and present the price data (e.g., recruitment and training of data collectors for field surveys or for retrieval of information from databases; establishment of processes for the review of the study protocol and of preliminary findings; decisions on presentation formats such as boxplots). Non-consideration of important elements in the planning phase (e.g., choice of a data source that does not allow retrieval of historic price data or does not cover medicines included in the product basket; lack of validation processes for checking the quality of the collected data) may result in impediments and delays at a later stage of the study, and corrections can be linked to considerable efforts and costs.

- **Medicine price surveys, analyses and comparisons can be time- and resource-intensive.** Some price studies can require substantial resources in terms of staff and other costs. A team of people might be needed for the data collection if this is done through visits to dispensaries but also if data are retrieved manually from (paper or not easy-to-handle electronic) data sources. Sufficient time for validating, analysing and interpreting the medicine price data should be scheduled, including buffer time in case of emergencies (e.g., no willingness of surveyed dispensaries to share prices, long waiting times or non-delivery of requested or ordered data). Additional information (e.g., patent status, volume data) might be needed for the analysis and have to be requested or surveyed elsewhere if they have not been included in the price databases. This may require further time and additional costs. Trainings might be needed for data collectors and researchers. For some methods (e.g., interrupted time-series analyses, price indices) further capacity (e.g., statisticians) might need to be involved.
- **Medicine price surveys, analyses and comparisons are policy relevant.** Medicine prices are a major factor that determines the affordability of medicines. Thus, any study addressing medicine price information is of policy interest. Researchers should be aware that their price

study findings may attract the interest of policy-makers and further stakeholders even if the research was conducted purely out of academic interest. As a result, findings could end up in being used in policy debates. Results that do not support statements of some stakeholders (e.g., that the medicine price level in a given country was the lowest or the highest in comparison) as well as the underlying methodology might be criticised.

Based on the findings presented in this book, the following principles appear to be helpful for **extending the knowledge base of medicine price information** and eventually also contributing to improved patient access to medicines:

- **Evidence and transparency:** Price transparency is a major asset for policy-makers. Information of medicine prices, and possible variations, in a country (e.g., inflated prices due to add-ons such as unregulated taxes or distribution mark-ups, high prices in the hospital sector) supports policy-makers in identifying critical areas for which government action (including price regulation) is required. Price transparency also helps policy-makers to (easier) follow up in reviewing and evaluating the impact of policy interventions. Given the widespread use of EPR, price transparency in terms of knowledge of 'real' (discounted) prices would offer policy-makers a more robust information base for their pricing decision, would reduce their 'overpaying' (as they do given their referencing to list prices that do not reflect reality) and would strengthen their purchasing power in negotiations since they would have a more complete picture of other public procurers. This would not only serve cost-containment purposes but could eventually also improve patient access since savings in the public bill could be used for funding other medicines and health technologies. Transparency is not only needed about medicine prices but also about inputs (e.g., production cost, research and development costs) and processes (e.g., transparent decision processes). Knowledge about new treatments in the pipeline would help policy-makers in their prioritisation decision, for instance. Furthermore, improved availability of price data would support researchers who could focus on analyses and evaluations instead of having to invest high efforts (time and costs) in the data collection.
- **Capacity:** Knowledgeable experts should conduct medicine price surveys, analyses and comparisons; data collectors and research assistants need to be trained. In addition, sufficient capacity has to be built to develop an appropriate EPR design and to implement this pricing

policy in accordance with its objectives. Guidance documents can help build this capacity.

- **Collaboration:** Collaboration of researchers, and of policy-makers, can contribute to improved transparency and capacity if there is interest to share price information and experiences. Finally, collaborative pricing policies beyond EPR may constitute a way forward to ensure sustainable access to medicines at affordable prices.

This book intends to improve knowledge of medicine price information. It is aimed to encourage experts in research and policy-making to further extend the evidence base of medicine prices. It is the editor's hope to have triggered interest in conducting medicine price studies, and, at the same time, have raised awareness about their particularities and limitations. Medicine price surveys, analyses or comparisons are challenging, but they are also interesting and inspiring. In conclusion, they are needed and valuable pieces of research since they may contribute to improved access to medicines that are affordable for public payers and patients.

Solutions of the Training Exercises

CHAPTER 7

7.2 Training Material: Exercises

7.2.1 Definitions – Multiple Choice Questions

Solutions:

1. All answers are correct (depending on the pricing policies in place of the respective country).
2. d), in practice, however, the three price types are usually only applicable in the outpatient sector
3. b)
4. c) but they increase price non-transparently and distort price comparisons.
5. c)

7.2.2 Cloze Text

Term	Definition
...Cost-plus.... pricing	Pricing policy that determines a medicine price by taking into account production costs, promotional expenses, research & ...development...., administration costs, overheads and ...profit.............
Pharmacy ...purchasing... price (Synonym: ...wholesale price, pharmacy purchase price)	The price charged by ...wholesalers... to the retailers (usually community pharmacies). It is based on the ex-factory price and additionally includes any ...remuneration.....for pharmaceutical wholesale (e.g., in the form of a wholesale ...mark-up.... or a wholesale margin)
Discounts	A ...price......reduction.... (2 words) granted to specified purchasers under specific conditions prior to ...purchase.............

Term	Definition
...Statutory............ pricing	Pricing procedure where medicine prices are set on a ...regulatory.....basis..... (2 words) (e.g., law, enactment, decree)
Hospital price	The price or amount paid by a purchaser in the ......hospital....setting (e.g., a hospital pharmacy) in order to take delivery of certain unit of medicines. Often, the hospital list price corresponds to the ...ex-factory.......price...... (2 words), in some cases to the pharmacy purchasing price. It may or may not include value-added tax/VAT. In addition, ...discounts.....and/or rebates may be granted to the hospitals by the suppliers

7.2.3 Crossword Puzzle

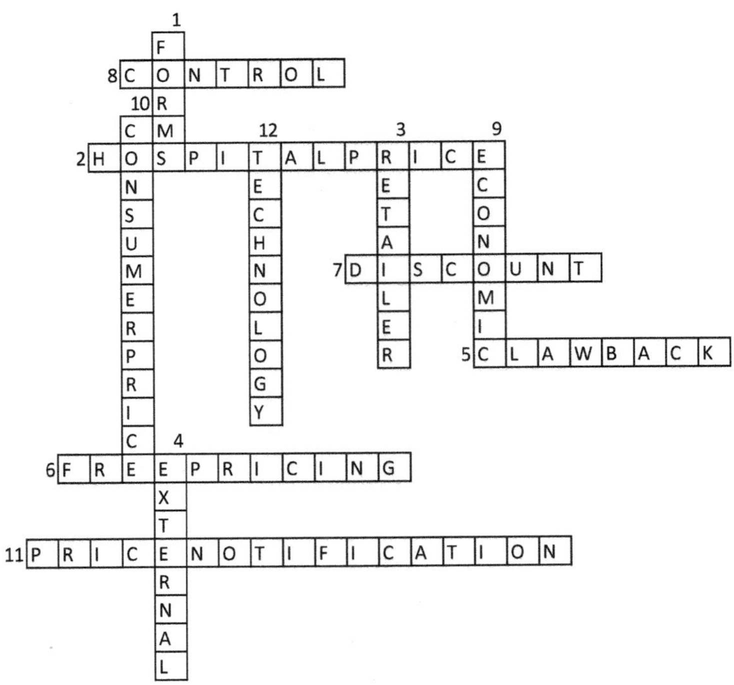

CHAPTER 10

Exercise 1 – Preparation of the study (methodology)

Q1:

1. the geographic area (country/countries, region(s), etc.),
2. sector (public/private, outpatient/inpatient)
3. the medicines included,
4. the price type depending on the perspective, and
5. the timing of the price data.

Q2:

The selection of medicines to be investigated depends on data availability and the research question of your study.

A medicine price study can be designed as individual price study for single medicines or as average price study for the overall market or sub-markets. Both approaches have their benefits and limitations. A limitation of the individual price study is that the product selection may not be representative of the overall market or the sub-market, or even the entire active ingredient. The relevance of a single medicine in a national context does not necessarily mean that this medicine is used as frequently as in other countries. In contrast, average price studies require price data of a large number of medicines, ideally supplemented by further information (e.g., volume) that may be needed for calculation (e.g., calculation of indices).

For this case study, you could select a representative sample, for example, the top 100 medicines which cause the highest expenditure for public payers and/or patients in the outpatient sector and/or in the inpatient sector or medicines with the highest volumes. If you are able to also get volume data, you could calculate price indices that would allow taking into account the relative importance of the medicines in your market. You may also decide to select medicines that are of major public health relevance for your country (e.g., high incidence of TB medicines), that have been in the focus of your Minister or the media (e.g., cancer medicines that have been criticised for the high prices) and that have been in the focus of campaigns of your Ministry.

The number of medicines selected can be lower if you do not have much time and you know that data collection will be a challenge (e.g., manual data retrieval from databases). If your Minister scheduled a price conference for the next day to present the results of the study, you might decide focussing on few medicines (e.g., five to seven products).

Q3:

Use of reliable and independent data sources is recommended, that is, if possible, official published prices by authorities in the surveyed countries. However, official price lists may not contain information on any possible discounts. Please consider assessing medicine price data sources according to the catalogue presented in chapter 8 of this book. You may also like to ask peers in the neighbouring countries (e.g., advisers to their Ministers of Health) for support in identifying and recommending medicine price databases.

Q4:

This depends on your research question and data availability:

a) if you would like to assess the impact of pricing policies, for example, statutory pricing on the level of the ex-factory price → select the ex-factory price

b) if you would like to analyse how wholesalers/pharmacies are remunerated in comparison to the neighbouring countries → select pharmacy purchasing or pharmacy retail prices

c) if you would like to explore how much patients have to (co-) pay → select the consumer/pharmacy retail price or the reimbursement price

Given the assignment of the Minister in the case study, there appears to be high interest in the final prices that patients pay (thus choose option c). If time allows, you may consider calculating additional scenarios to gain a more complete picture and to be prepared to critical questions that findings of the price study may cause (e.g., ex-factory prices can help inform about price differences between your country and the neighbouring countries from an industry's perspective).

Q5:

As a prerequisite, you need to know the reimbursement status and the applied reimbursement regulation of the specific product in your country as well as in the neighbouring countries. In fact, the comparison of reimbursement prices in practice presents some methodological difficulties: By definition the reimbursement price 'is the maximum amount paid for by a third party payer'. If the reimbursement rate is 70% of the pharmacy retail price — would you then only compare the reimbursed part (70%) of the price?

Q6:

Since exchange rates may be subject to strong fluctuations, results of the price study might be affected by the selected date of the exchange rate even though actual prices in national currencies do not alternate.

Price studies account for this volatility by using average exchange rates over longer periods ranging from 1 to 12 months. The choice which average to use has major implications for price studies. It has to be balanced between equalising short-term fluctuations and avoiding too long periods. Monthly or quarterly exchange rates appear to be appropriate, but yearly exchange rates are also feasible.

For instance, knowing about high exchange rate fluctuations that have been observed in recent years due to the financial crisis in the region, you decide to choose rather long intervals of 6 or even 12 months in the price study.

Q7:

It has been argued that not all medicines included in a study have the same relevance. This is of particular interest if different medicines are aggregated and average prices are calculated. In order to account for national utilisation patterns and local epidemiologic patterns, weights can be applied to the prices of pharmaceutical specialities. The size of these weights can be determined by sales, market shares or number of prescriptions. Weighting prices by GDP per capita or PPP is an adjustment that accounts for economic indicators such as the ability-to-pay.

In your preliminary research with advisers to the Minister in the neighbouring countries you learned that some top-selling medicines in your country do not account for large sales in the other countries and that their top-selling products are different ones. To account for these differences, you consider weighting by volume. However, to your disappointment, a check of data availability shows that neither in your country nor in the neighbouring countries volume data are available. Thus, you cannot calculate volume-based price indices. You decide to talk to your Minister with the aim to convince him to establish volume data collection mechanisms to allow for such analyses in future.

Exercise 2 – Price data calculation

Q1:

Solution table:

Product	Home country	Fantasia	Belladonna	Heavensgate	Redland
Ex-factory prices in Euro					
Glupic, 100 mg, 60 film-coated tablets	1126.41	940.29	1362.28	(862.14)*	838.46
Ex-factory prices per unit in Euro					
Glupic, 100 mg, 60 film-coated tablets	18.77	15.67	22.71	(14.37)*	13.97

*Different pack size (120).

Fantasia:

Calculate the ex-factory price in Fantasian Crowns by applying the 10% margin (= 10% of the wholesale price; it is NOT an add-on on the ex-factory price) on the wholesale price in Fantasian Crowns: 7769.90 *[(100–10)/100] = 6992.91. Convert the ex-factory price in Fantasian Crowns into Euro: 6992.91/7.437 = 940.29 (ex-factory price in Euro). This approach first determines the missing price types and then converts the price data into Euro. In principle, you may like to convert price data and then do the calculations. Results may slightly differ due to rounding differences.

Belladonna:

Calculate the ex-factory price by deducting the VAT of 5%:

1430.39/[(100 + 5)/100] = 1362.28.

In Belladonna the medicine is only available in capsules and not in tablets. However, tablets and capsules are designed so that the active ingredient is released immediately after the medicine is taken. While some solid oral pharmaceutical forms (e.g., plain tablets, film-coated tablets or plain capsules) can be considered as equivalent, their comparison with modified release formulations is disadvised. Please consider that national price sources may differ with regard to the use of periods and commas.

Heavensgate:

The medicine in the requested pack size, strength and pharmaceutical form is not available in Heavensgate. Glupic 100 mg f/c tablets are only available in a pack size of 120. Given the large difference it is advised against using this data for the comparison. Medicine prices of similar/closest pack sizes (e.g., 56 compared to the requested 60 units per pack, 28 compared to the requested 30 units per pack) would, however, be acceptable.

However, you assume that your Minister does not like missing data and is not interested in methodological discussions. He may pressure you to provide the data for Heavensgate. To be on the safe side, you will calculate the price for Heavensgate.

The data source you consult is the national positive list that contains medicines included for reimbursement. Thus, the prices listed are for reimbursed products – hence VAT exempt. Calculate the ex-factory price by deducting the linear pharmacy mark-up (18%) and the linear wholesale mark-up (3%):

2095.70/[(100 + 18)/100] = 1776.02 (wholesale price)/[(100 + 3)/100] = 1724.29 Euro (ex-factory price)

Since this product has 120 units per package (and we would like to compare with the package containing 60 units), the price is divided by 120 units and multiplied by 60 units:

1724.29 Euro/120 = 14.37 * 60 = 862.14 Euro.

Redland:

The ex-factory price of 838.46 Euro has to be taken since the price of 814.47 is only valid starting from 01/07/2018 and the date of our price comparison is of May 2018.

Exercise 3 – Price data presentation and data analysis

Q1:

	In %
Price difference in home country/min	= (price of your home country – minimum price)/minimum price * 100 = (1126.41–838.46)/838.46*100 = **34.3**
Price difference in home country/∅	= (price of your home country - average of the other countries' prices)/average *100 = [(1126.41-(940.28 + 1362.28 + 838.46)/3]/1047 *100 = **7.6**
Price difference in home country/max	= (price of your home country – maximum price)/maximum price * 100 = (1126.41–1362.28)/1362.28 *100 = **–17.31**

Interpretation: The price of the product in your home country is higher than the average price in the comparator countries, but is not the highest price. Overall, there is a rather large variation for the prices of Glupic, with the price in the highest country being approx. 63% higher than in the lowest priced country.

Calculation of the 63% = (price of maximum price − minimum price)/minimum price * 100 = (1362.28−838.46)/838.46 * 100 = **62.47**.

Q2:

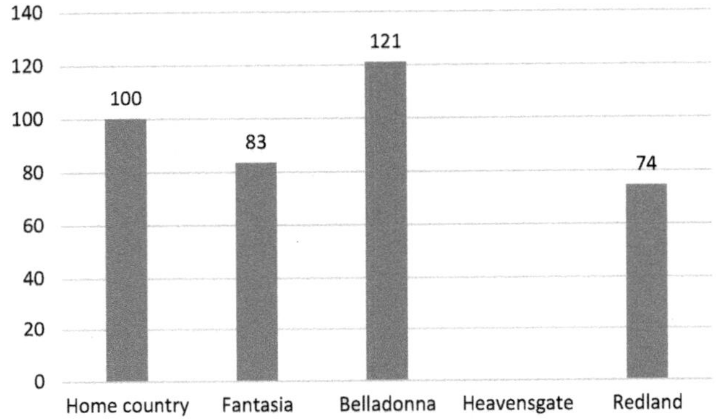

In comparison with three other countries, the product has the second highest price in the region. The lowest price in the region is 26% below the price in the home country. Please note that the difference to the answer in Question 1 is the reference point. The percentages in Q1 referred to the lowest (or average or highest) price in the region as denominator, whereas in this exercise all prices refer to the home region, for example, the price in Belladonna is 21% above the price in the home country.

A weighted index (e.g., by taking the number of prescriptions into account) for one product equals the price ratio as the weights cross out in the equation.

Q3:

To optimise visualisation, data of a range should be considered for a box plot. Thus, in this case, it is suggested drawing the box plot for per unit ex-factory prices of Braintrain, Glupic, Heart Core, Respira, Sanita and Supermills and excluding the data for Injectao (per unit ex-factory prices are comparably too high for this kind of visualisation) and SomePills (per unit ex-factory prices are comparably too low).

Product	Ex-factory prices in Euro (per unit)				
	Home country	Fantasia	Belladonna	Heavensgate	Redland
Glupic, 100 mg, 60 film-coated tablets	18.77	15.67	22.71	(14.37)*	13.97
Heart Core, 150 mg, 28 capsules	14.5	12.6	25.75	11.54	12.55
SomePills, 100 mg, 14 film-coated tablets**	0.17	0.22	0.23	0.11	0.12
Respira, 25 mg, 1 vial containing powder and solvent for prolonged-release suspension for injection	13.77	15.12	14.21	9	8.5
Supermill, 300 mg, 30 modified release tablets	18.22	19.78	23.77	17.64	17.68
Injectao, 50 mg, 1 vial solution for injection**	3500	3555	4500	3500	3500
Braintrain, 500 mg, 21 capsules	19.59	22.82	24.38	21.53	20.84
Sanita, 300 mg, 1 pre-filled syringe	24.59	28.54	26.7	22.67	19.32

* Different pack size (120) included in the box plot.
** Excluded for visualisation in the box plot.

As a result, the box plot for the ex-factory prices per unit (in Euro) for the six selected products looks as follows:

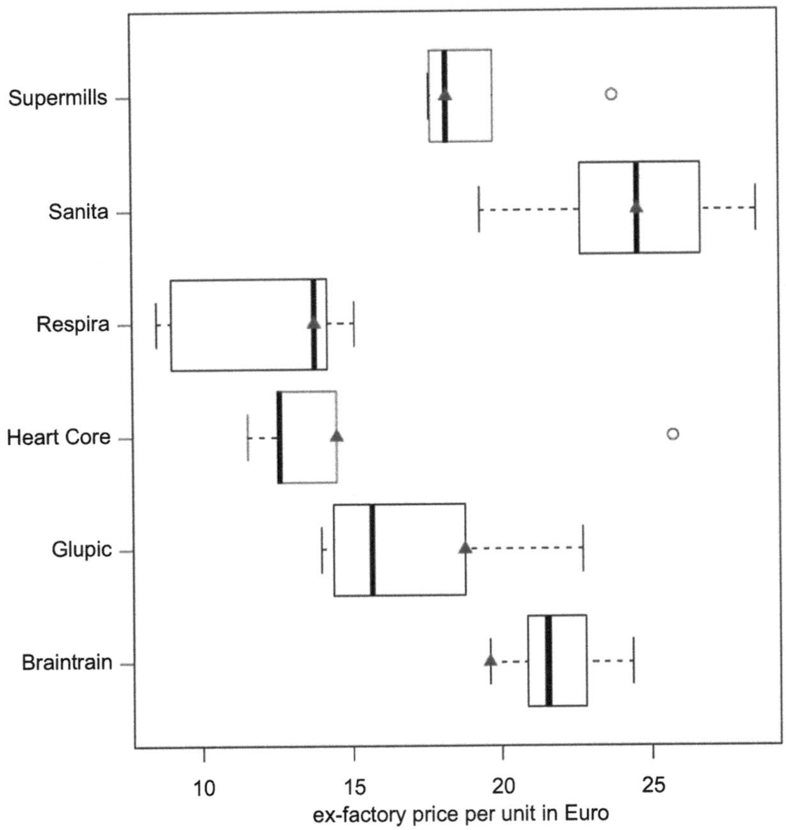

A box plot is a visual method that allows quick graphical examination of one or more data sets. In this example, you can see at first glance that the price in your country is frequently the median and that, overall, the range between the prices of the investigated countries is not extremely large (rather short 'whiskers'/'antennas', rarely outliers). Belladonna is an upper outlier for two medicines.

The Minister may like this type of visualisation. It confirms that, at least for the selected product, prices in your country are not the highest. While the table of data already offered an overview for the data of the five countries, a box plot gains relevance if you compare data of more countries. Its drawback, however, is that the inclusion of data that are of different extent (in this case, of Injectao and SomePills) would limit its visual representation.

Q4.

Why would you calculate prices in purchasing power parities (PPP)?

Comparing prices between two or more countries does not take into account the different income and price levels of the respective countries. For the same amount of money you may not be able to buy exactly the same goods and services in different countries. Purchasing power parities (PPP) are indicators of price level differences across countries. They indicate how many currency units a particular quantity of goods and services costs in different countries. However, usually PPP are calculated for a general consumer basket and do not specifically reflect a pharmaceutical basket.

For the example of the four countries an exchange rate in EUR PPP of 0.84 for Fantasia and 0.98 for Belladonna means that these countries have higher price levels compared to the rest of the (fictive) Eurozone. Therefore, by spending the same amount of money in these two countries fewer products can be bought. They are presumably rich countries.

International organisations such as EUROSTAT or OECD offer PPP exchange rates for download.

	Home country	**Fantasia**	**Belladonna**	**Heavensgate**	**Redland**
Exchange rate in EUR PPP	1.056	0.84	0.98	–	1.06
Glupic, 100 mg, 60 film-coated tablets – ex-factory prices in Euro	1126.41	940.28	1362.28	–	838.46
Glupic, 100 mg, 60 film-coated tablets – ex-factory prices in Euro PPP	1189.49	789.84	1335.03	–	888.77

Interpretation:

In the home country, the ex-factory price of the given product is 1126.41 Euro. Since the price level is lower in the home country than the rest of the Eurozone (= reference value of the exchange rate), the product has a value of 1189.49 Euro PPP as compared to the average price in the Eurozone. With one Euro spent in the home country you are able to buy more products compared to the average Eurozone.

INDEX

'*Note*: Page numbers followed by "f" indicate figures, "t" indicate tables.'

B

C

D

E

M

N

Q

R

Kolibri 360 GmbH
Ferdinand-Jühlke-Straße 7
99095 Erfurt, Deutschland
produktsicherheit@kolibri360.de